THE OTHER SIDE OF THE MIRROR

By
Jo Chen

HAMBURG // LONDON // LOS ANGELES // TOKYO

The Other Side of the Mirror Volume 1
Created by Jo Chen

Translation - J.Y. Standaert
English Adaptation - Kereth Cowe-Spigai
Copy Editor - Nikhil Burman
Retouch and Lettering - Star Print Brokers
Production Artist - Bowen Park
Graphic Designer - Fawn Lau

Editor - Katherine Schilling
Digital Imaging Manager - Chris Buford
Pre-Production Supervisor - Erika Terriquez
Production Manager - Elisabeth Brizzi
Managing Editor - Vy Nguyen
Creative Director - Anne Marie Horne
Editor-in-Chief - Rob Tokar
Publisher - Mike Kiley
President and C.O.O. - John Parker
C.E.O. and Chief Creative Officer - Stuart Levy

A  Manga

TOKYOPOP and 🐛 are trademarks or registered trademarks of TOKYOPOP Inc.

TOKYOPOP Inc.
5900 Wilshire Blvd. Suite 2000
Los Angeles, CA 90036

E-mail: info@TOKYOPOP.com
Come visit us online at www.TOKYOPOP.com

ISBN: 978-1-4278-0316-0

First TOKYOPOP printing: December 2007
10 9 8 7 6 5 4 3 2 1
Printed in the USA

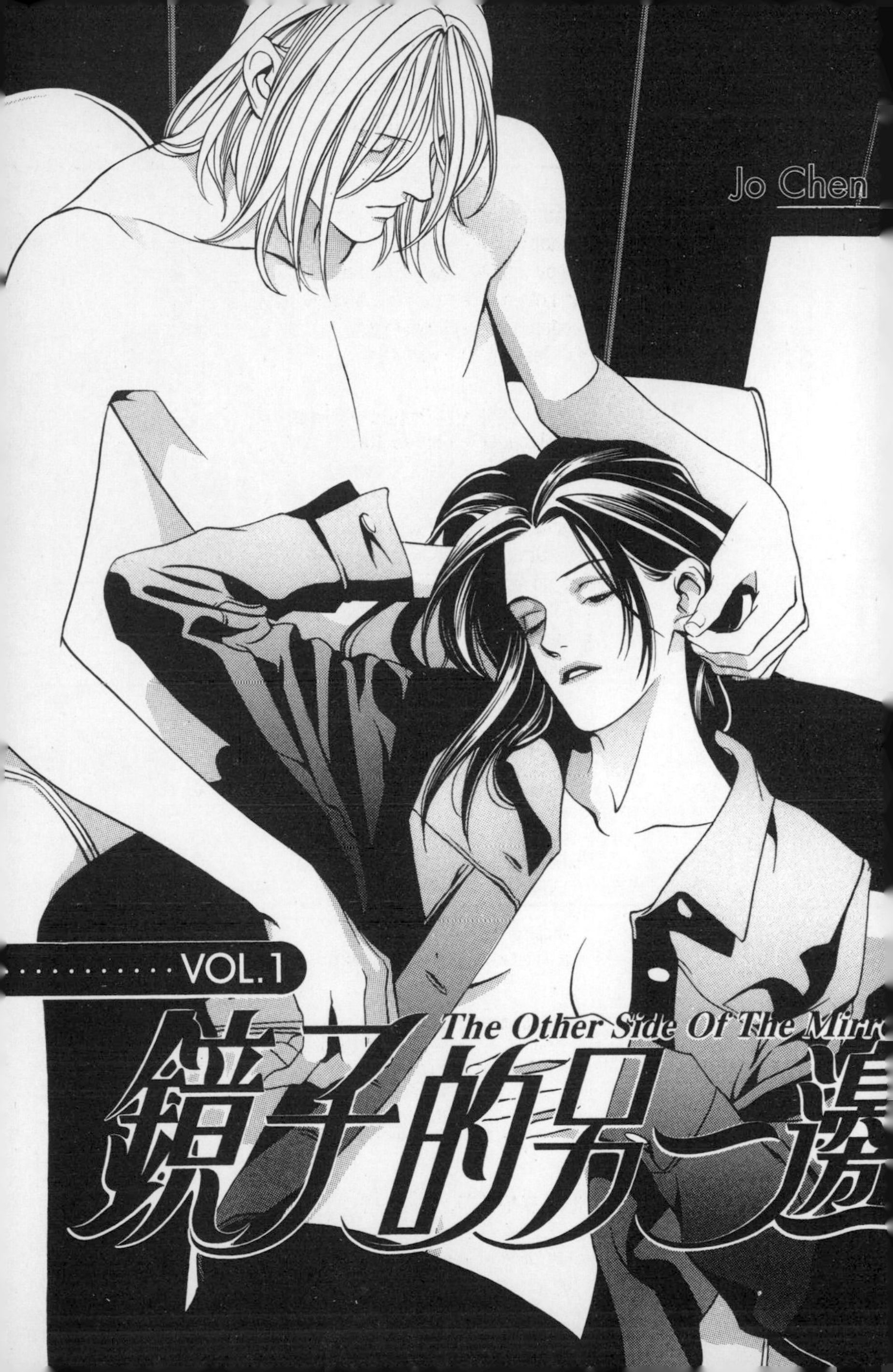
Jo Chen
VOL. 1
The Other Side Of The Mirr
鏡子的另一邊

CONTENTS

NO ONE KNOWS WHAT THE FUTURE HOLDS.
STILL--WE LURCH FORWARD, STUMBLING DAY AFTER DAY
TOWARD SOMETHING BETTER.
MAYBE IT'S JUST ON THE OTHER SIDE OF THE MIRROR.
OR MAYBE NOT EVERYONE FINDS A HAPPY ENDING.

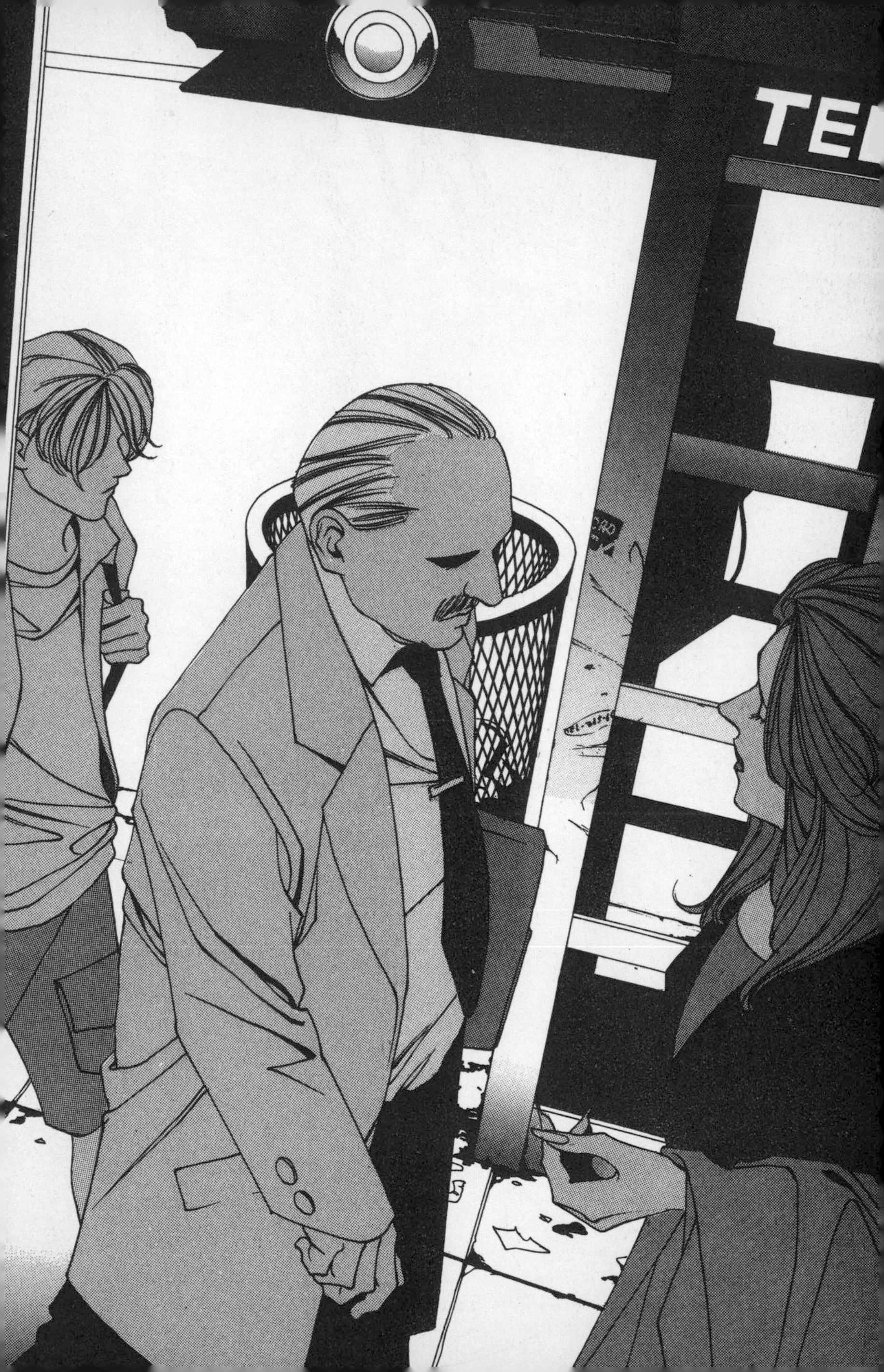
TE

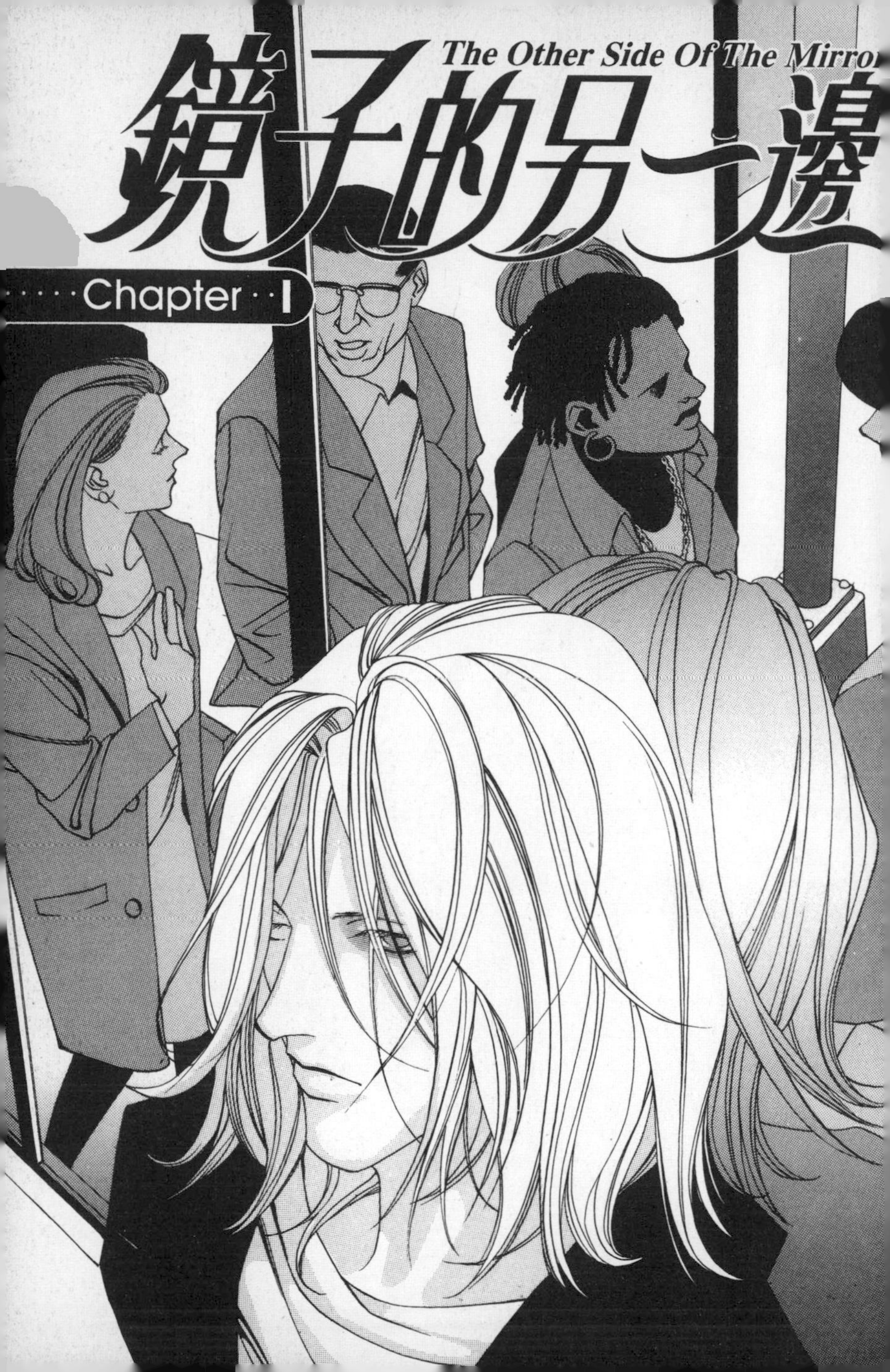
鏡子的另一邊
The Other Side Of The Mirro
Chapter I

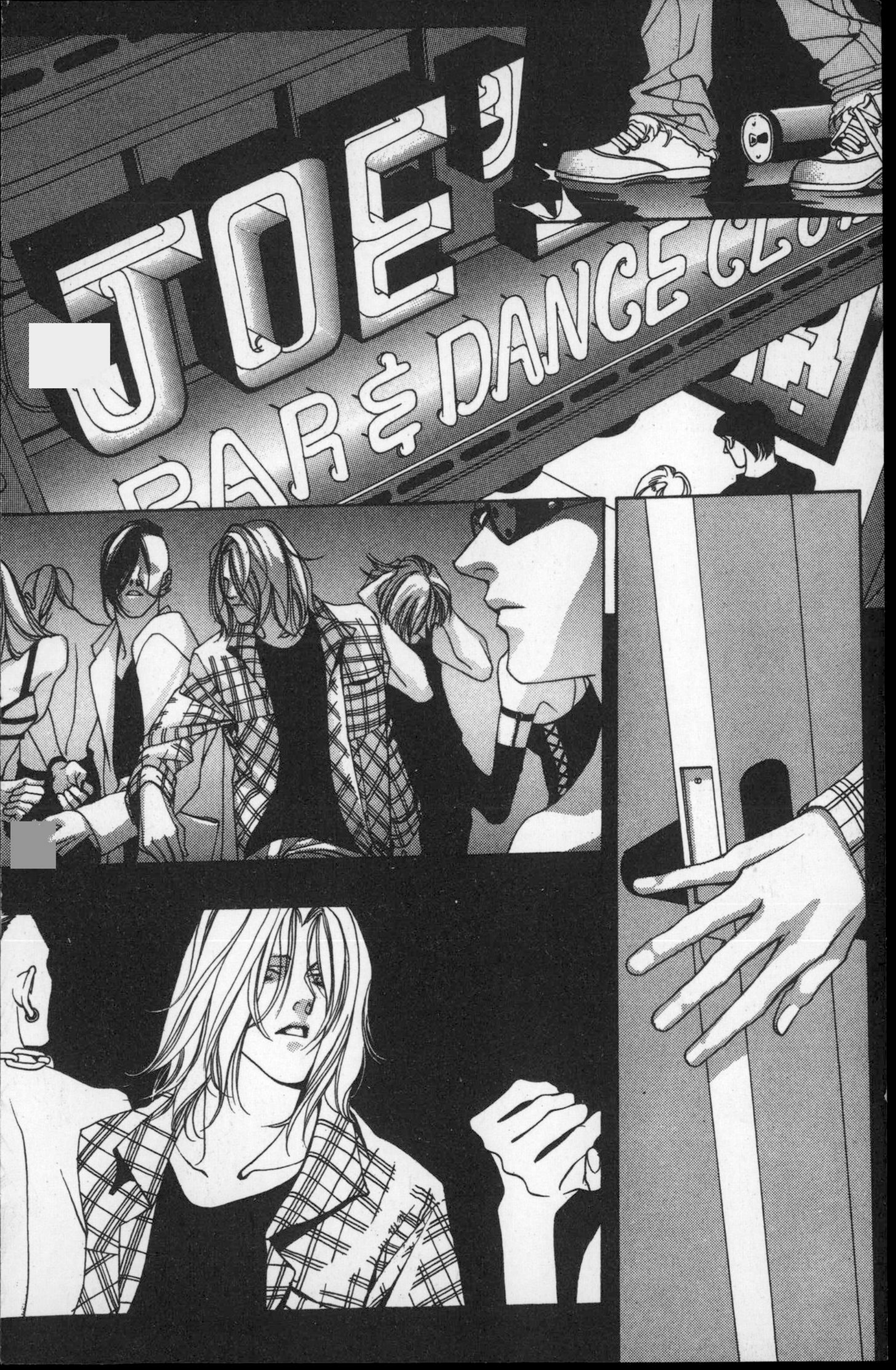
JOE
BAR & DANCE

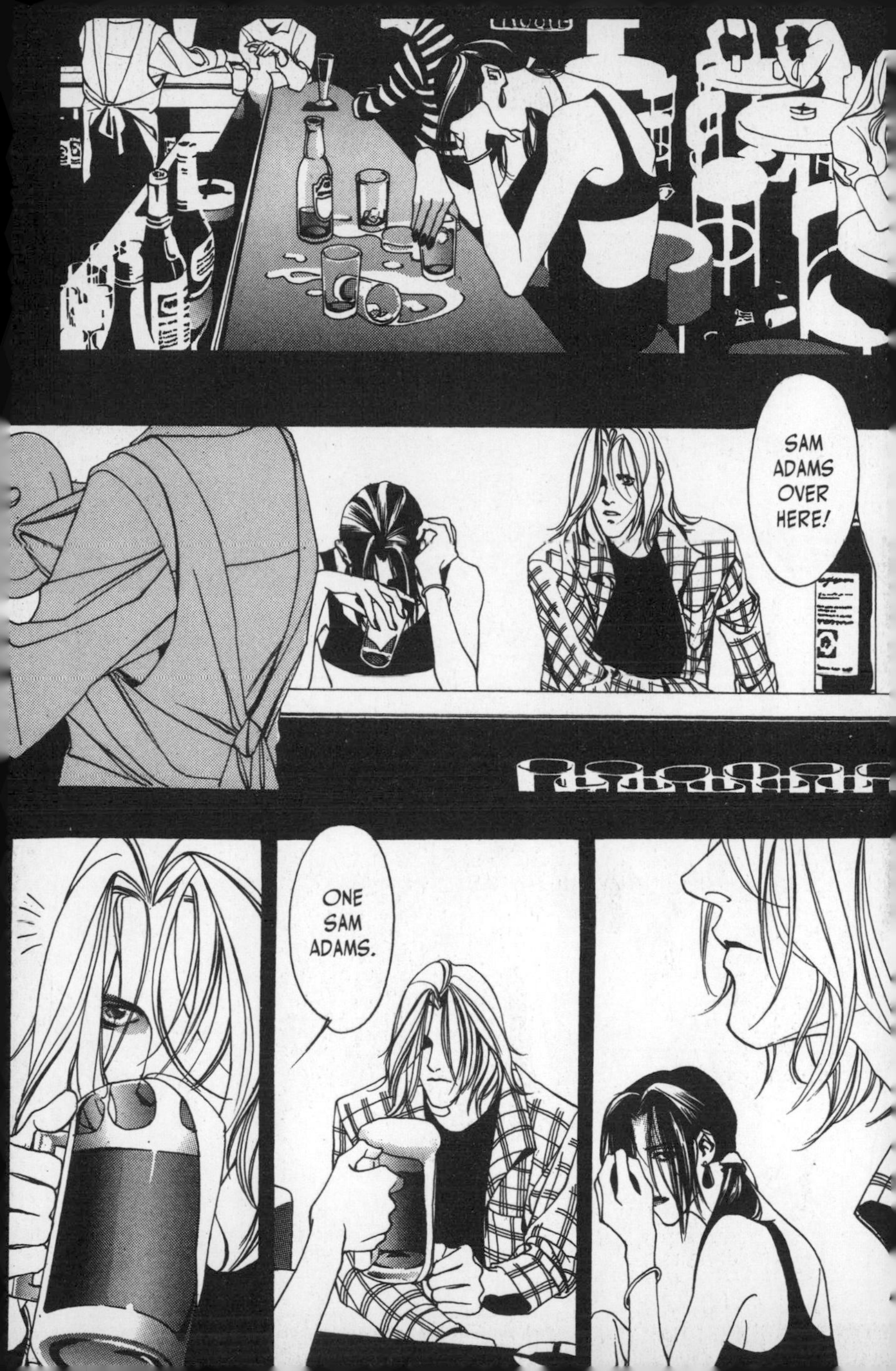
SAM ADAMS OVER HERE!
ONE SAM ADAMS.

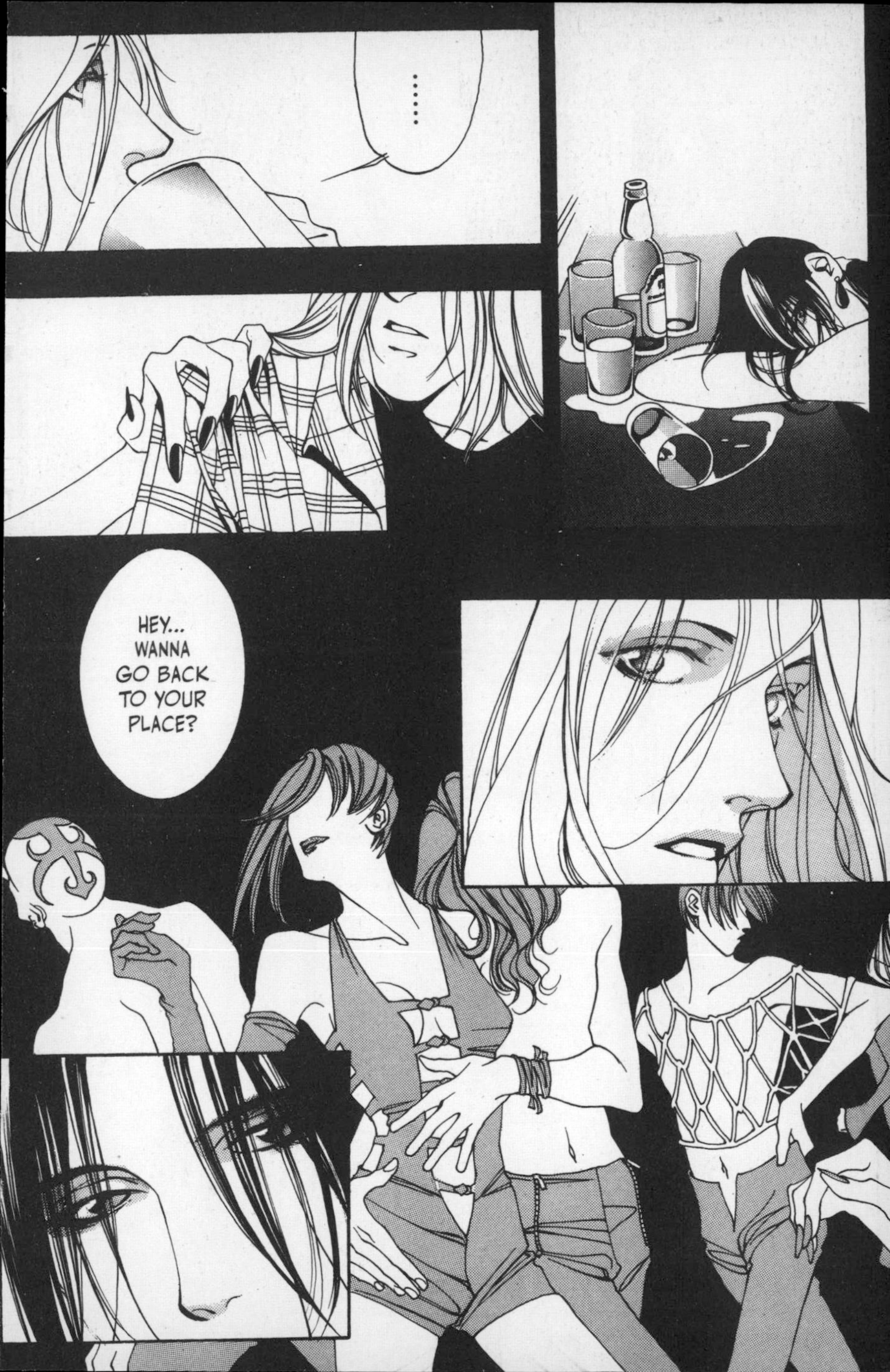
......
HEY... WANNA GO BACK TO YOUR PLACE?

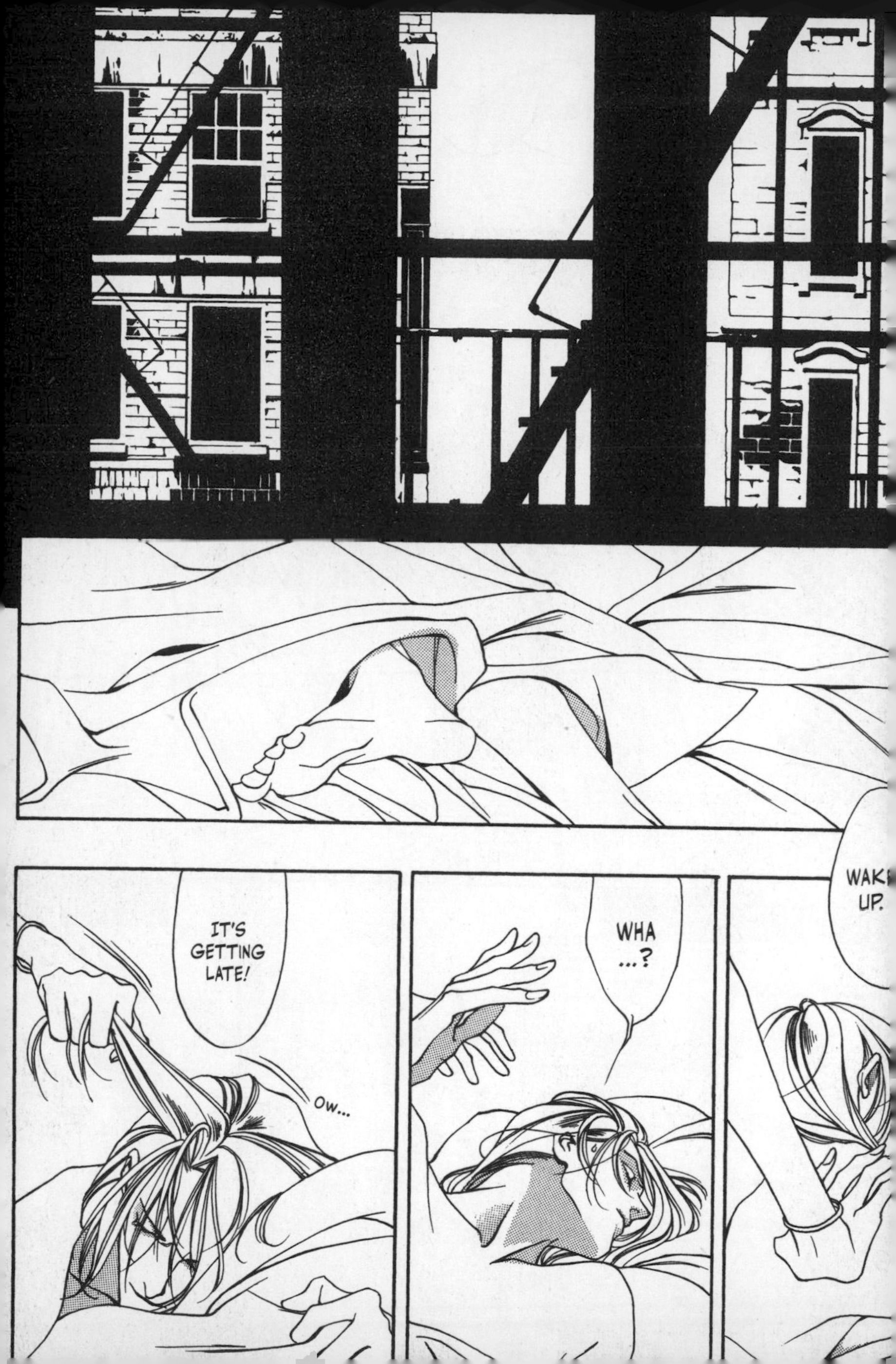
WAKE UP.
WHA ...?
IT'S GETTING LATE!
OW...

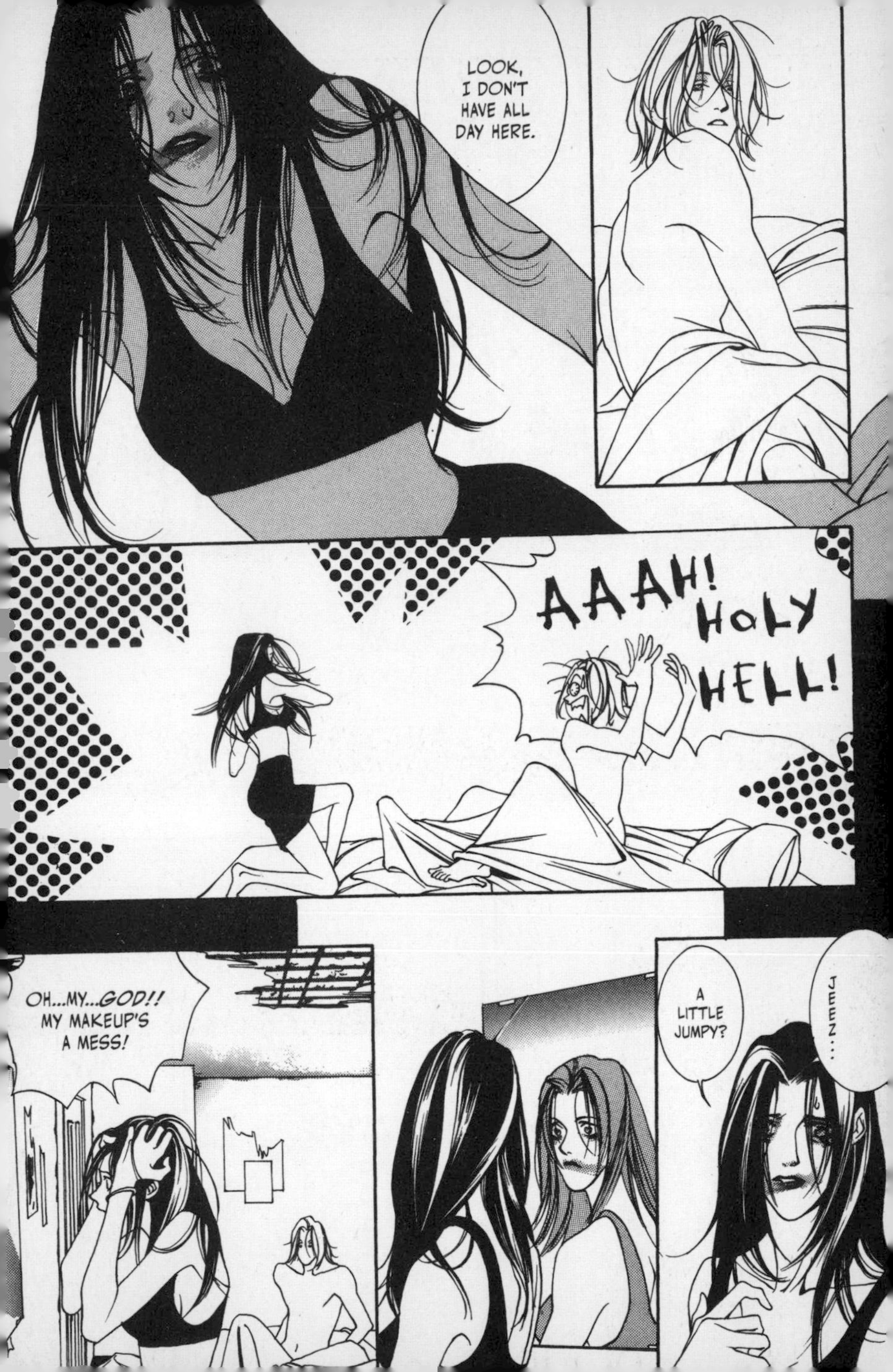
LOOK, I DON'T HAVE ALL DAY HERE.
AAAH! HOLY HELL!
JEEZ...
A LITTLE JUMPY?
OH...MY...GOD!! MY MAKEUP'S A MESS!

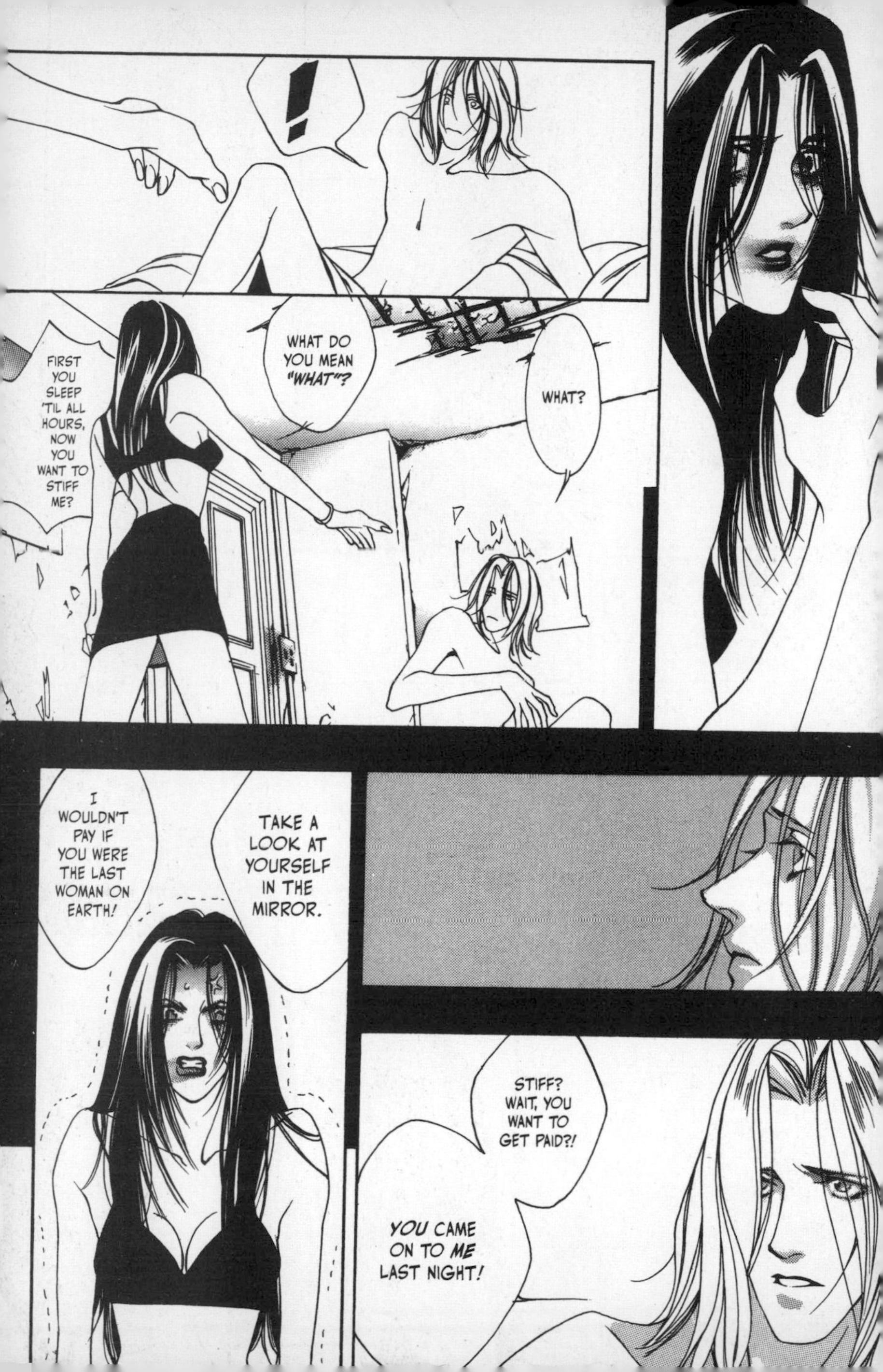
!
WHAT?
WHAT DO YOU MEAN *"WHAT"?*
FIRST YOU SLEEP 'TIL ALL HOURS, NOW YOU WANT TO STIFF ME?
STIFF? WAIT, YOU WANT TO GET PAID?!
YOU CAME ON TO *ME* LAST NIGHT!
TAKE A LOOK AT YOURSELF IN THE MIRROR.
I WOULDN'T PAY IF YOU WERE THE LAST WOMAN ON EARTH!

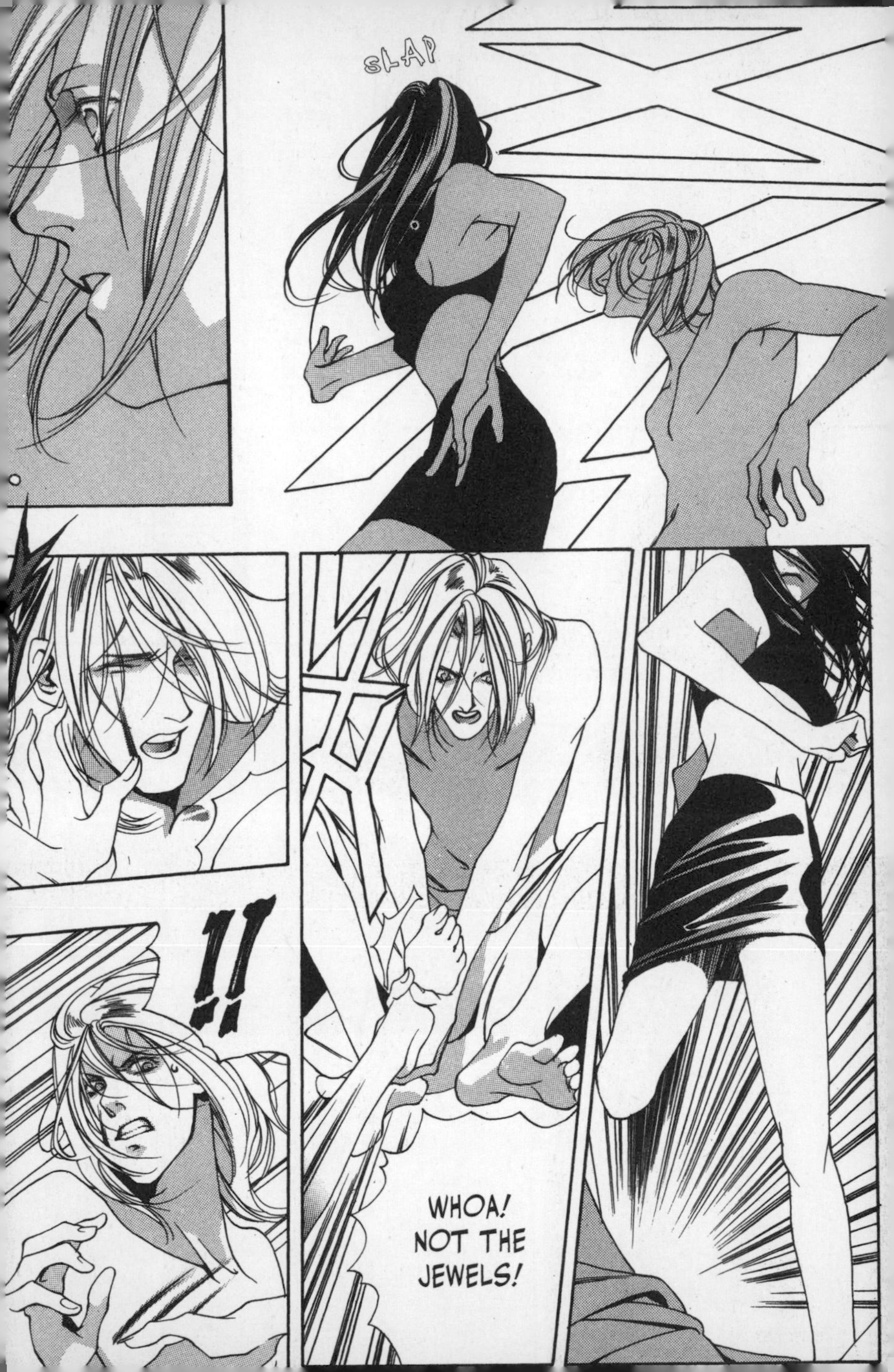
SLAP
WHOA! NOT THE JEWELS!
!!

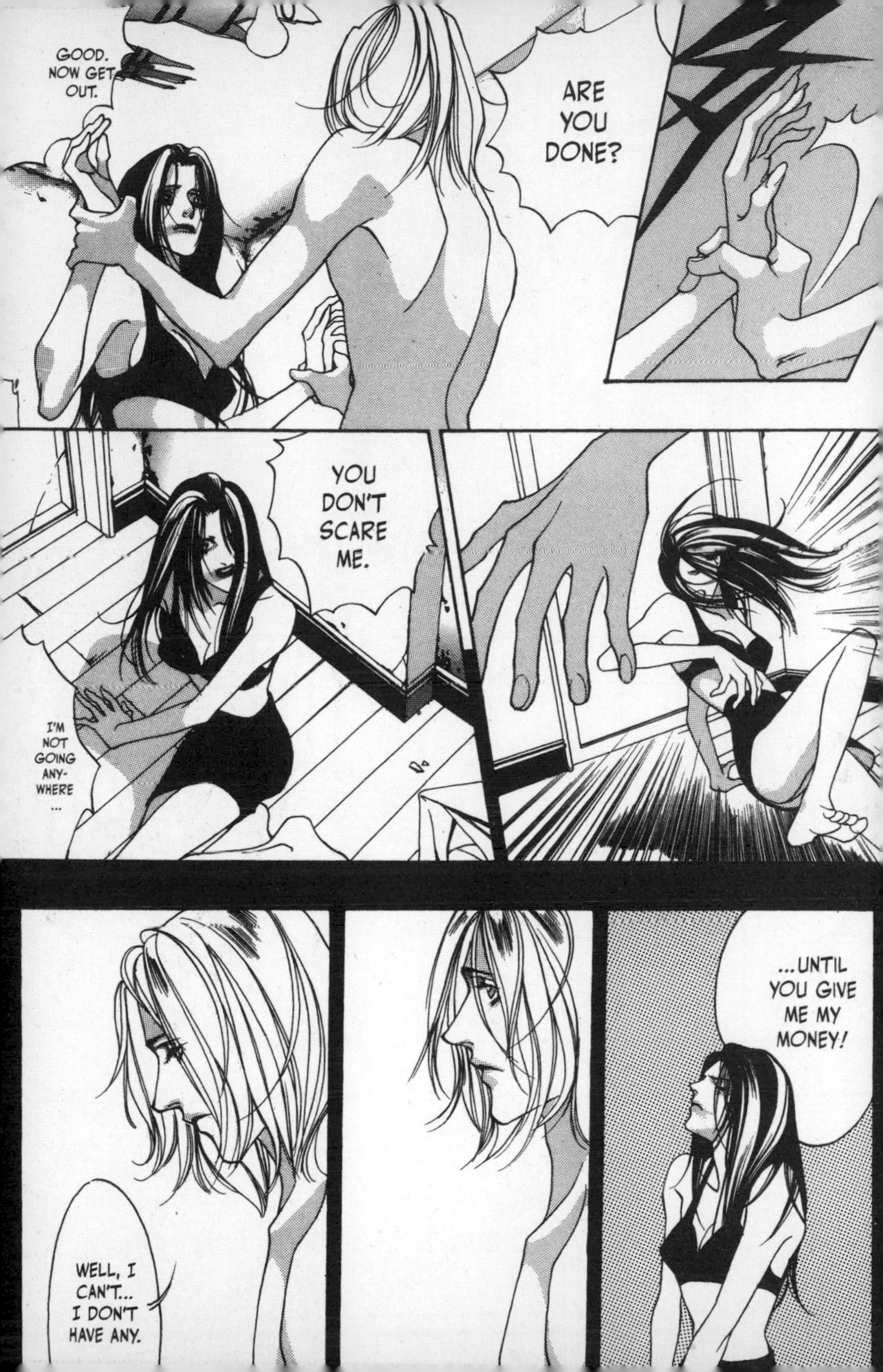
ARE YOU DONE?
GOOD. NOW GET OUT.
YOU DON'T SCARE ME.
I'M NOT GOING ANY-WHERE ...
...UNTIL YOU GIVE ME MY MONEY!
WELL, I CAN'T... I DON'T HAVE ANY.

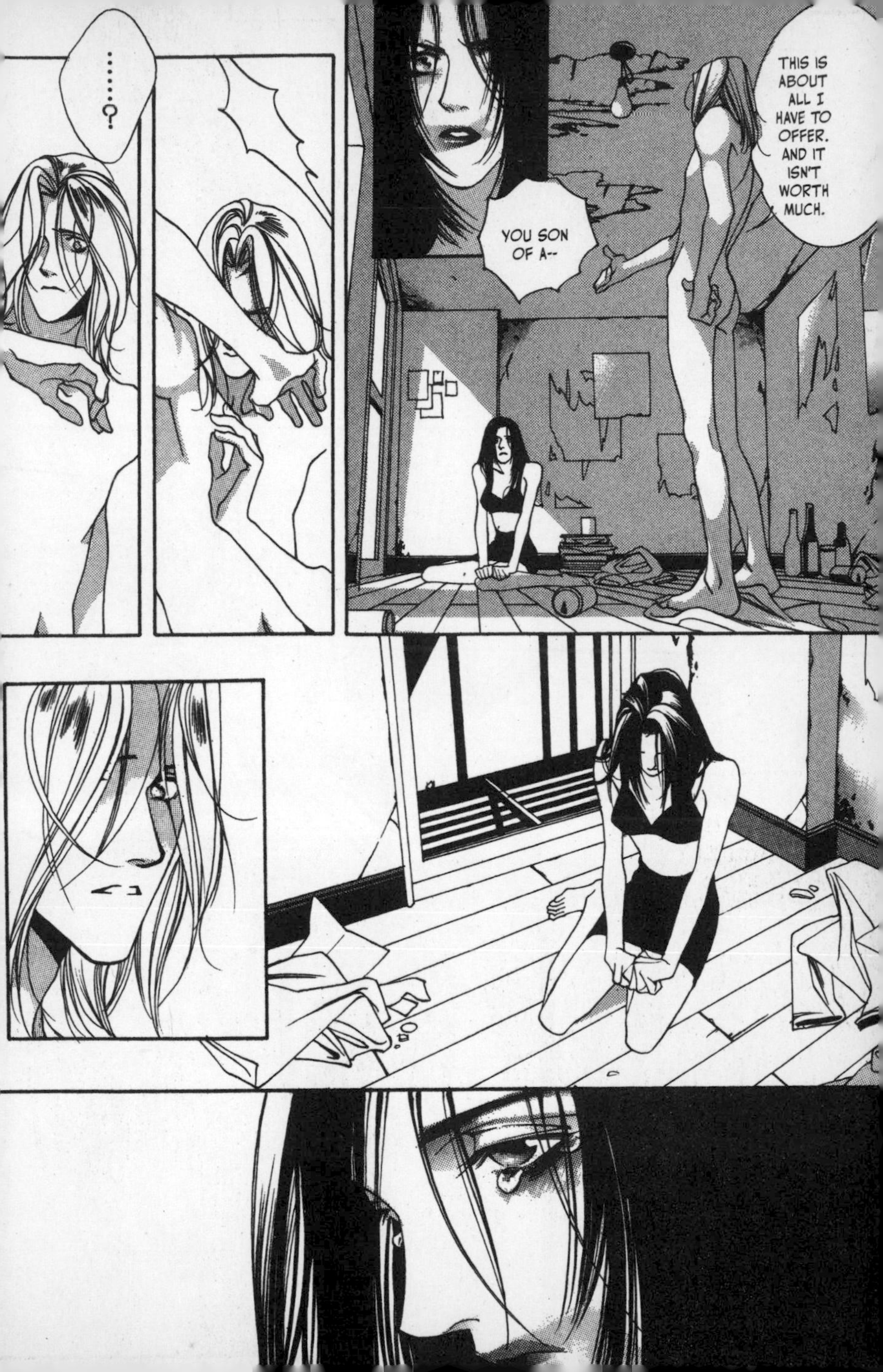
THIS IS ABOUT ALL I HAVE TO OFFER. AND IT ISN'T WORTH MUCH.
YOU SON OF A--
......?

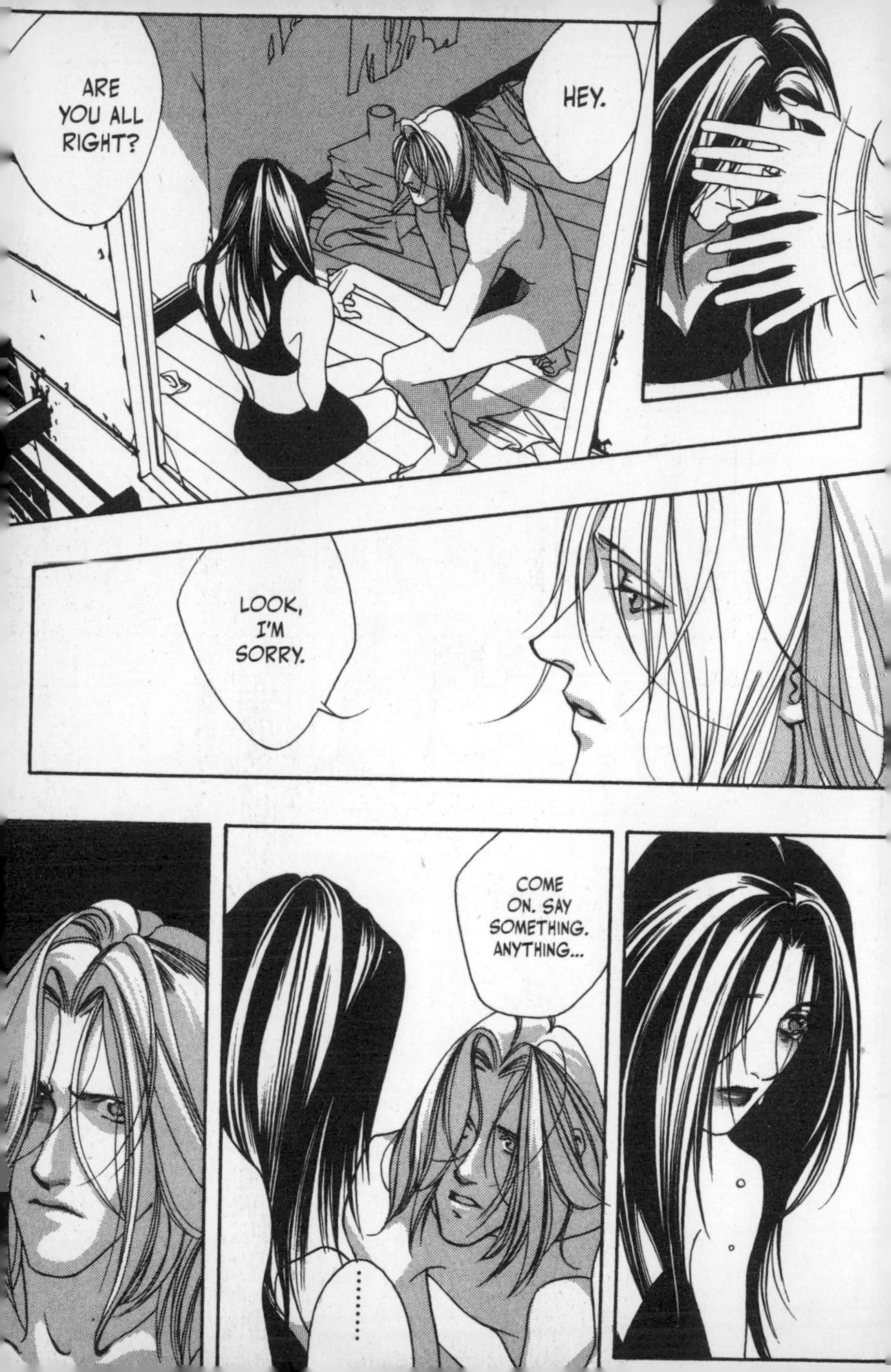
HEY.
ARE YOU ALL RIGHT?
LOOK, I'M SORRY.
COME ON. SAY SOMETHING. ANYTHING...
......

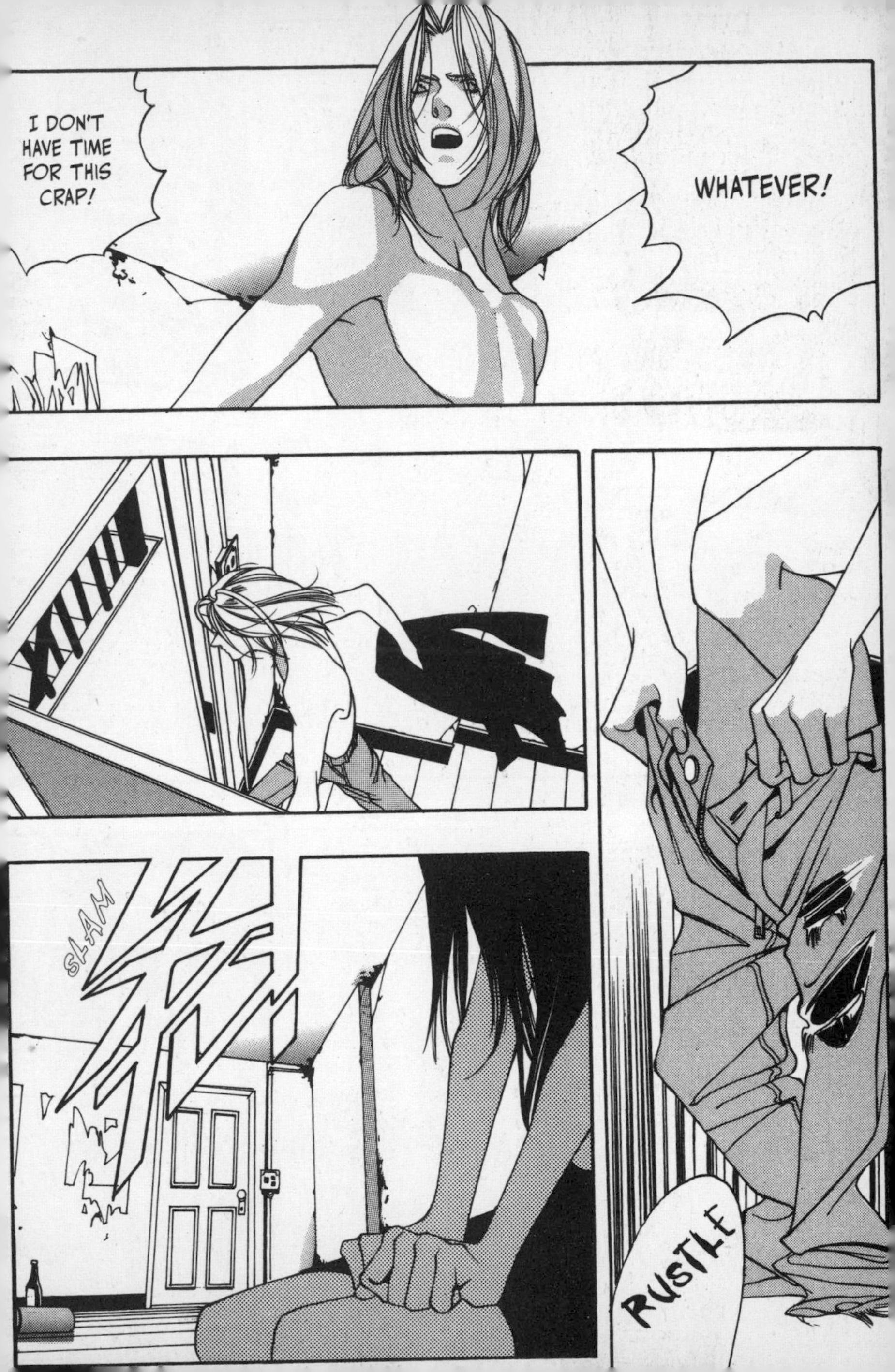
WHATEVER!
I DON'T HAVE TIME FOR THIS CRAP!
RUSTLE
SLAM

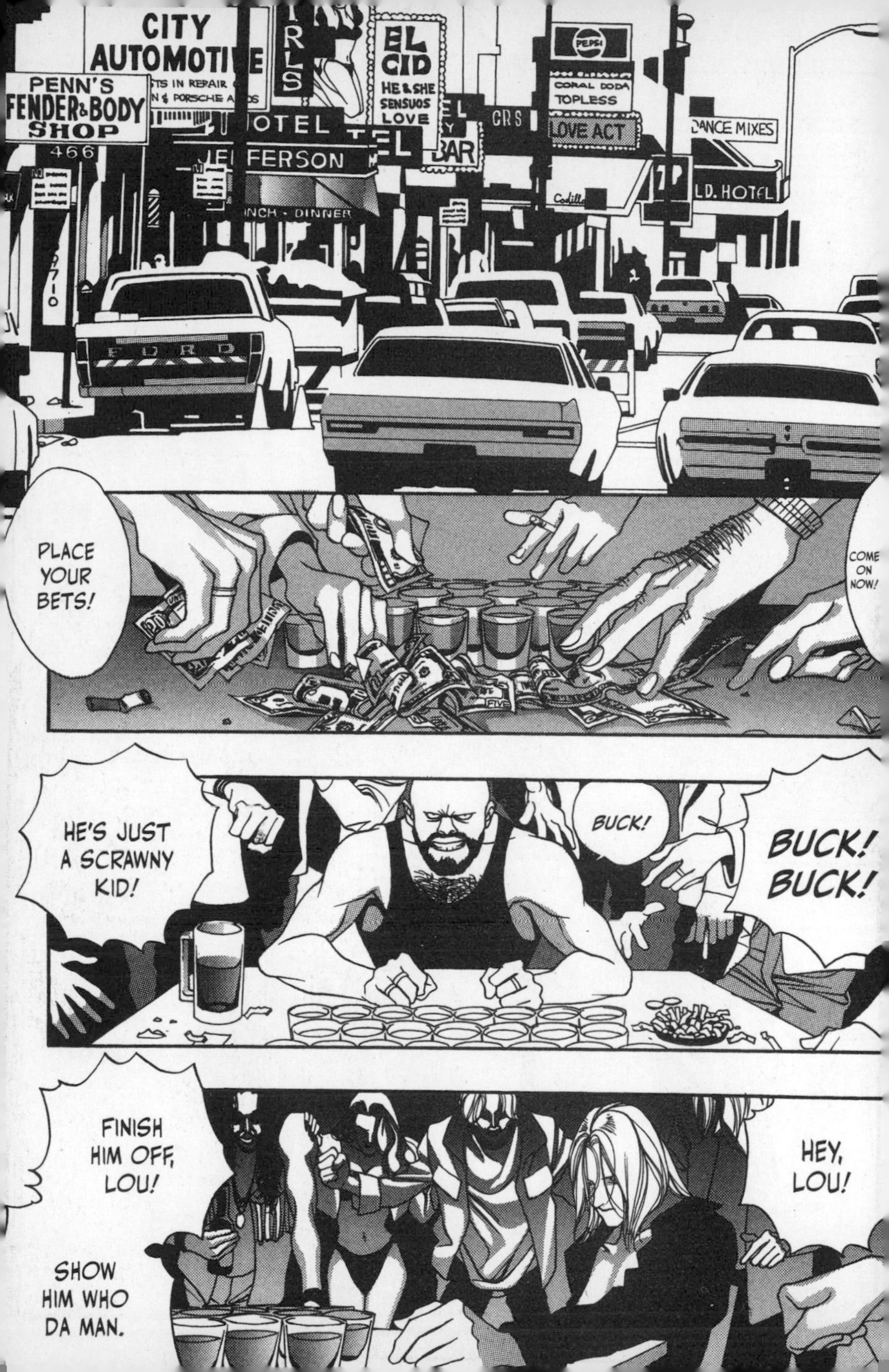
DANCE MIXES
CORAL DODA
TOPLESS
LOVE ACT
PEPSI
BAR
EL CID
HE & SHE
SENSUOS
LOVE
HOTEL
JEFFERSON
CITY
AUTOMOTIVE
PENN'S
FENDER & BODY
SHOP
466
FORD
COME ON NOW!
PLACE YOUR BETS!
BUCK! BUCK!
BUCK!
HE'S JUST A SCRAWNY KID!
HEY, LOU!
FINISH HIM OFF, LOU!
SHOW HIM WHO DA MAN.

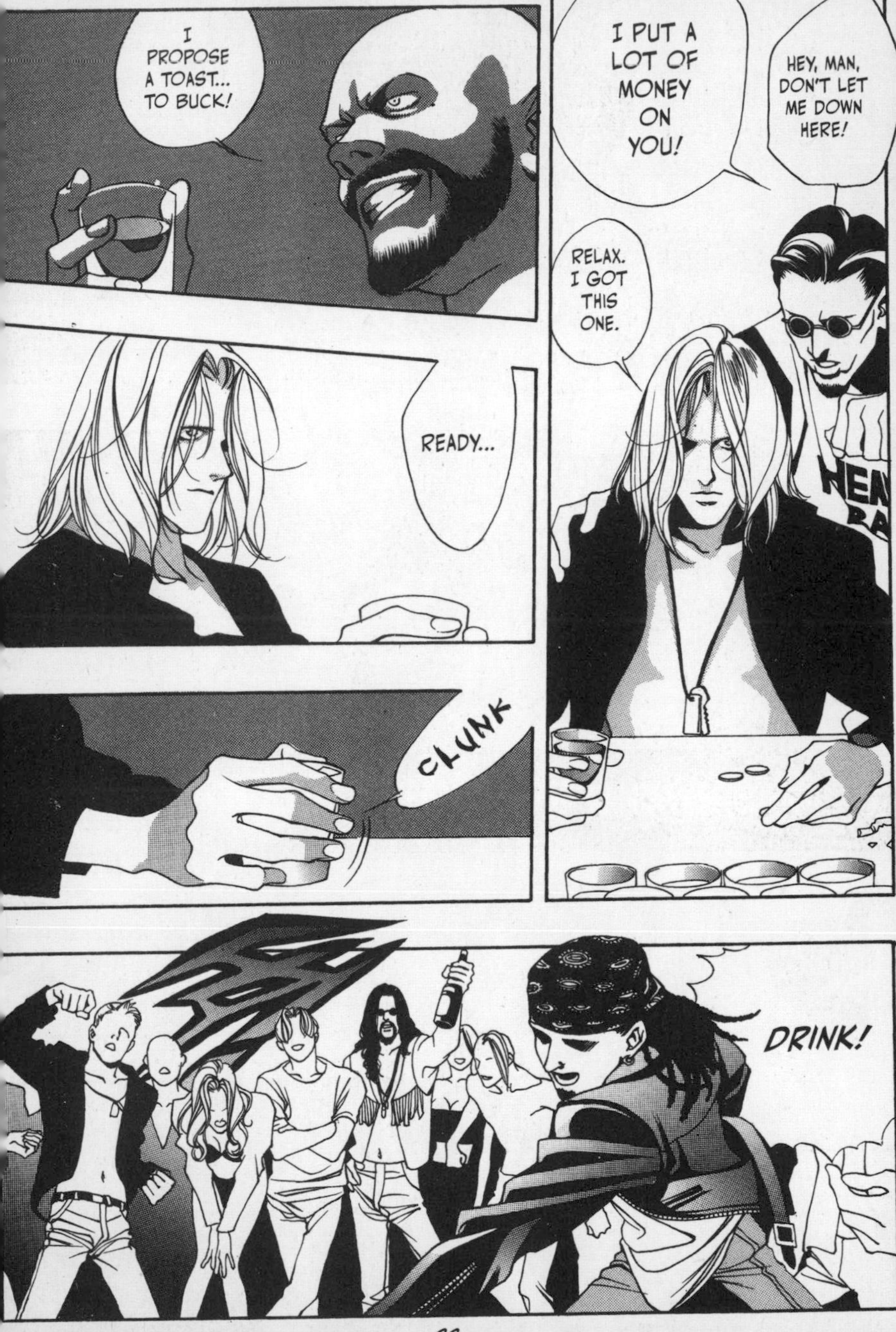
HEY, MAN, DON'T LET ME DOWN HERE!
I PUT A LOT OF MONEY ON YOU!
RELAX. I GOT THIS ONE.
I PROPOSE A TOAST... TO BUCK!
READY...
CLUNK
DRINK!

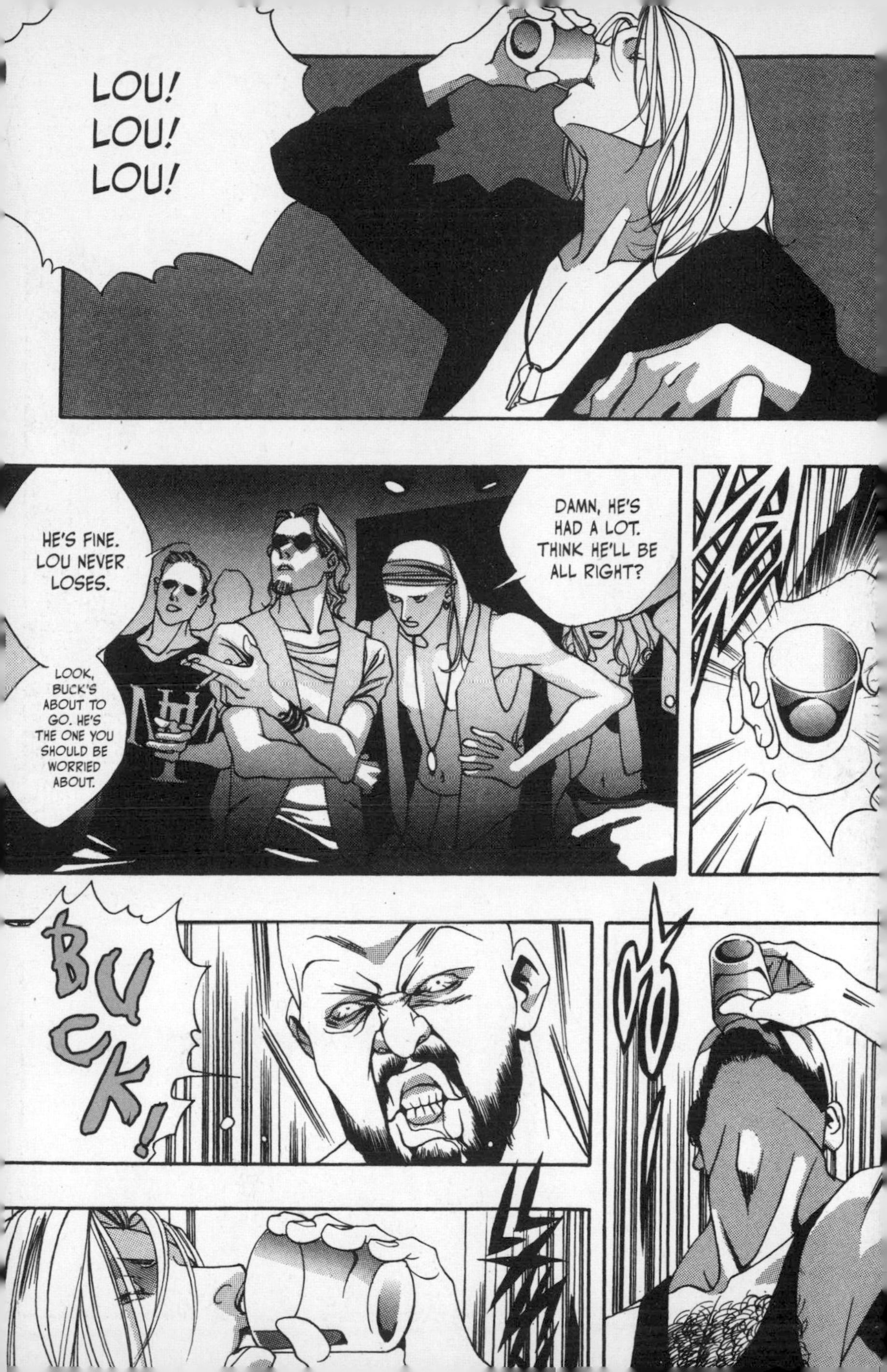
LOU!
LOU!
LOU!
DAMN, HE'S HAD A LOT. THINK HE'LL BE ALL RIGHT?
HE'S FINE. LOU NEVER LOSES.
LOOK, BUCK'S ABOUT TO GO. HE'S THE ONE YOU SHOULD BE WORRIED ABOUT.
BUCK!

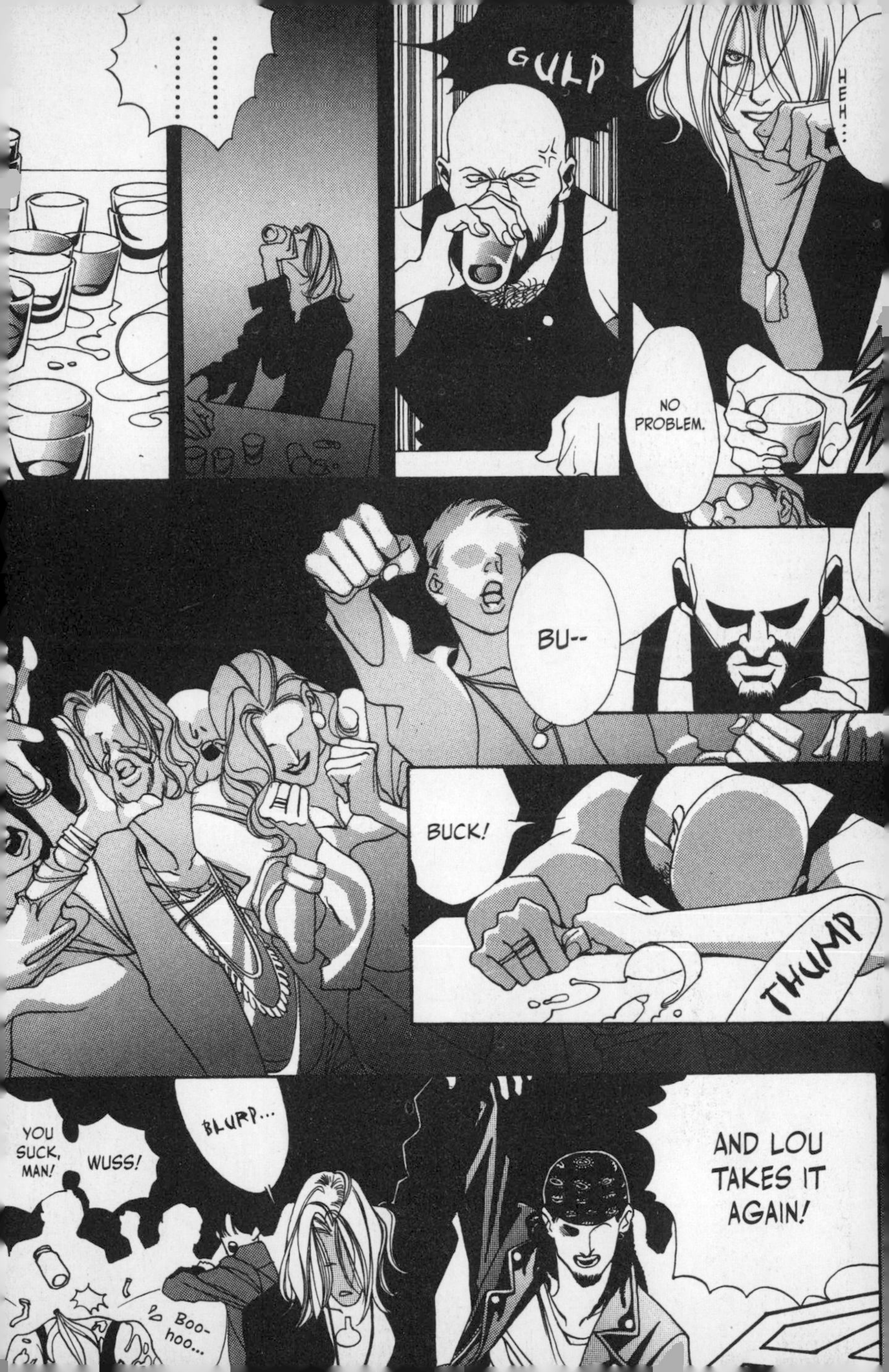
HEH...
NO PROBLEM.
GULP
......
BU--
BUCK!
THUMP
AND LOU TAKES IT AGAIN!
BLURP...
WUSS!
YOU SUCK, MAN!
Boo-hoo...

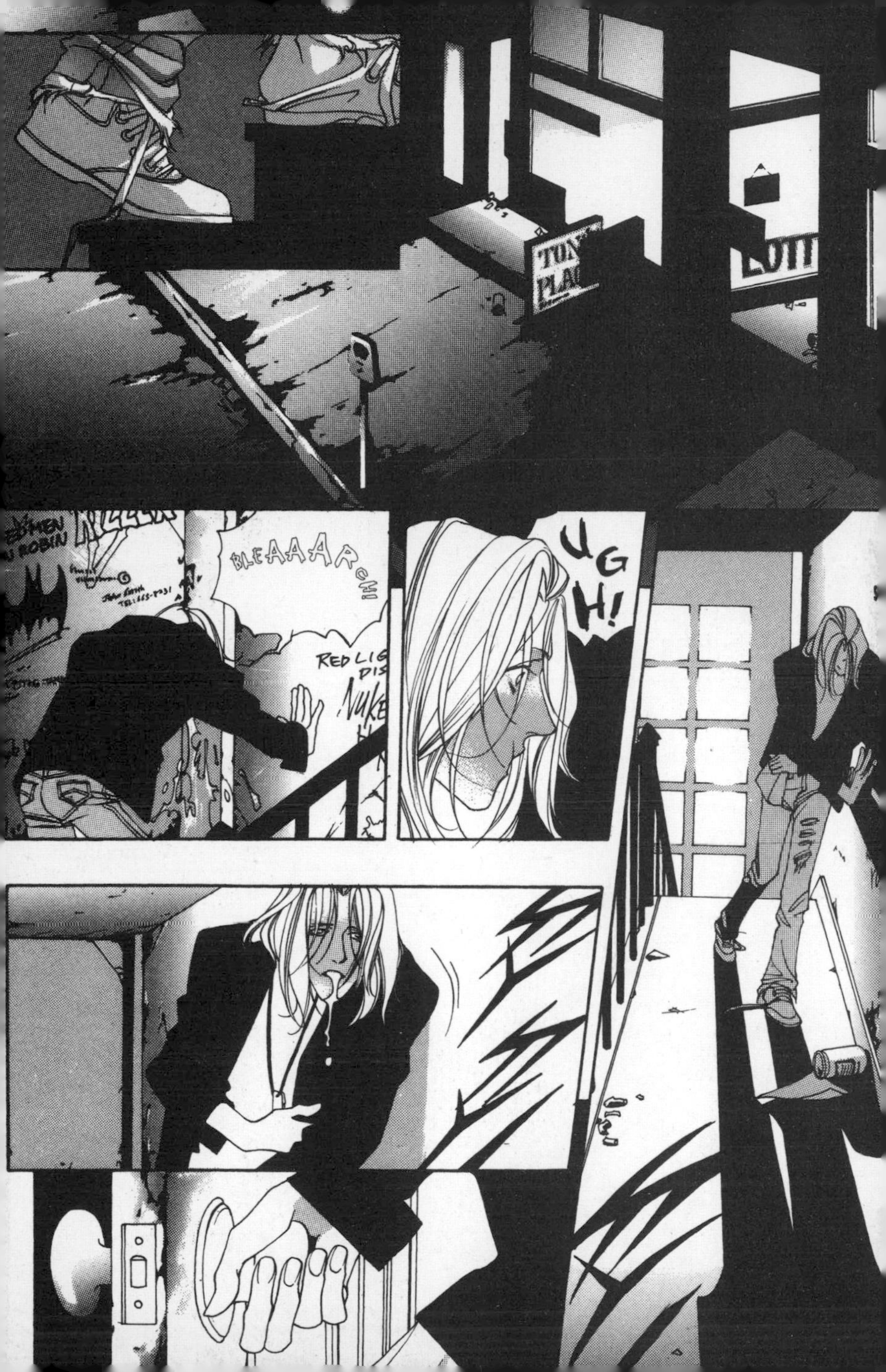
UGH!
BLEAAAARCH!
NUKE

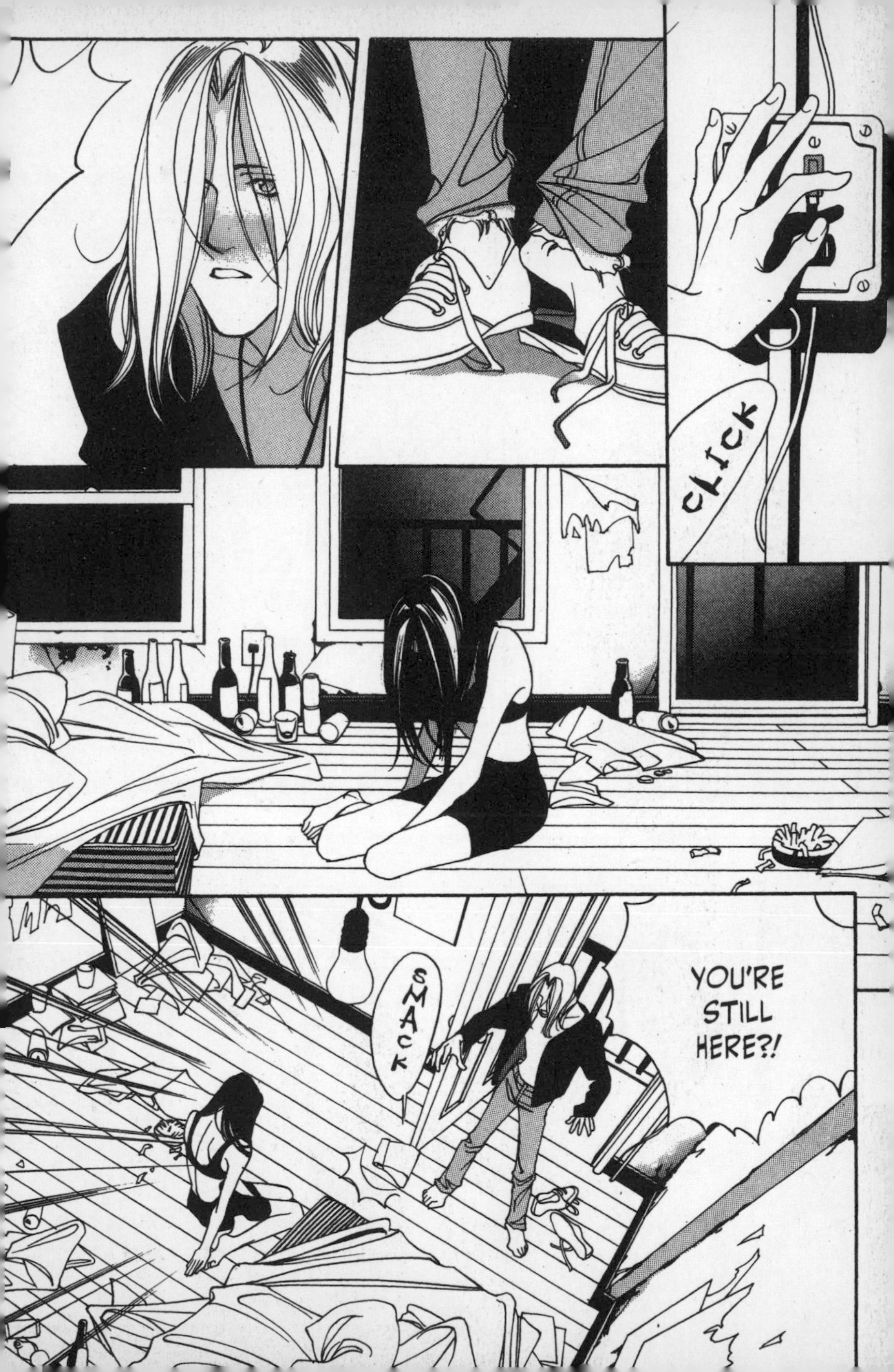
CLICK
YOU'RE STILL HERE?!
SMACK

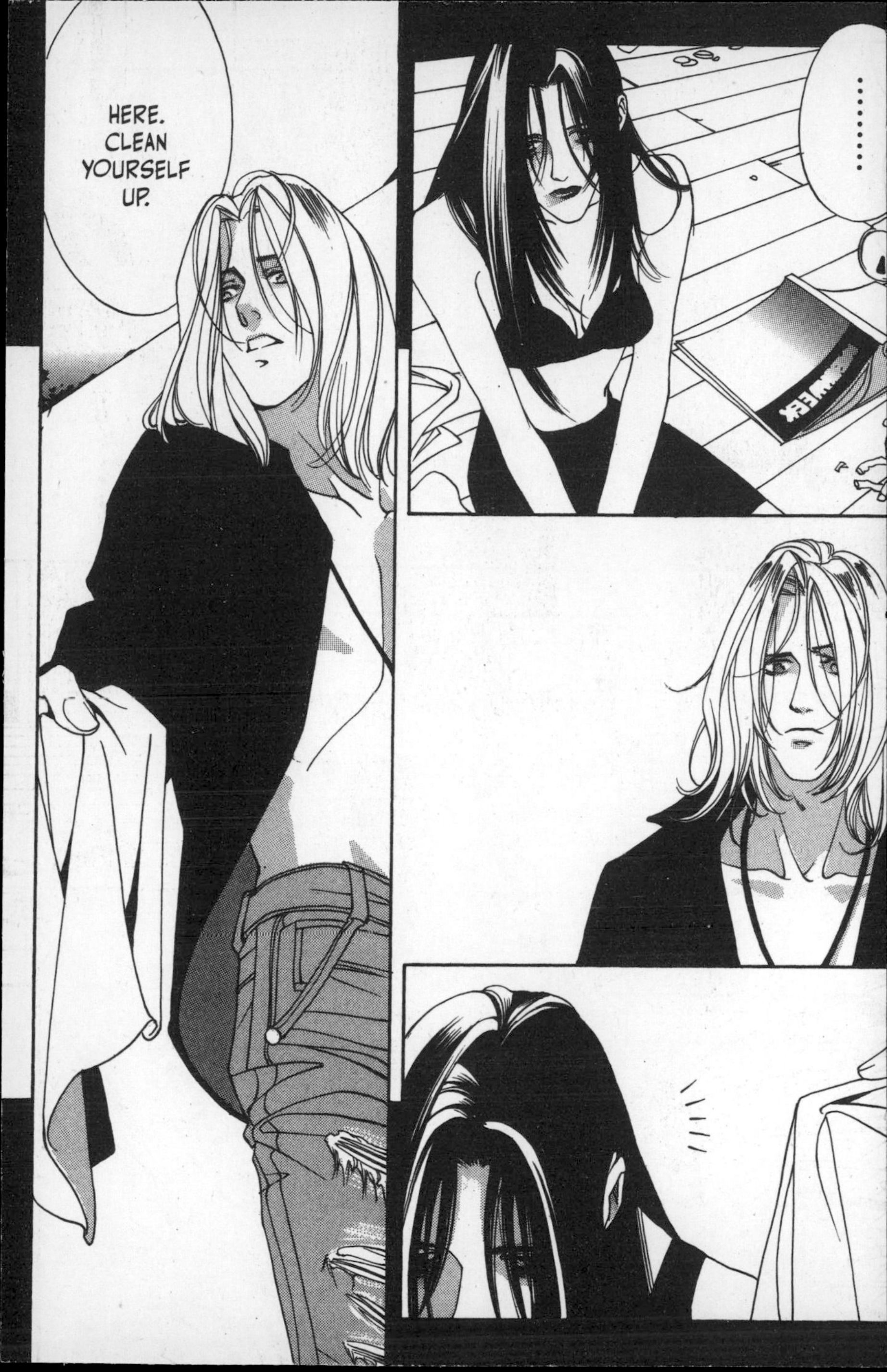
......
HERE. CLEAN YOURSELF UP.

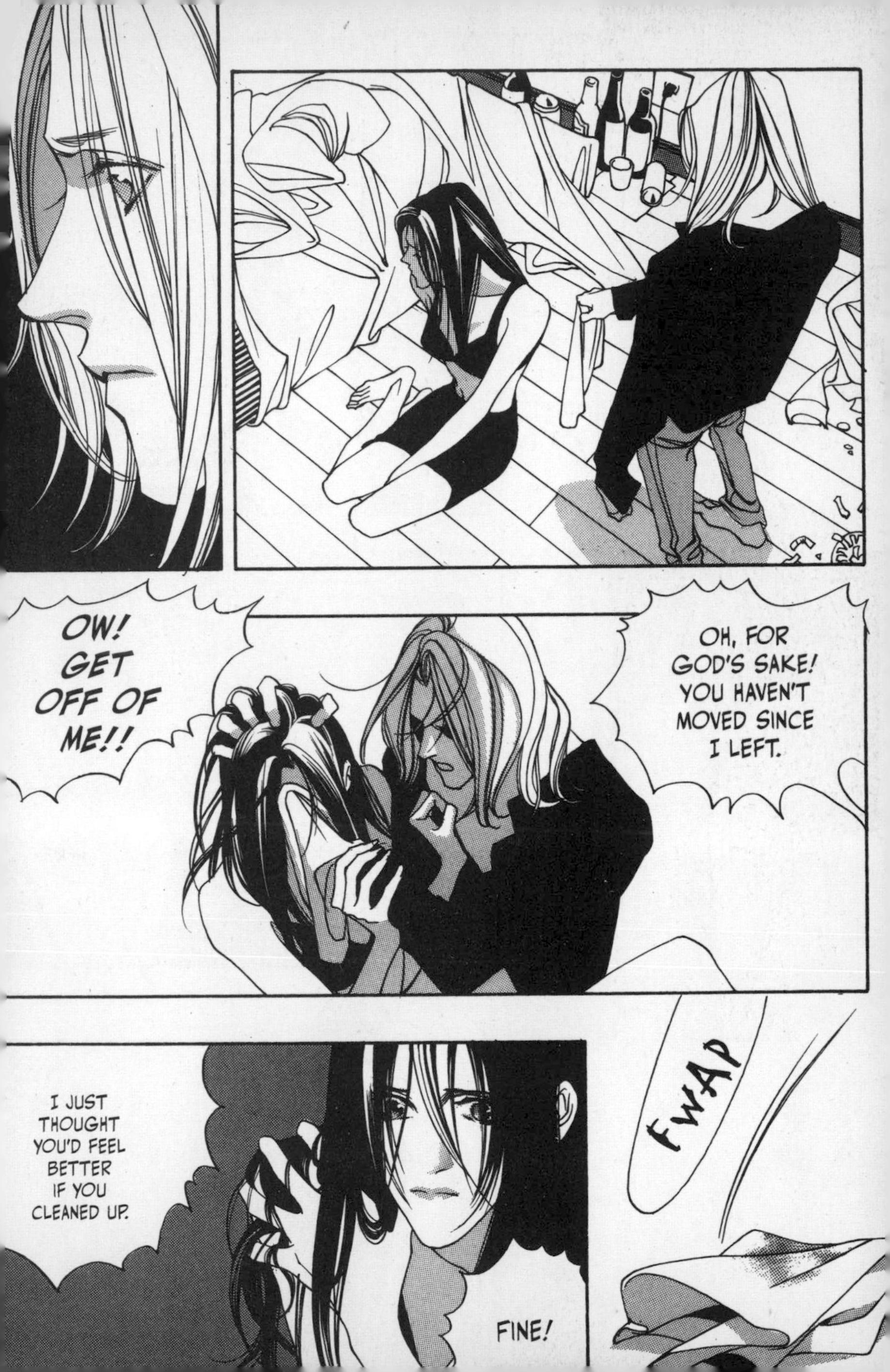
OH, FOR GOD'S SAKE! YOU HAVEN'T MOVED SINCE I LEFT.
OW! GET OFF OF ME!!
FWAP
I JUST THOUGHT YOU'D FEEL BETTER IF YOU CLEANED UP.
FINE!

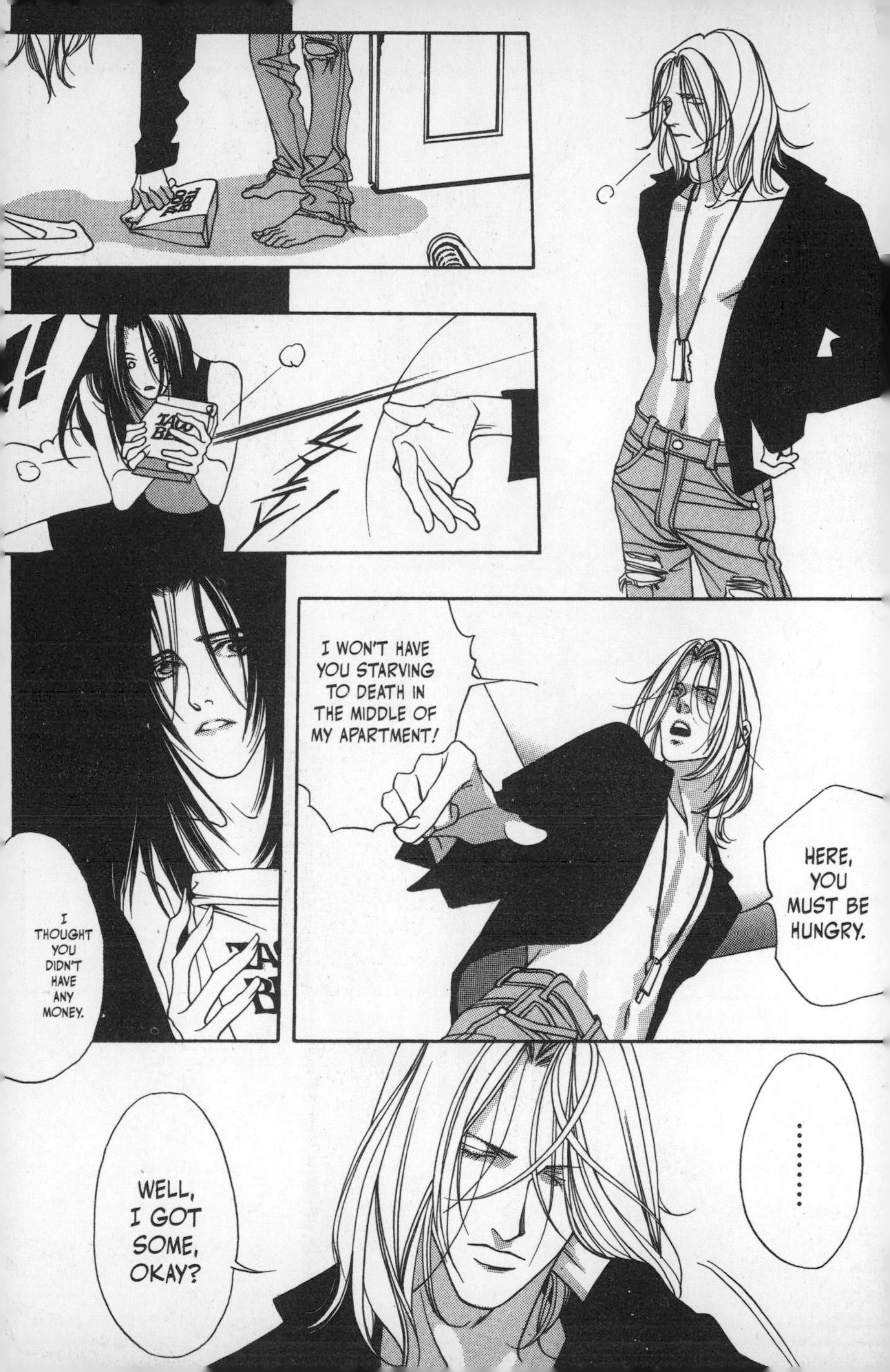
HERE, YOU MUST BE HUNGRY.
I WON'T HAVE YOU STARVING TO DEATH IN THE MIDDLE OF MY APARTMENT!
I THOUGHT YOU DIDN'T HAVE ANY MONEY.
......
WELL, I GOT SOME, OKAY?

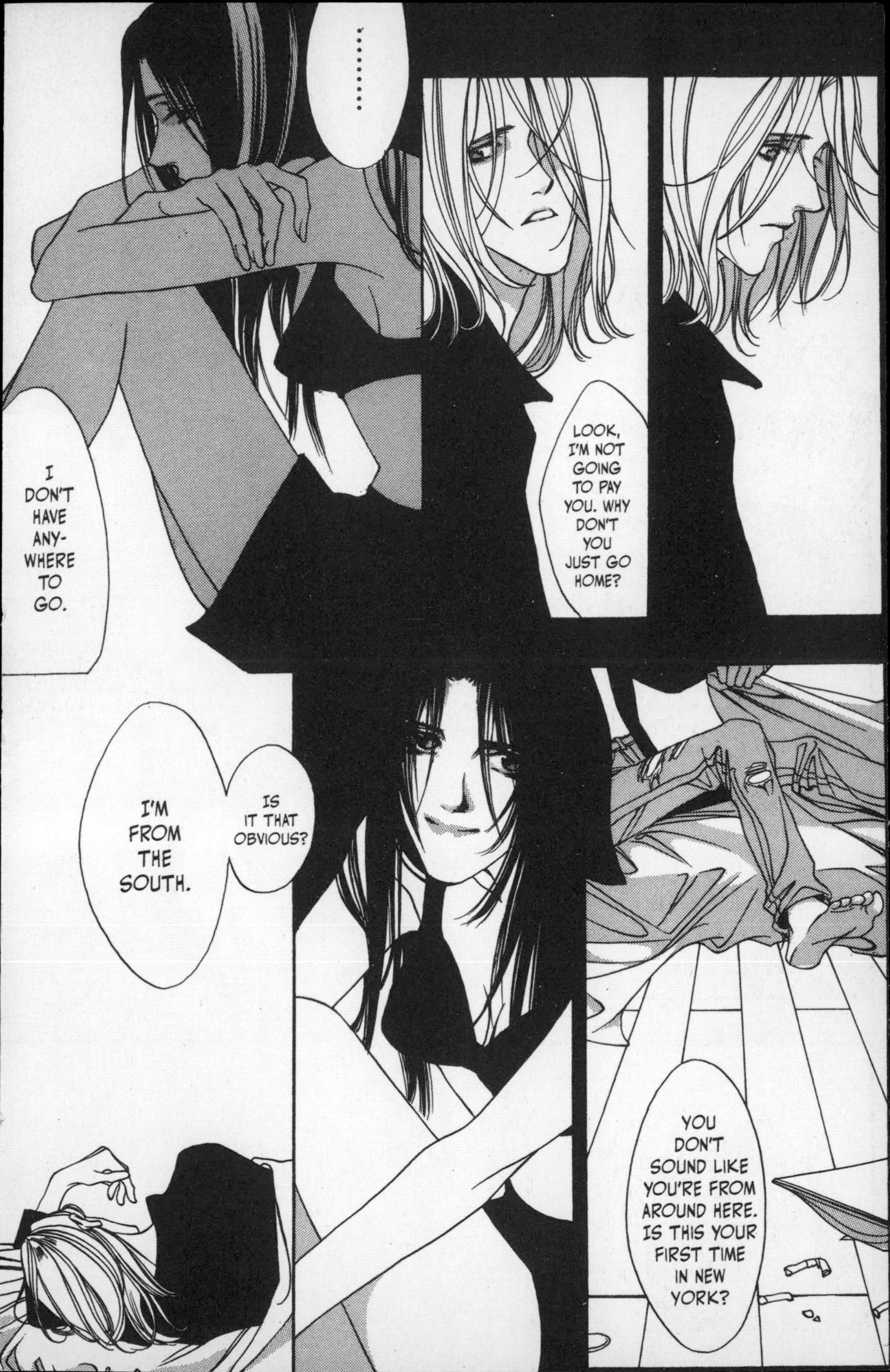
LOOK, I'M NOT GOING TO PAY YOU. WHY DON'T YOU JUST GO HOME?
......
I DON'T HAVE ANY-WHERE TO GO.
YOU DON'T SOUND LIKE YOU'RE FROM AROUND HERE. IS THIS YOUR FIRST TIME IN NEW YORK?
IS IT THAT OBVIOUS?
I'M FROM THE SOUTH.

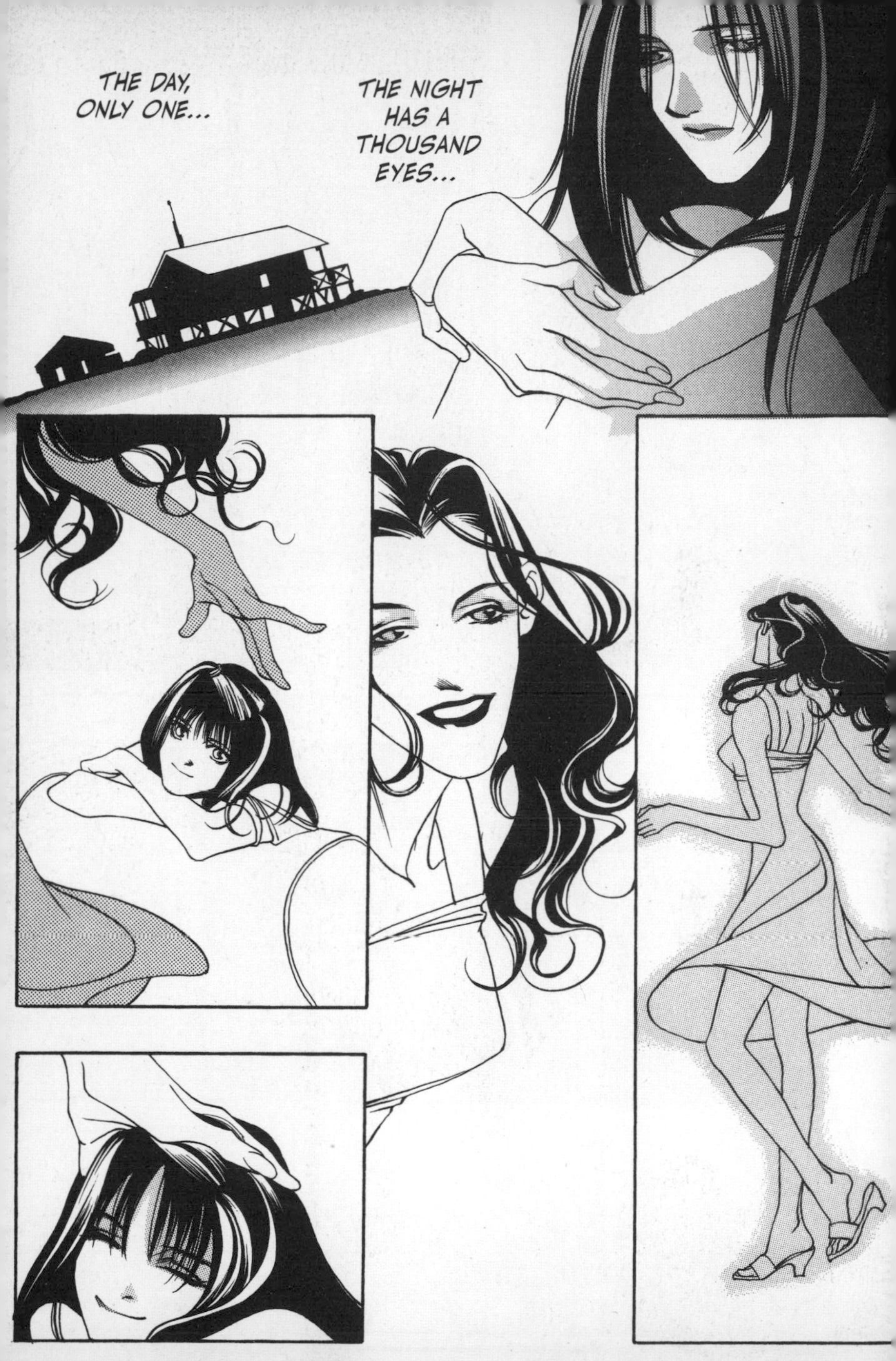
THE NIGHT HAS A THOUSAND EYES...
THE DAY, ONLY ONE...

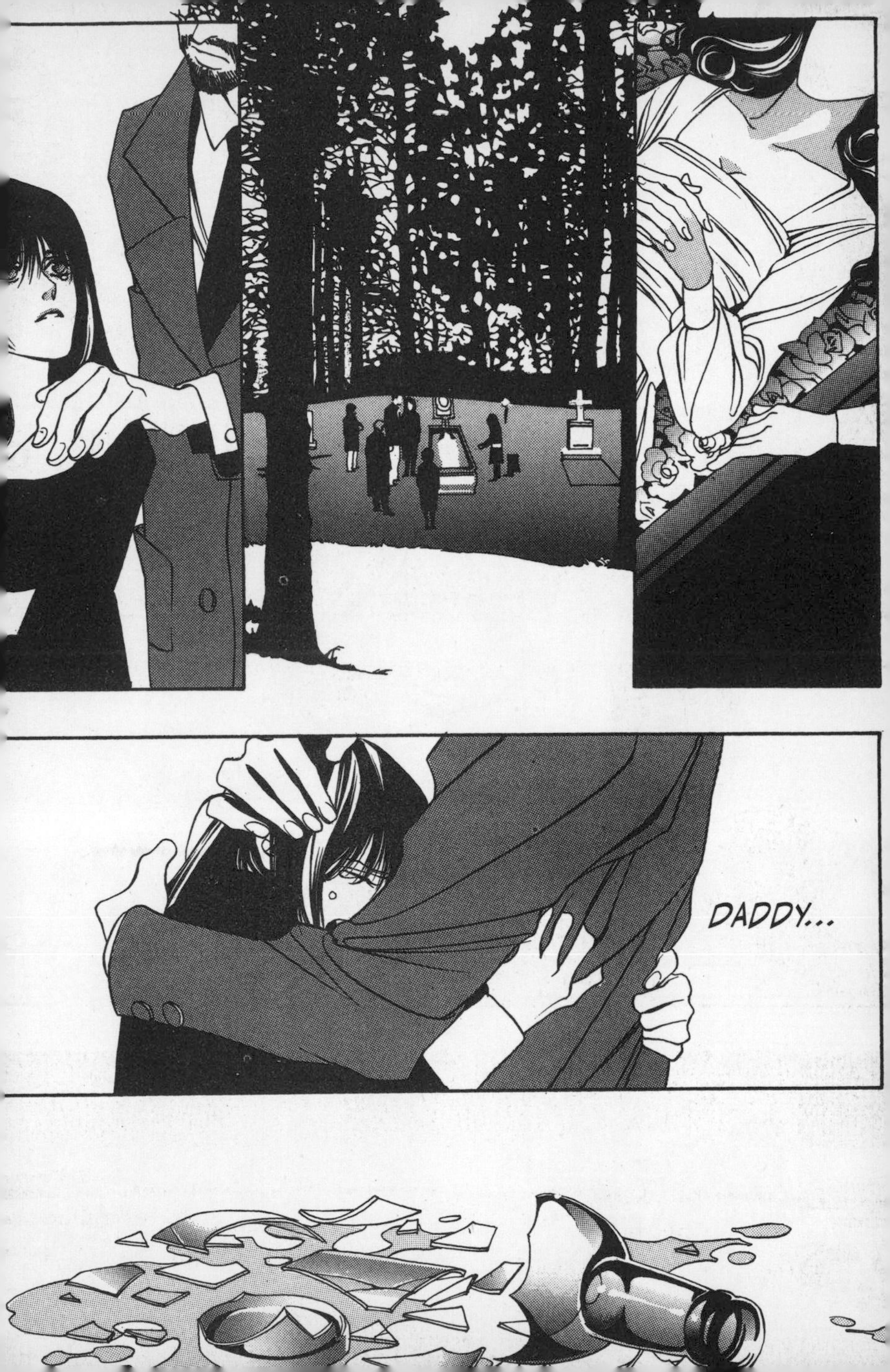
DADDY...

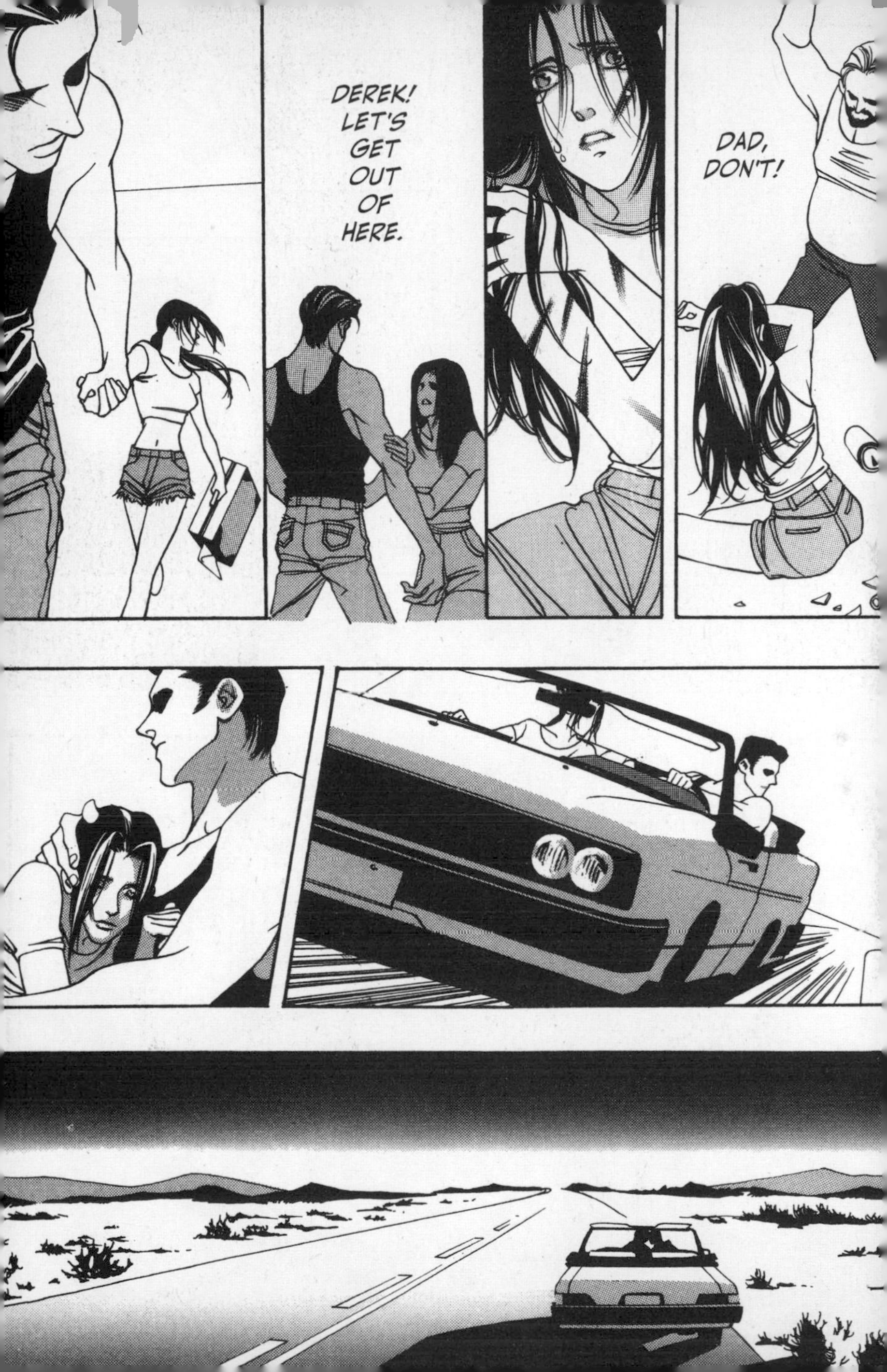
DAD, DON'T!
DEREK! LET'S GET OUT OF HERE.

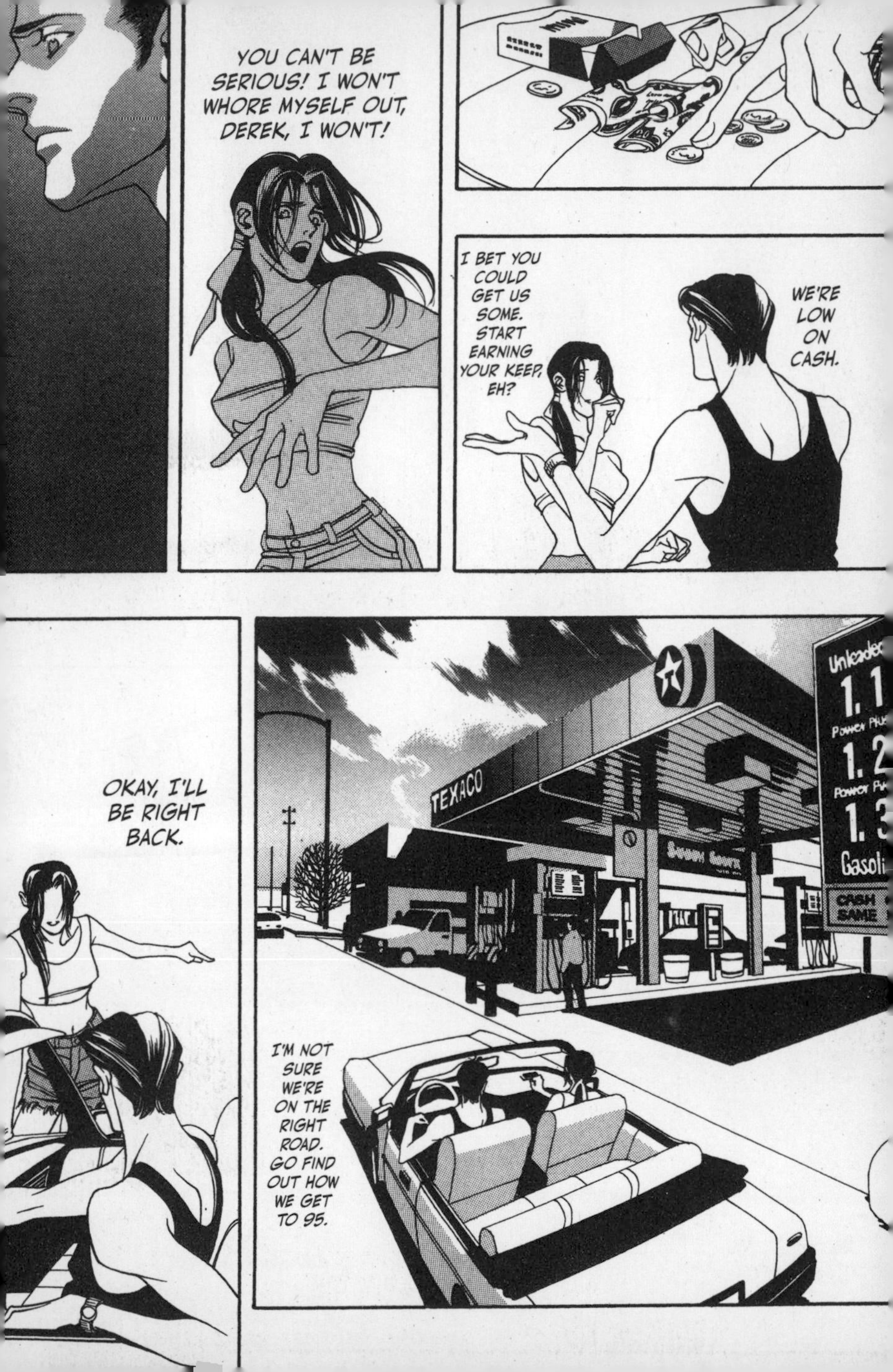
WE'RE LOW ON CASH.
I BET YOU COULD GET US SOME. START EARNING YOUR KEEP, EH?
YOU CAN'T BE SERIOUS! I WON'T WHORE MYSELF OUT, DEREK, I WON'T!
TEXACO
CASH SAME
I'M NOT SURE WE'RE ON THE RIGHT ROAD. GO FIND OUT HOW WE GET TO 95.
OKAY, I'LL BE RIGHT BACK.

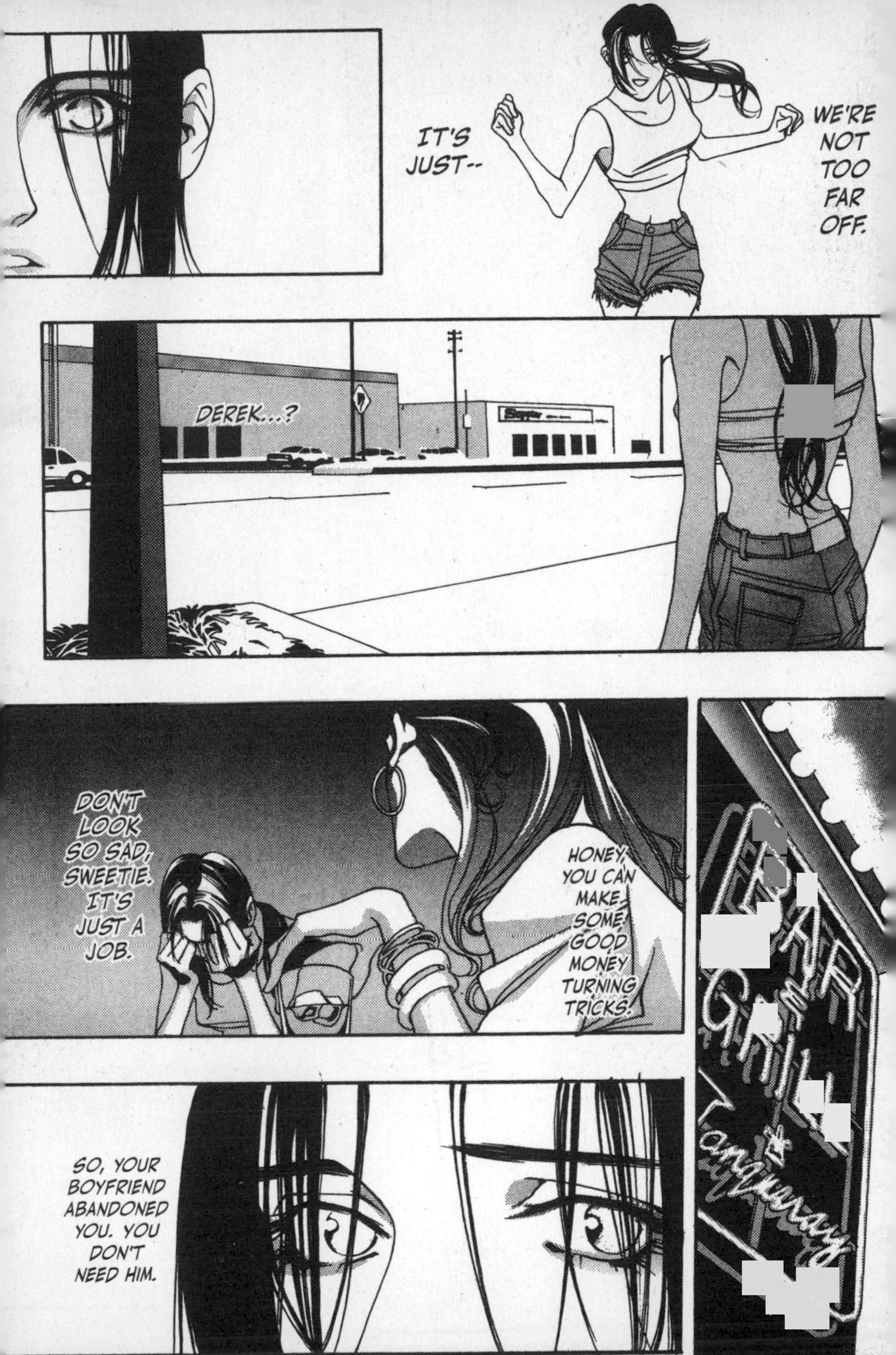
WE'RE NOT TOO FAR OFF.
IT'S JUST--
DEREK...?
HONEY, YOU CAN MAKE SOME GOOD MONEY TURNING TRICKS!
DON'T LOOK SO SAD, SWEETIE. IT'S JUST A JOB.
SO, YOUR BOYFRIEND ABANDONED YOU. YOU DON'T NEED HIM.

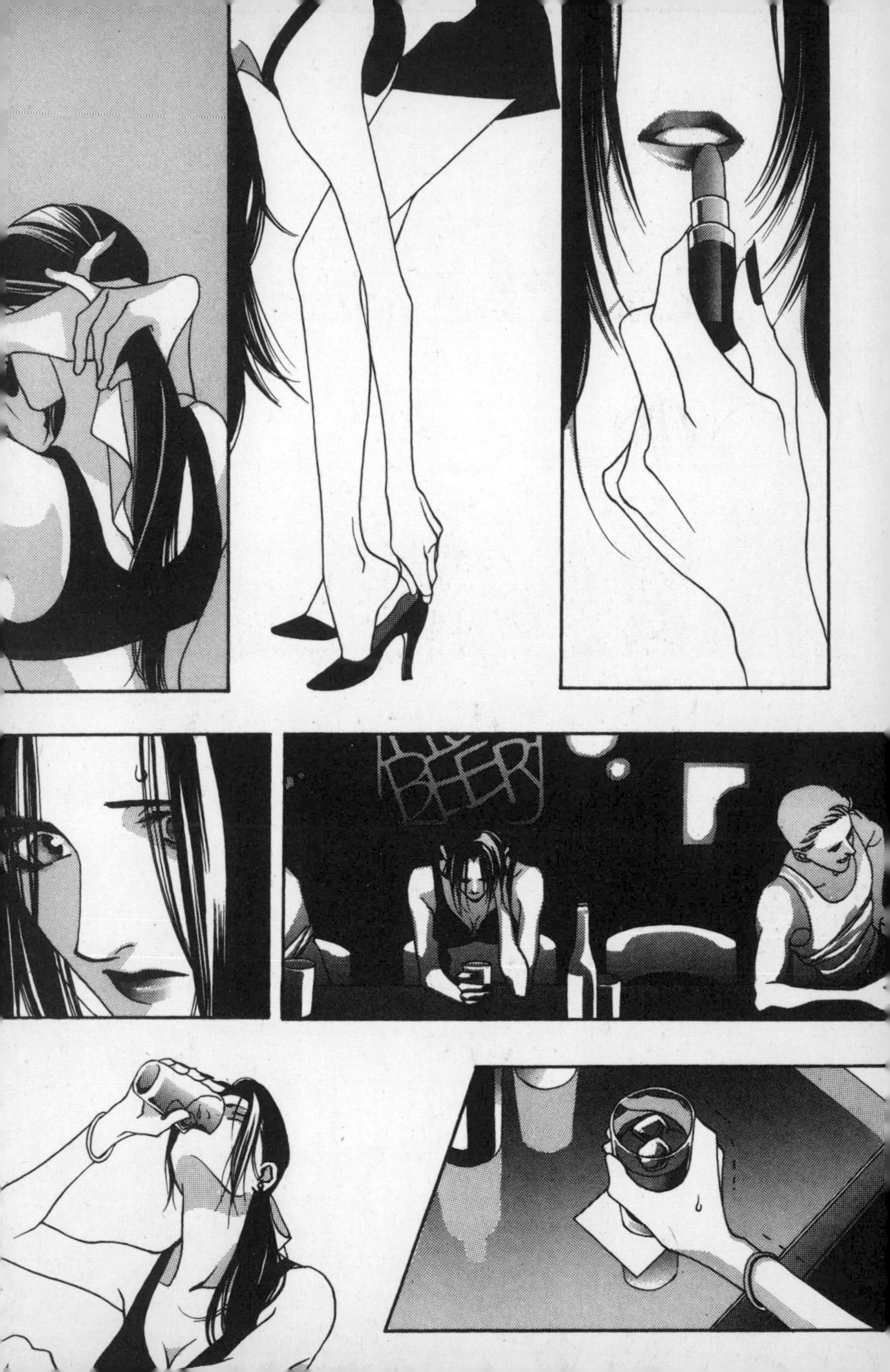
BEER

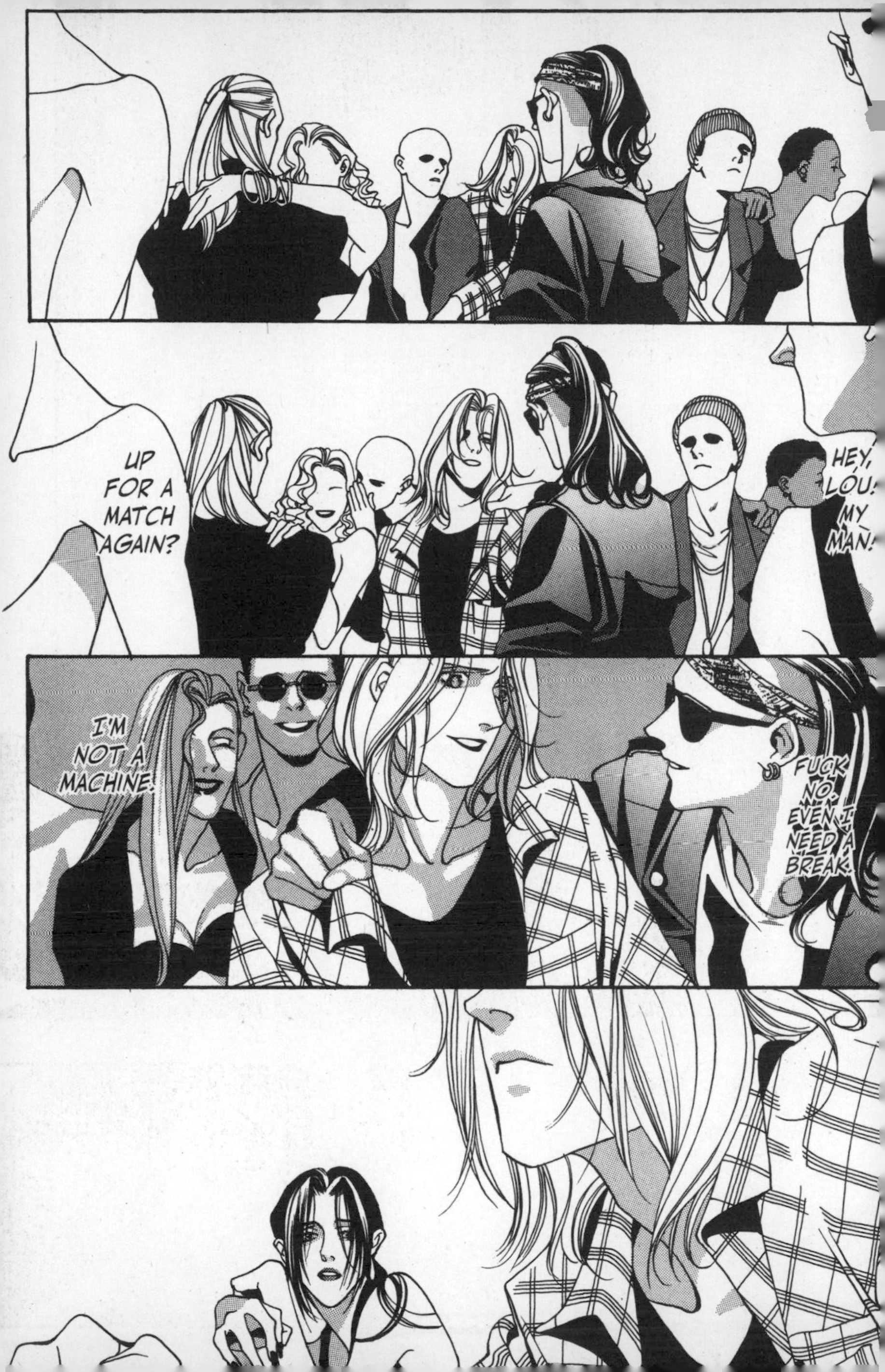
HEY, LOU! MY MAN!
UP FOR A MATCH AGAIN?
FUCK NO. EVEN I NEED A BREAK.
I'M NOT A MACHINE.

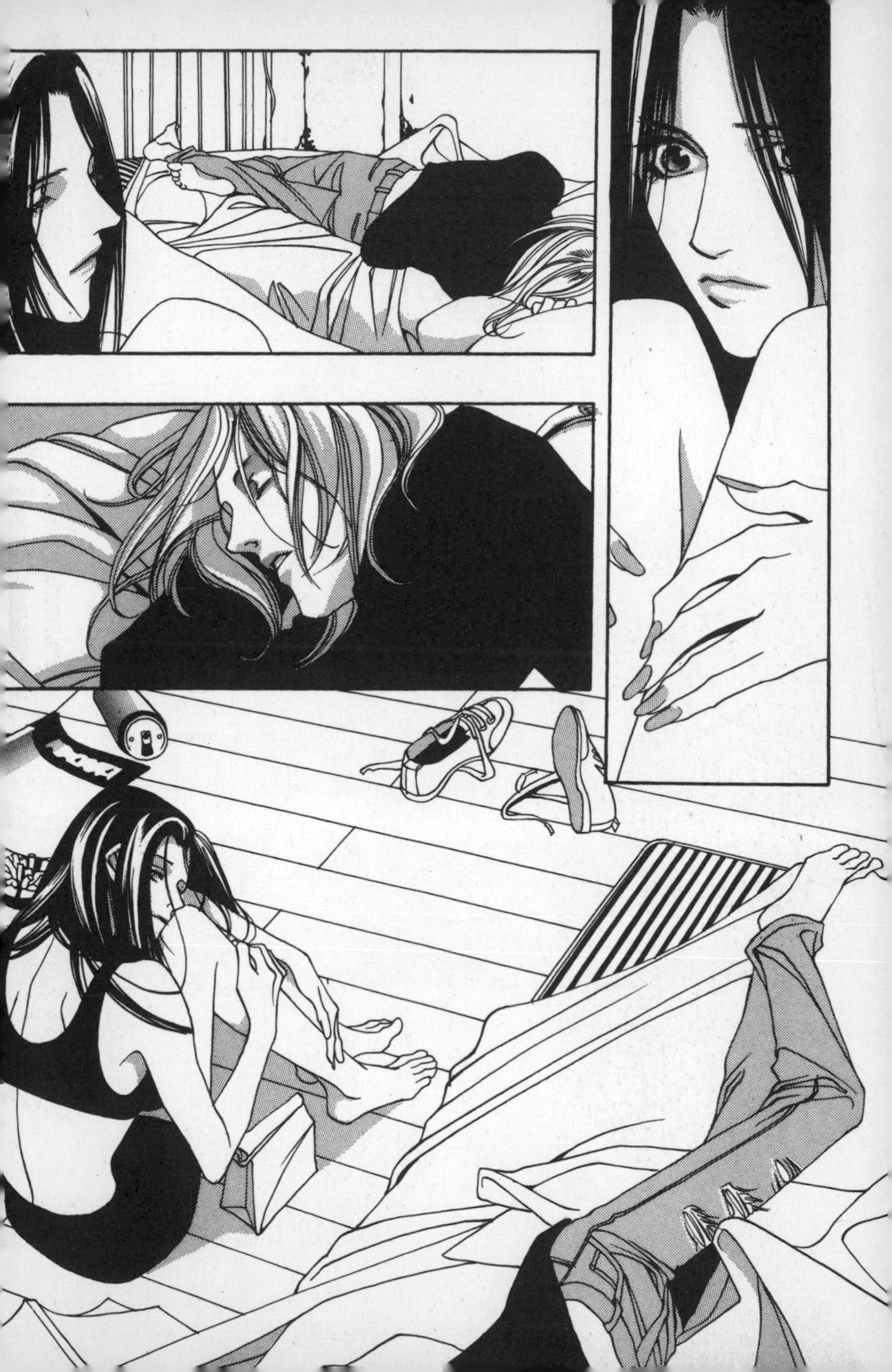

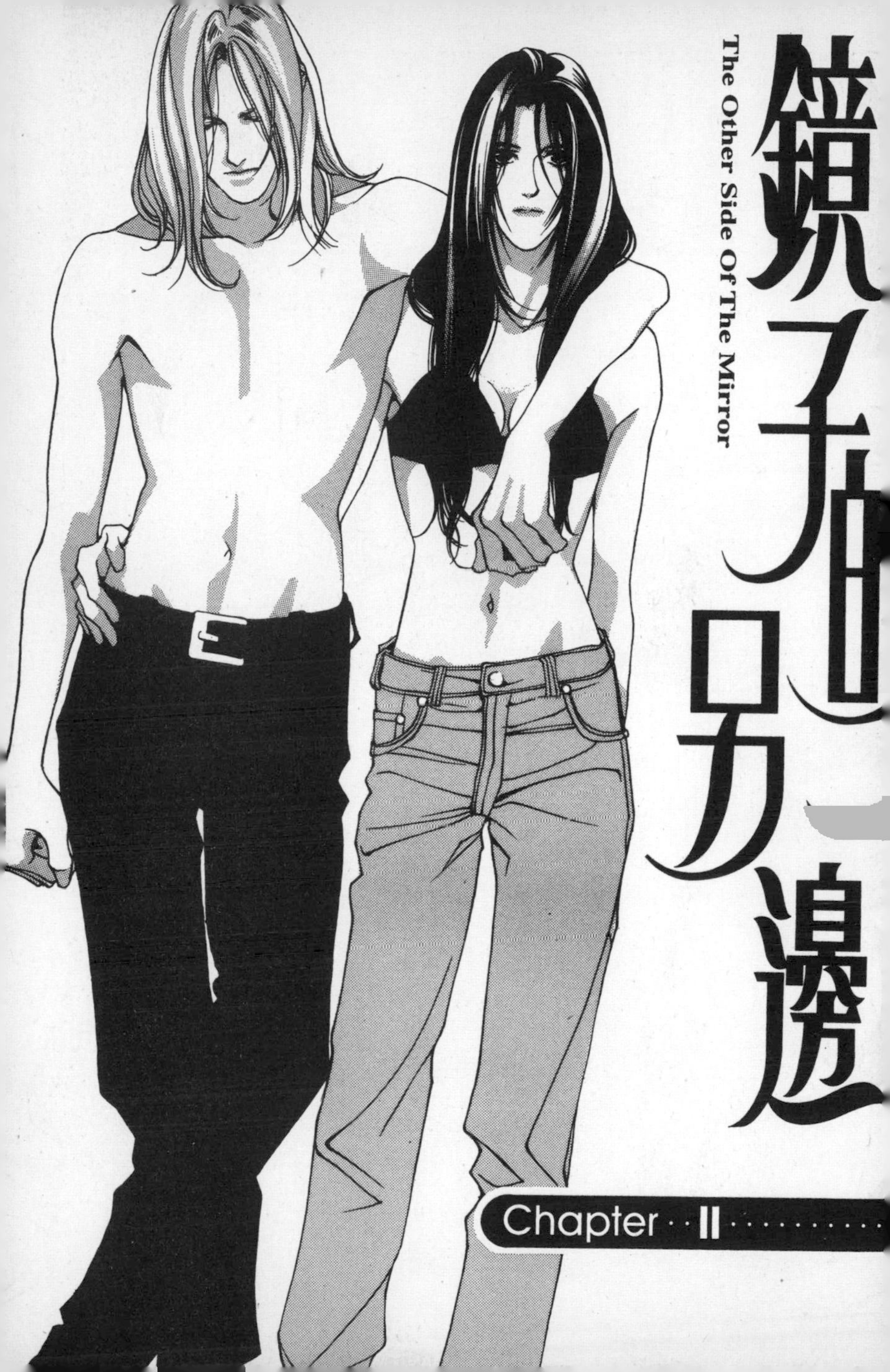
鏡子的另一邊
The Other Side Of The Mirror
Chapter · · II

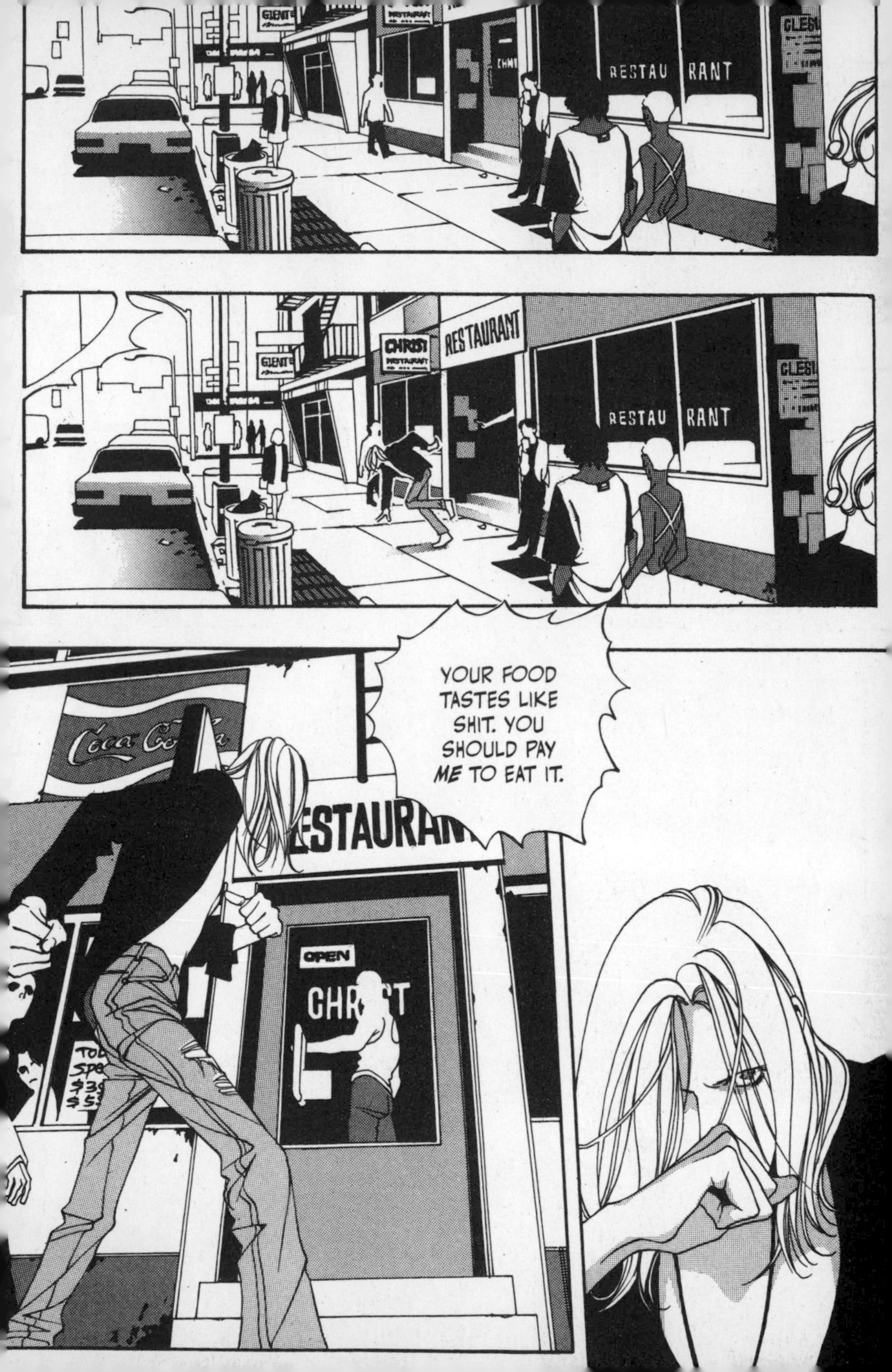
RESTAU RANT
RESTAURANT
RESTAU RANT
YOUR FOOD TASTES LIKE SHIT. YOU SHOULD PAY *ME* TO EAT IT.
OPEN

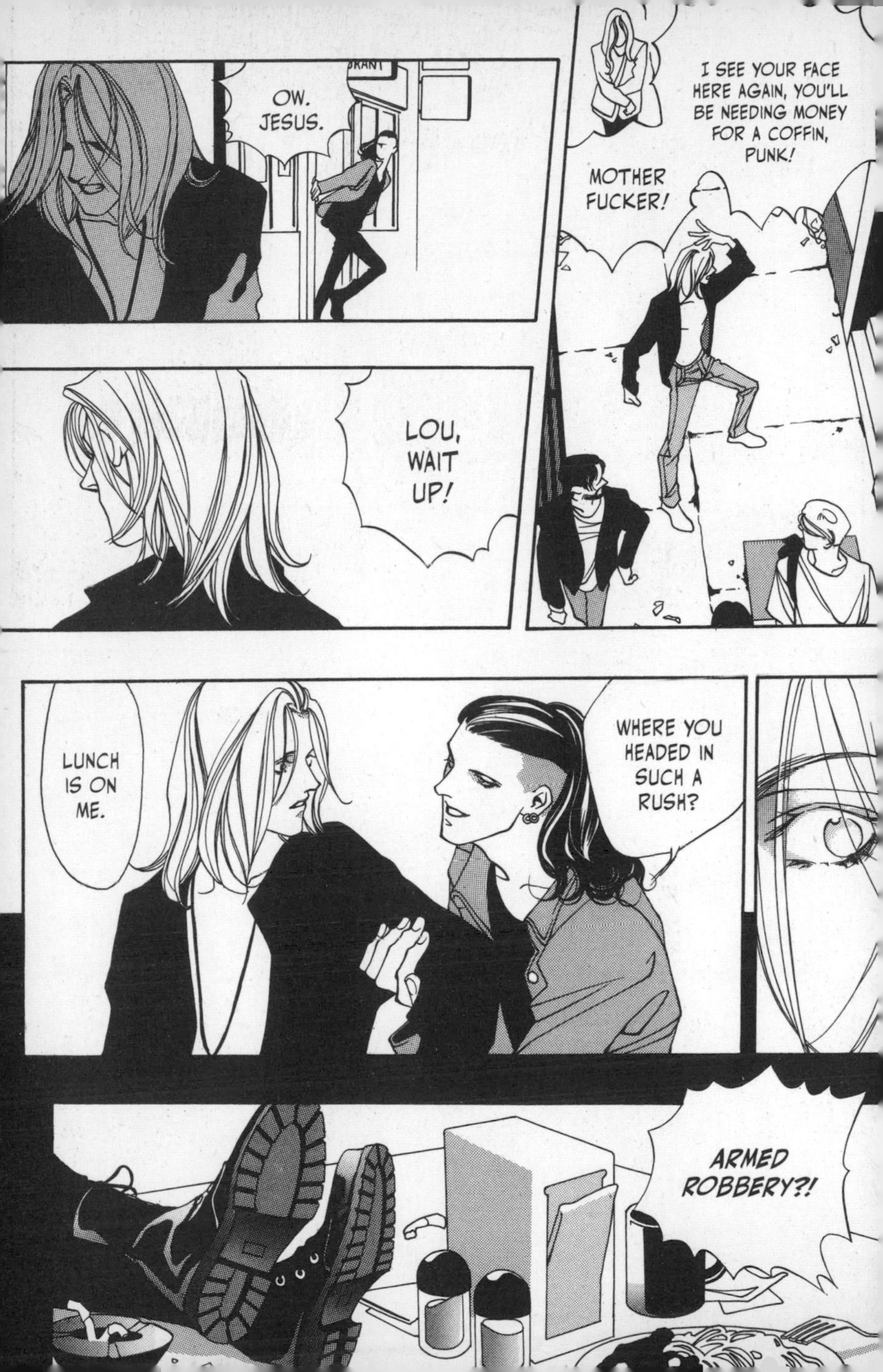
I SEE YOUR FACE HERE AGAIN, YOU'LL BE NEEDING MONEY FOR A COFFIN, PUNK!
MOTHER FUCKER!
OW. JESUS.
LOU, WAIT UP!
WHERE YOU HEADED IN SUCH A RUSH?
LUNCH IS ON ME.
ARMED ROBBERY?!

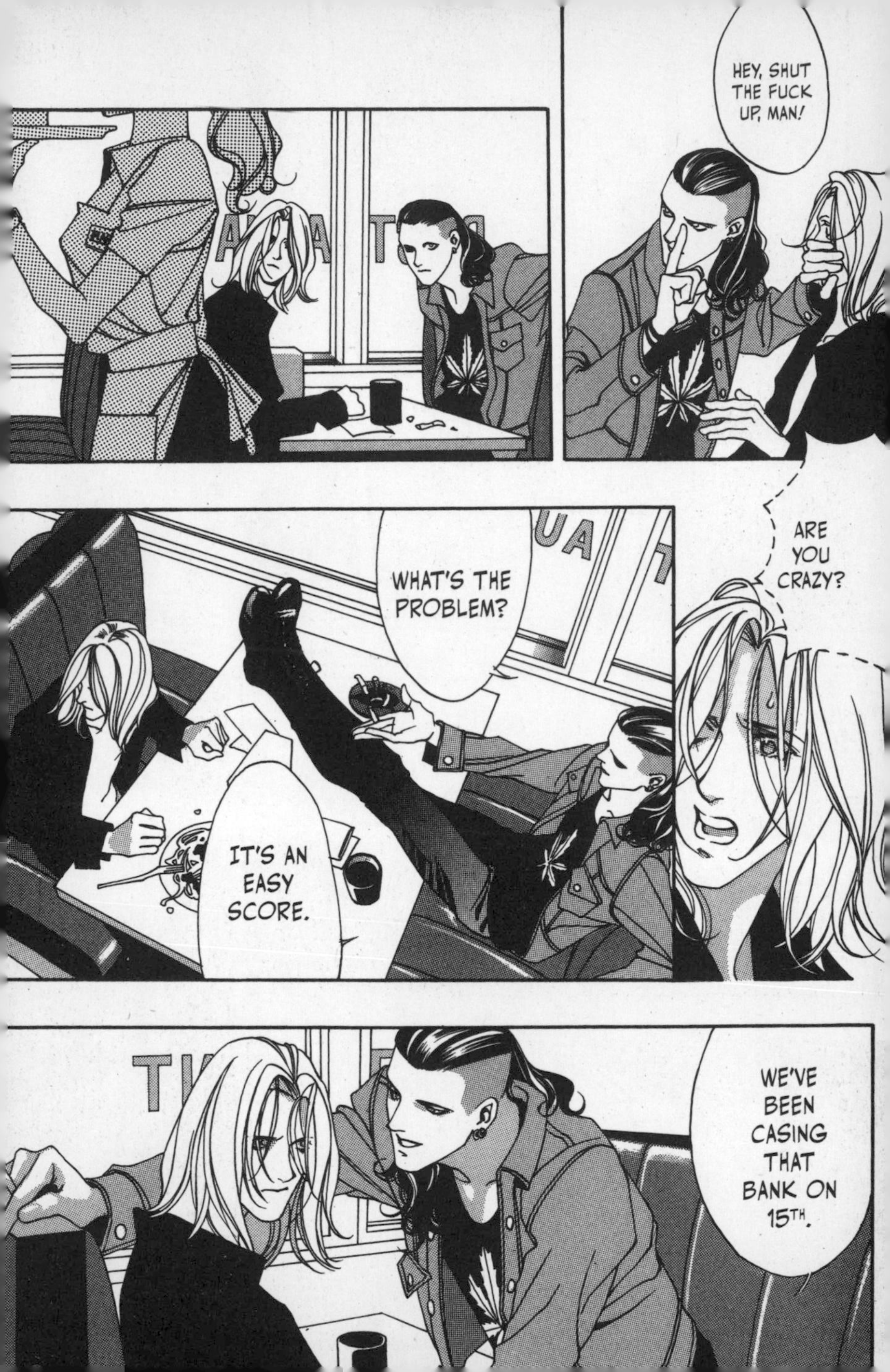
HEY, SHUT THE FUCK UP, MAN!
ARE YOU CRAZY?
WHAT'S THE PROBLEM?
IT'S AN EASY SCORE.
WE'VE BEEN CASING THAT BANK ON 15TH.

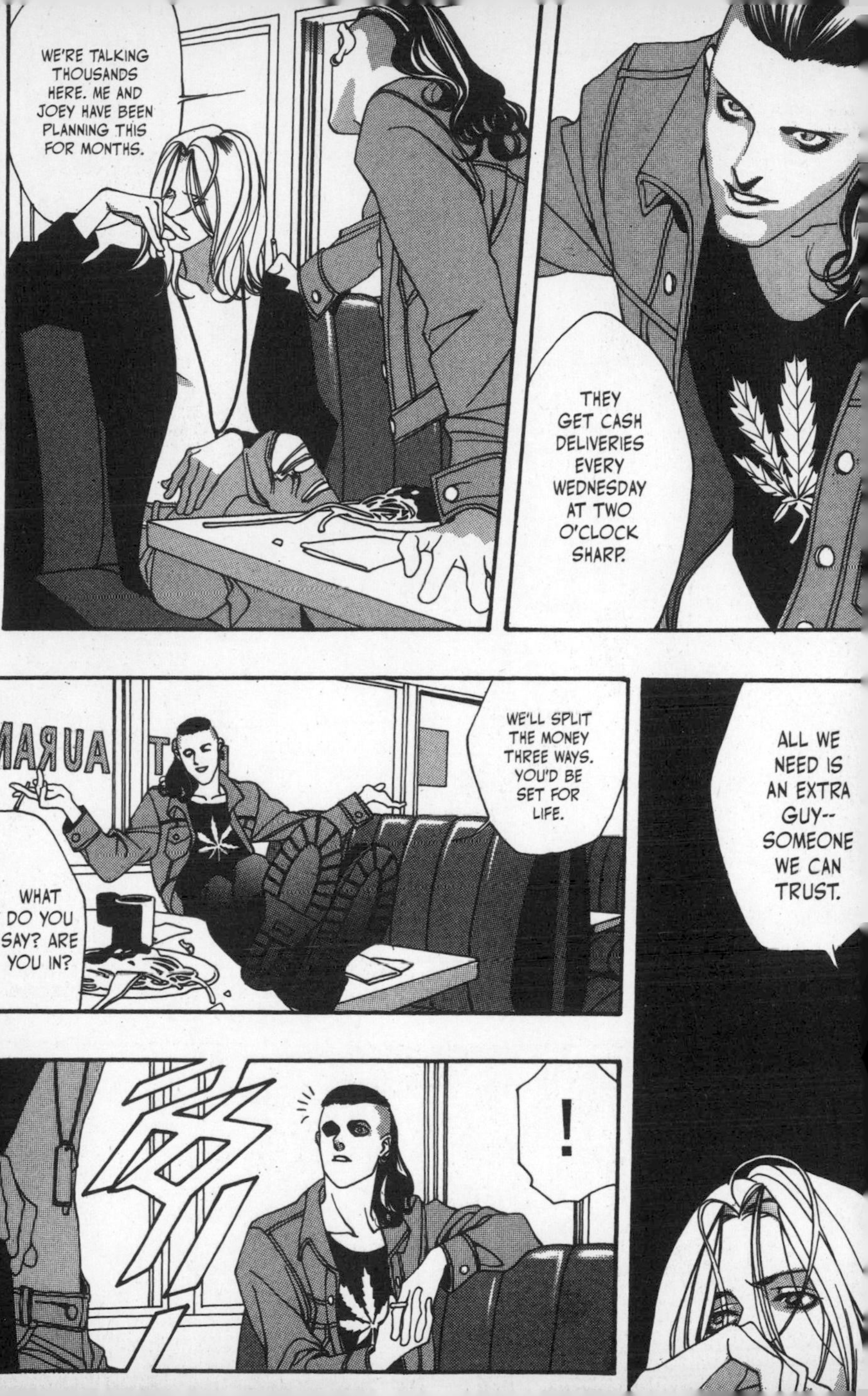
THEY GET CASH DELIVERIES EVERY WEDNESDAY AT TWO O'CLOCK SHARP.
WE'RE TALKING THOUSANDS HERE. ME AND JOEY HAVE BEEN PLANNING THIS FOR MONTHS.
ALL WE NEED IS AN EXTRA GUY-- SOMEONE WE CAN TRUST.
WE'LL SPLIT THE MONEY THREE WAYS. YOU'D BE SET FOR LIFE.
WHAT DO YOU SAY? ARE YOU IN?
!

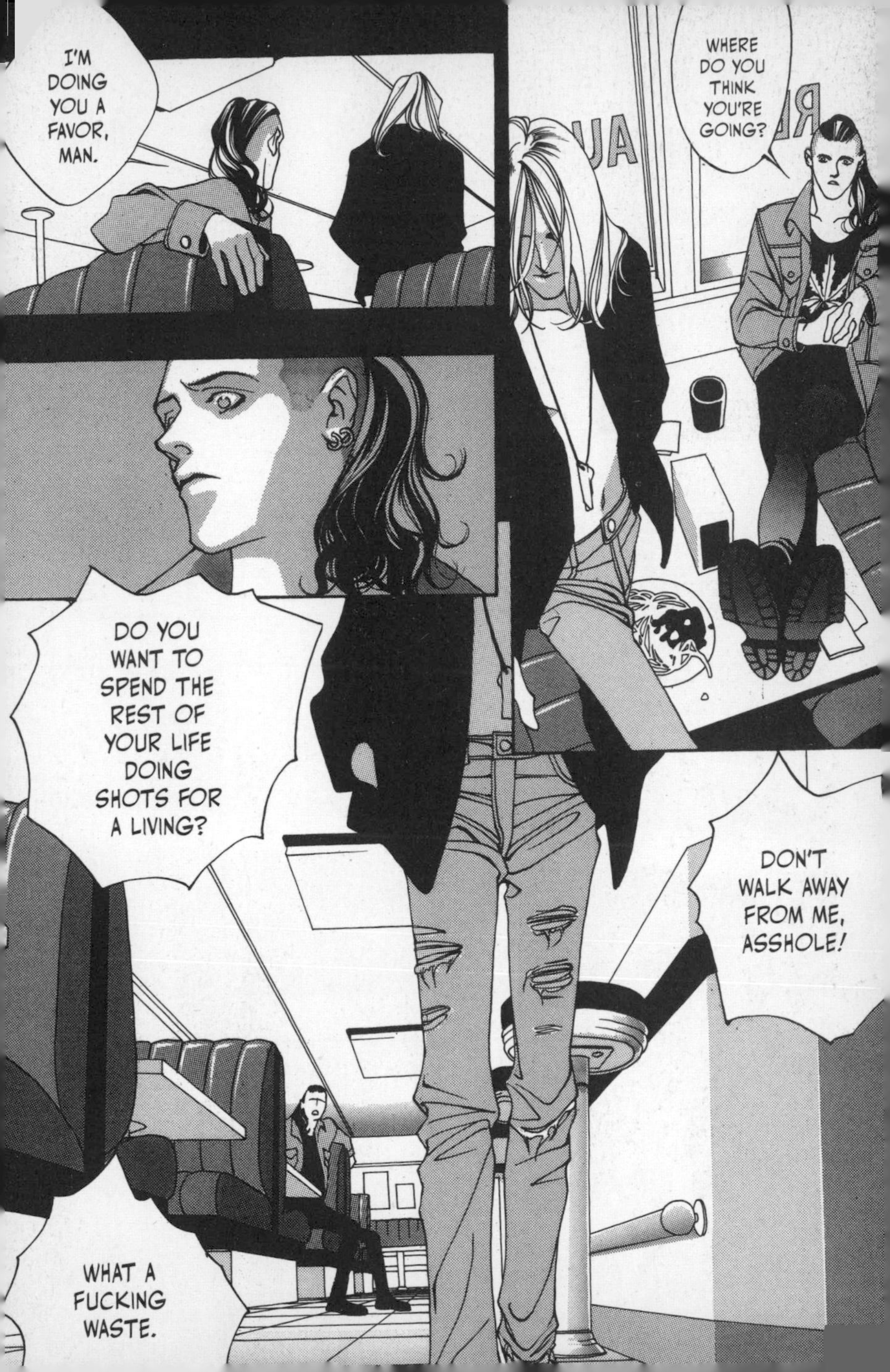
WHERE DO YOU THINK YOU'RE GOING?
I'M DOING YOU A FAVOR, MAN.
DO YOU WANT TO SPEND THE REST OF YOUR LIFE DOING SHOTS FOR A LIVING?
DON'T WALK AWAY FROM ME, ASSHOLE!
WHAT A FUCKING WASTE.

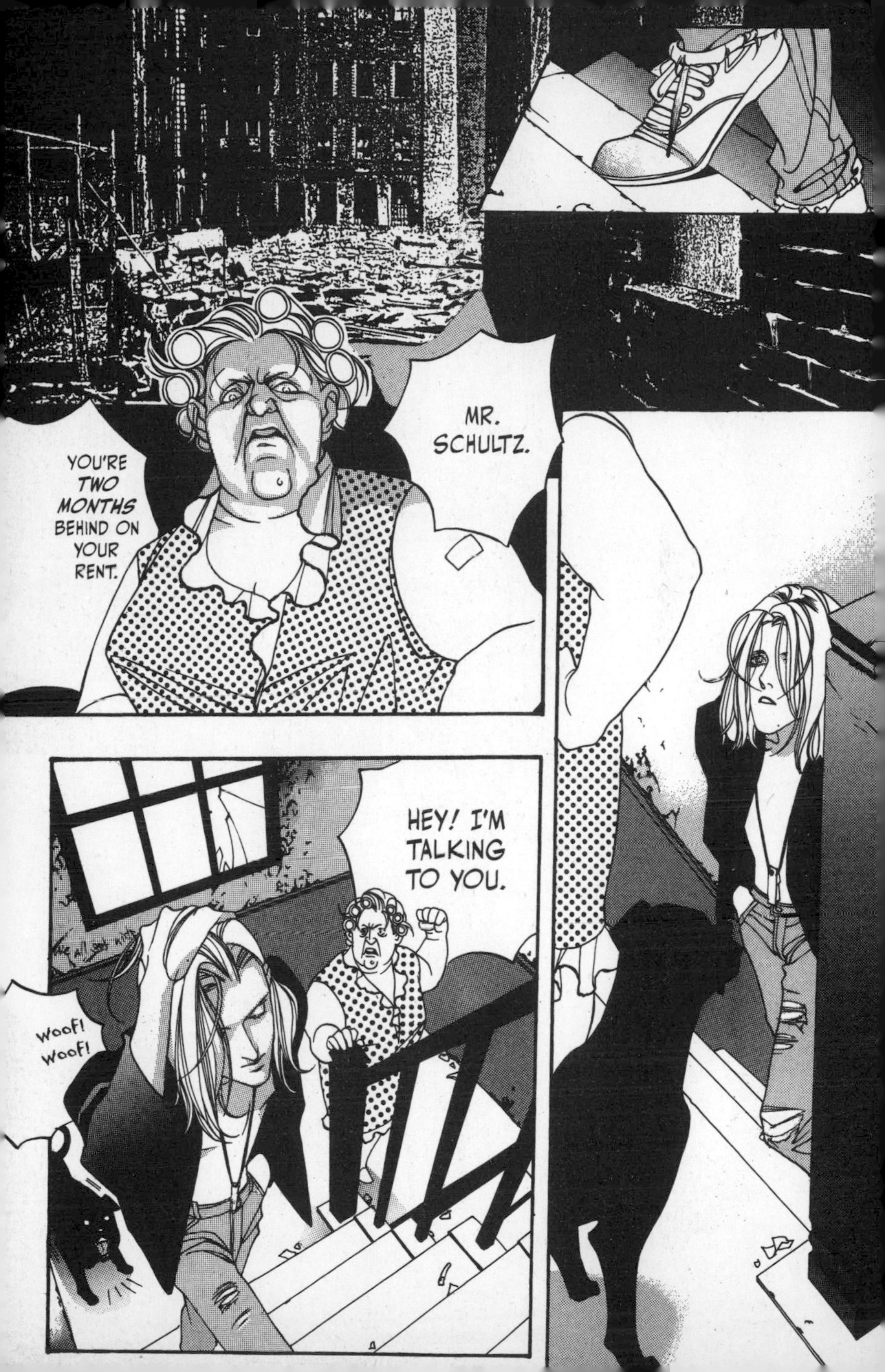
MR. SCHULTZ.
YOU'RE TWO MONTHS BEHIND ON YOUR RENT.
HEY! I'M TALKING TO YOU.
Woof! Woof!

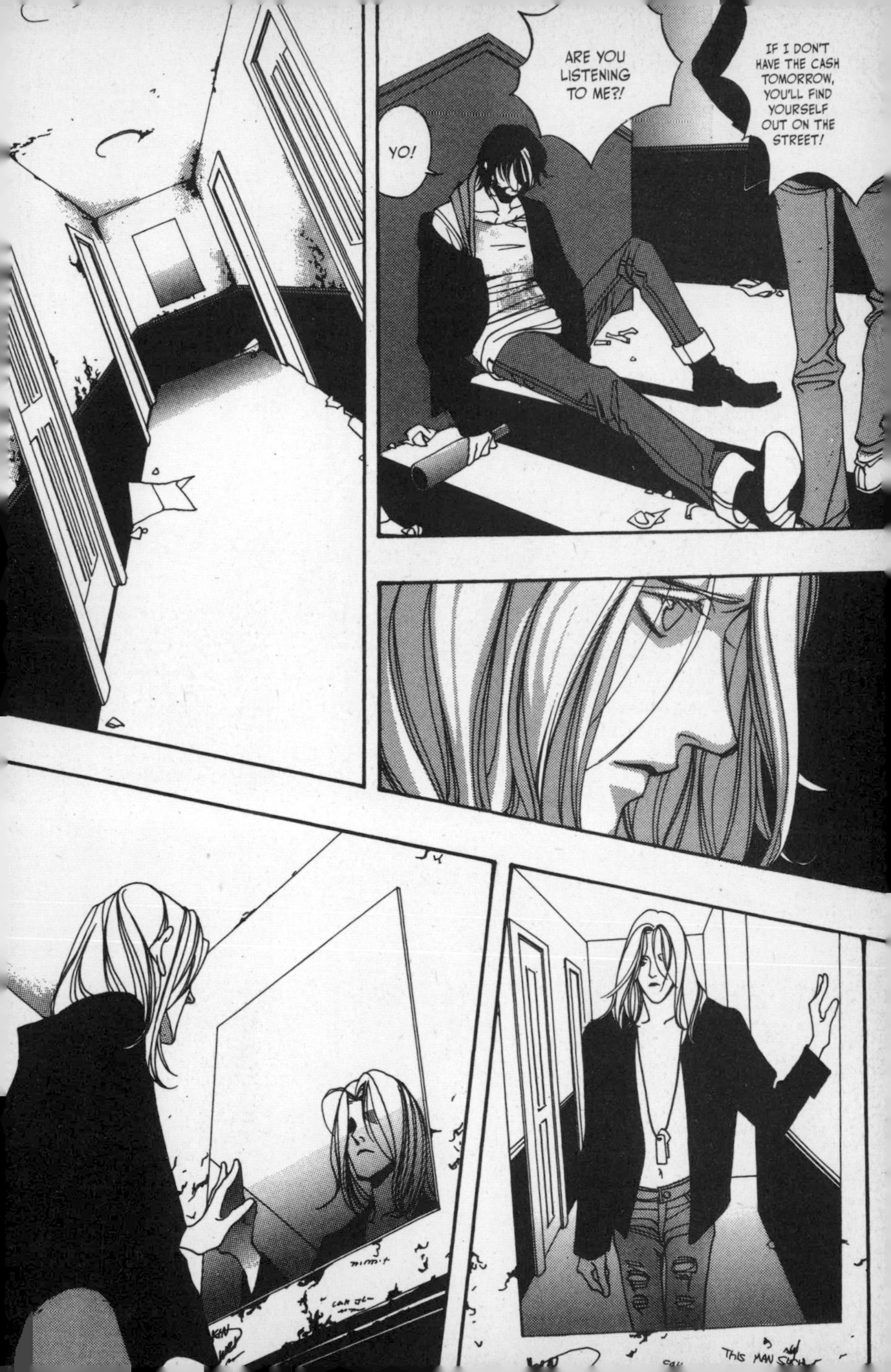
IF I DON'T HAVE THE CASH TOMORROW, YOU'LL FIND YOURSELF OUT ON THE STREET!
ARE YOU LISTENING TO ME?!
YO!
THIS MAN

HERE IT
IS, BOYS
AND
GIRLS--
THE FACE
OF A
LOSER.

HE SPENDS
HIS NIGHTS IN
BARS GETTING
WASTED AND
THEN HAS THE
NERVE TO PASS
UP A REAL
OPPORTUNITY.

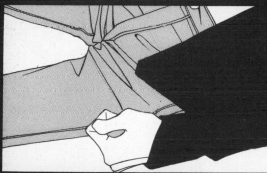

SELF-RIGHTEOUS
IDIOT IS
AFRAID TO GET
HIS HANDS A
LITTLE DIRTY.

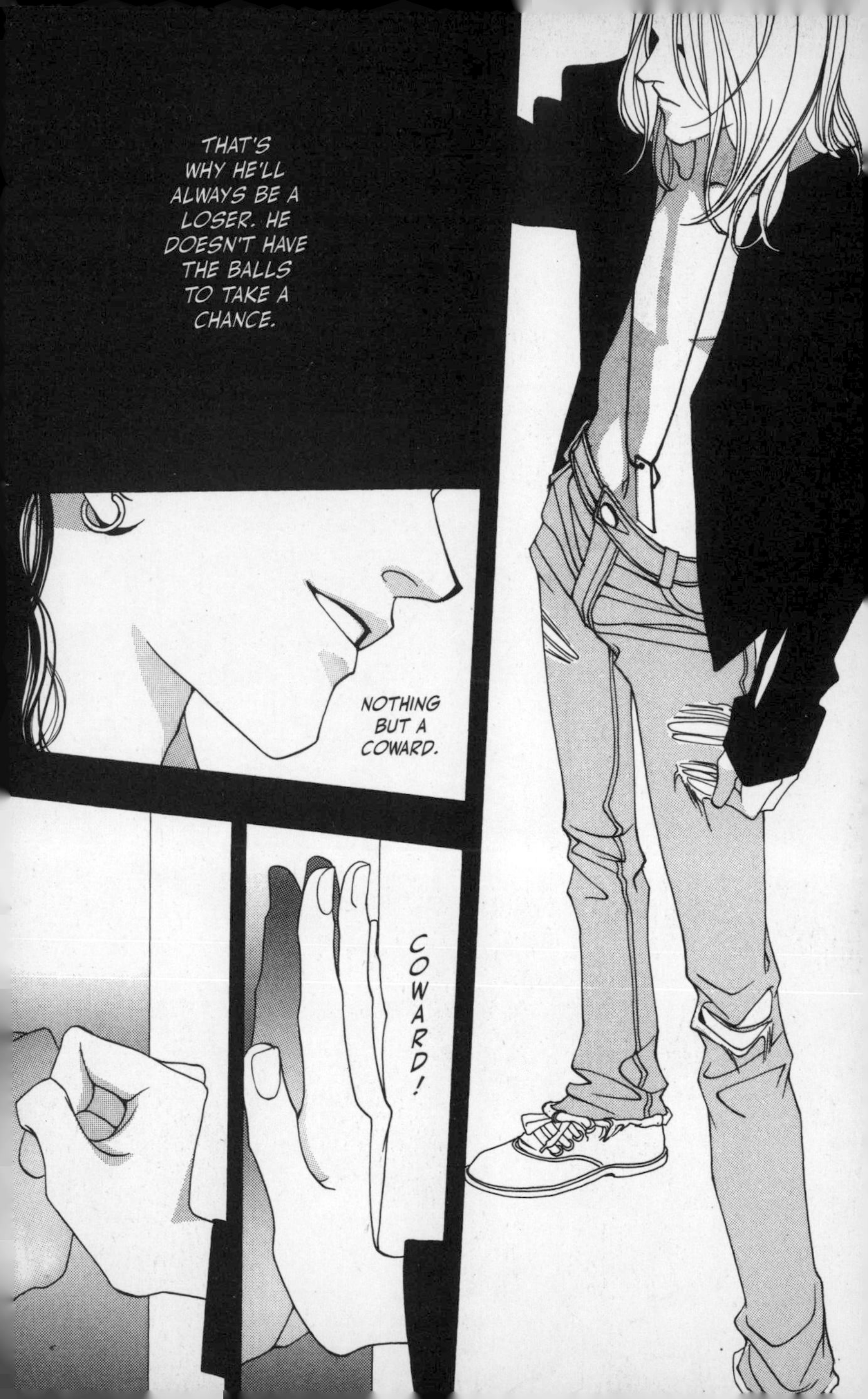
THAT'S WHY HE'LL ALWAYS BE A LOSER. HE DOESN'T HAVE THE BALLS TO TAKE A CHANCE.
NOTHING BUT A COWARD.
COWARD!

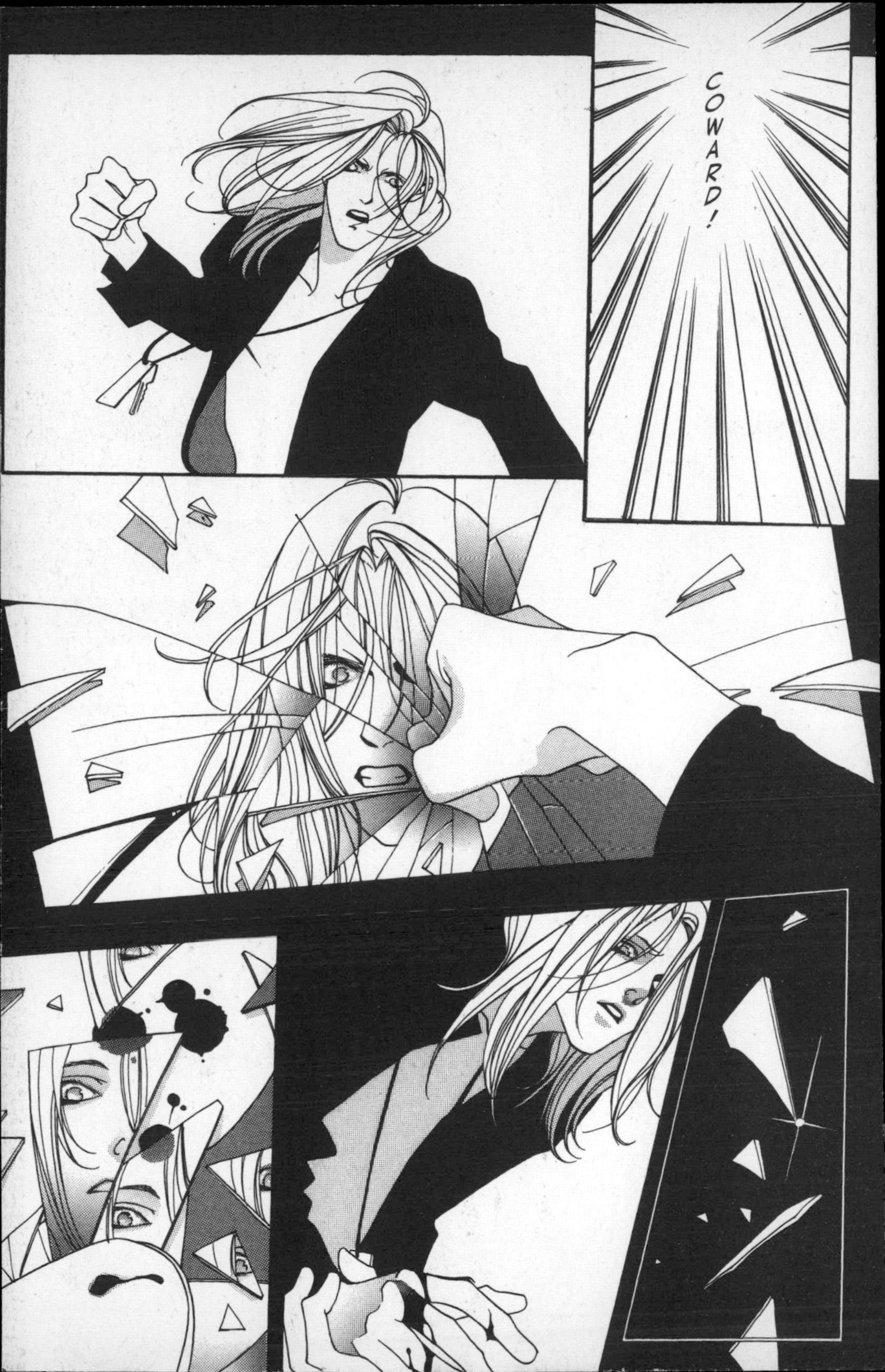
COWARD!

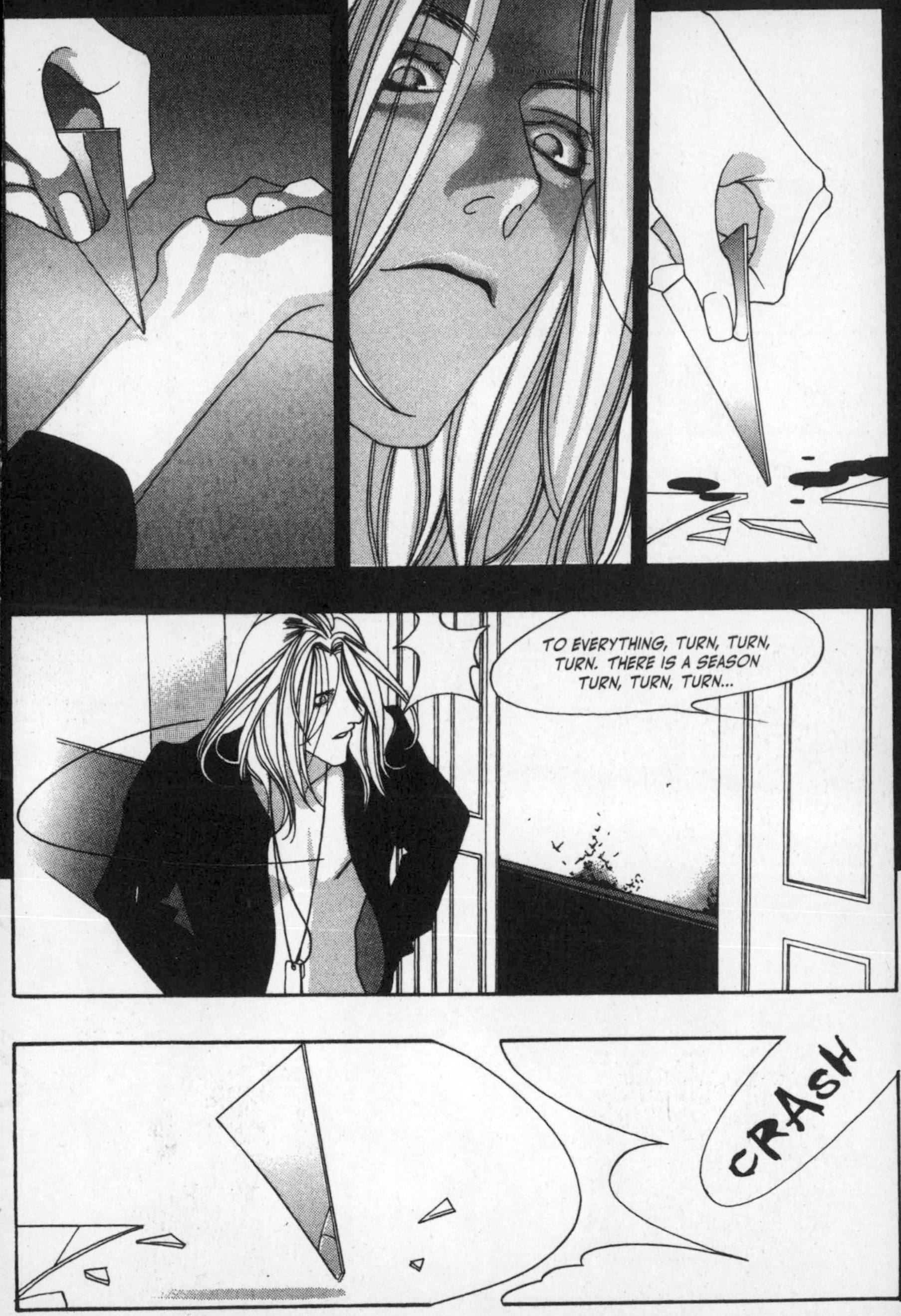
TO EVERYTHING, TURN, TURN, TURN. THERE IS A SEASON TURN, TURN, TURN...
CRASH

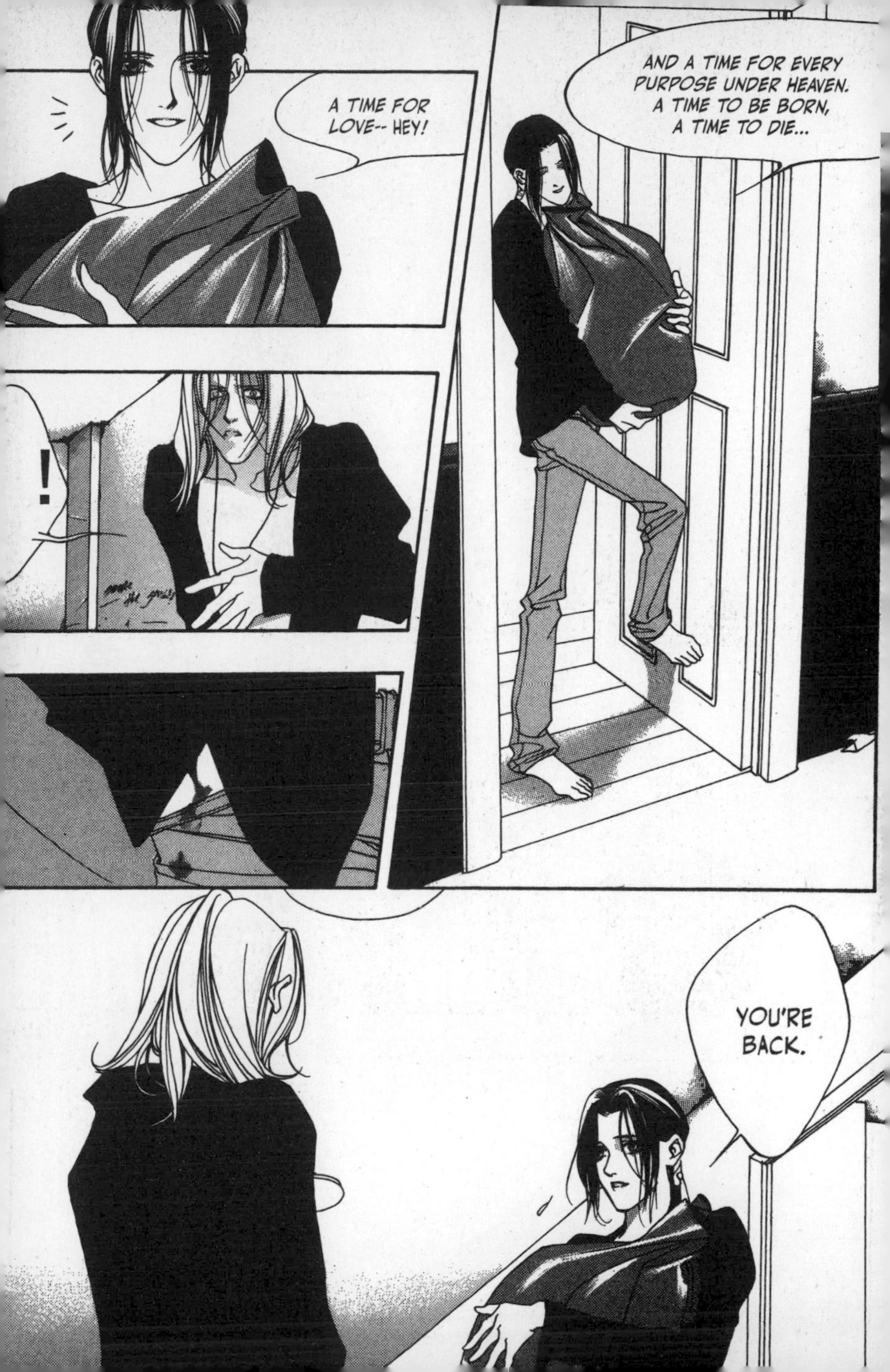
AND A TIME FOR EVERY PURPOSE UNDER HEAVEN. A TIME TO BE BORN, A TIME TO DIE...
A TIME FOR LOVE-- HEY!
!
YOU'RE BACK.

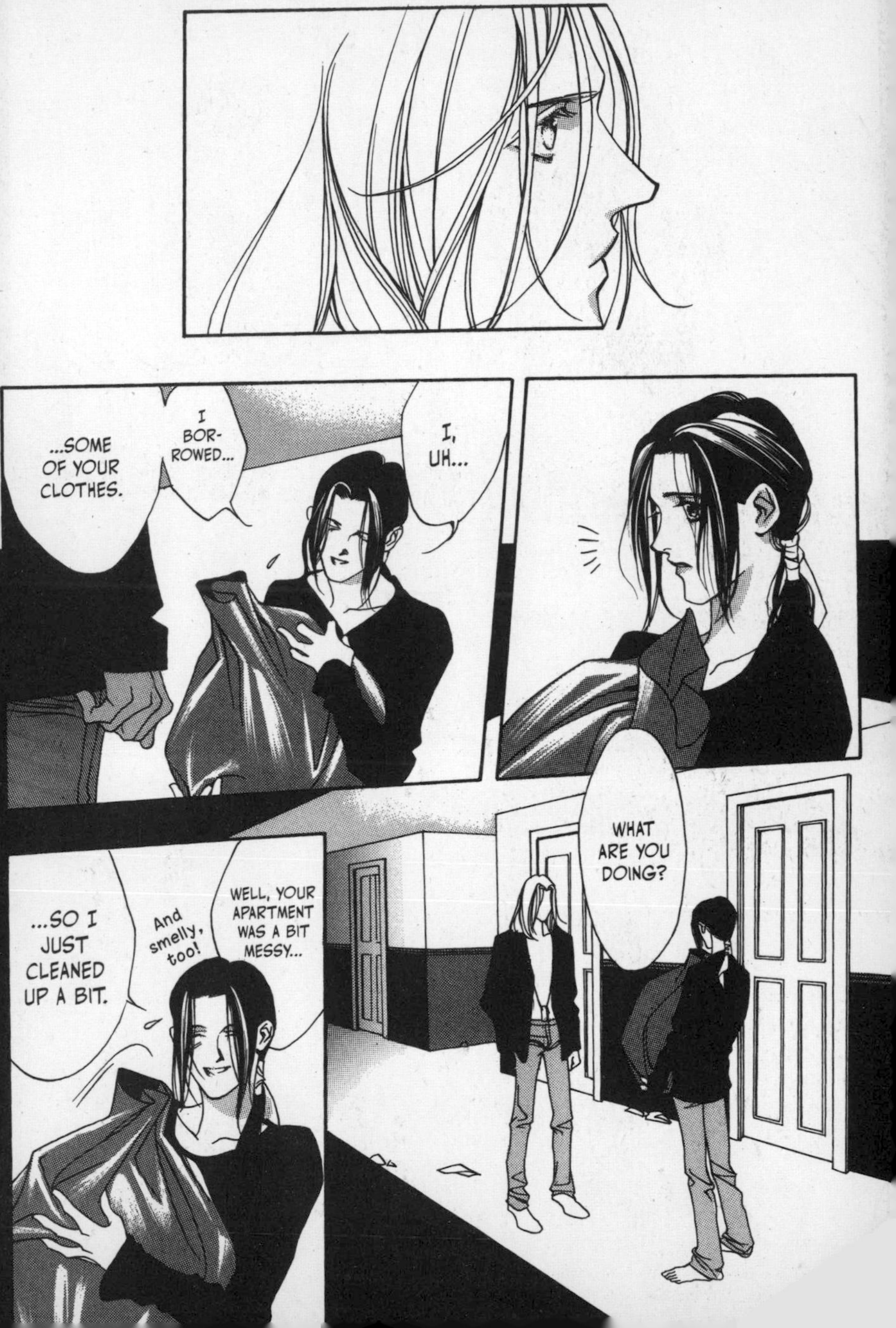
WHAT ARE YOU DOING?
I, UH...
I BOR-ROWED...
...SOME OF YOUR CLOTHES.
WELL, YOUR APARTMENT WAS A BIT MESSY...
And smelly, too!
...SO I JUST CLEANED UP A BIT.

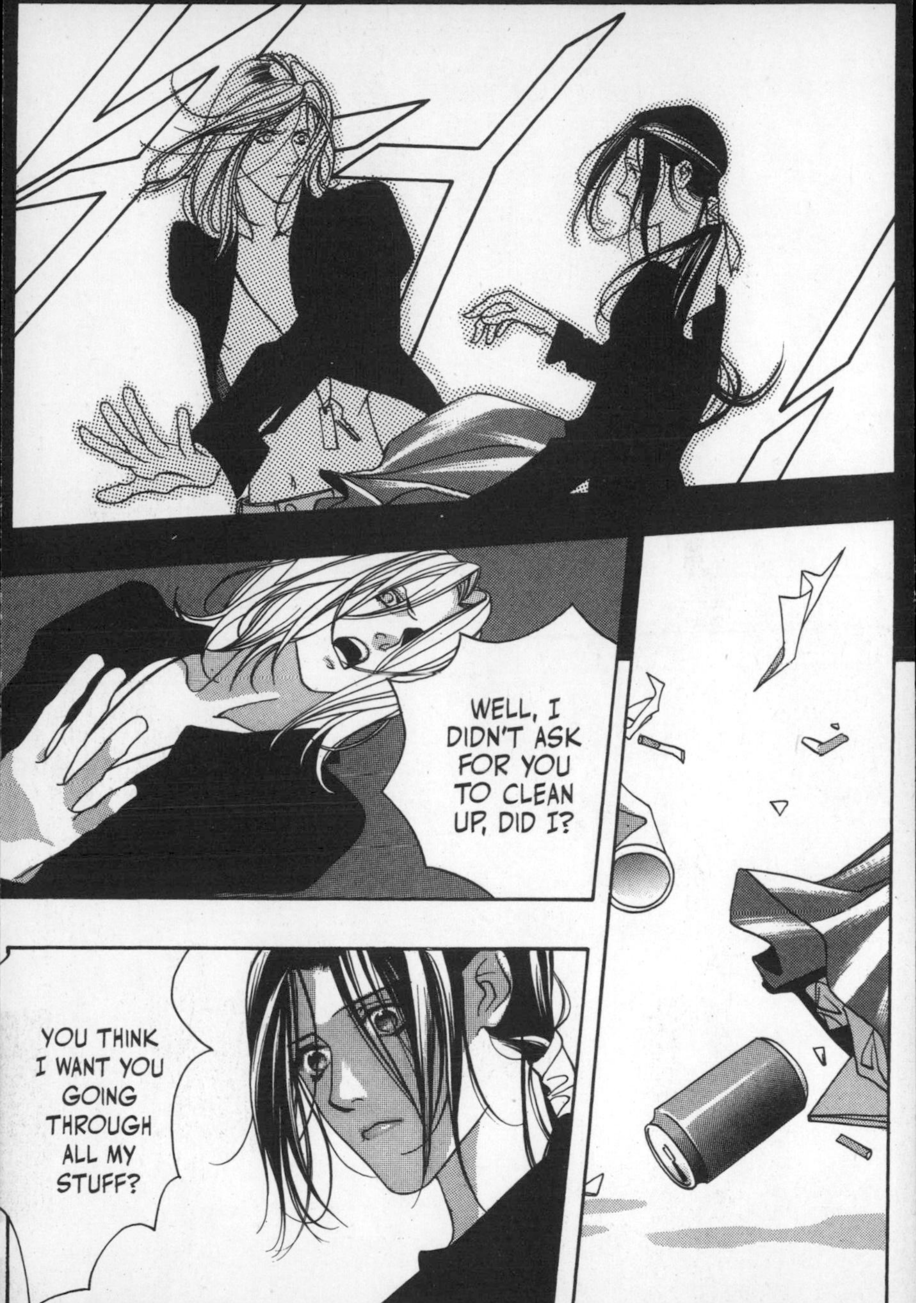
WELL, I DIDN'T ASK FOR YOU TO CLEAN UP, DID I?
YOU THINK I WANT YOU GOING THROUGH ALL MY STUFF?

Jo's note: "Sifting through trash is more like it."

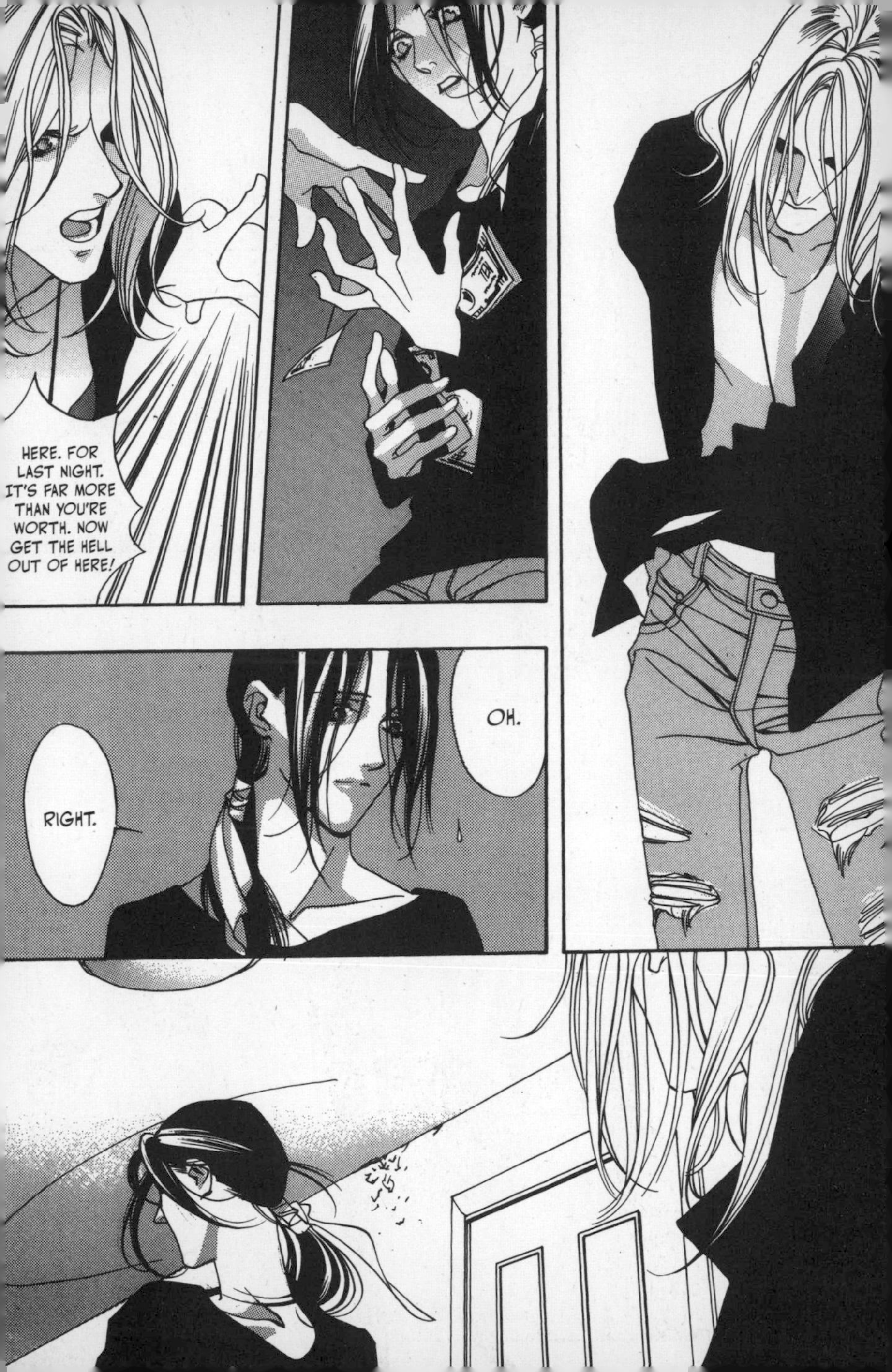
HERE. FOR LAST NIGHT. IT'S FAR MORE THAN YOU'RE WORTH. NOW GET THE HELL OUT OF HERE!
OH.
RIGHT.

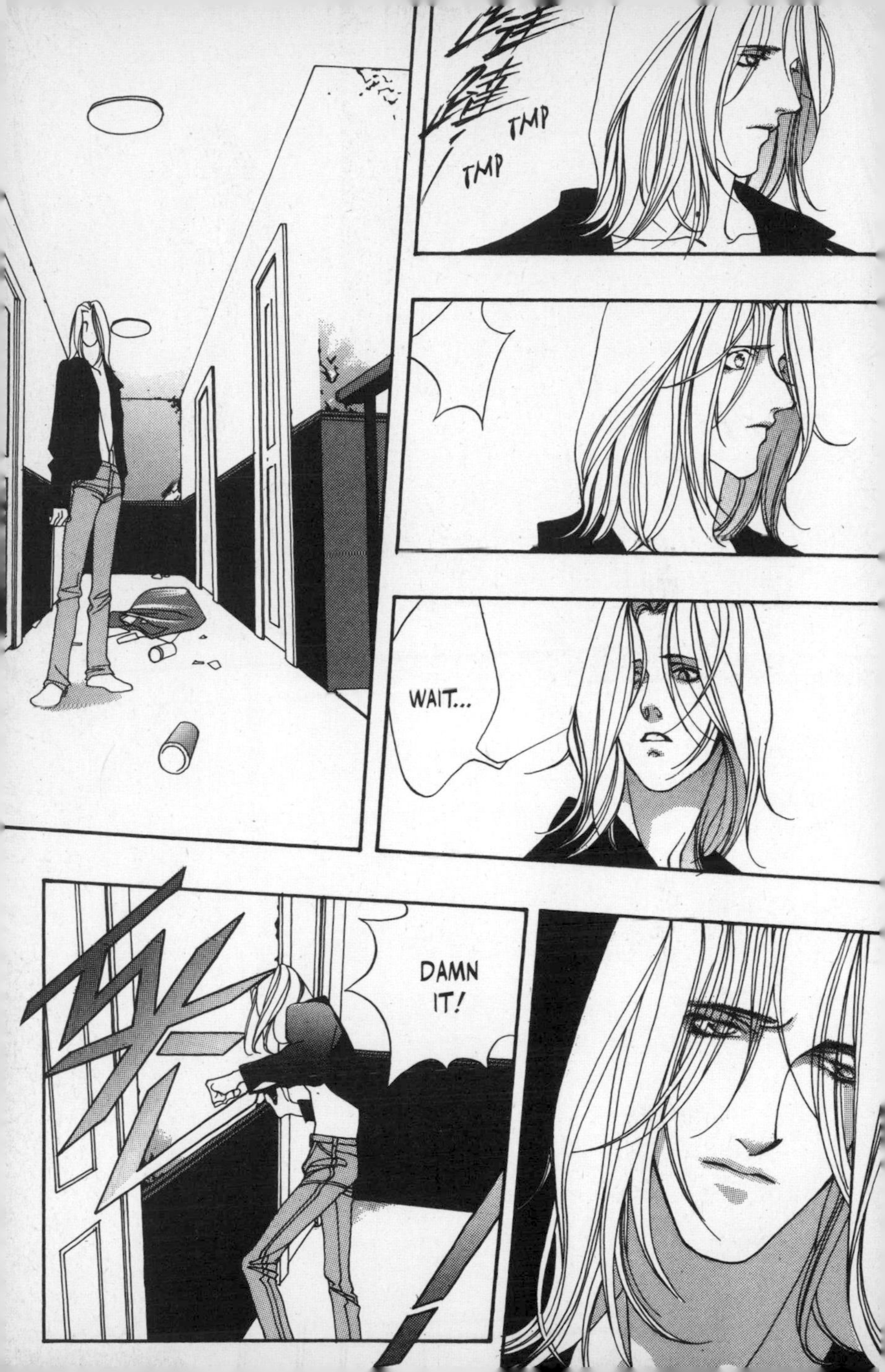
TMP
TMP
WAIT...
DAMN IT!

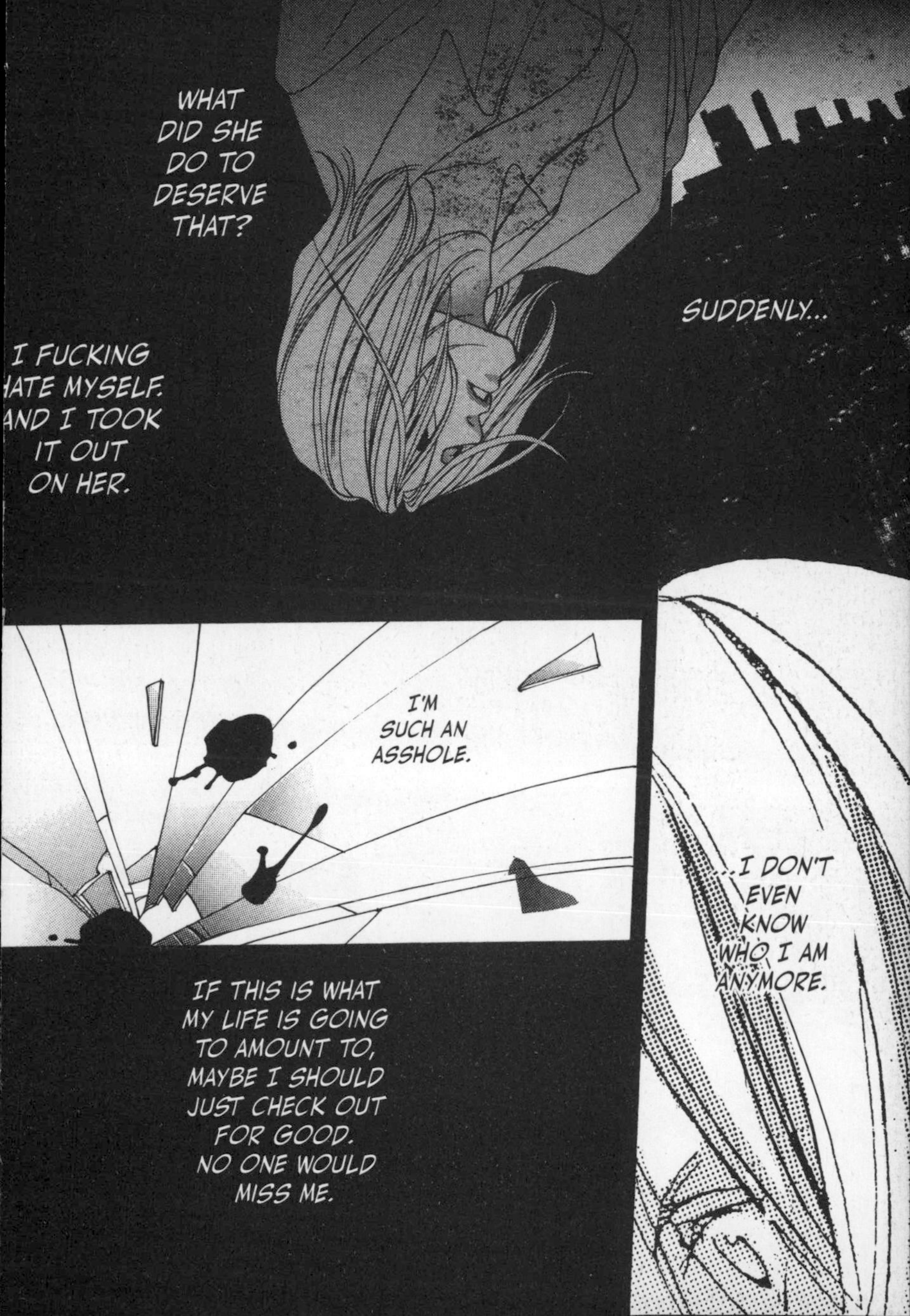
WHAT DID SHE DO TO DESERVE THAT?
I FUCKING HATE MYSELF. AND I TOOK IT OUT ON HER.
SUDDENLY...
...I DON'T EVEN KNOW WHO I AM ANYMORE.
I'M SUCH AN ASSHOLE.
IF THIS IS WHAT MY LIFE IS GOING TO AMOUNT TO, MAYBE I SHOULD JUST CHECK OUT FOR GOOD. NO ONE WOULD MISS ME.

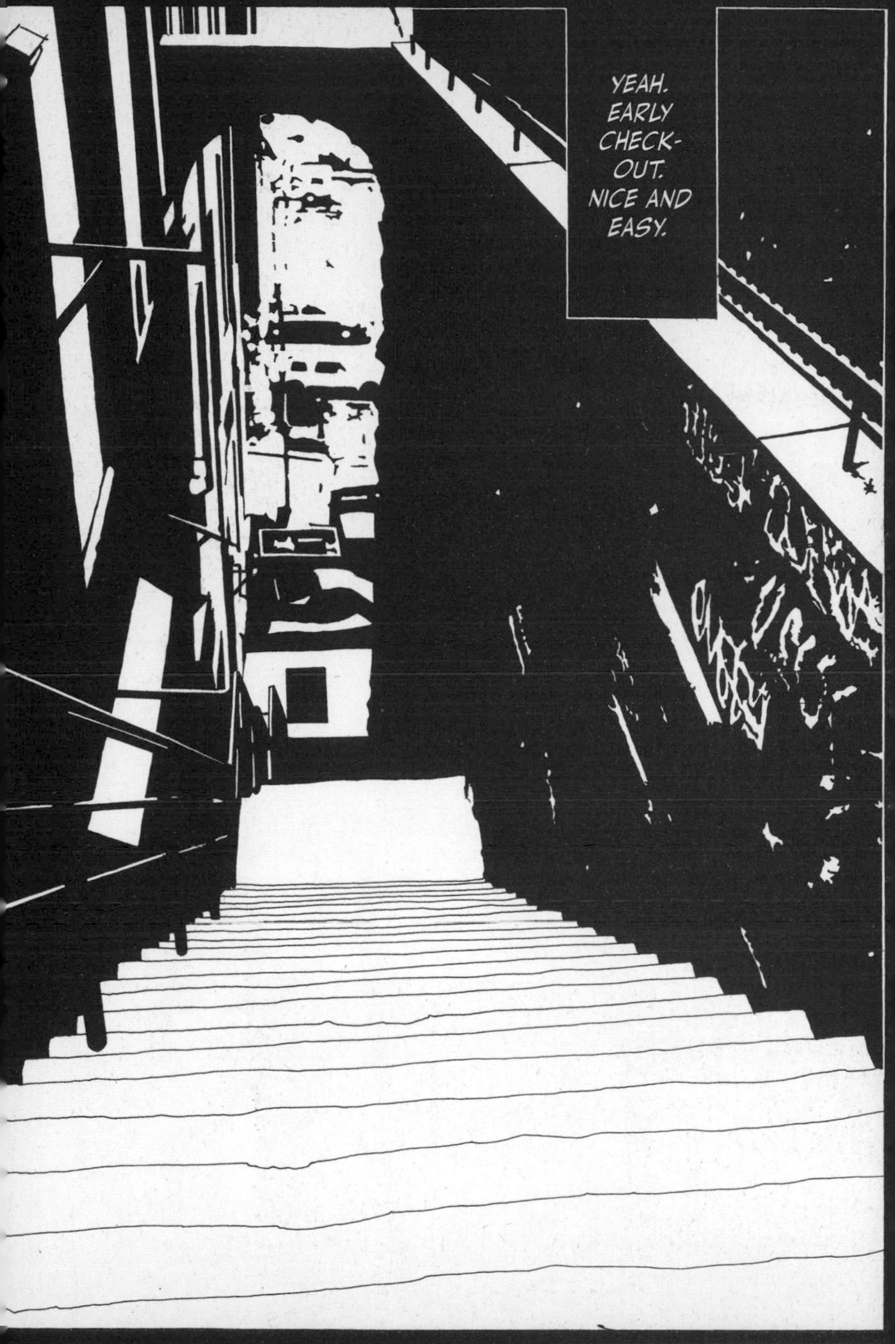
YEAH. EARLY CHECK-OUT. NICE AND EASY.

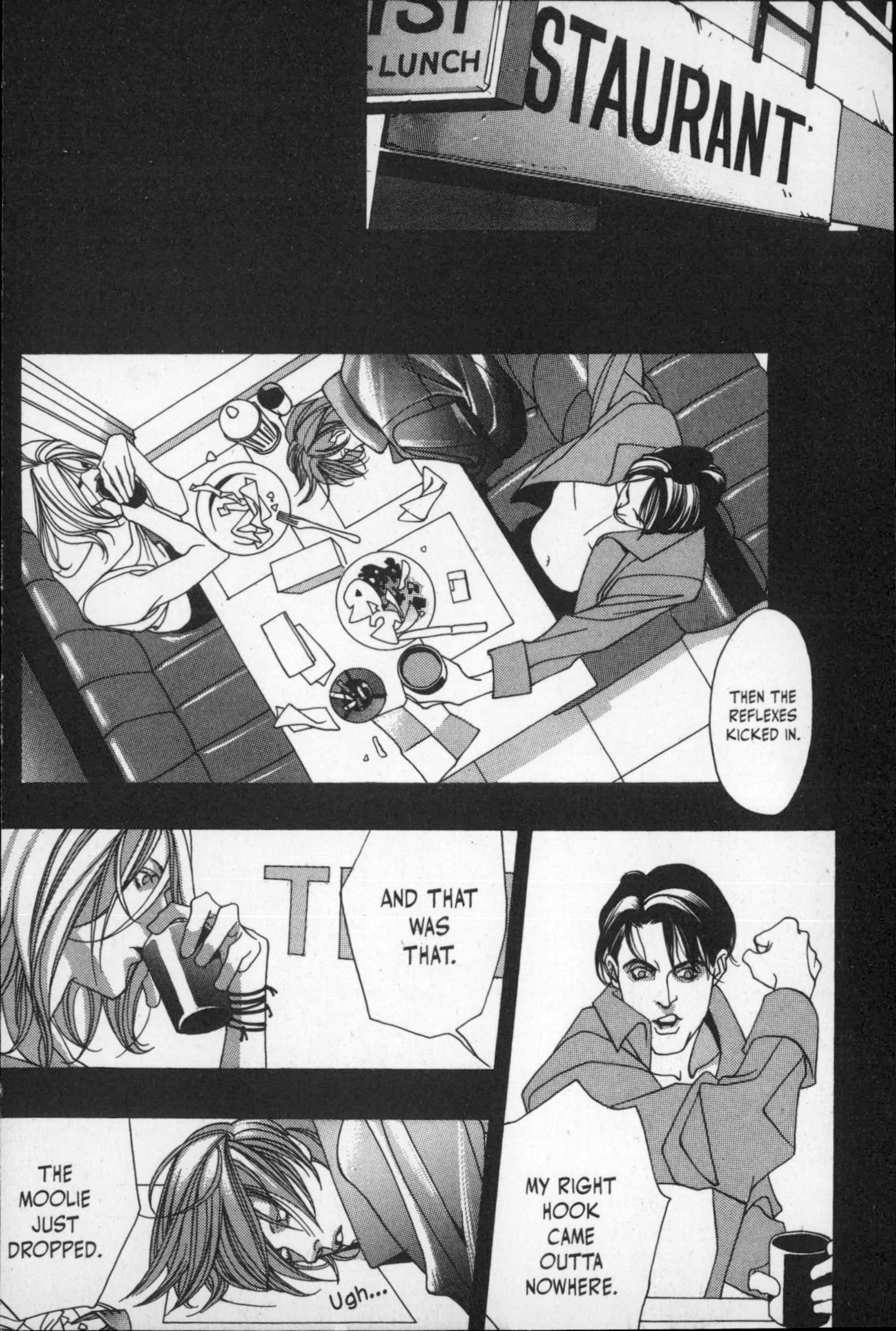
LUNCH
STAURANT
THEN THE REFLEXES KICKED IN.
MY RIGHT HOOK CAME OUTTA NOWHERE.
AND THAT WAS THAT.
THE MOOLIE JUST DROPPED.
Ugh...

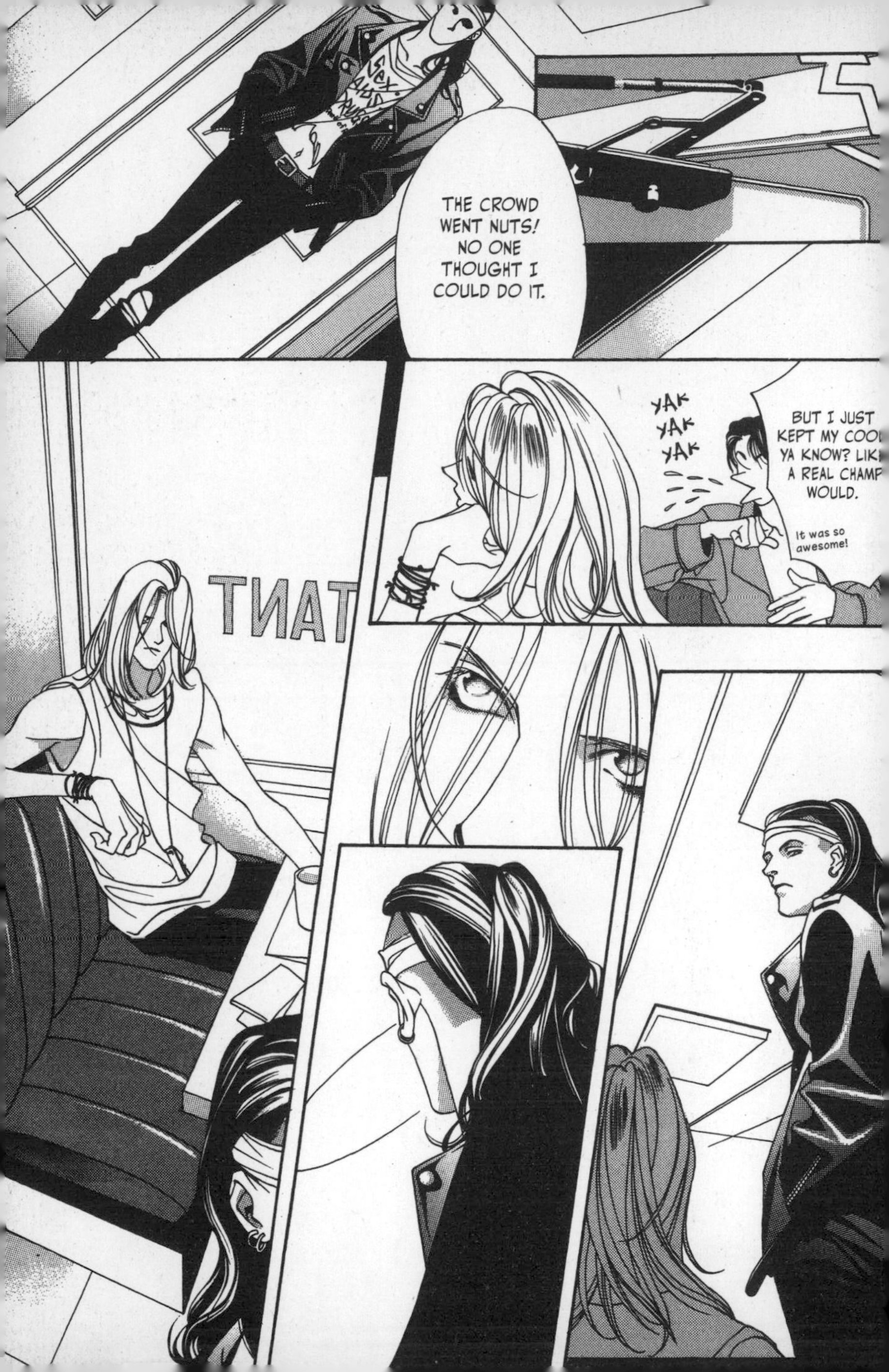
THE CROWD WENT NUTS! NO ONE THOUGHT I COULD DO IT.
YAK YAK YAK
BUT I JUST KEPT MY COO YA KNOW? LIK A REAL CHAMP WOULD.
It was so awesome!
TNAT

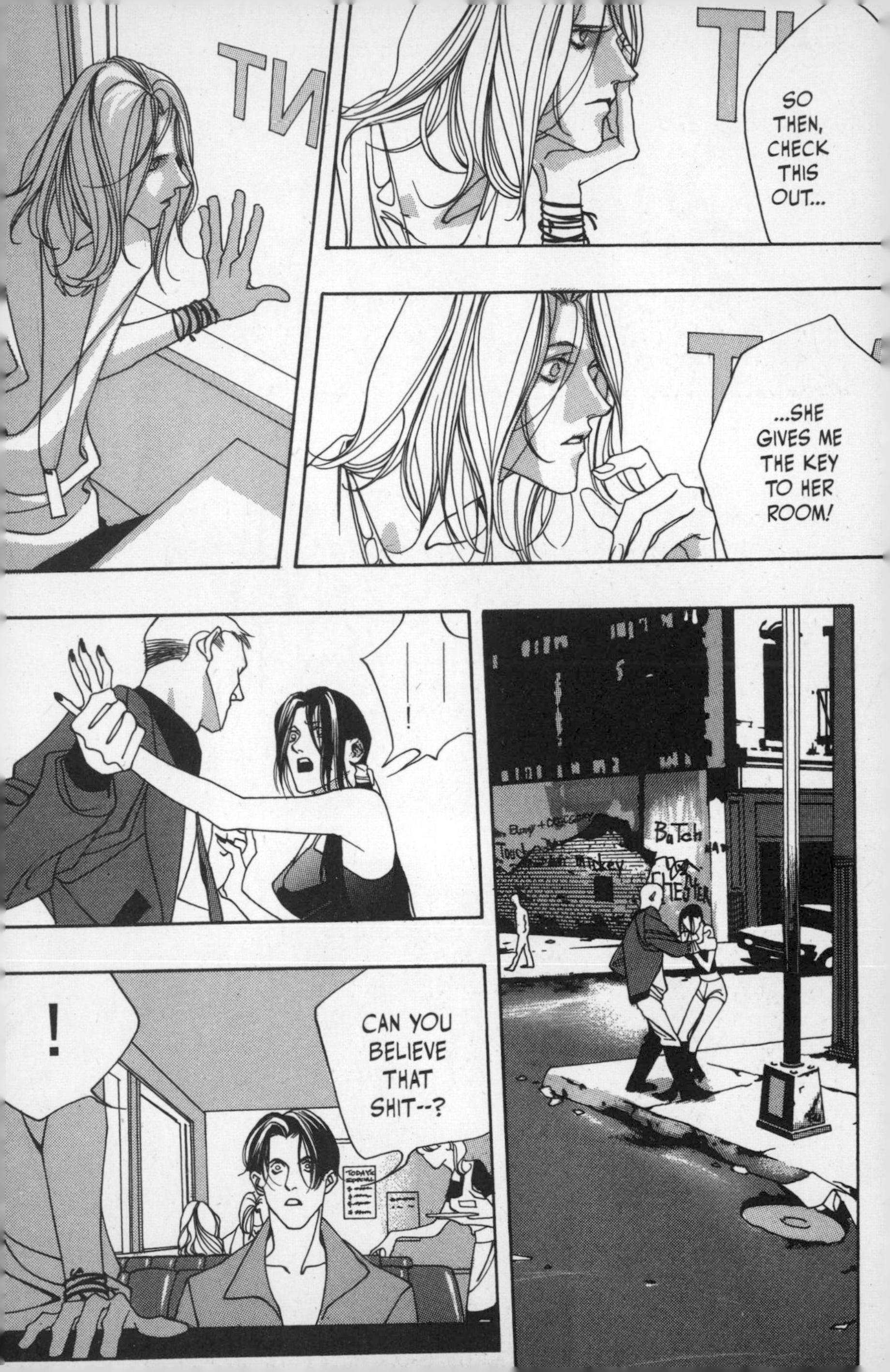

TH
SO THEN, CHECK THIS OUT...
T
...SHE GIVES ME THE KEY TO HER ROOM!
TH
BuTch
Mickey
CHESTER
!
!
CAN YOU BELIEVE THAT SHIT--?

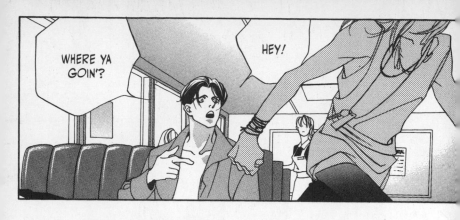

HEY!
WHERE YA GOIN'?
WHAT'S WITH THIS CITY? YOU'RE THE SECOND GUY WHO'S TRIED TO STIFF ME!
FUCK OFF, BITCH. YOU'RE OVERCHARGING FOR YOUR BONEY ASS.
DAMN.
GET LOST, WILL YA?

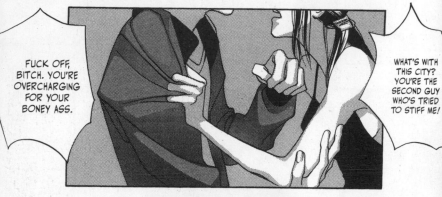

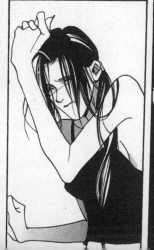

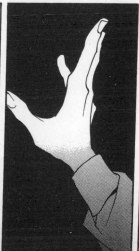

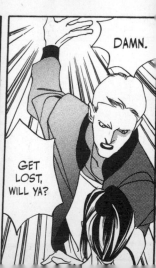

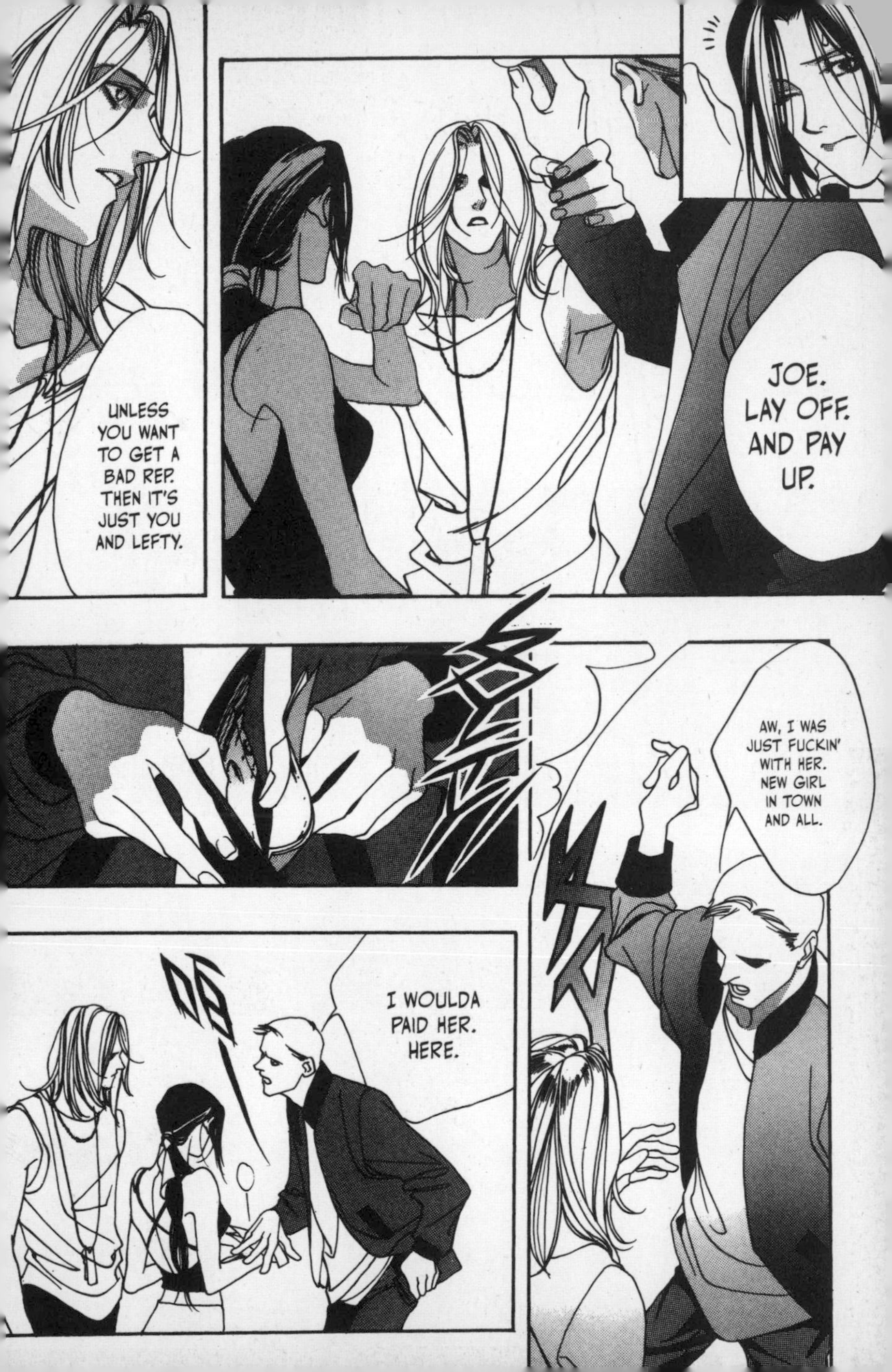
JOE. LAY OFF. AND PAY UP.
UNLESS YOU WANT TO GET A BAD REP. THEN IT'S JUST YOU AND LEFTY.
AW, I WAS JUST FUCKIN' WITH HER. NEW GIRL IN TOWN AND ALL.
I WOULDA PAID HER. HERE.

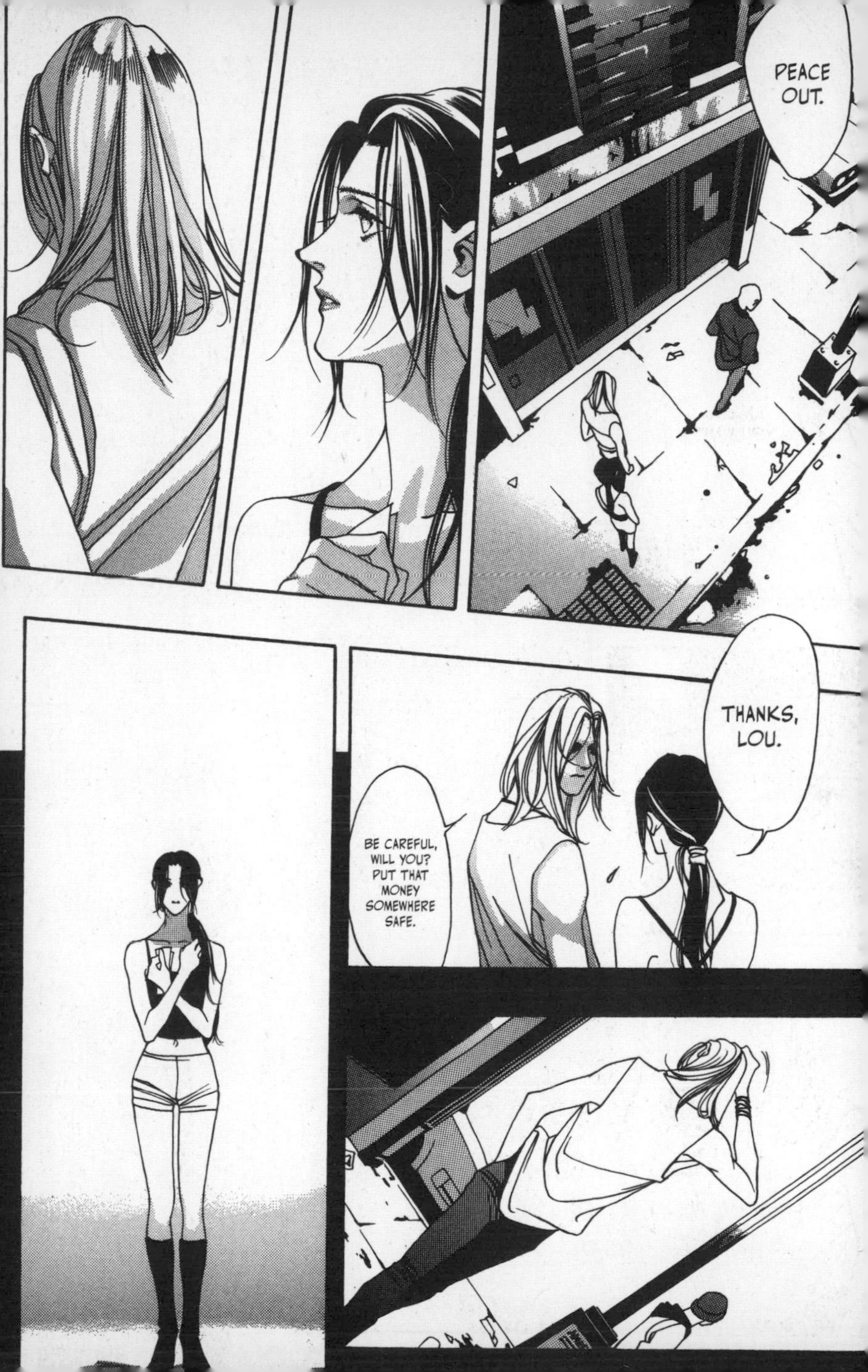
PEACE OUT.
THANKS, LOU.
BE CAREFUL, WILL YOU? PUT THAT MONEY SOMEWHERE SAFE.

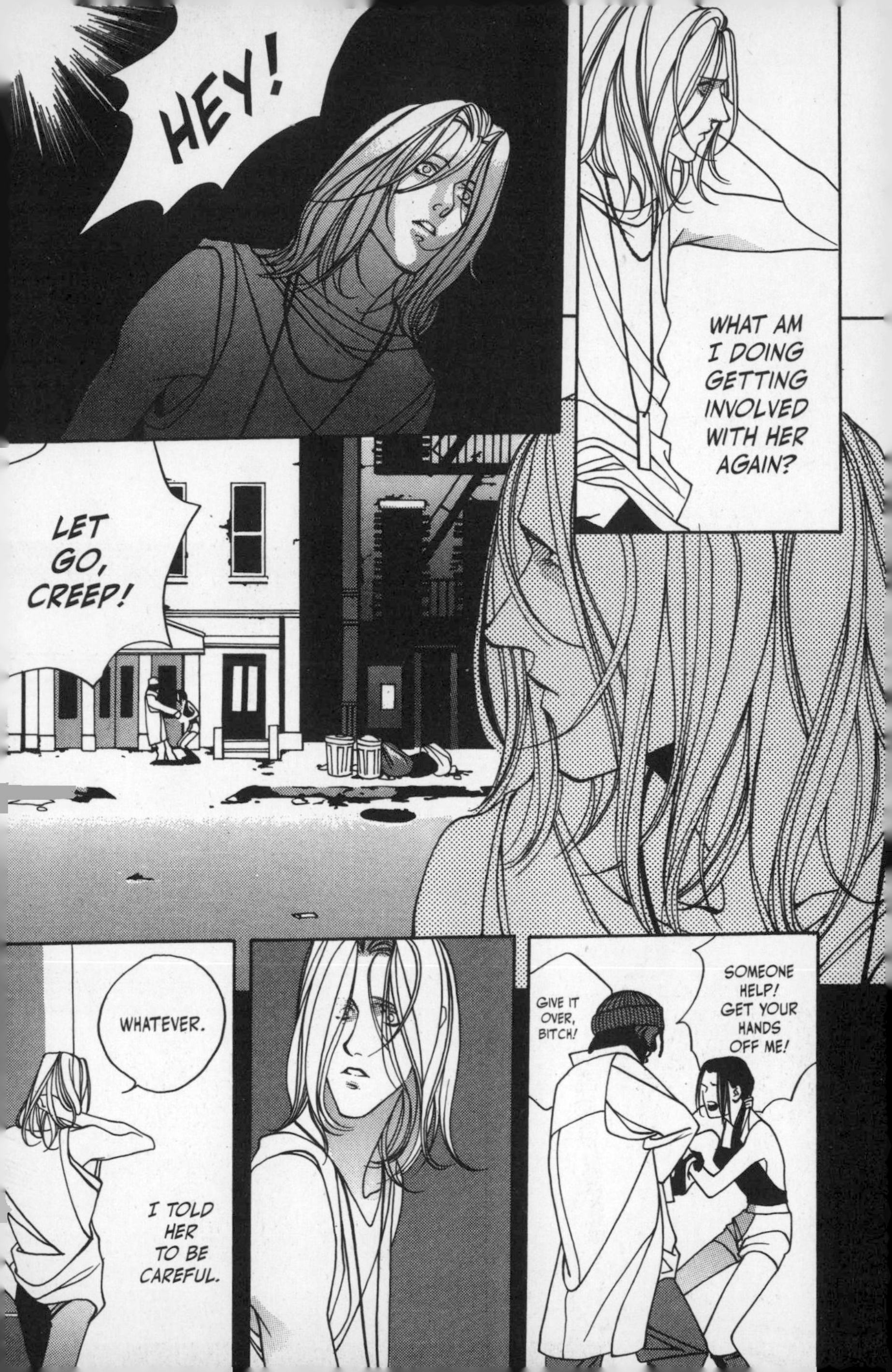
WHAT AM I DOING GETTING INVOLVED WITH HER AGAIN?
HEY!
LET GO, CREEP!
SOMEONE HELP! GET YOUR HANDS OFF ME!
GIVE IT OVER, BITCH!
WHATEVER.
I TOLD HER TO BE CAREFUL.

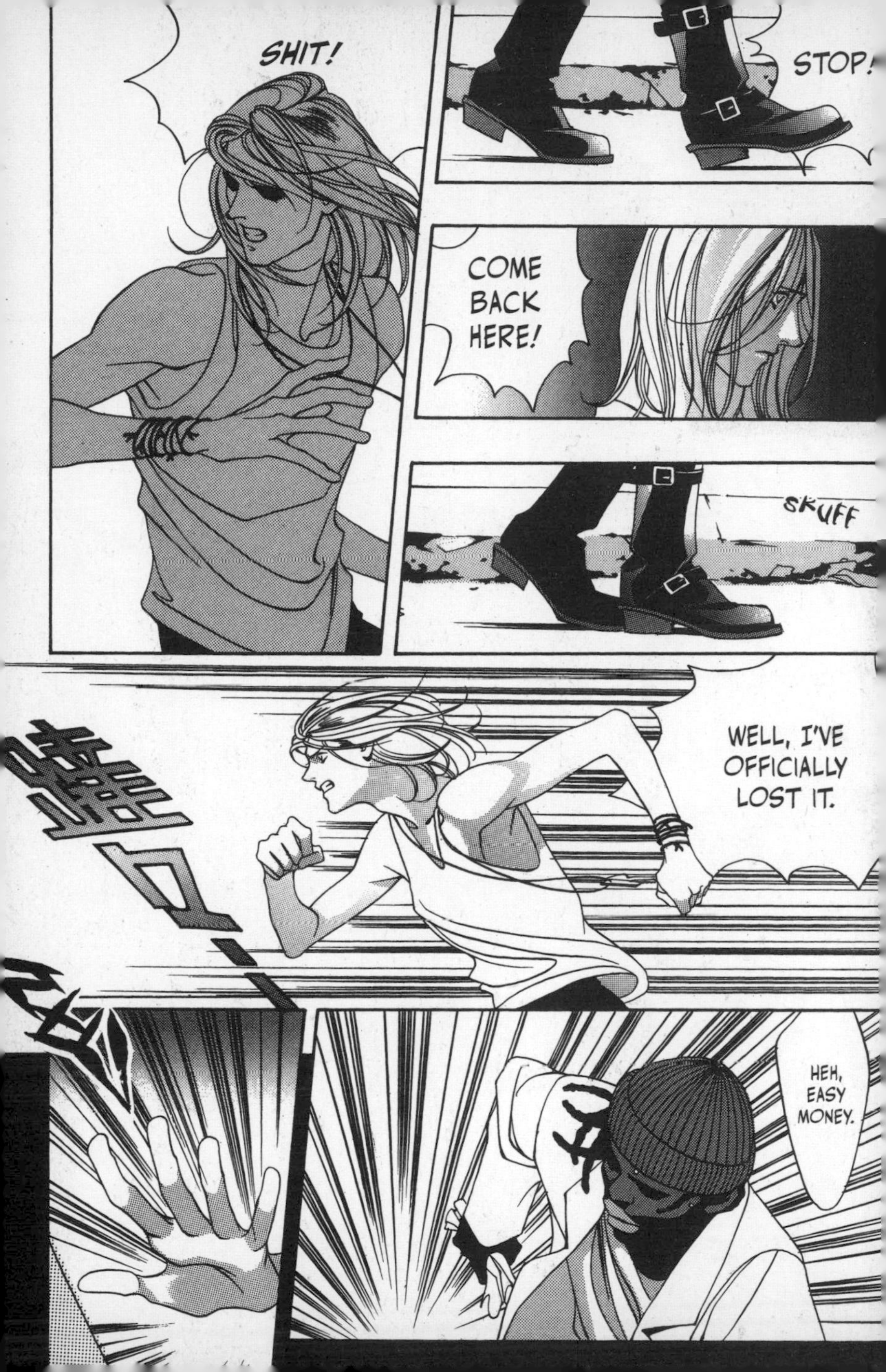
STOP!
COME BACK HERE!
SKUFF
SHIT!
WELL, I'VE OFFICIALLY LOST IT.
HEH, EASY MONEY.

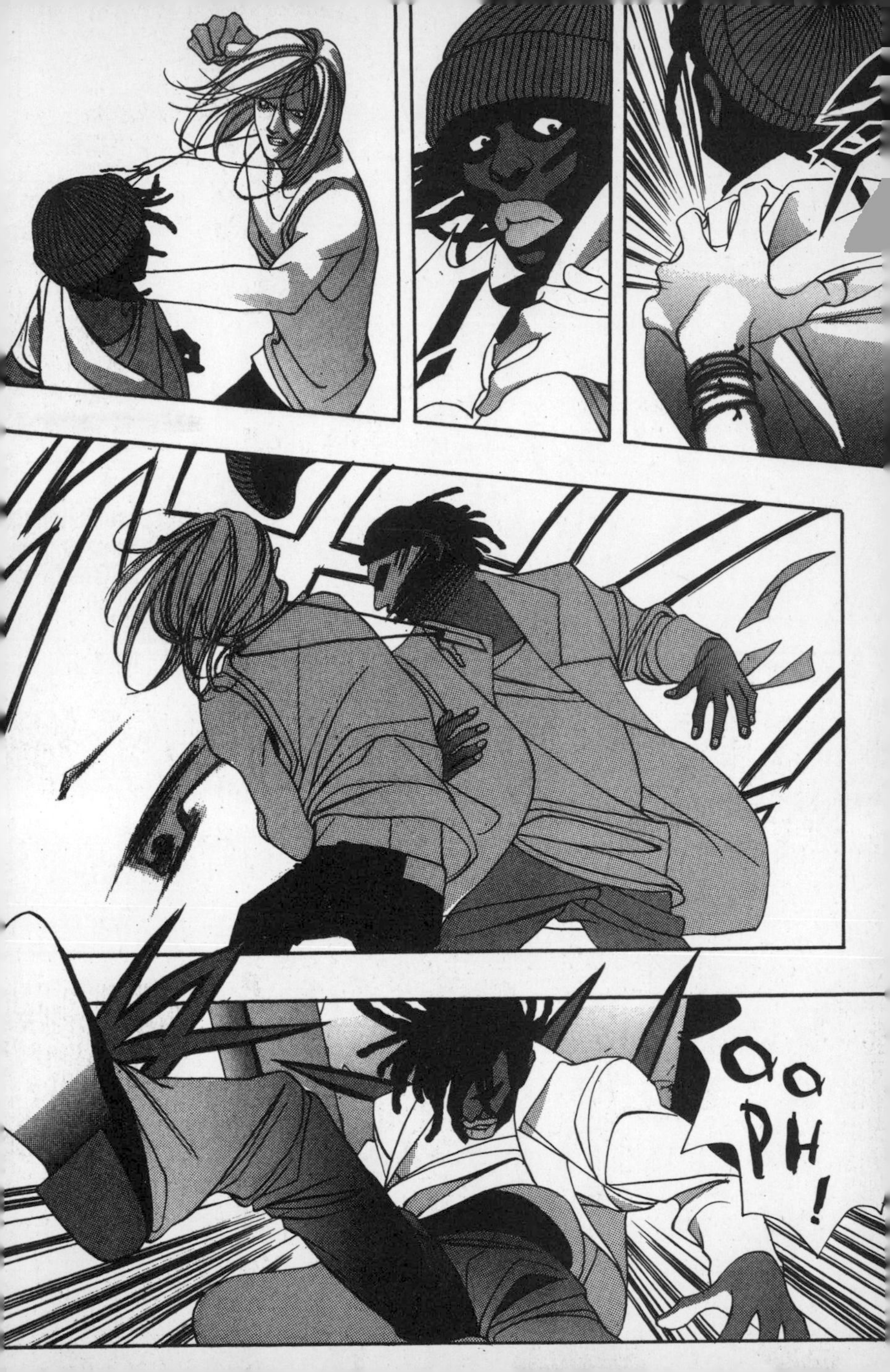
aaPH!

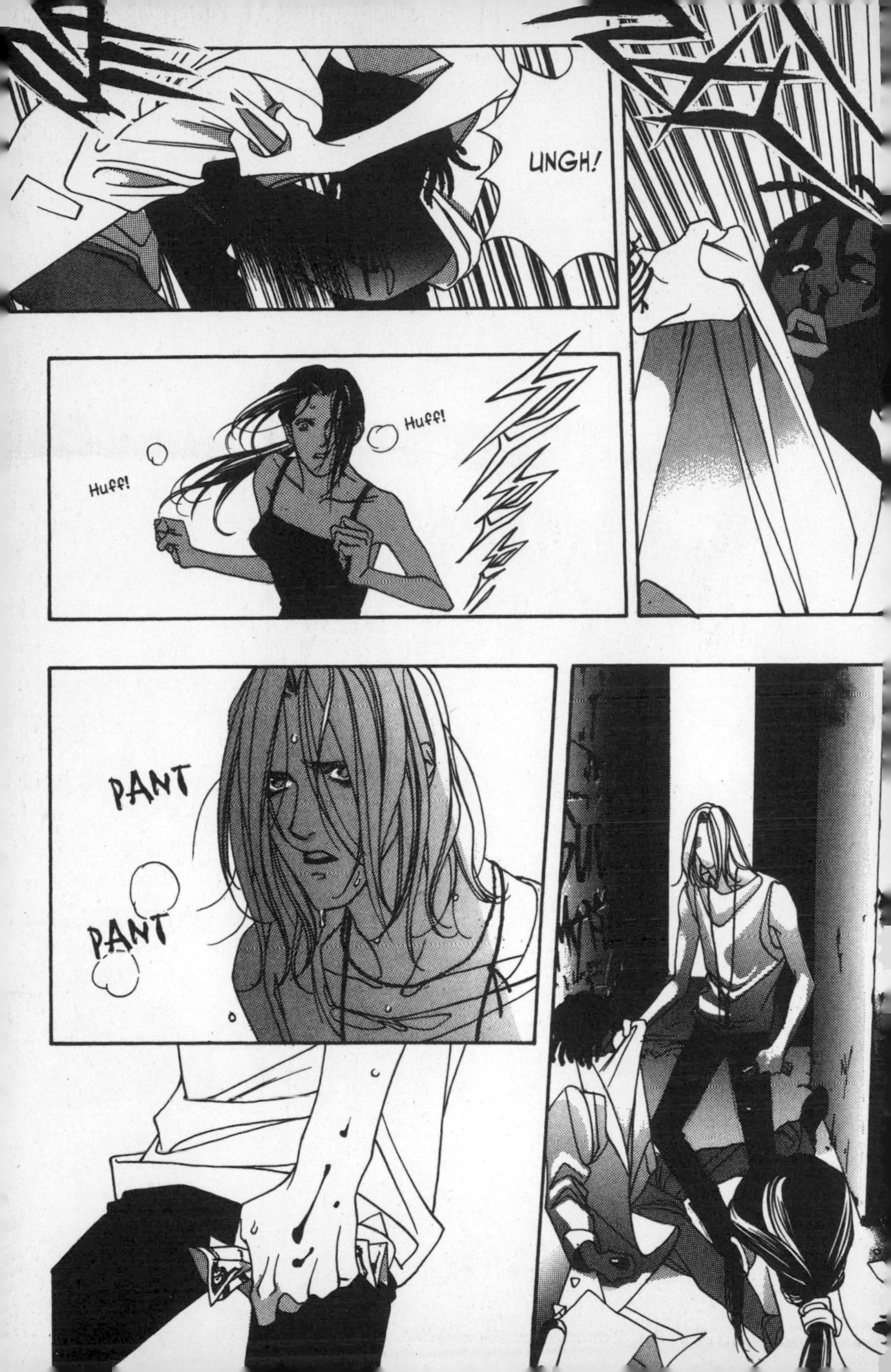
UNGH!
Huff!
Huff!
PANT
PANT

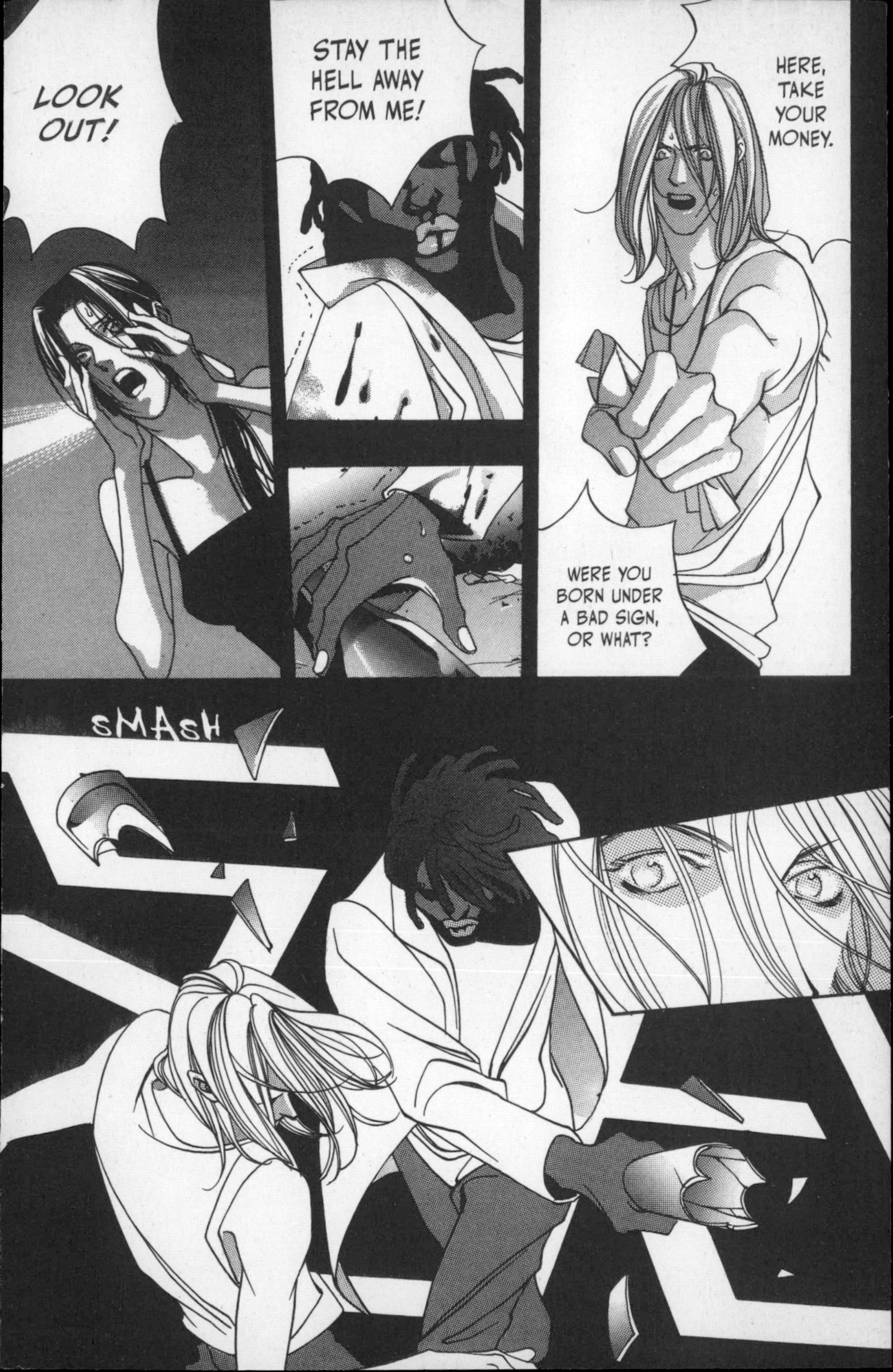
HERE, TAKE YOUR MONEY.
WERE YOU BORN UNDER A BAD SIGN, OR WHAT?
STAY THE HELL AWAY FROM ME!
LOOK OUT!
SMASH

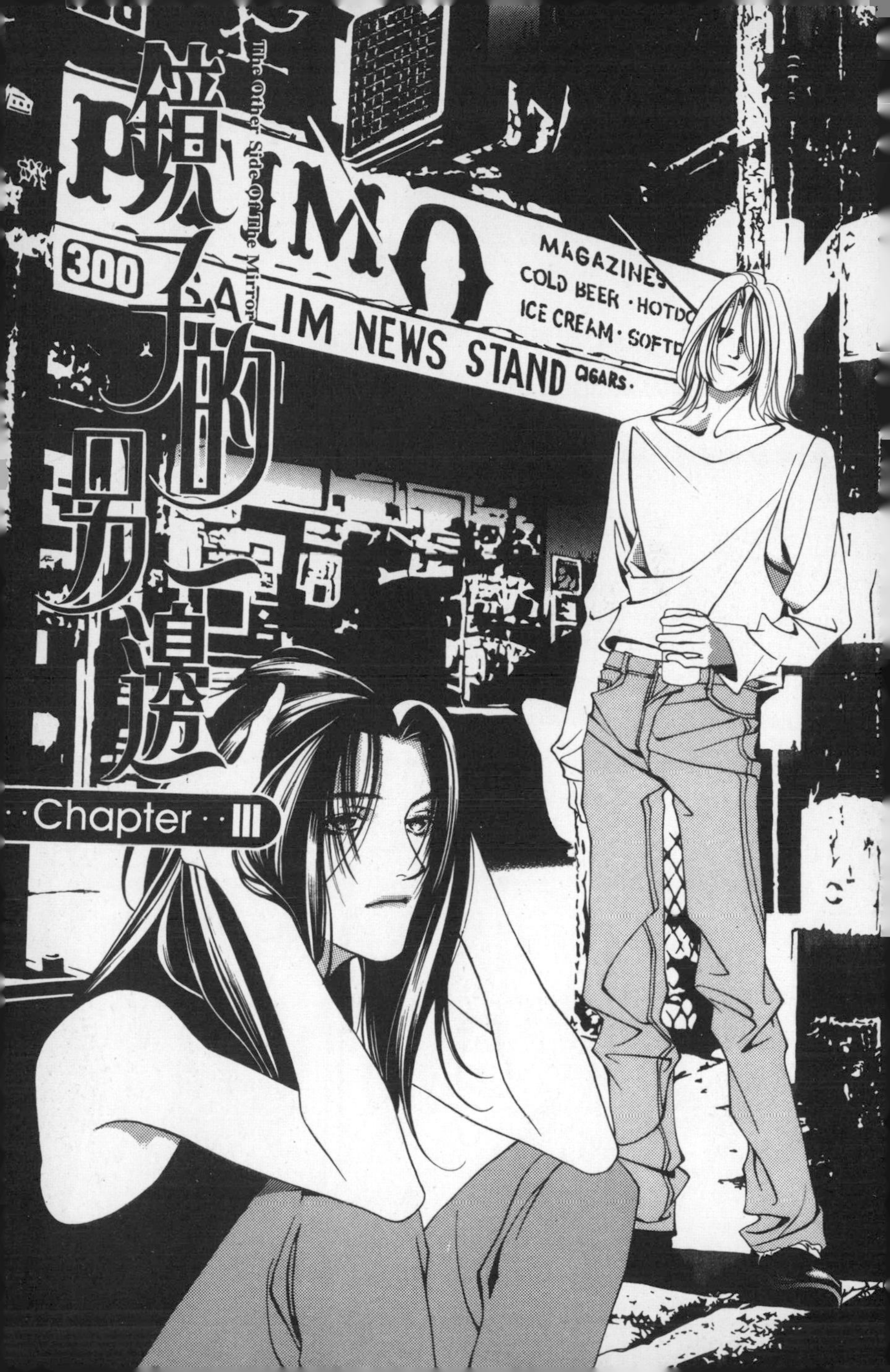
鏡子的另一邊
The Other Side Of The Mirror
Chapter III
MAGAZINES
COLD BEER · HOTDO
ICE CREAM · SOFT
LIM NEWS STAND
CIGARS.
300
IMO

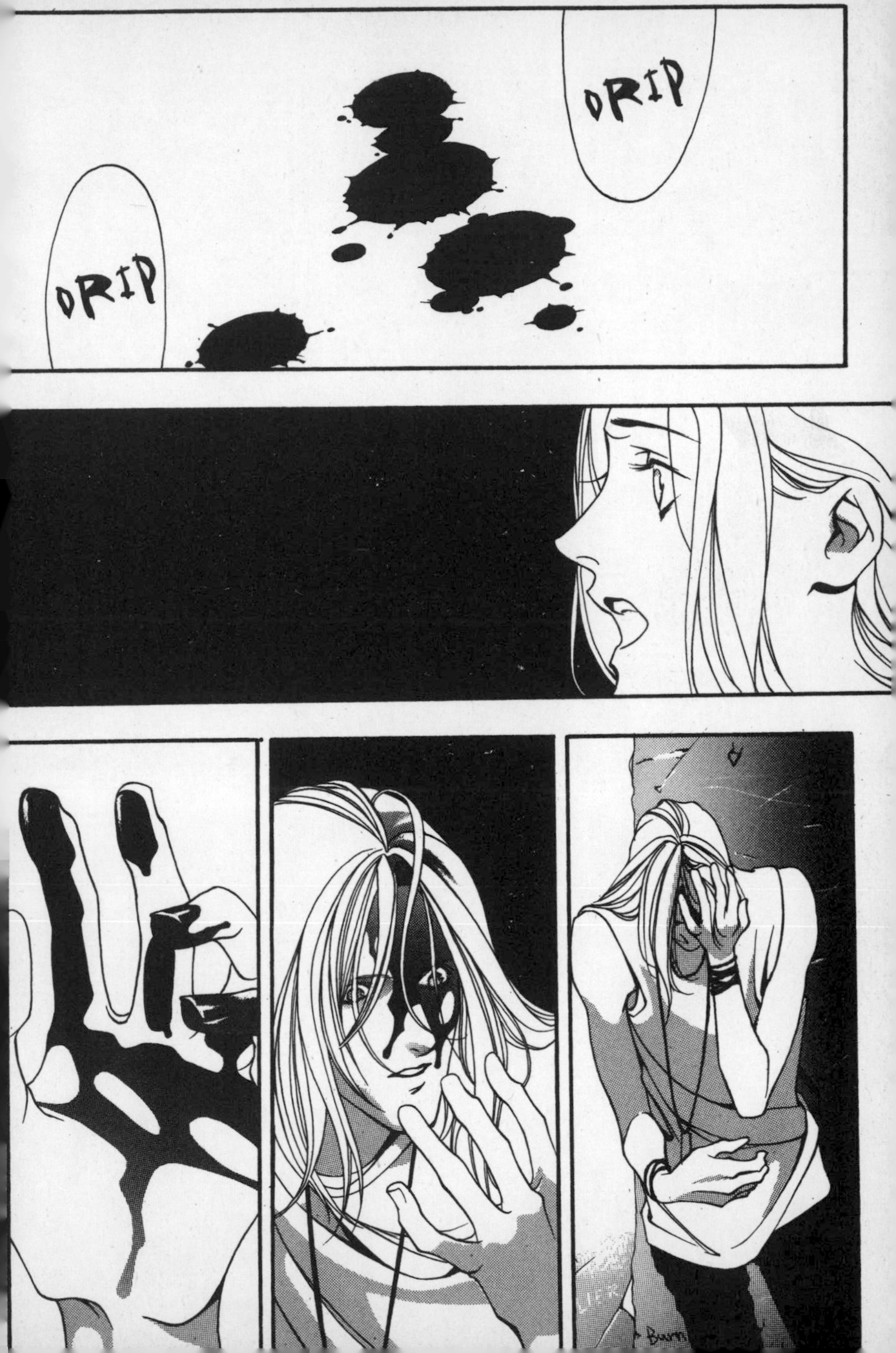
DRIP
DRIP

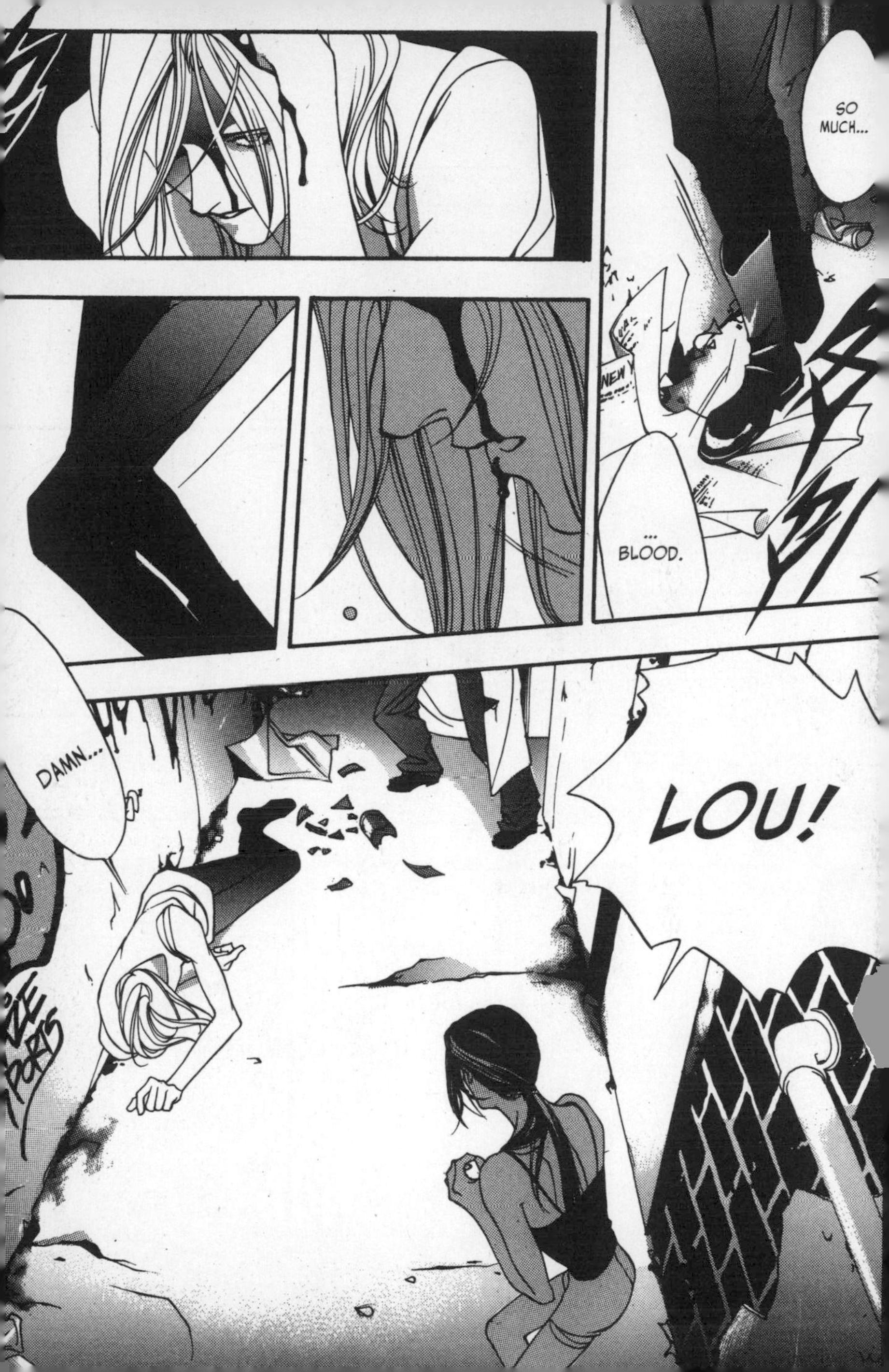

SO MUCH...
... BLOOD.
LOU!
DAMN...

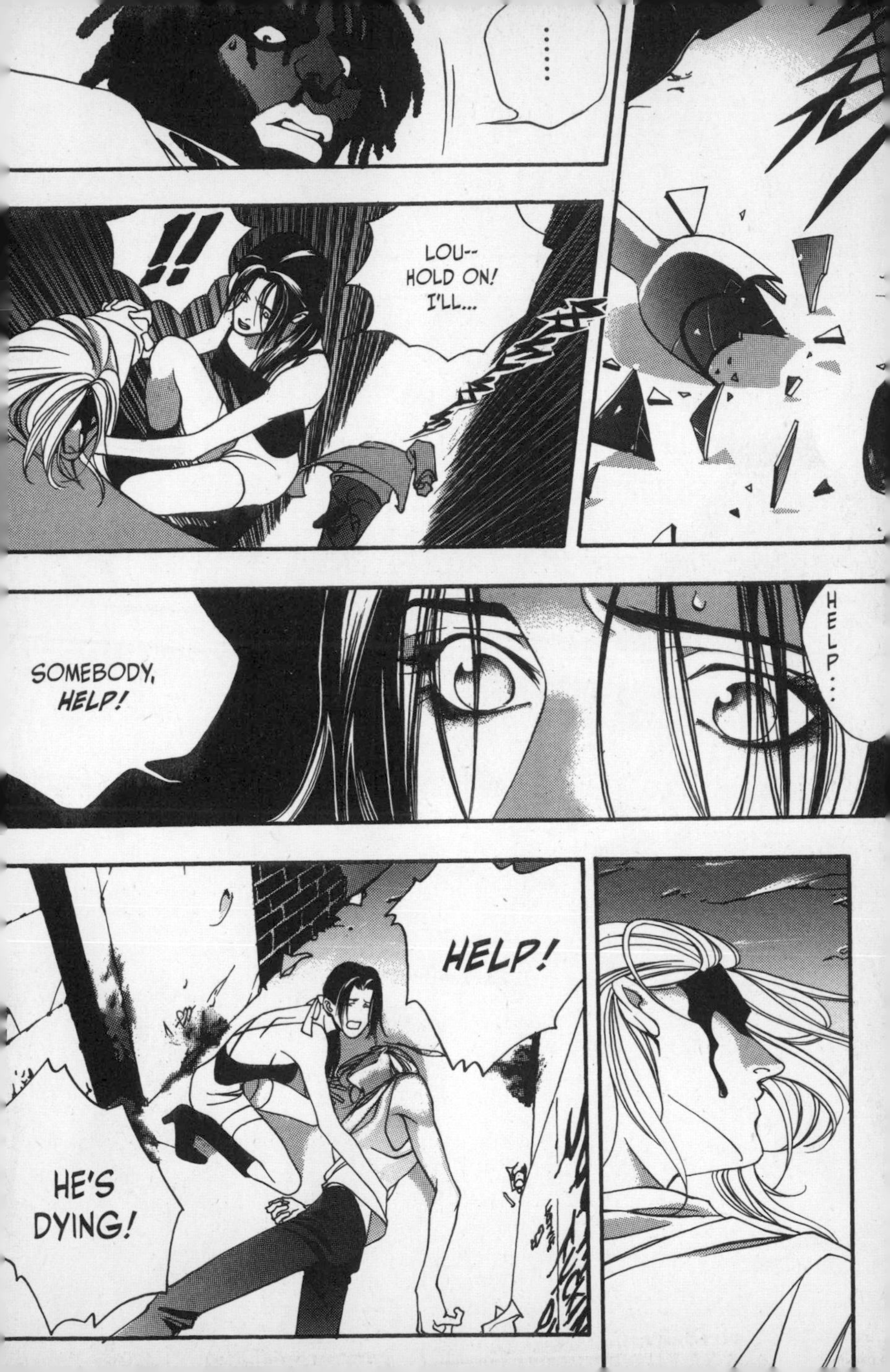
......
!!
LOU-- HOLD ON! I'LL...
HELP...
SOMEBODY, HELP!
HELP!
HE'S DYING!

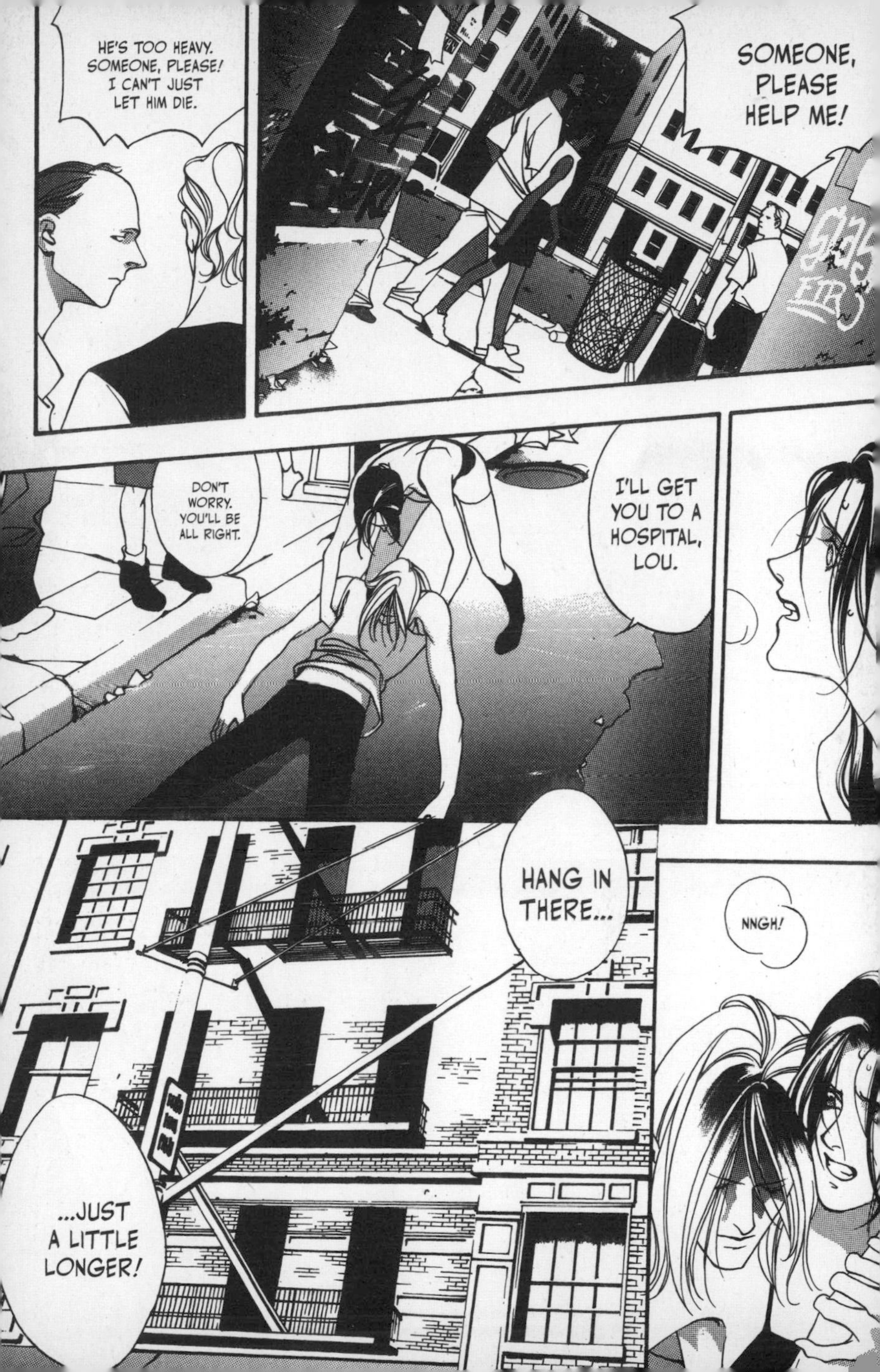
SOMEONE, PLEASE HELP ME!
HE'S TOO HEAVY. SOMEONE, PLEASE! I CAN'T JUST LET HIM DIE.
I'LL GET YOU TO A HOSPITAL, LOU.
DON'T WORRY. YOU'LL BE ALL RIGHT.
NNGH!
HANG IN THERE...
...JUST A LITTLE LONGER!

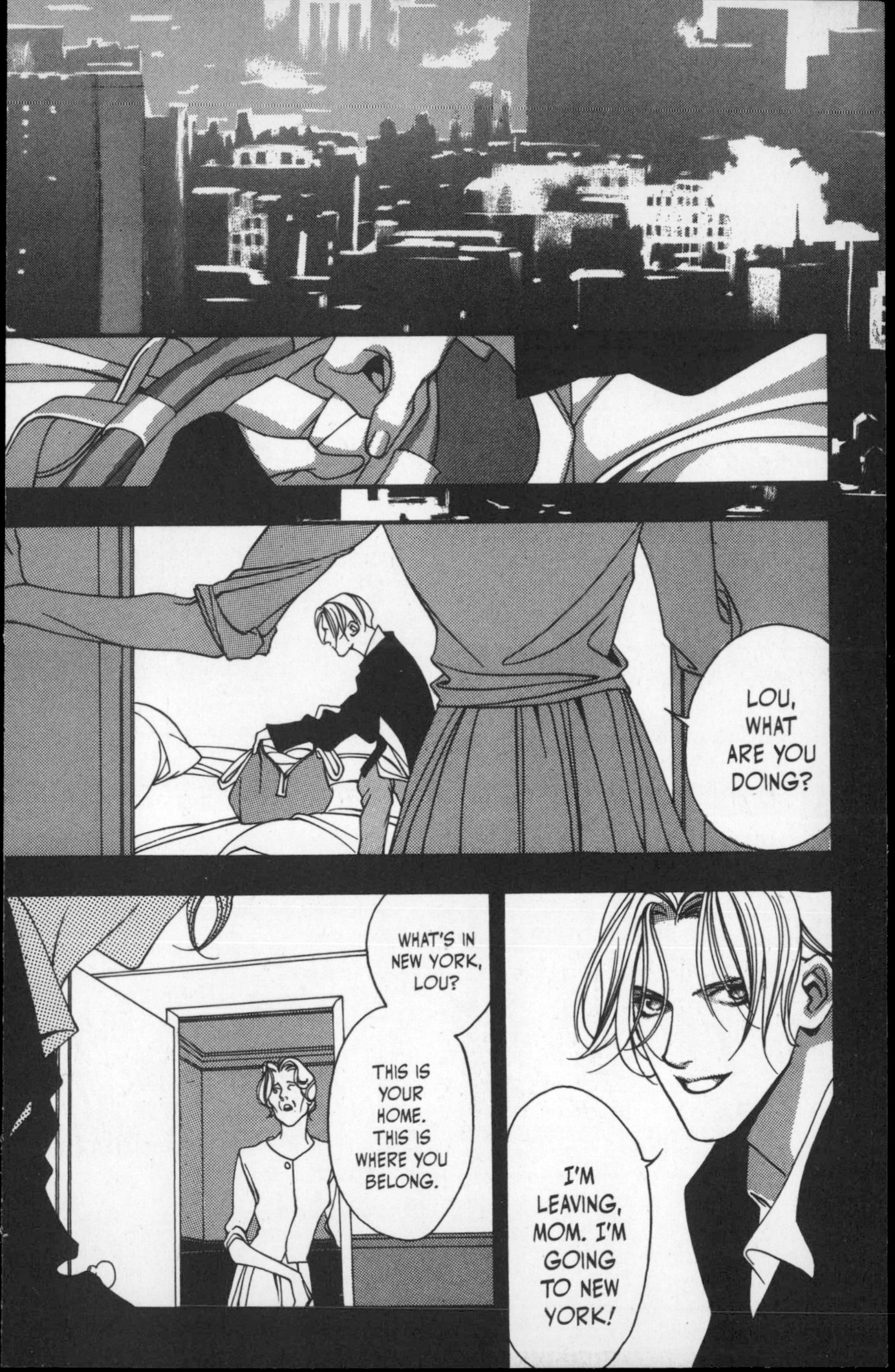
LOU, WHAT ARE YOU DOING?
I'M LEAVING, MOM. I'M GOING TO NEW YORK!
WHAT'S IN NEW YORK, LOU?
THIS IS YOUR HOME. THIS IS WHERE YOU BELONG.

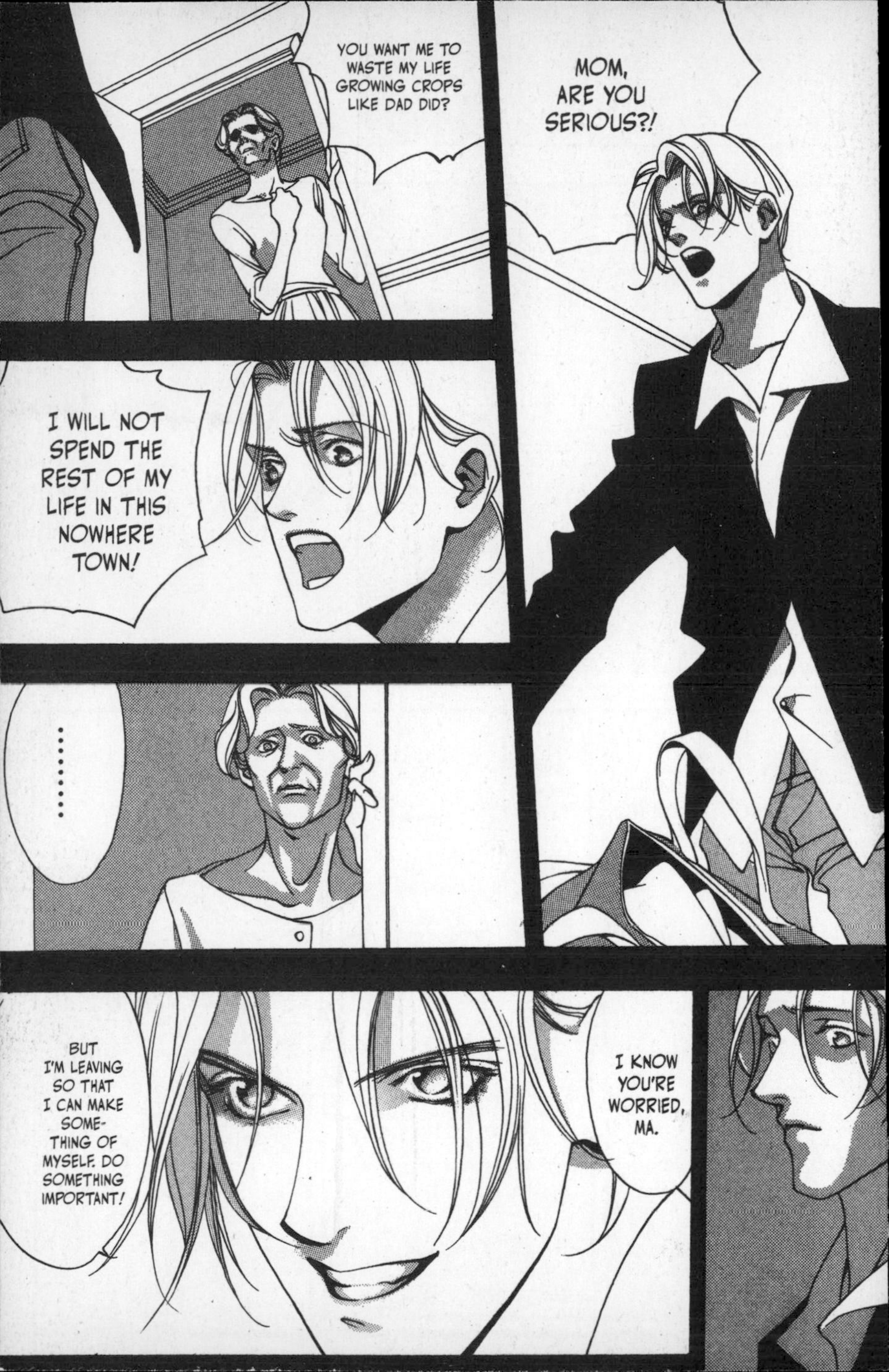
MOM, ARE YOU SERIOUS?!
YOU WANT ME TO WASTE MY LIFE GROWING CROPS LIKE DAD DID?
I WILL NOT SPEND THE REST OF MY LIFE IN THIS NOWHERE TOWN!
....
I KNOW YOU'RE WORRIED, MA.
BUT I'M LEAVING SO THAT I CAN MAKE SOME-THING OF MYSELF. DO SOMETHING IMPORTANT!

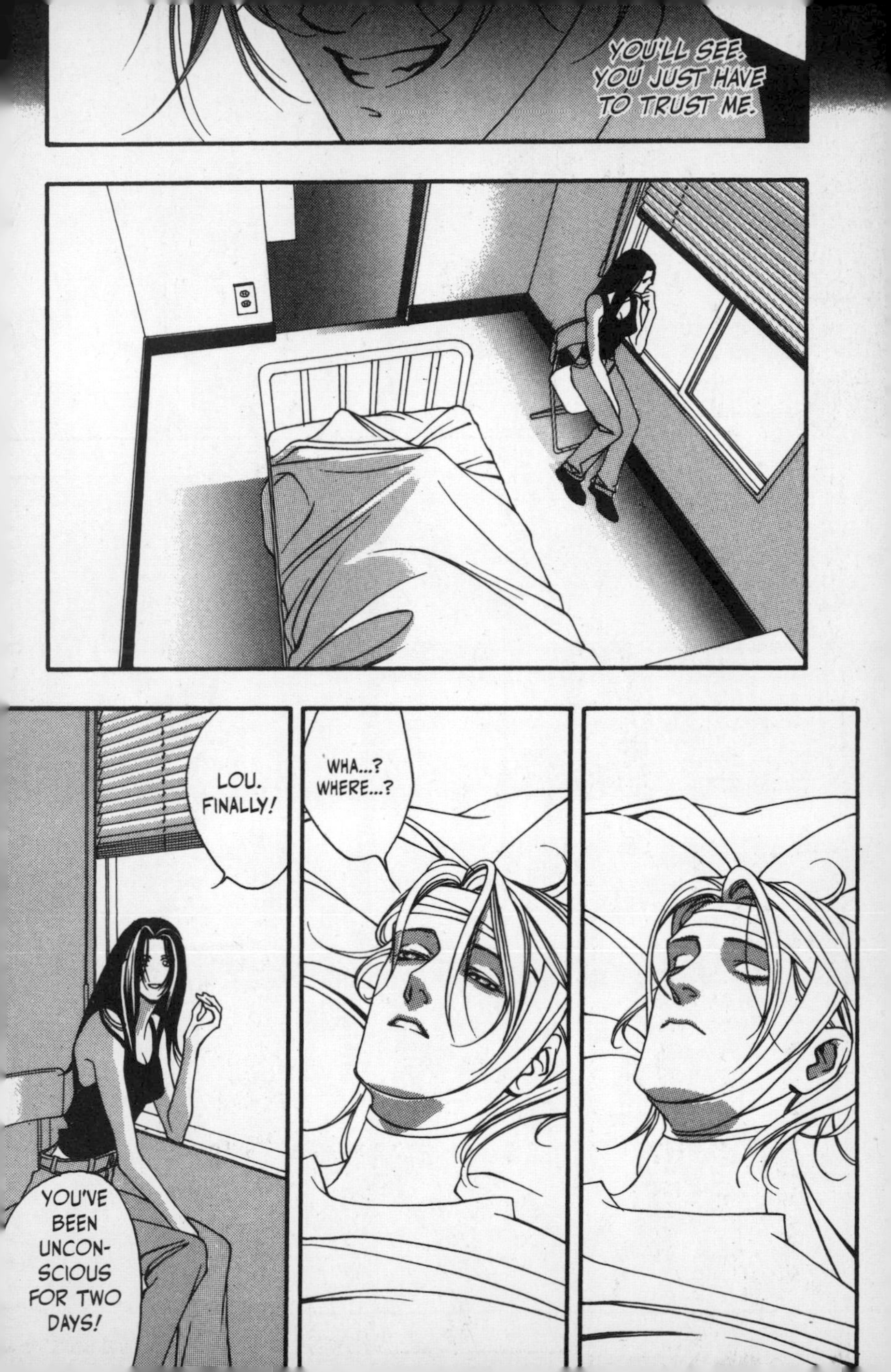
YOU'LL SEE. YOU JUST HAVE TO TRUST ME.
WHA...? WHERE...?
LOU. FINALLY!
YOU'VE BEEN UNCON-SCIOUS FOR TWO DAYS!

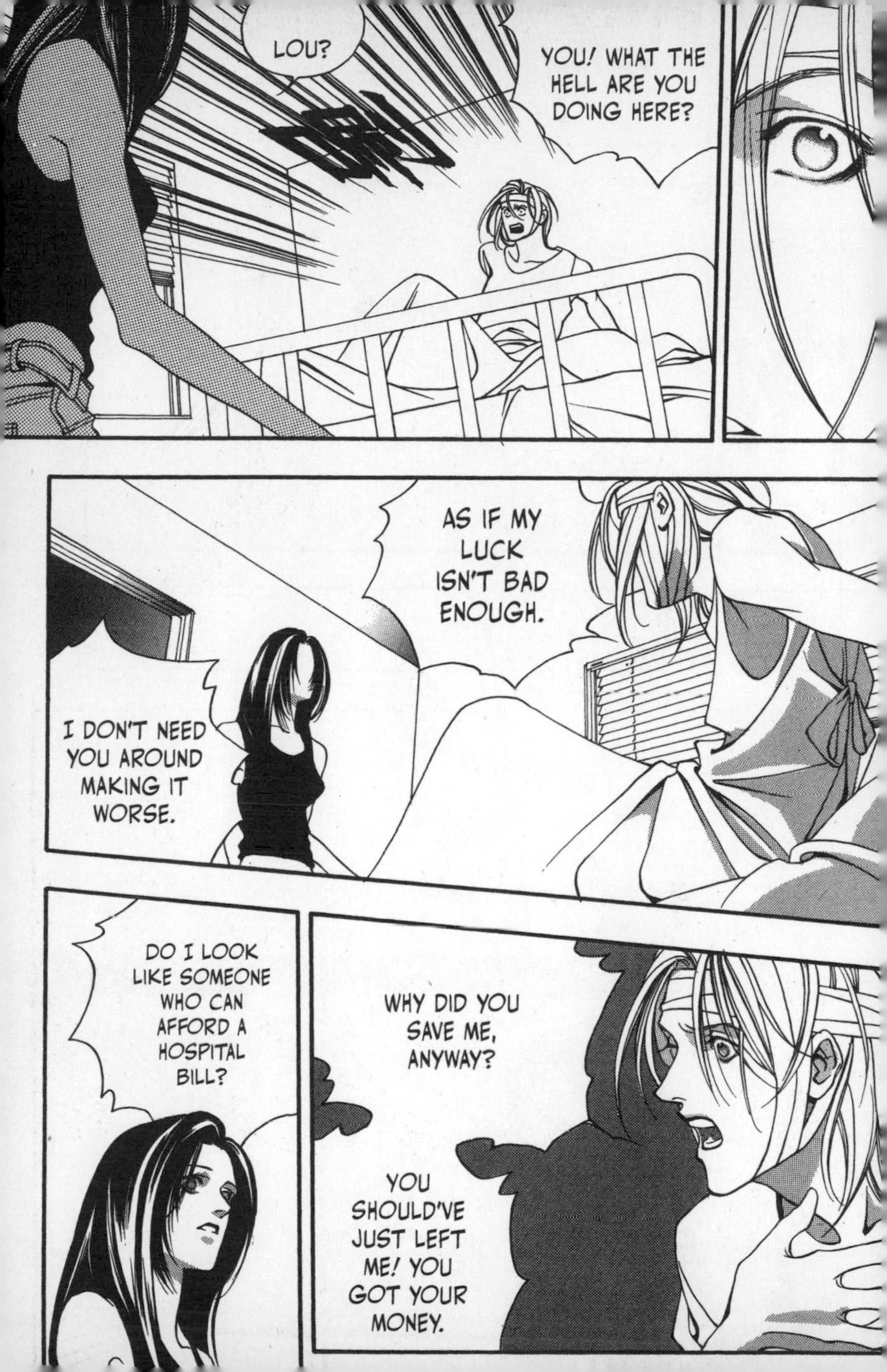
LOU?
YOU! WHAT THE HELL ARE YOU DOING HERE?
AS IF MY LUCK ISN'T BAD ENOUGH.
I DON'T NEED YOU AROUND MAKING IT WORSE.
WHY DID YOU SAVE ME, ANYWAY?
YOU SHOULD'VE JUST LEFT ME! YOU GOT YOUR MONEY.
DO I LOOK LIKE SOMEONE WHO CAN AFFORD A HOSPITAL BILL?

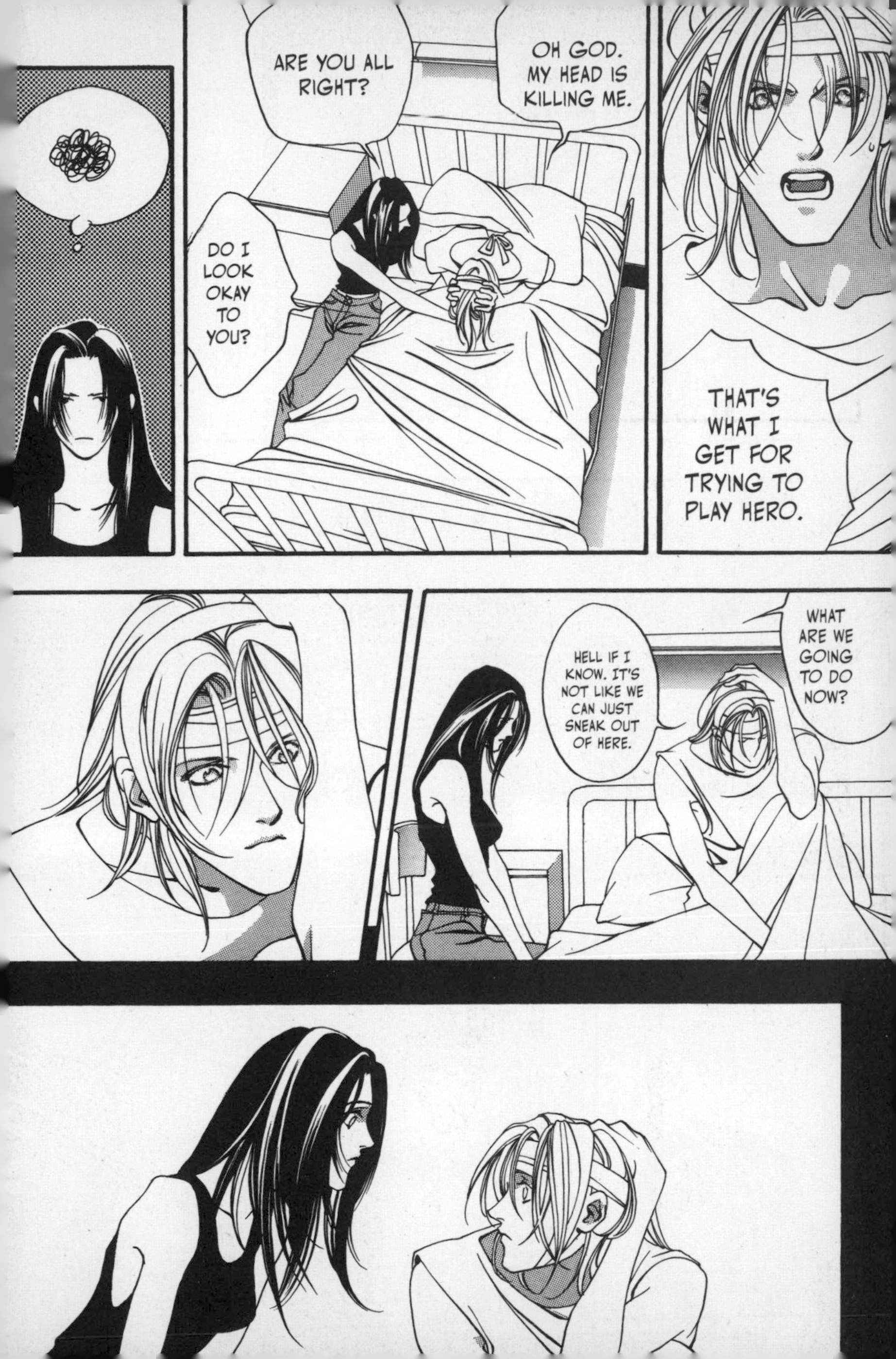
THAT'S WHAT I GET FOR TRYING TO PLAY HERO.
OH GOD. MY HEAD IS KILLING ME.
ARE YOU ALL RIGHT?
DO I LOOK OKAY TO YOU?
WHAT ARE WE GOING TO DO NOW?
HELL IF I KNOW. IT'S NOT LIKE WE CAN JUST SNEAK OUT OF HERE.

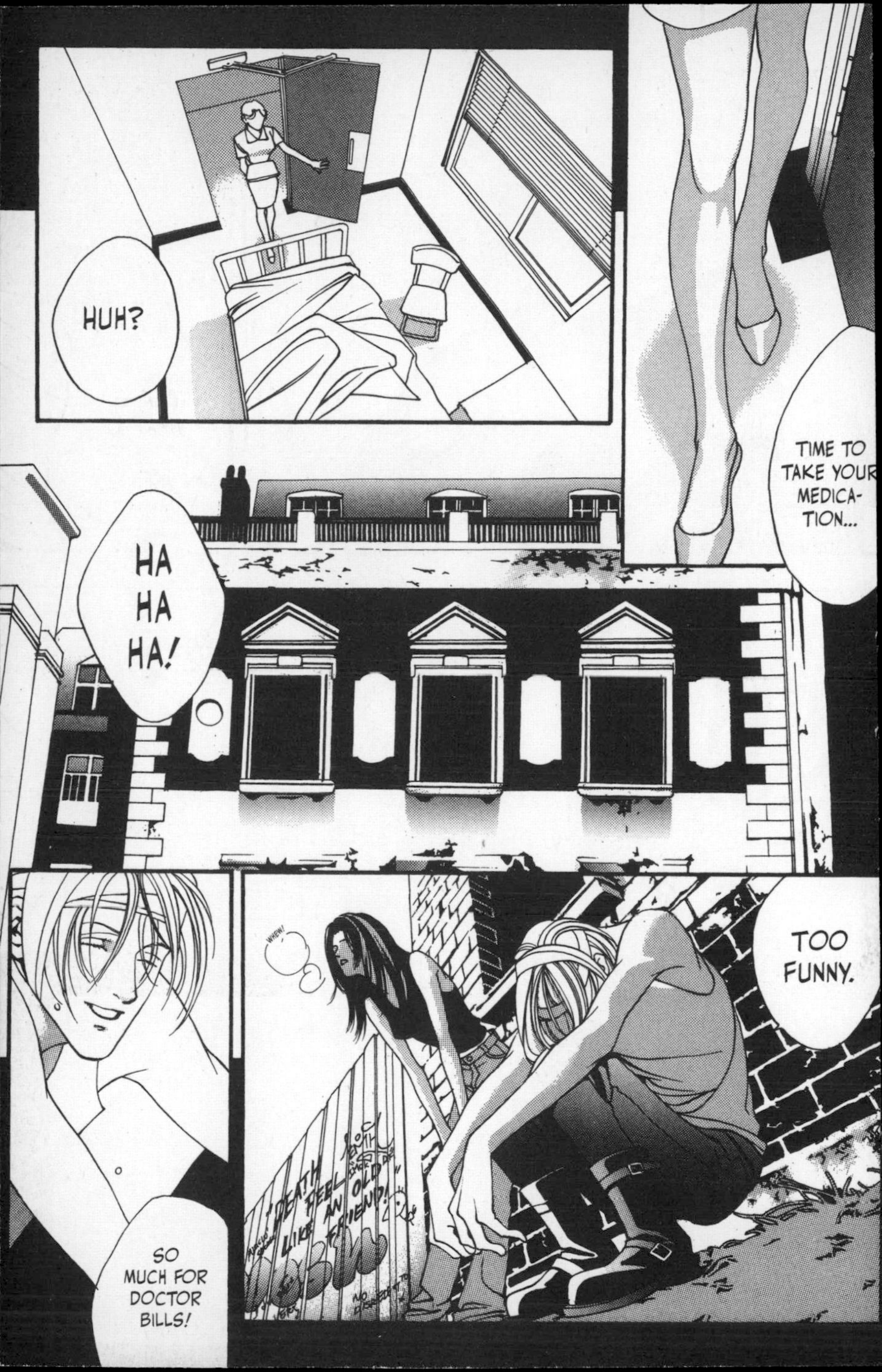
TIME TO TAKE YOUR MEDICATION...
HUH?
HA HA HA!
TOO FUNNY.
WHEW!
DEATH FEEL LIKE AN OLD FRIEND!
SO MUCH FOR DOCTOR BILLS!

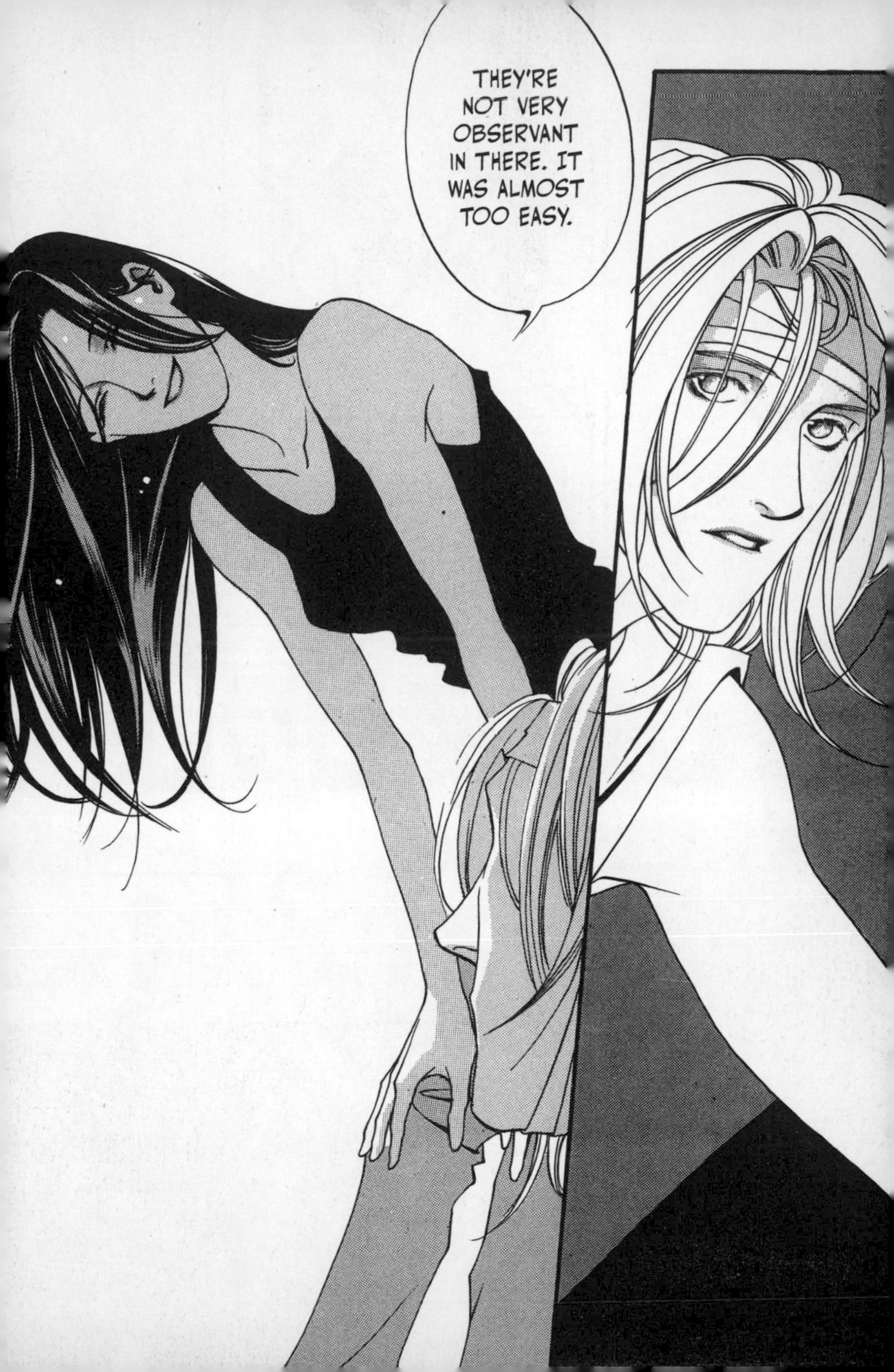
THEY'RE NOT VERY OBSERVANT IN THERE. IT WAS ALMOST TOO EASY.

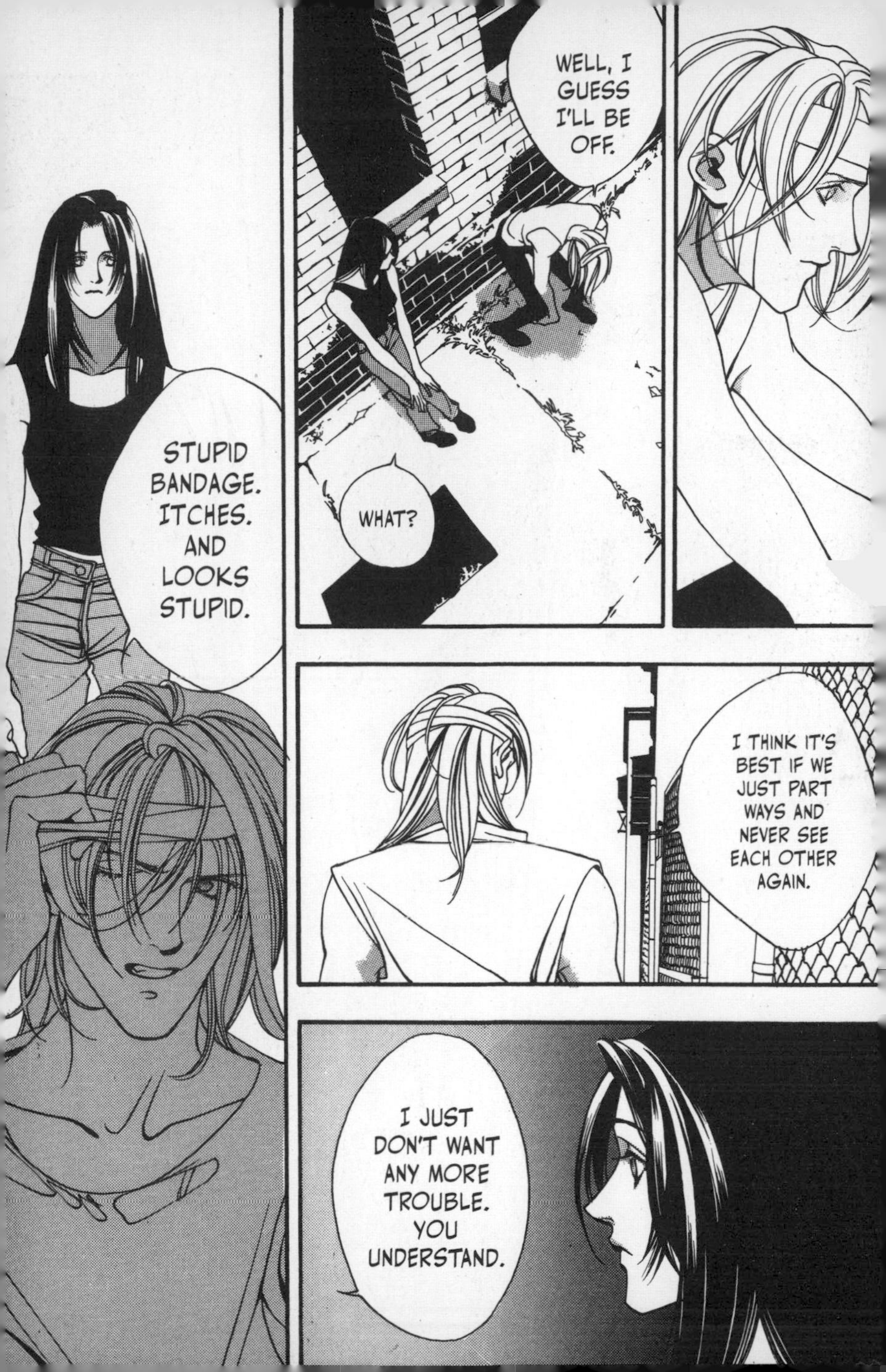
WELL, I GUESS I'LL BE OFF.
WHAT?
I THINK IT'S BEST IF WE JUST PART WAYS AND NEVER SEE EACH OTHER AGAIN.
I JUST DON'T WANT ANY MORE TROUBLE. YOU UNDERSTAND.
STUPID BANDAGE. ITCHES. AND LOOKS STUPID.

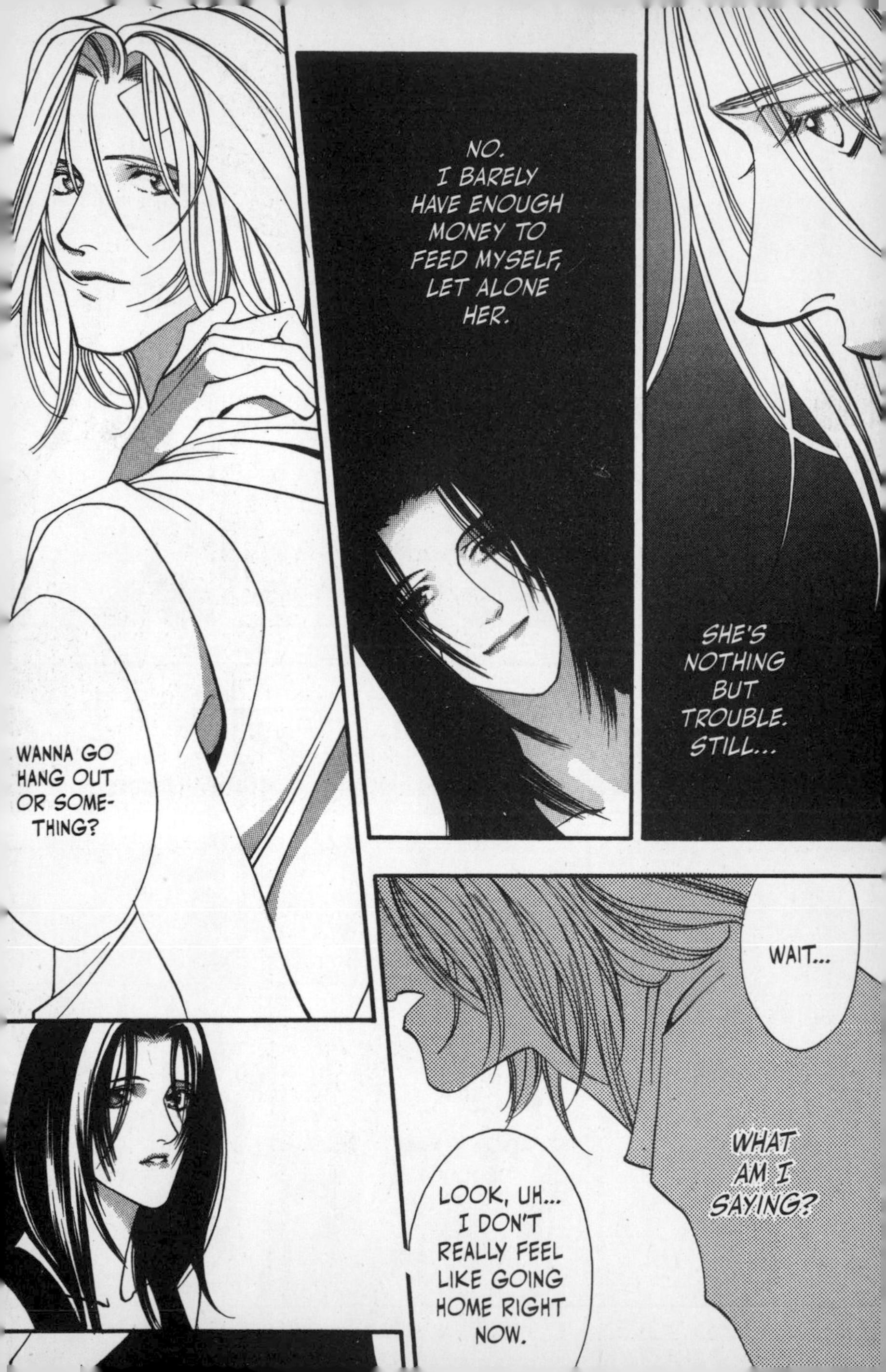
SHE'S NOTHING BUT TROUBLE. STILL...
NO. I BARELY HAVE ENOUGH MONEY TO FEED MYSELF, LET ALONE HER.
WANNA GO HANG OUT OR SOME-THING?
WAIT...
WHAT AM I SAYING?
LOOK, UH... I DON'T REALLY FEEL LIKE GOING HOME RIGHT NOW.

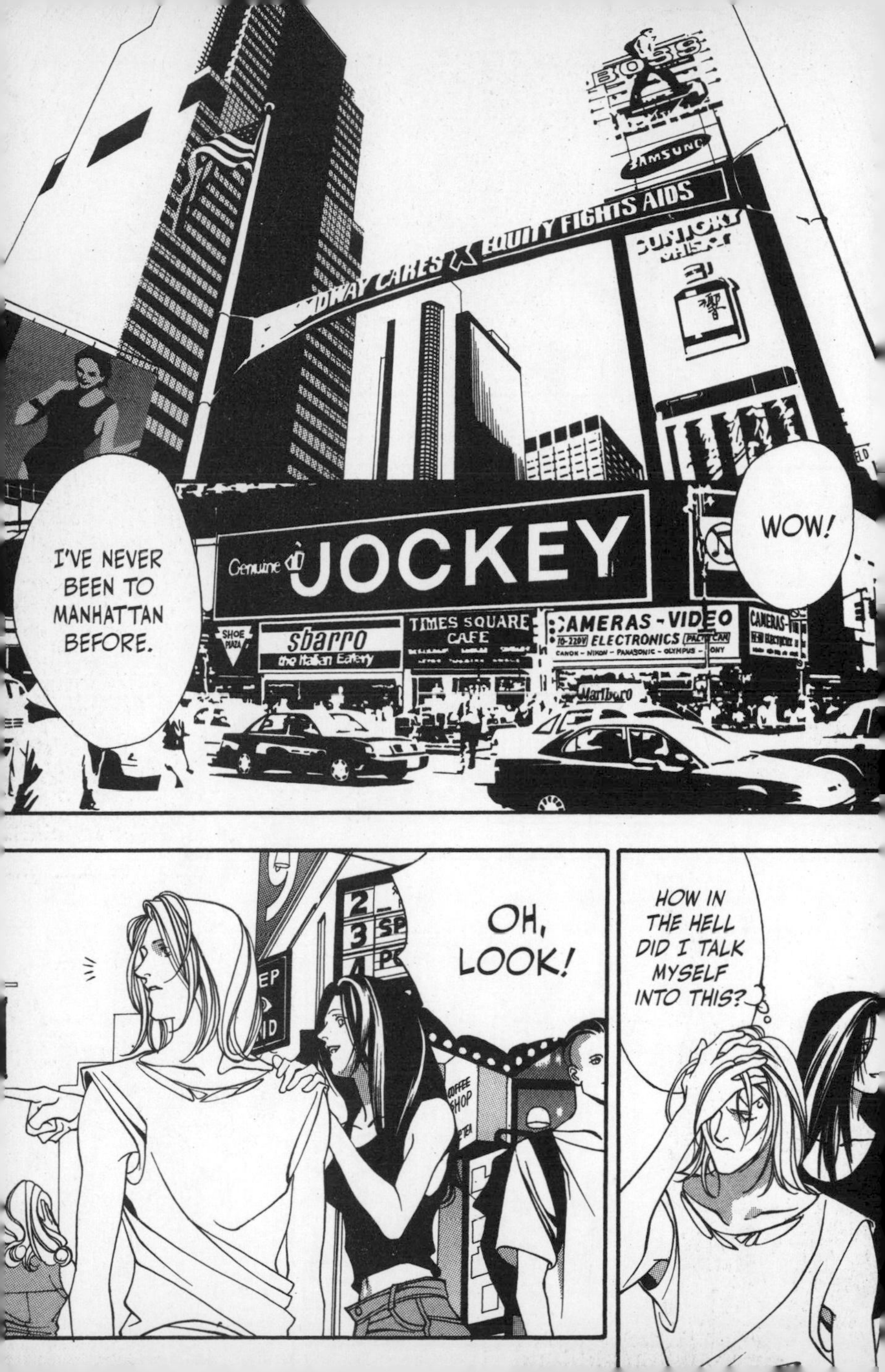
BOSS
SAMSUNG
EQUITY FIGHTS AIDS
WOW!
Genuine JOCKEY
I'VE NEVER BEEN TO MANHATTAN BEFORE.
CAMERAS - VIDEO ELECTRONICS
TIMES SQUARE CAFE
sbarro the Italian Eatery
SHOE PLAZA
HOW IN THE HELL DID I TALK MYSELF INTO THIS?
OH, LOOK!

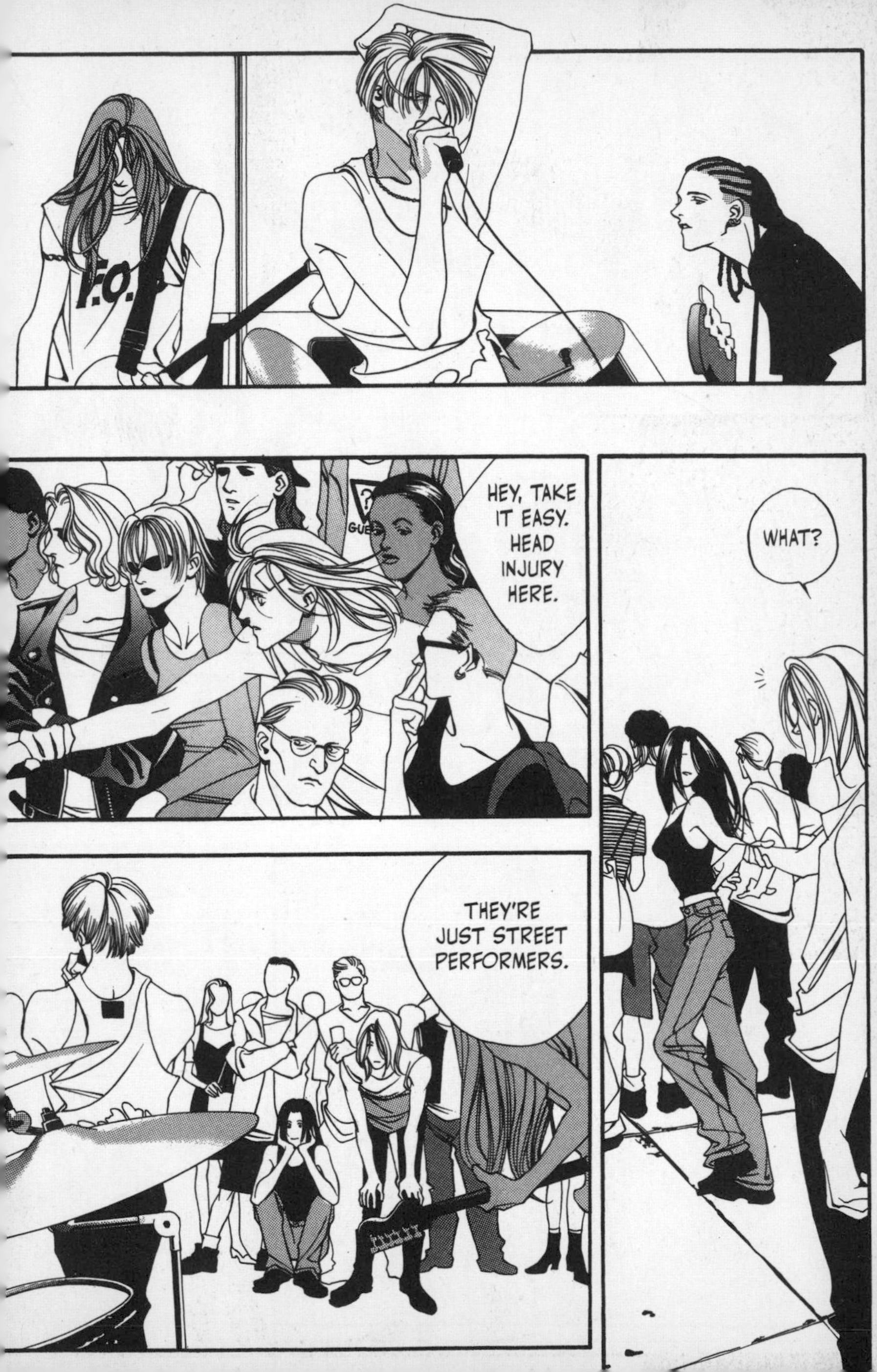
WHAT?
HEY, TAKE IT EASY. HEAD INJURY HERE.
THEY'RE JUST STREET PERFORMERS.

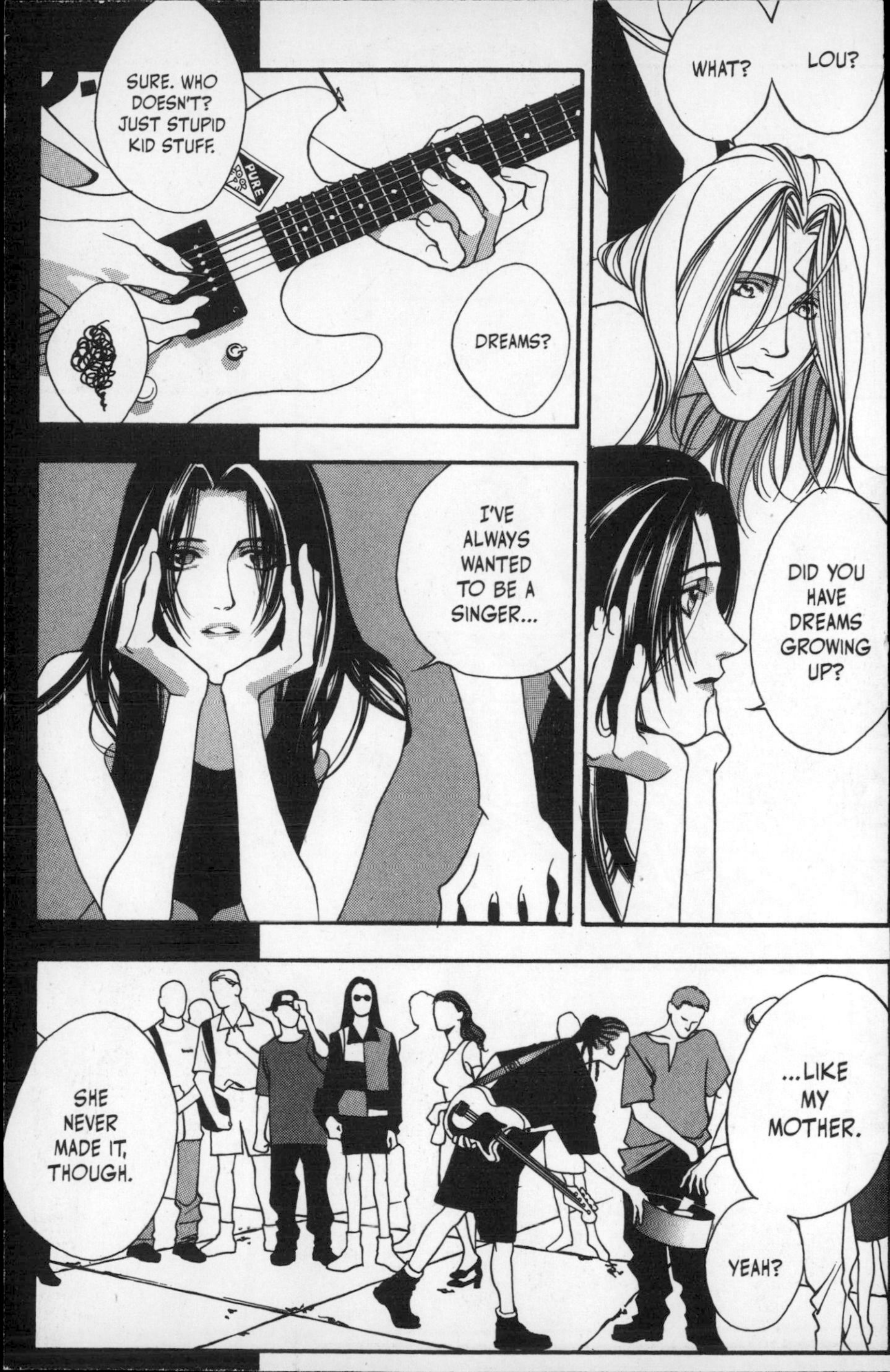
LOU?
WHAT?
DID YOU HAVE DREAMS GROWING UP?
DREAMS?
SURE. WHO DOESN'T? JUST STUPID KID STUFF.
PURE
I'VE ALWAYS WANTED TO BE A SINGER...
...LIKE MY MOTHER.
YEAH?
SHE NEVER MADE IT, THOUGH.

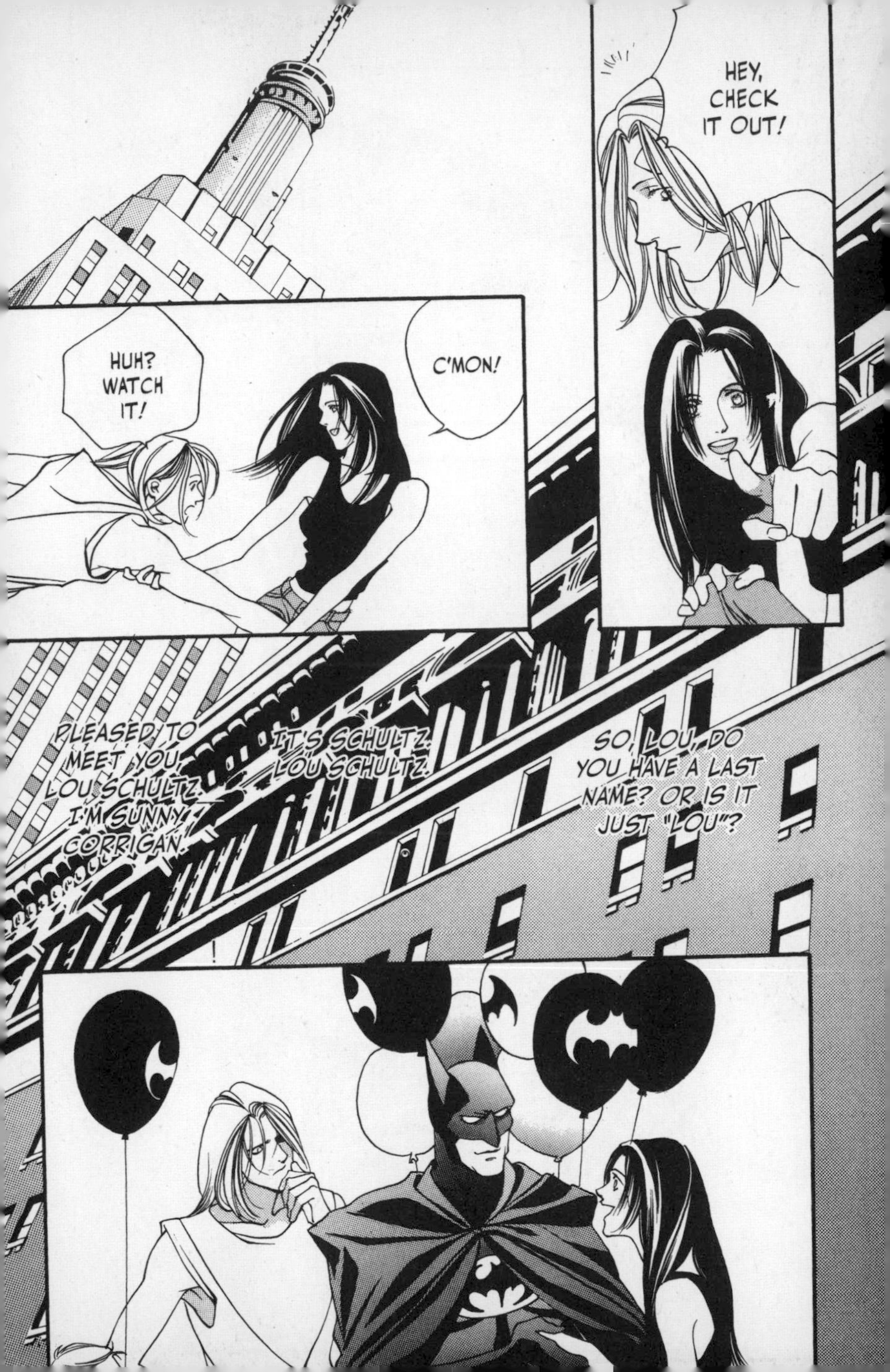
HEY, CHECK IT OUT!
C'MON!
HUH? WATCH IT!
SO, LOU, DO YOU HAVE A LAST NAME? OR IS IT JUST "LOU"?
IT'S SCHULTZ. LOU SCHULTZ.
PLEASED TO MEET YOU, LOU SCHULTZ. I'M SUNNY CORRIGAN.

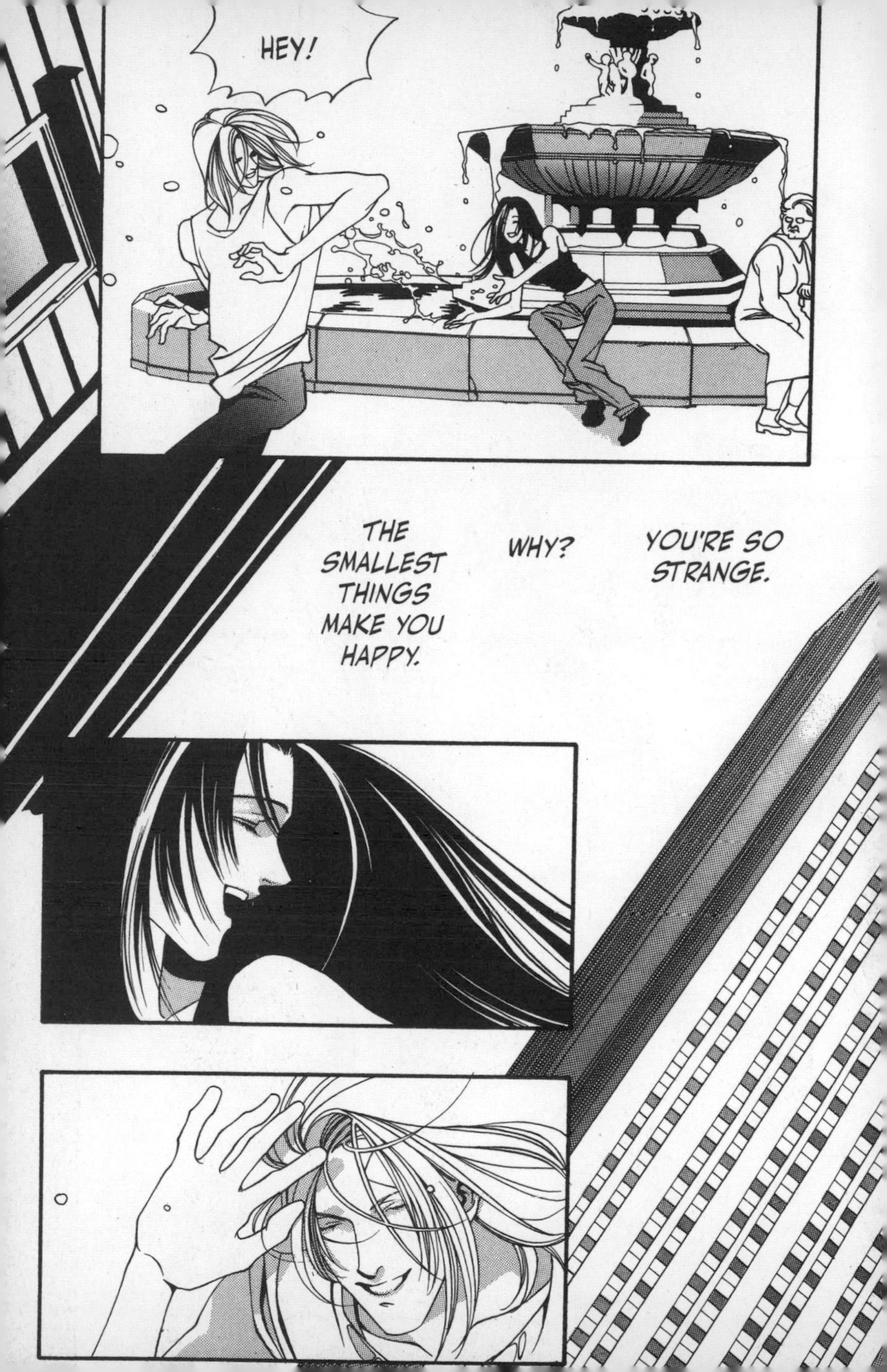
HEY!
YOU'RE SO STRANGE.
WHY?
THE SMALLEST THINGS MAKE YOU HAPPY.

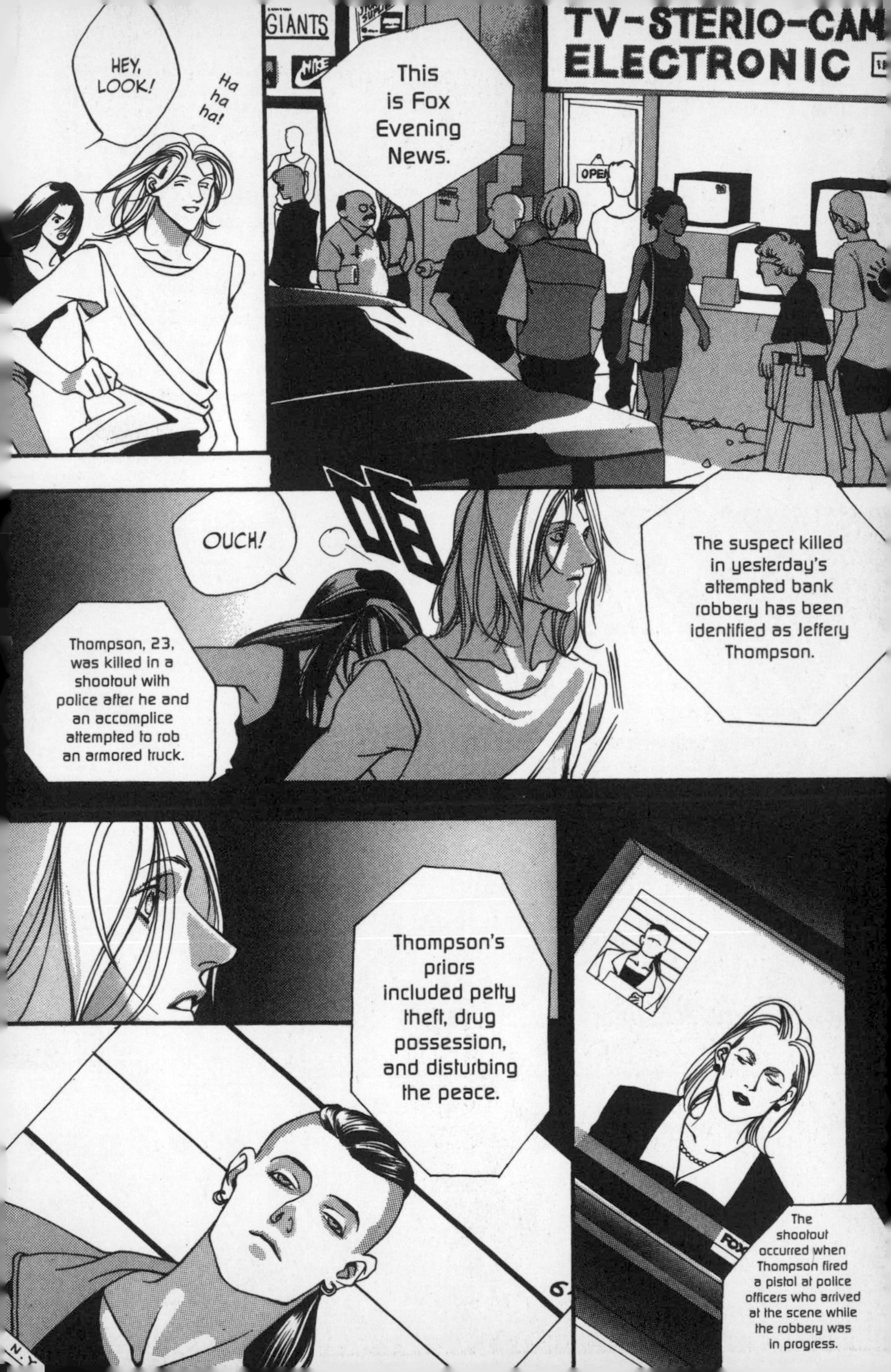
TV-STERIO-CAM
ELECTRONIC
GIANTS
NIKE
OPEN
This is Fox Evening News.
HEY, LOOK!
Ha ha ha!
The suspect killed in yesterday's attempted bank robbery has been identified as Jeffery Thompson.
OUCH!
Thompson, 23, was killed in a shootout with police after he and an accomplice attempted to rob an armored truck.
Thompson's priors included petty theft, drug possession, and disturbing the peace.
FOX
The shootout occurred when Thompson fired a pistol at police officers who arrived at the scene while the robbery was in progress.

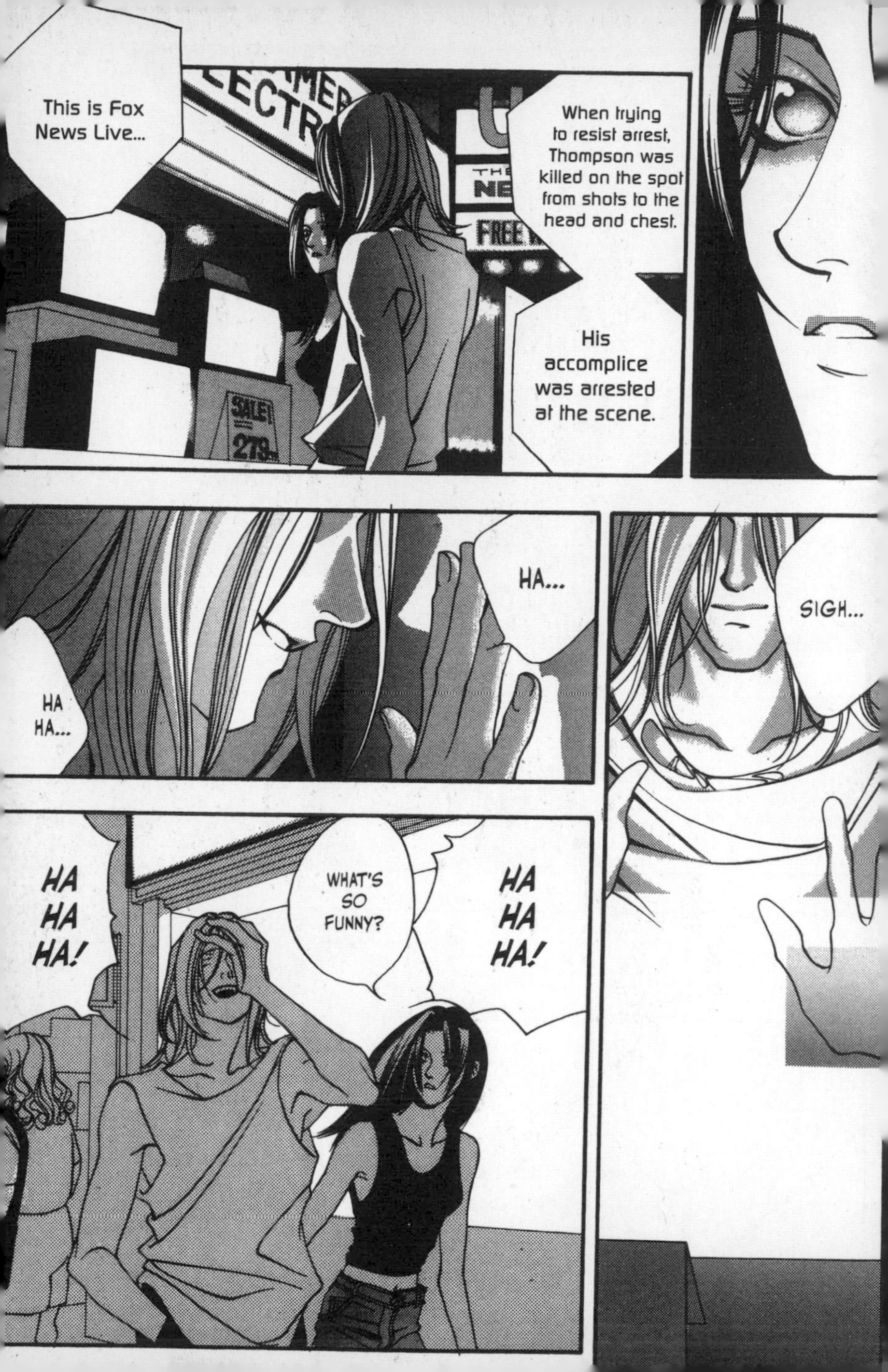
This is Fox News Live...
When trying to resist arrest, Thompson was killed on the spot from shots to the head and chest.
His accomplice was arrested at the scene.
SIGH...
HA...
HA HA...
HA HA HA!
WHAT'S SO FUNNY?
HA HA HA!

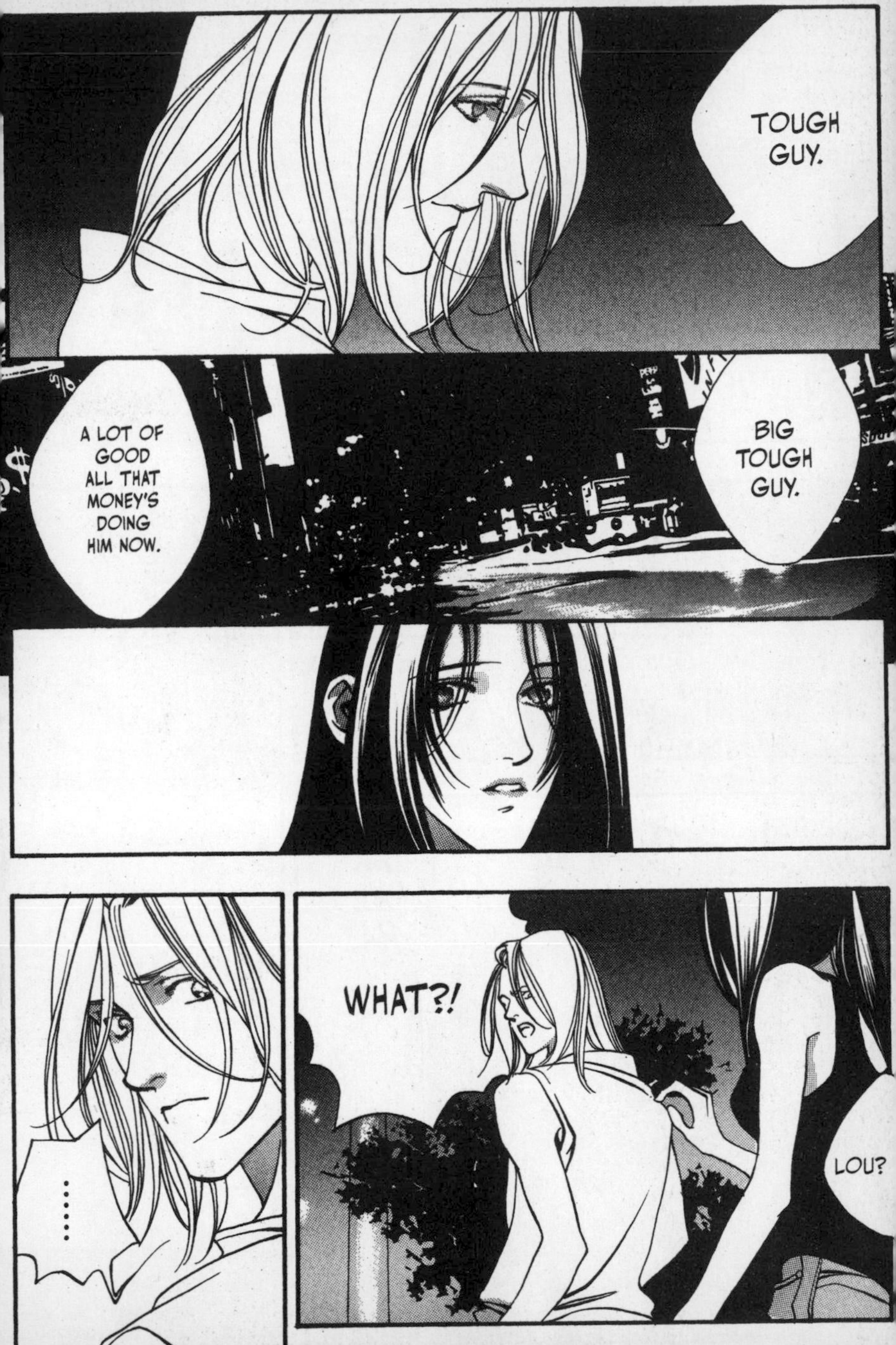
TOUGH GUY.
BIG TOUGH GUY.
A LOT OF GOOD ALL THAT MONEY'S DOING HIM NOW.
LOU?
WHAT?!
......

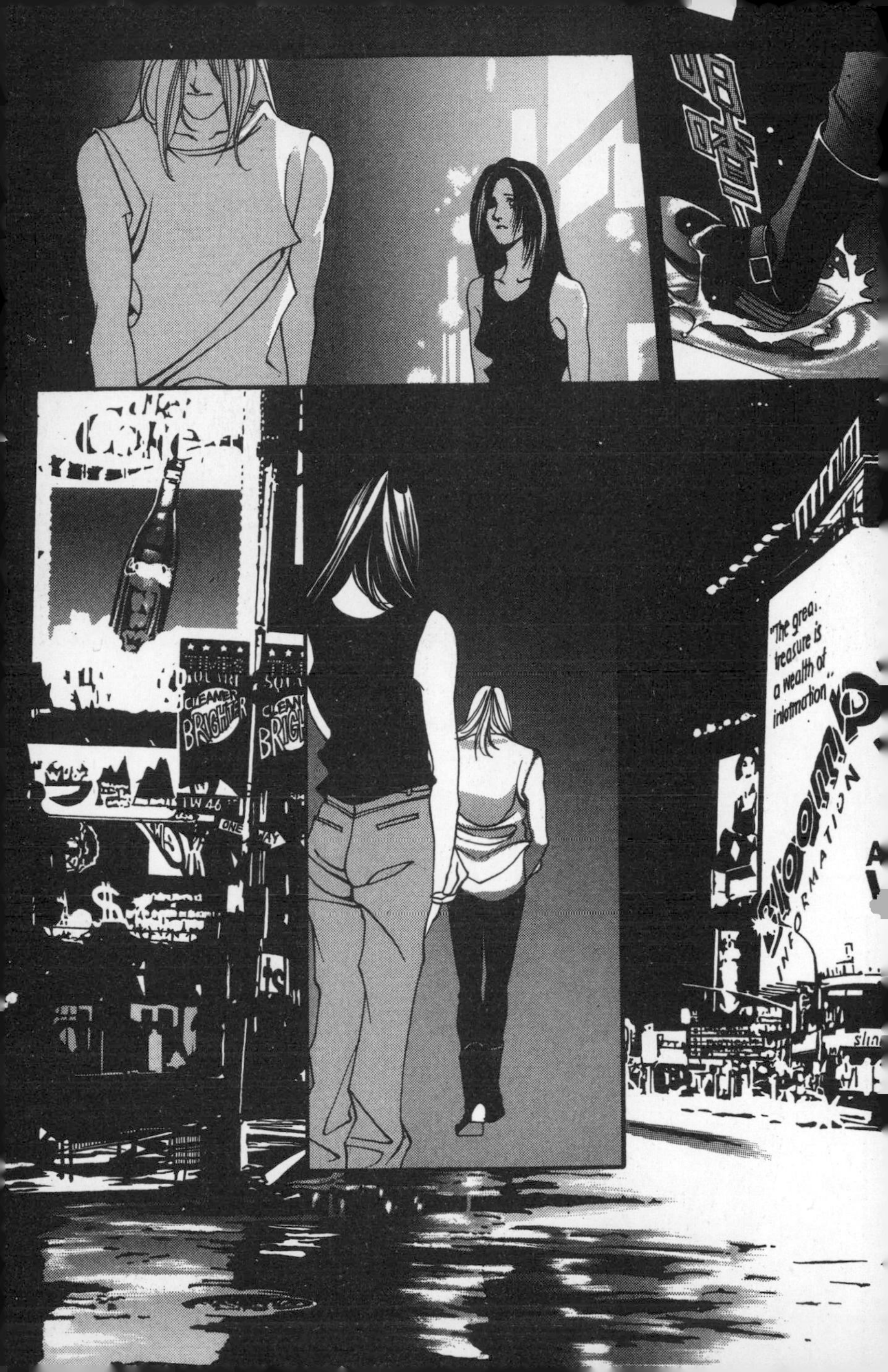
"The great
treasure is
a wealth of
information"
INFORMATION
CLEANER
BRIGHTER
ONE WAY

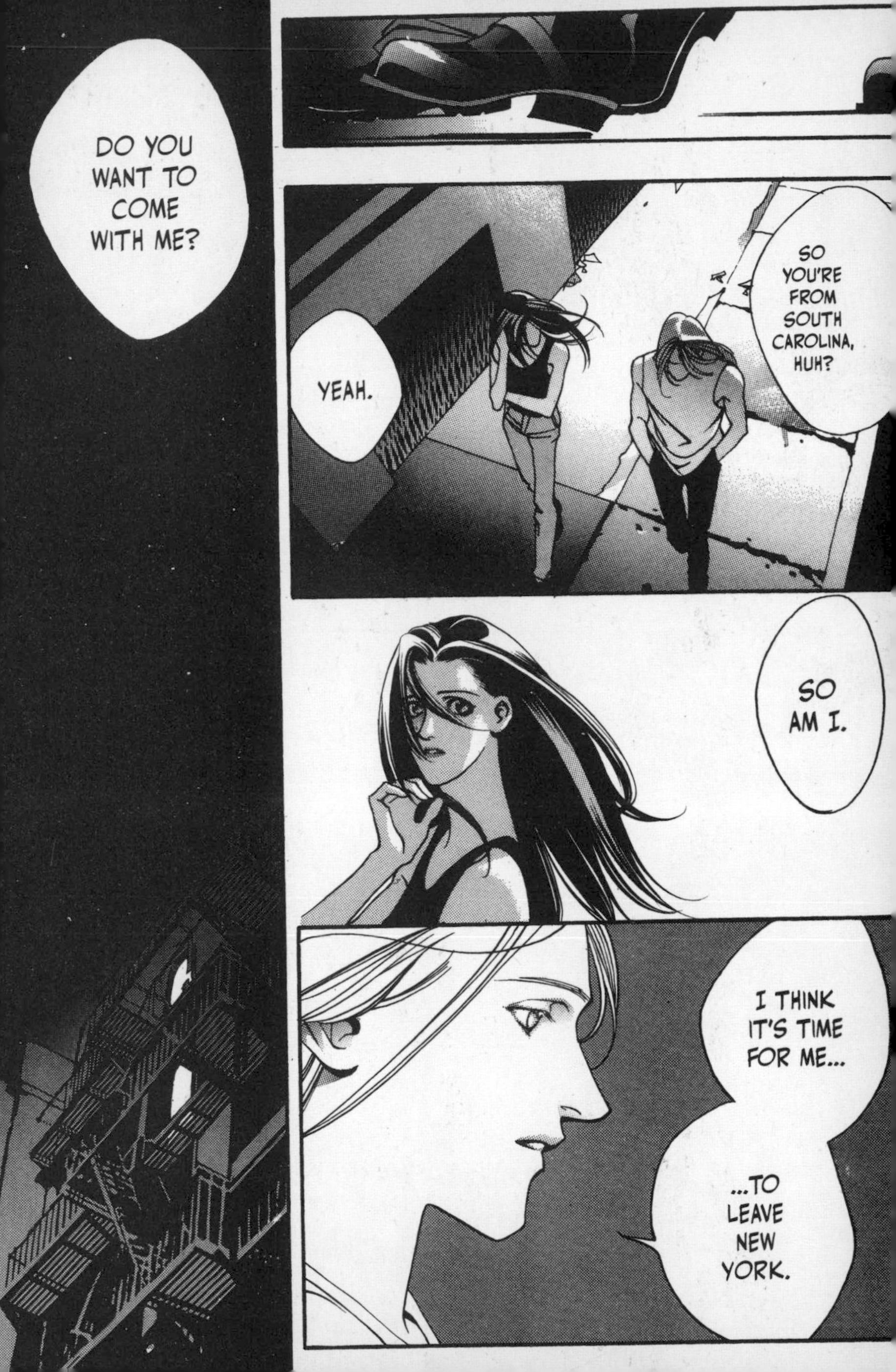
SO YOU'RE FROM SOUTH CAROLINA, HUH?
YEAH.
SO AM I.
I THINK IT'S TIME FOR ME...
...TO LEAVE NEW YORK.
DO YOU WANT TO COME WITH ME?

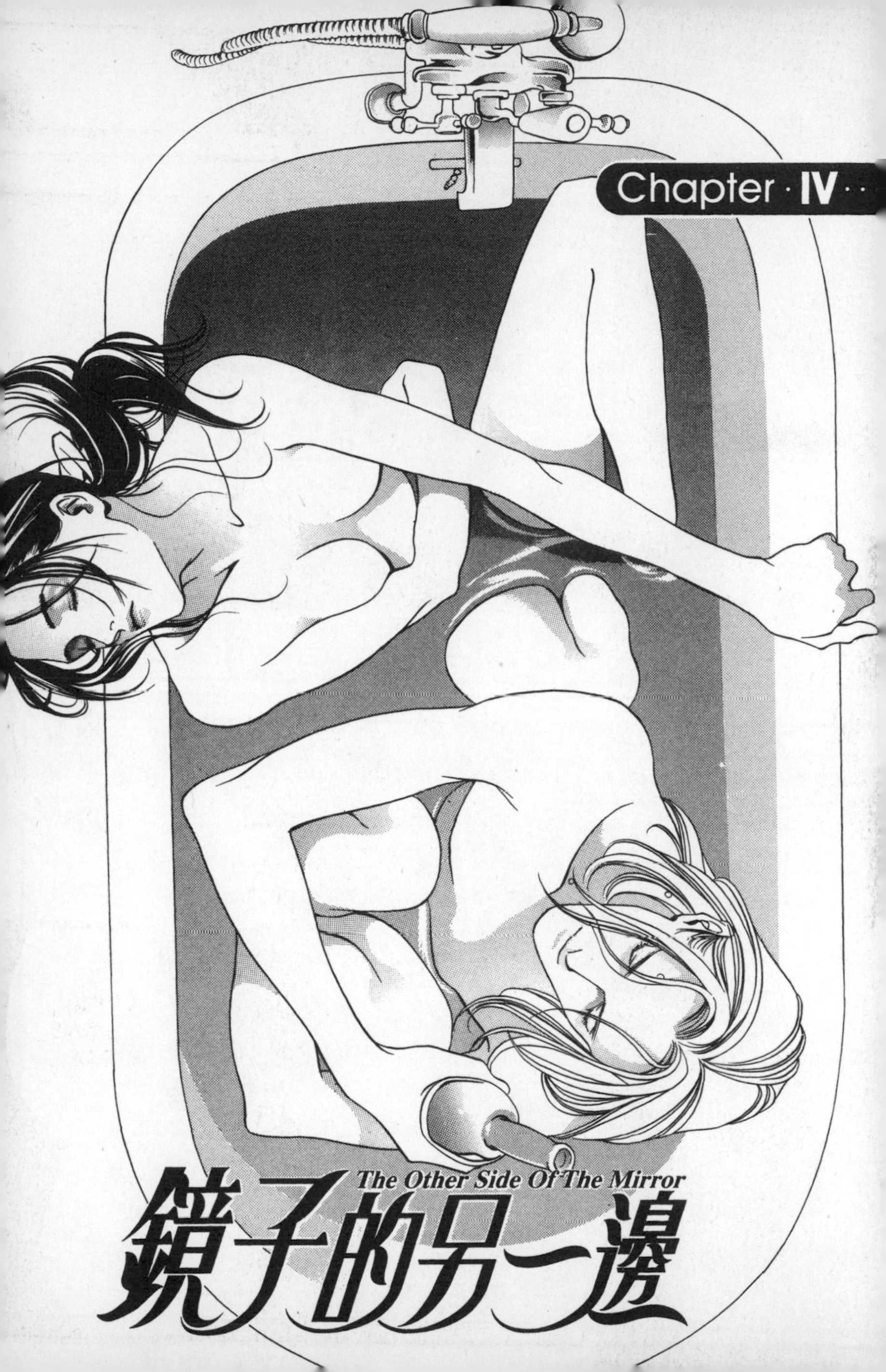
Chapter · IV · ·
The Other Side Of The Mirror
鏡子的另一邊

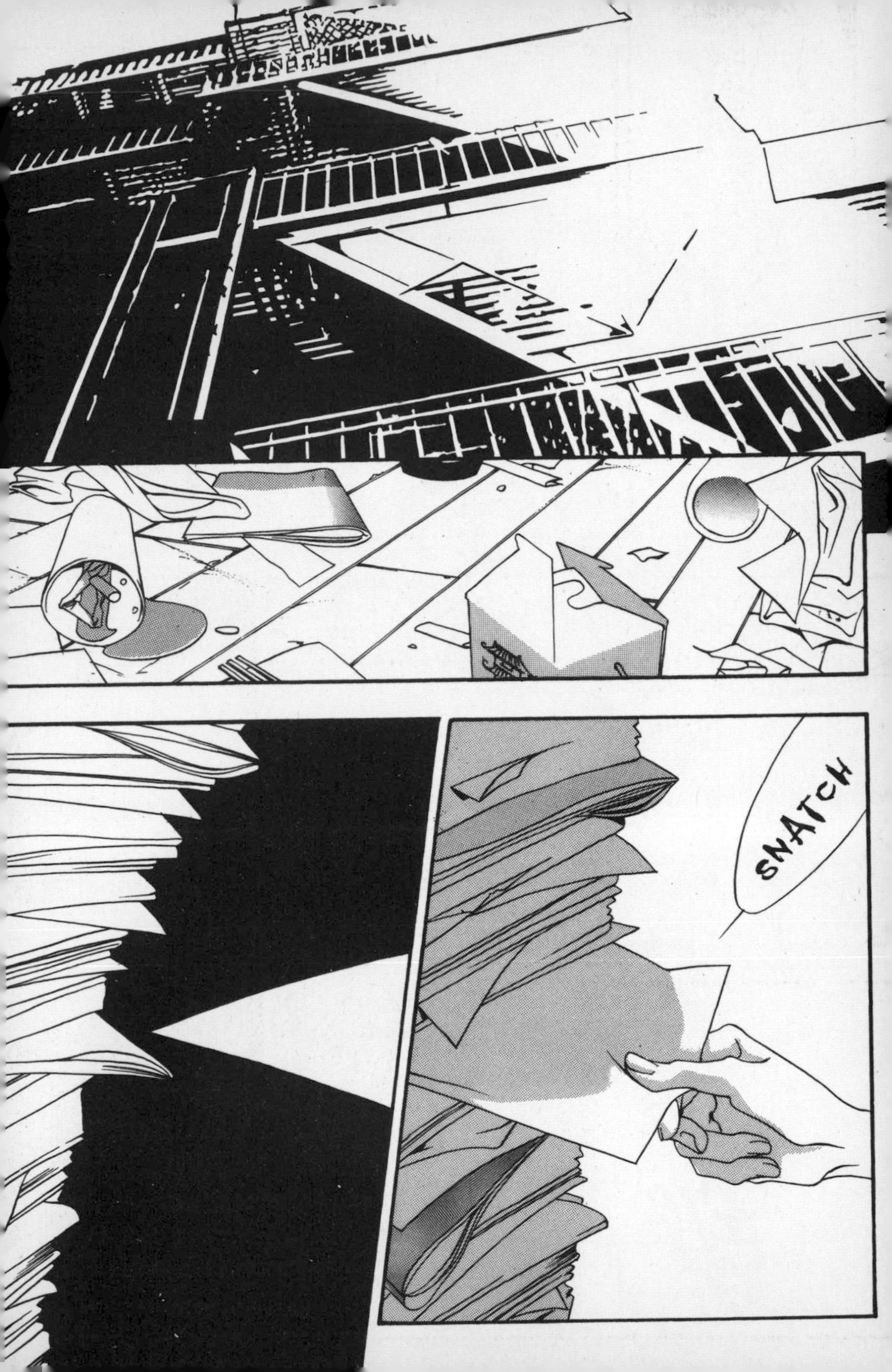
SNATCH

DO YOU HAVE TO BE SUCH A SLOB? THIS PLACE IS A MESS.

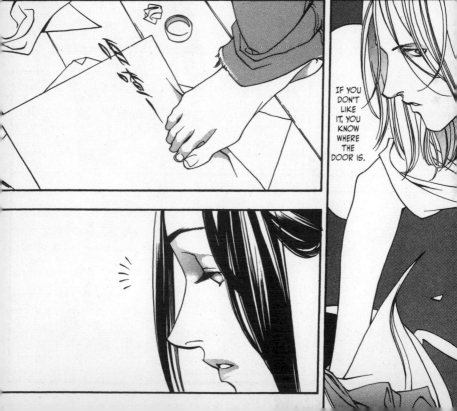

IF YOU DON'T LIKE IT, YOU KNOW WHERE THE DOOR IS.

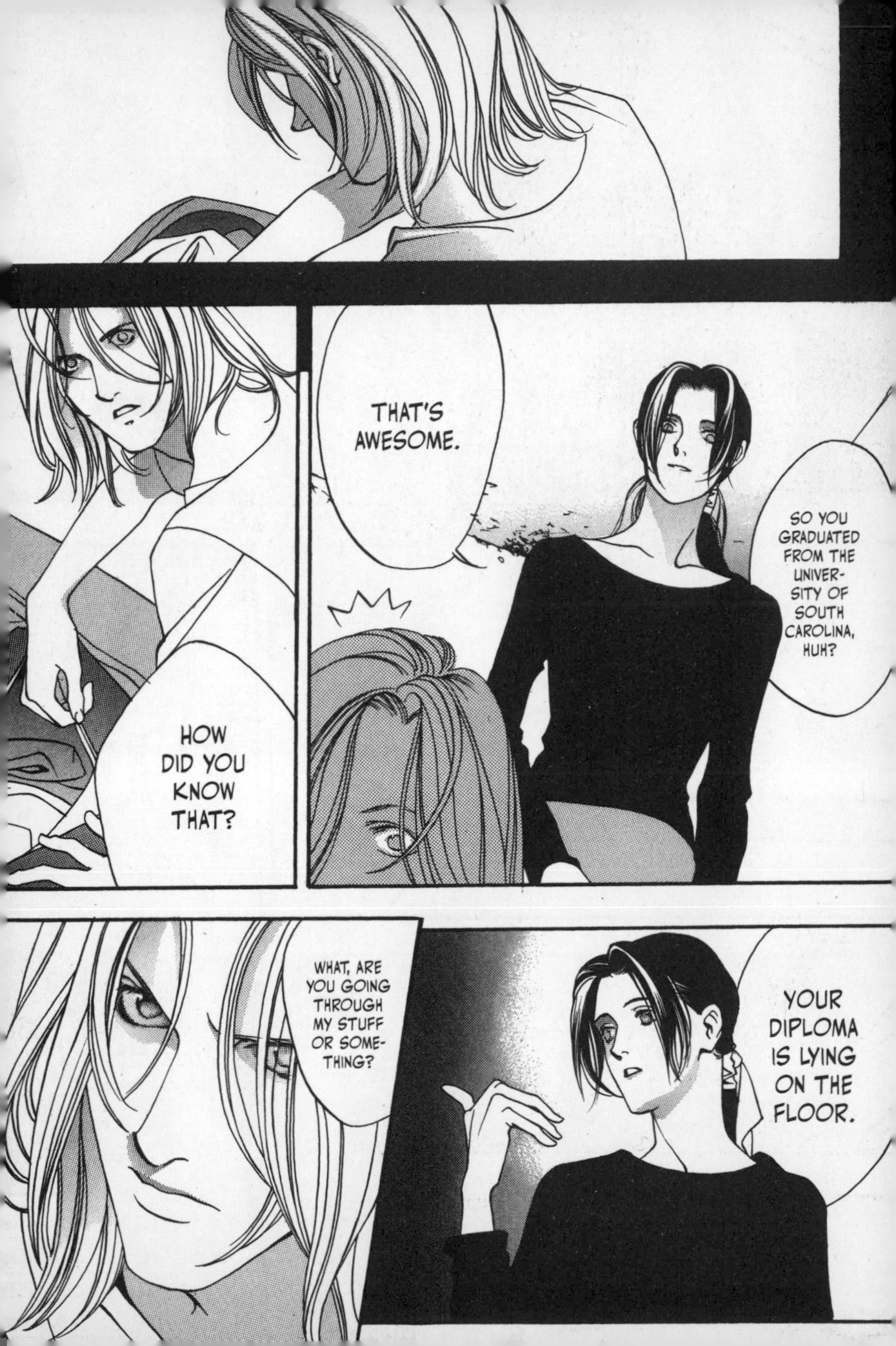
SO YOU GRADUATED FROM THE UNIVER-SITY OF SOUTH CAROLINA, HUH?
THAT'S AWESOME.
HOW DID YOU KNOW THAT?
YOUR DIPLOMA IS LYING ON THE FLOOR.
WHAT, ARE YOU GOING THROUGH MY STUFF OR SOME-THING?

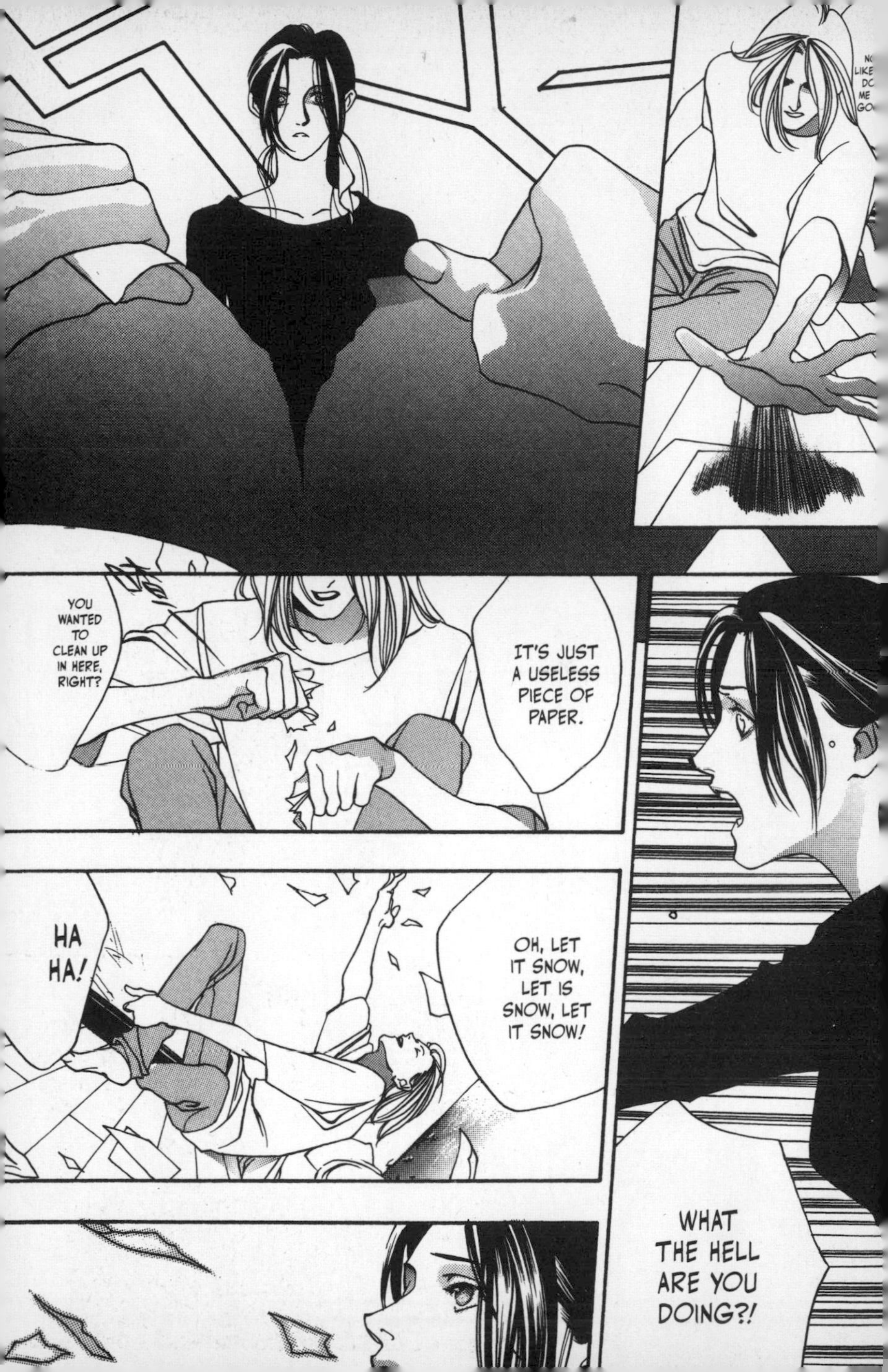
WHAT THE HELL ARE YOU DOING?!
IT'S JUST A USELESS PIECE OF PAPER.
YOU WANTED TO CLEAN UP IN HERE, RIGHT?
OH, LET IT SNOW, LET IS SNOW, LET IT SNOW!
HA HA!

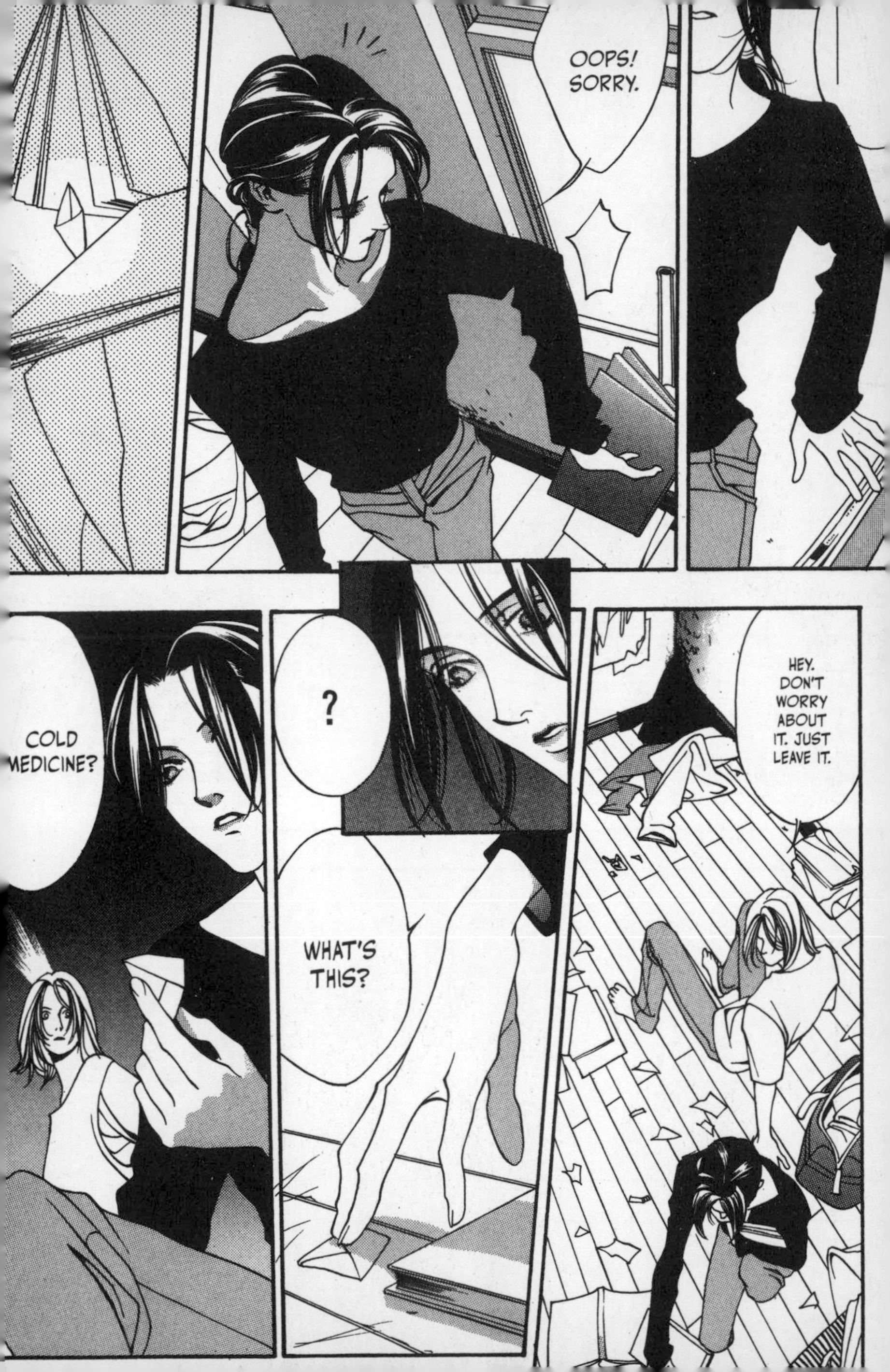
OOPS! SORRY.
HEY. DON'T WORRY ABOUT IT. JUST LEAVE IT.
?
WHAT'S THIS?
COLD MEDICINE?

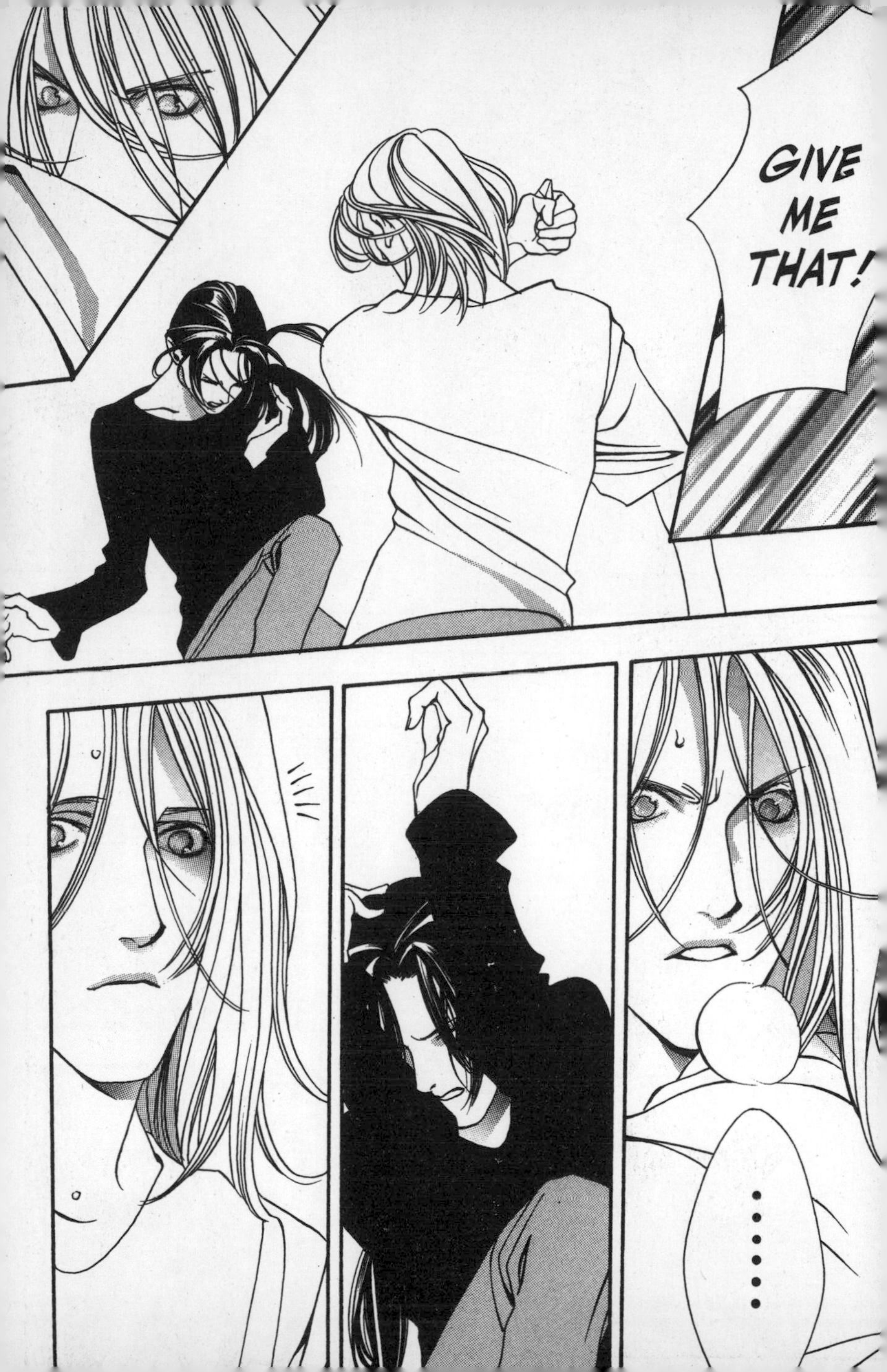
GIVE ME THAT!
......

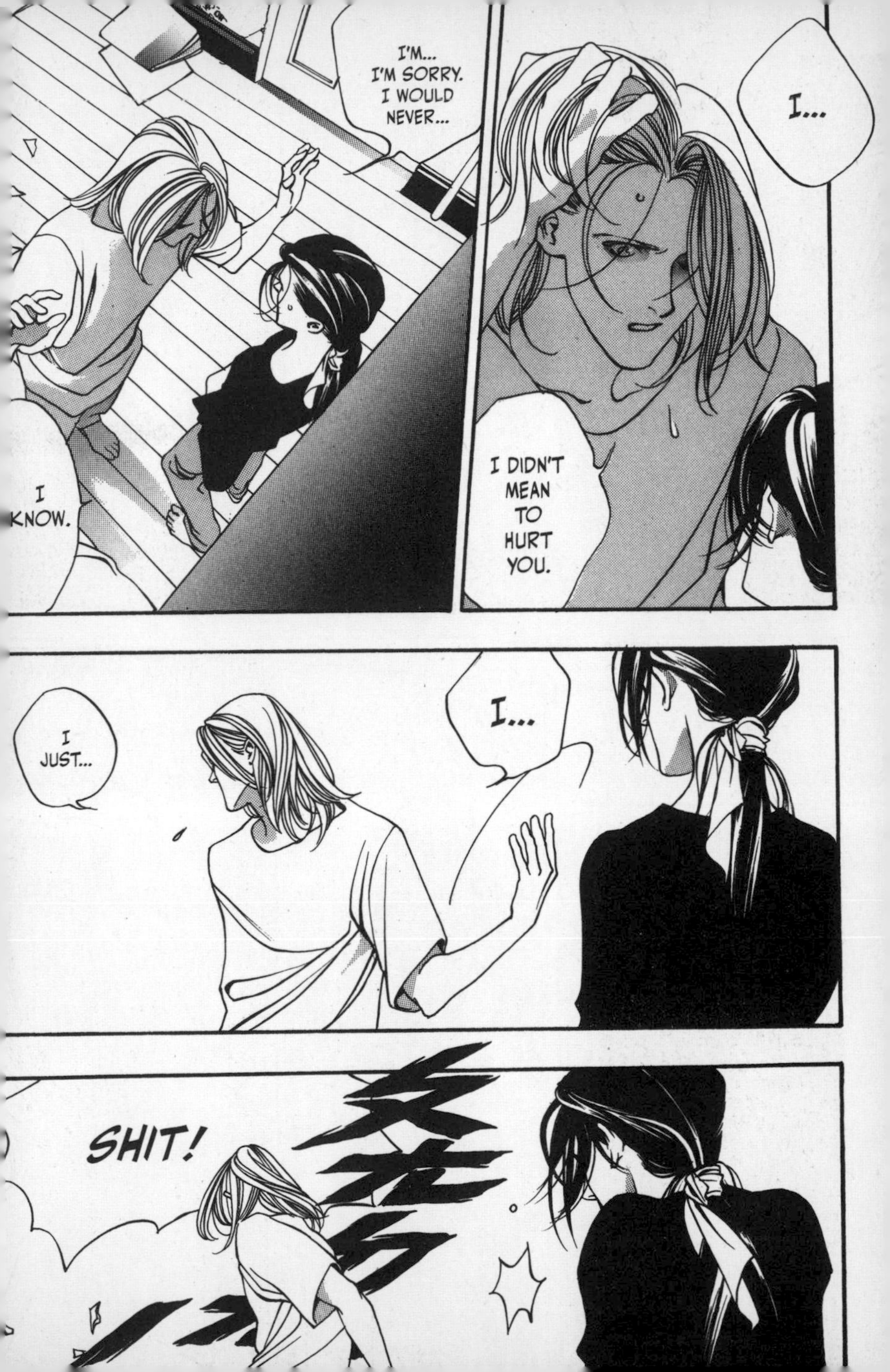
I...
I DIDN'T MEAN TO HURT YOU.
I'M... I'M SORRY. I WOULD NEVER...
I KNOW.
I...
I JUST...
SHIT!

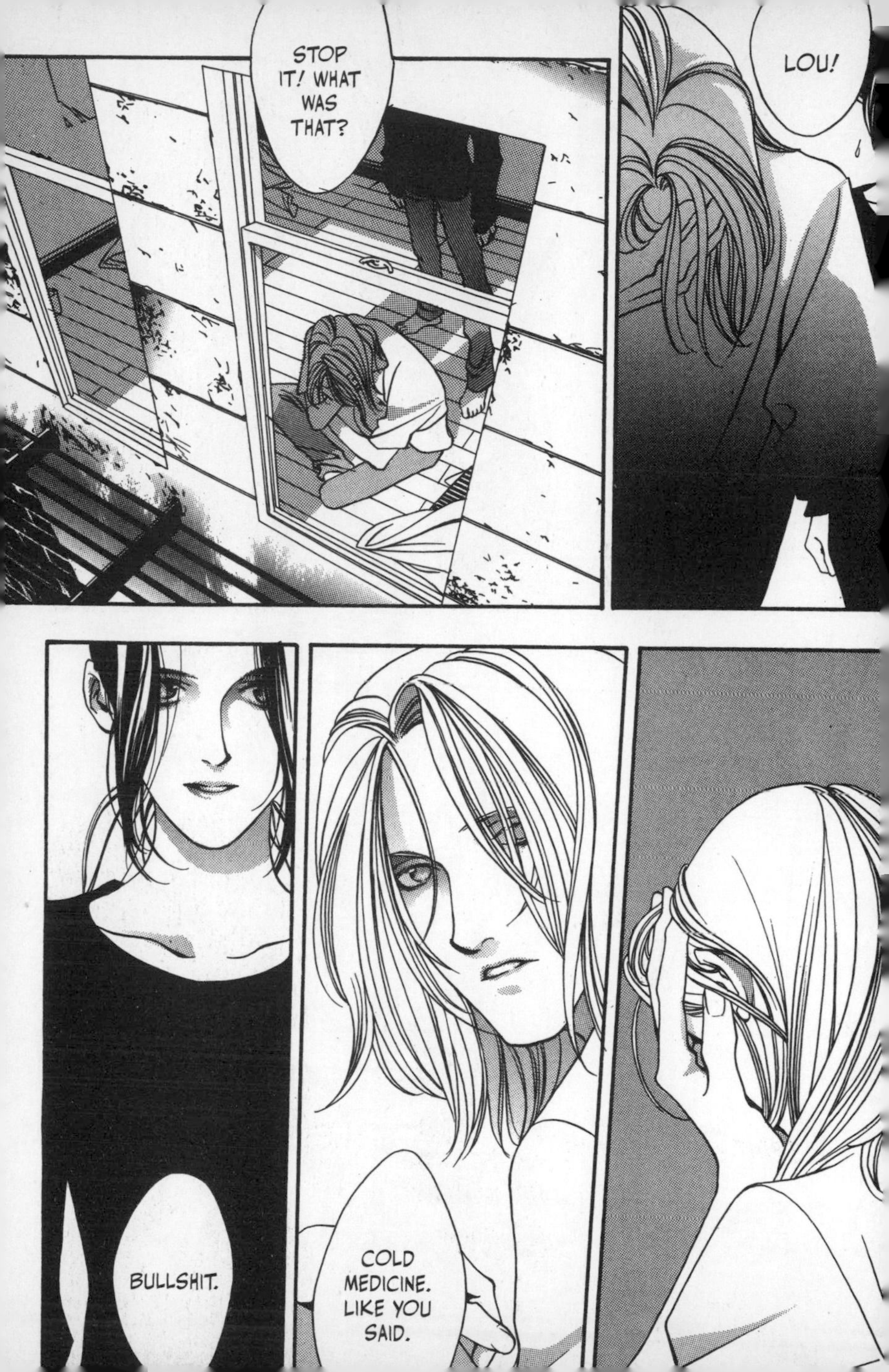
LOU!
STOP IT! WHAT WAS THAT?
COLD MEDICINE. LIKE YOU SAID.
BULLSHIT.

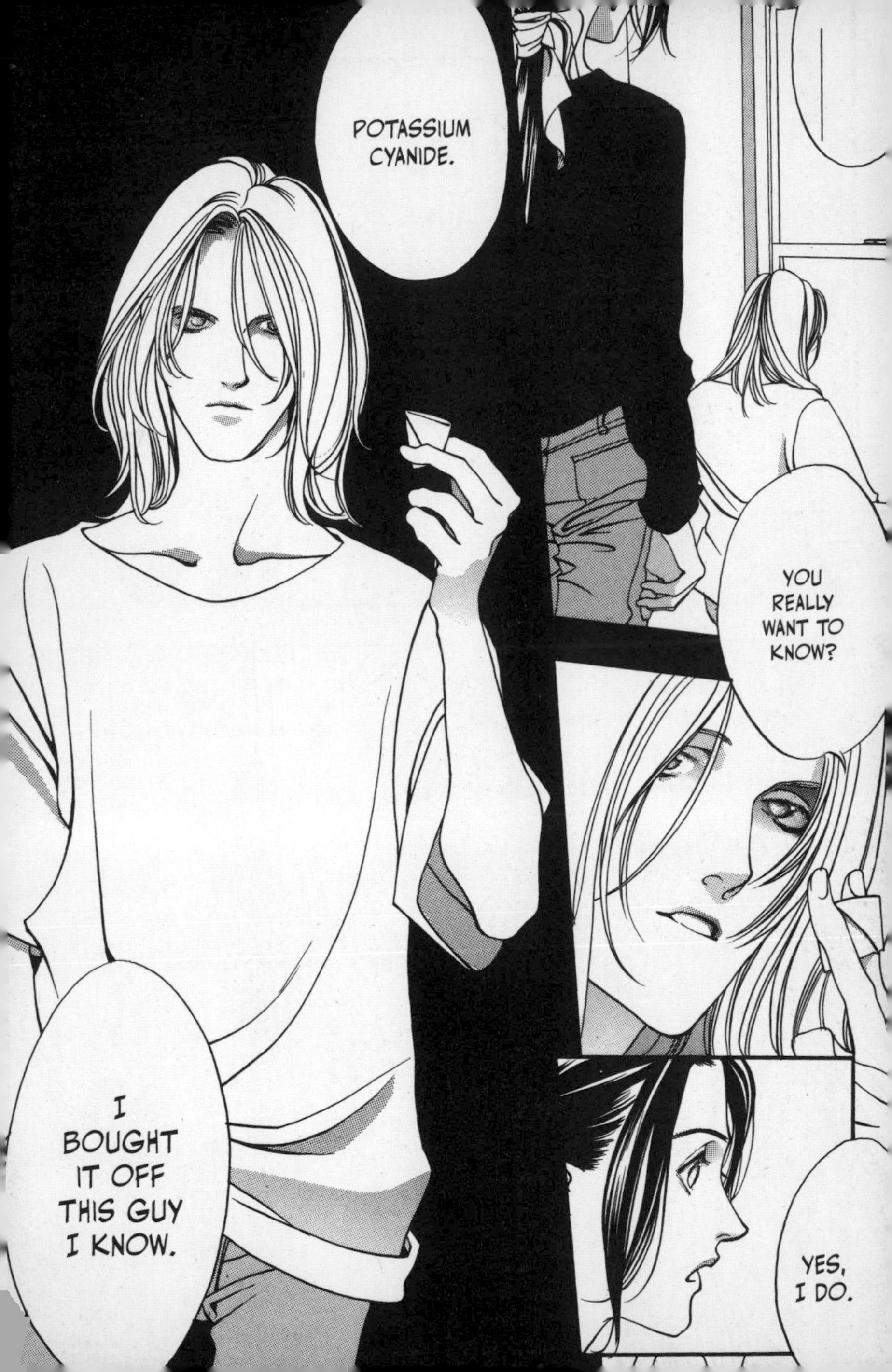
YOU REALLY WANT TO KNOW?
YES, I DO.
POTASSIUM CYANIDE.
I BOUGHT IT OFF THIS GUY I KNOW.

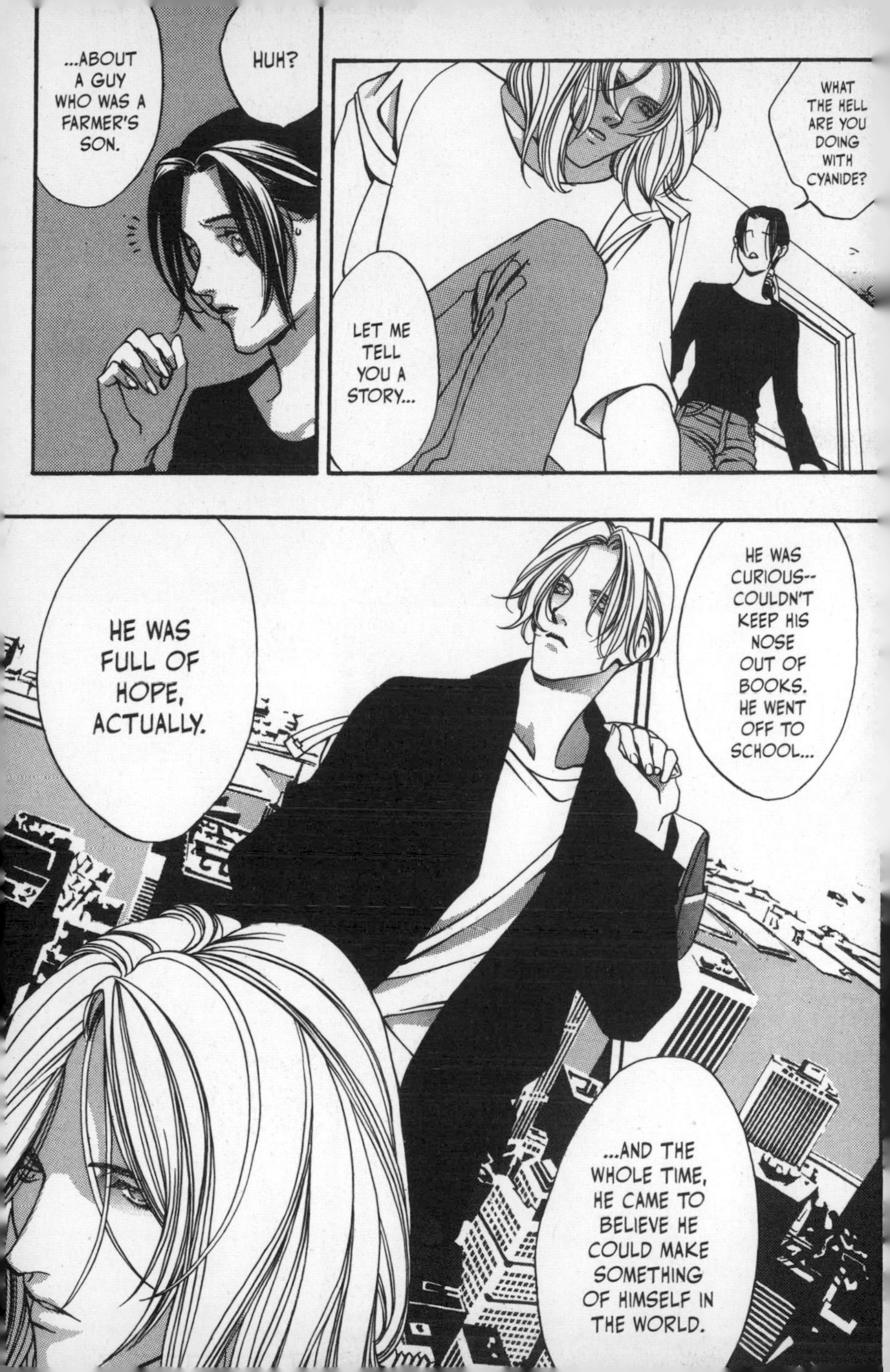

WHAT THE HELL ARE YOU DOING WITH CYANIDE?
LET ME TELL YOU A STORY...
HUH?
...ABOUT A GUY WHO WAS A FARMER'S SON.
HE WAS CURIOUS--COULDN'T KEEP HIS NOSE OUT OF BOOKS. HE WENT OFF TO SCHOOL...
HE WAS FULL OF HOPE, ACTUALLY.
...AND THE WHOLE TIME, HE CAME TO BELIEVE HE COULD MAKE SOMETHING OF HIMSELF IN THE WORLD.

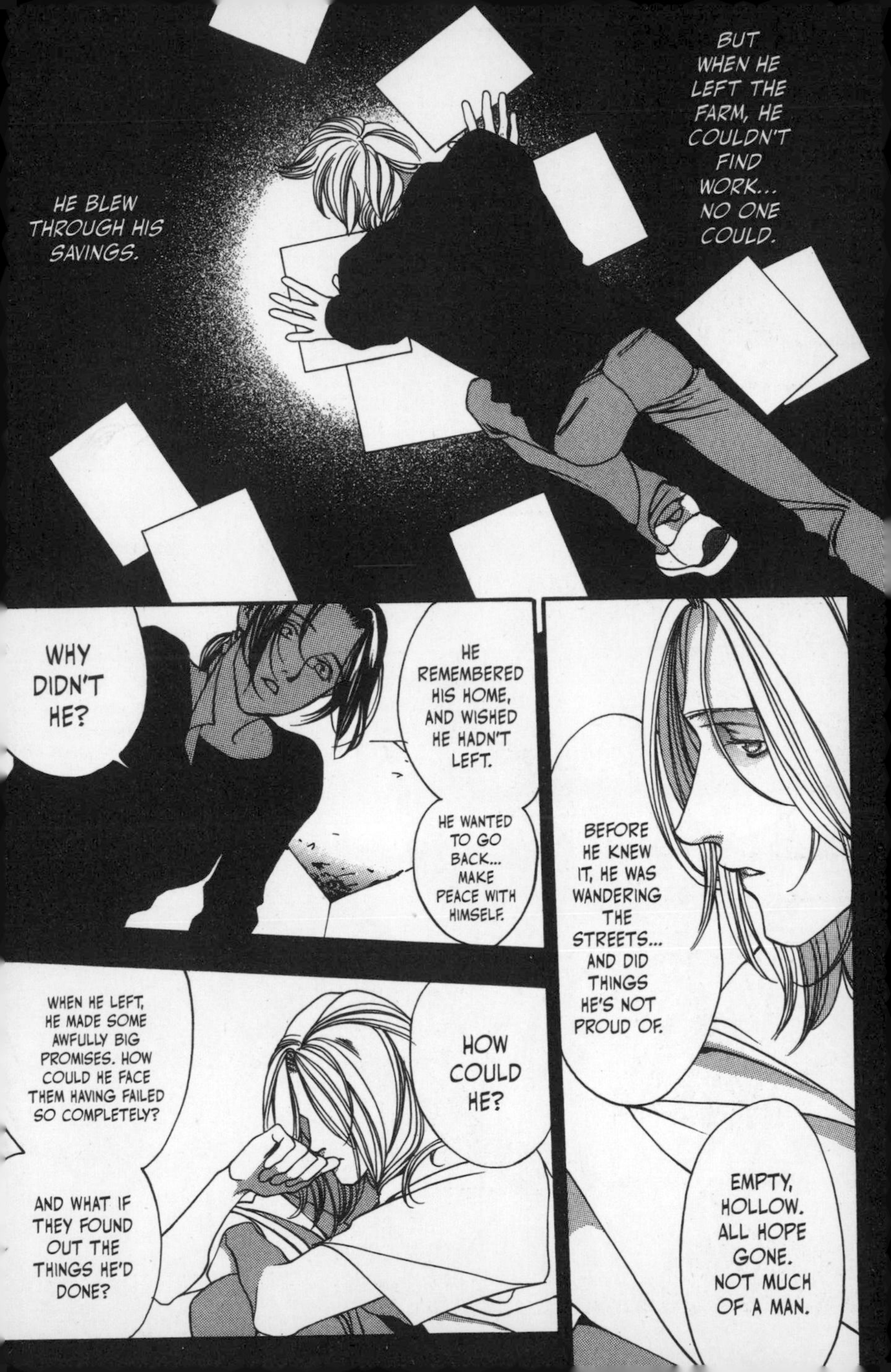
BUT WHEN HE LEFT THE FARM, HE COULDN'T FIND WORK... NO ONE COULD.
HE BLEW THROUGH HIS SAVINGS.
BEFORE HE KNEW IT, HE WAS WANDERING THE STREETS... AND DID THINGS HE'S NOT PROUD OF.
EMPTY, HOLLOW. ALL HOPE GONE. NOT MUCH OF A MAN.
HE REMEMBERED HIS HOME, AND WISHED HE HADN'T LEFT.
HE WANTED TO GO BACK... MAKE PEACE WITH HIMSELF.
WHY DIDN'T HE?
HOW COULD HE?
WHEN HE LEFT, HE MADE SOME AWFULLY BIG PROMISES. HOW COULD HE FACE THEM HAVING FAILED SO COMPLETELY?
AND WHAT IF THEY FOUND OUT THE THINGS HE'D DONE?

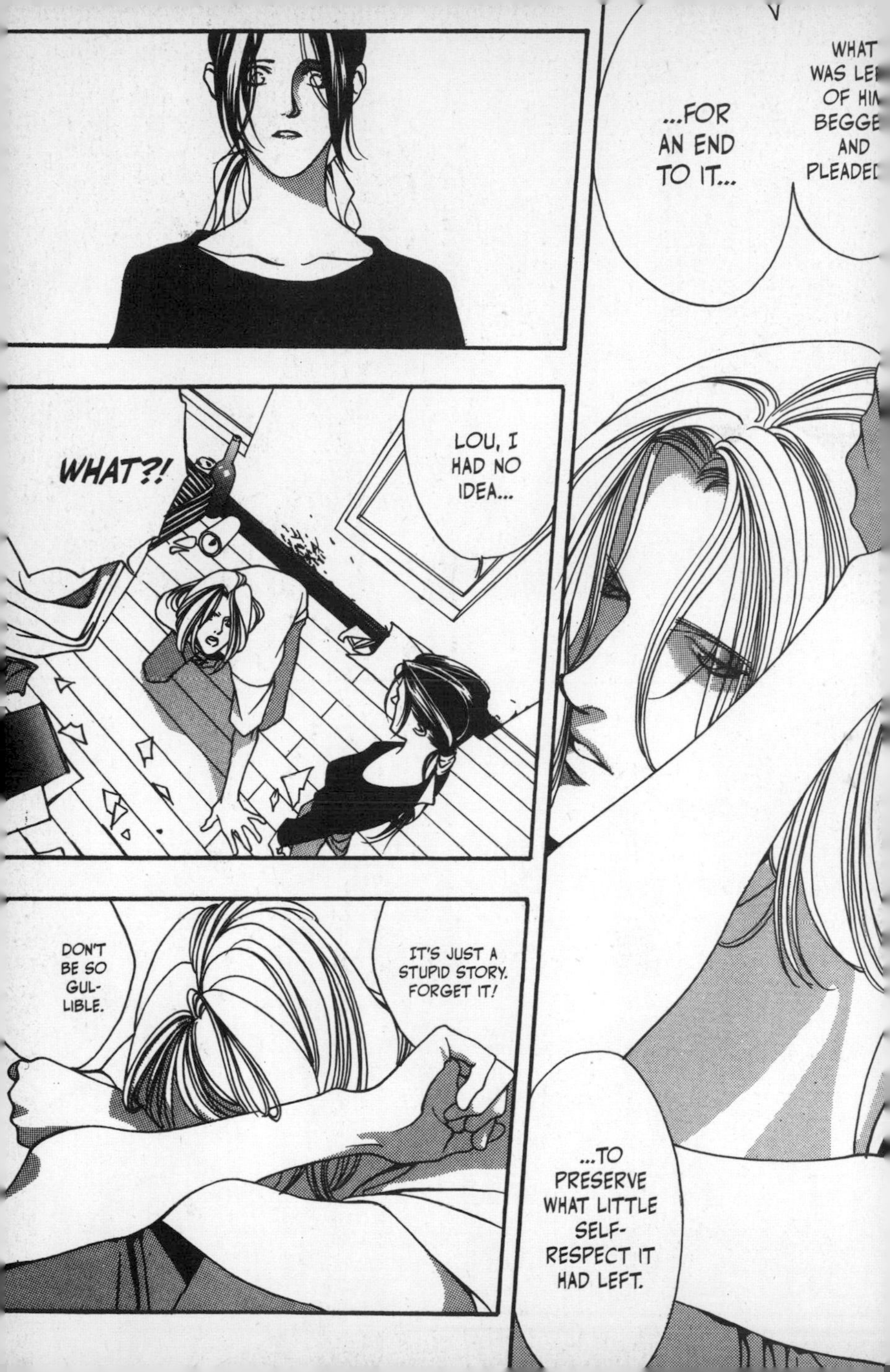
WHAT WAS LE OF HIM BEGGE AND PLEADED
...FOR AN END TO IT...
...TO PRESERVE WHAT LITTLE SELF-RESPECT IT HAD LEFT.
LOU, I HAD NO IDEA...
WHAT?!
IT'S JUST A STUPID STORY. FORGET IT!
DON'T BE SO GUL-LIBLE.

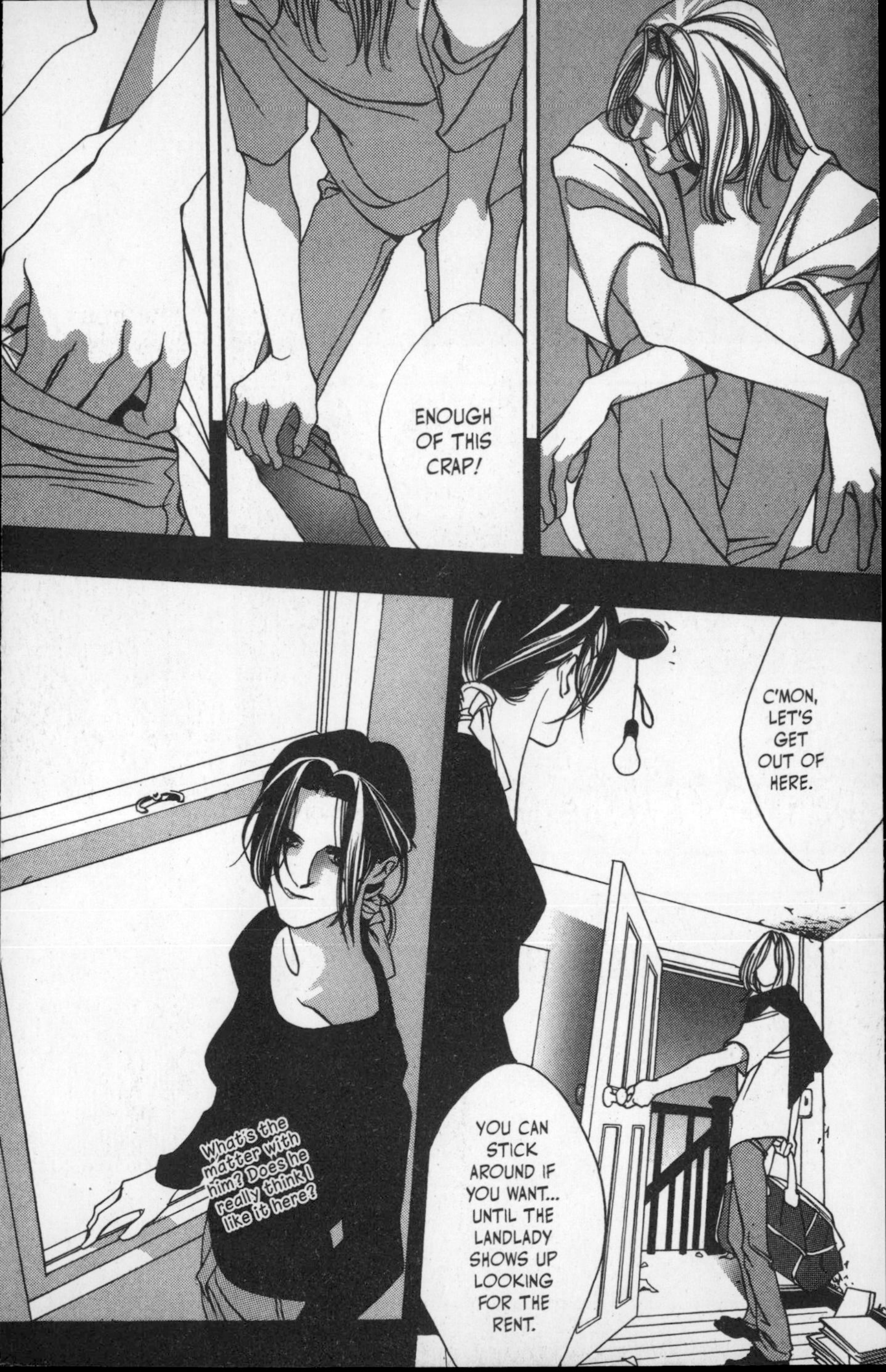
ENOUGH OF THIS CRAP!
C'MON, LET'S GET OUT OF HERE.
YOU CAN STICK AROUND IF YOU WANT... UNTIL THE LANDLADY SHOWS UP LOOKING FOR THE RENT.
What's the matter with him? Does he really think I like it here?

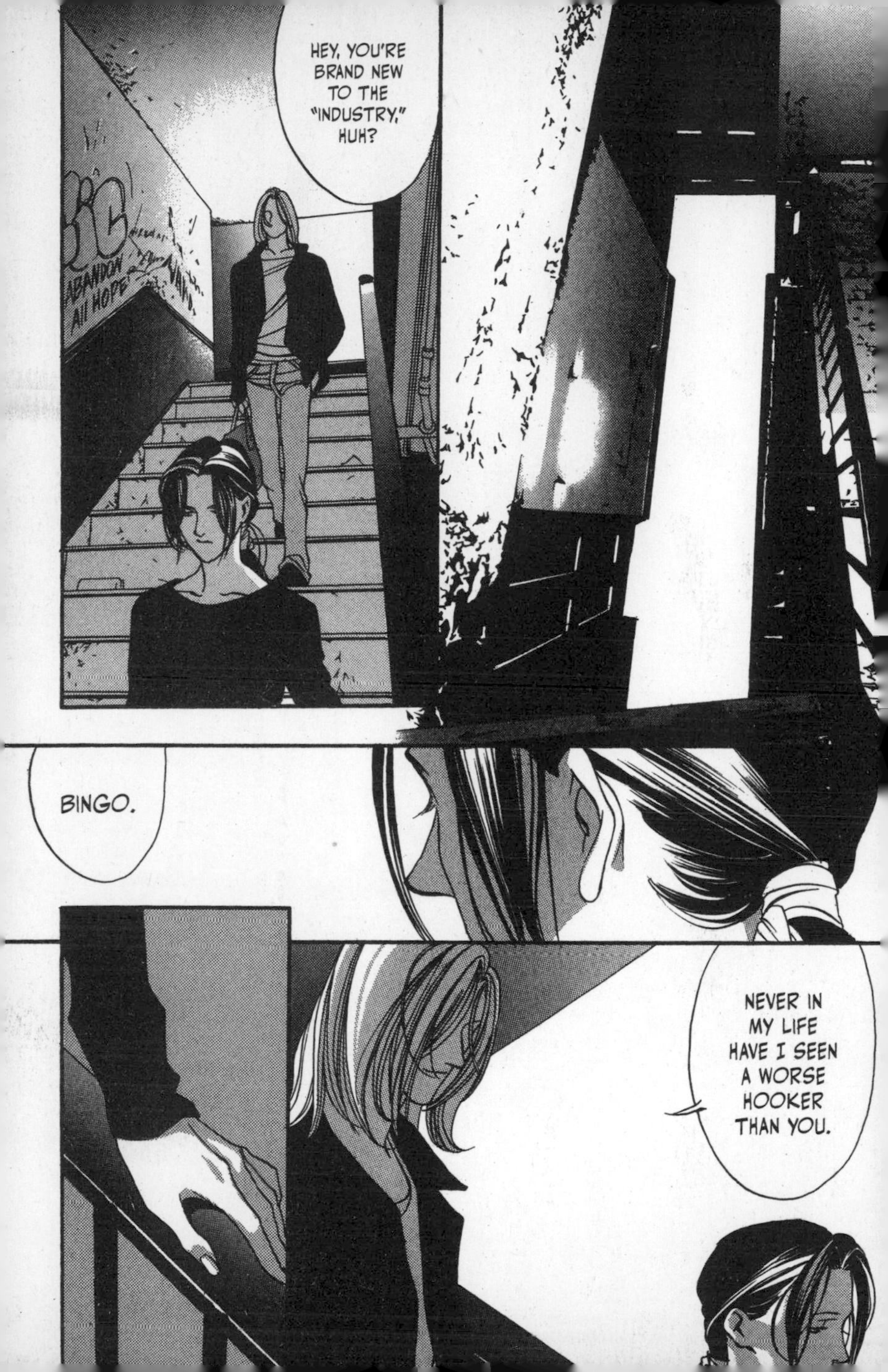
HEY, YOU'RE BRAND NEW TO THE "INDUSTRY," HUH?
ABANDON All HOPE
BINGO.
NEVER IN MY LIFE HAVE I SEEN A WORSE HOOKER THAN YOU.

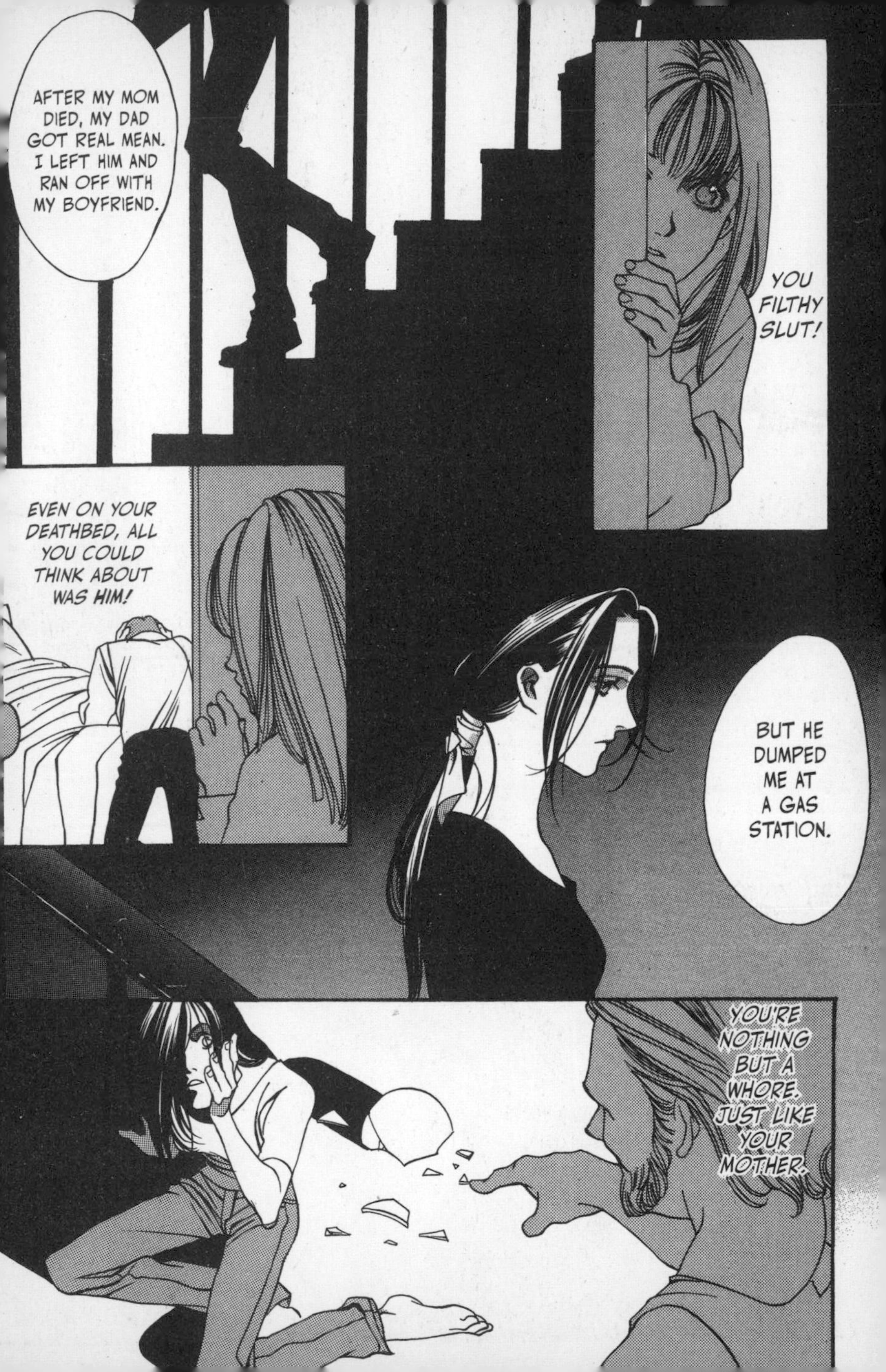
YOU FILTHY SLUT!
AFTER MY MOM DIED, MY DAD GOT REAL MEAN. I LEFT HIM AND RAN OFF WITH MY BOYFRIEND.
BUT HE DUMPED ME AT A GAS STATION.
EVEN ON YOUR DEATHBED, ALL YOU COULD THINK ABOUT WAS HIM!
YOU'RE NOTHING BUT A WHORE. JUST LIKE YOUR MOTHER.

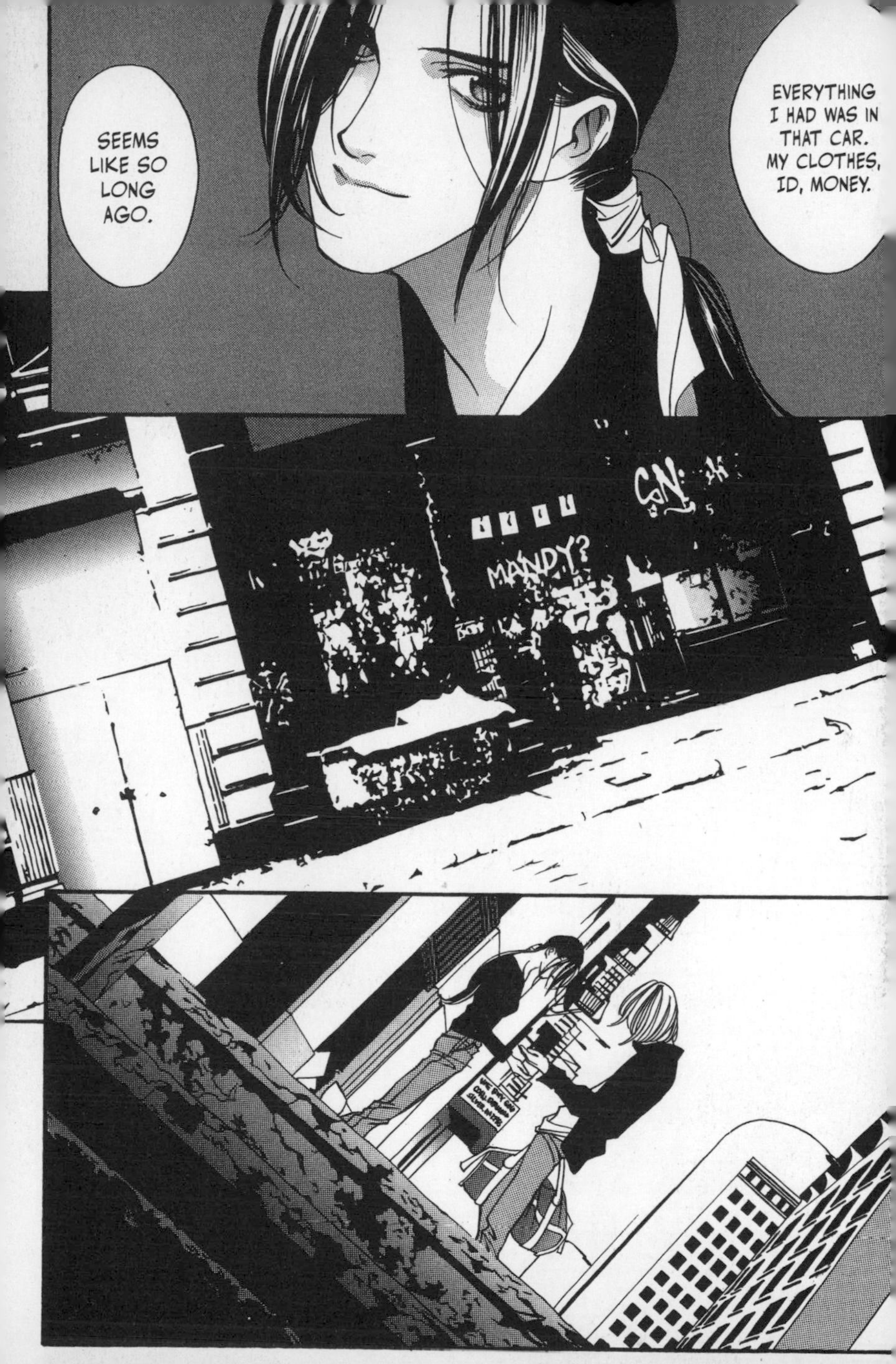
EVERYTHING I HAD WAS IN THAT CAR. MY CLOTHES, ID, MONEY.
SEEMS LIKE SO LONG AGO.
MANDY?

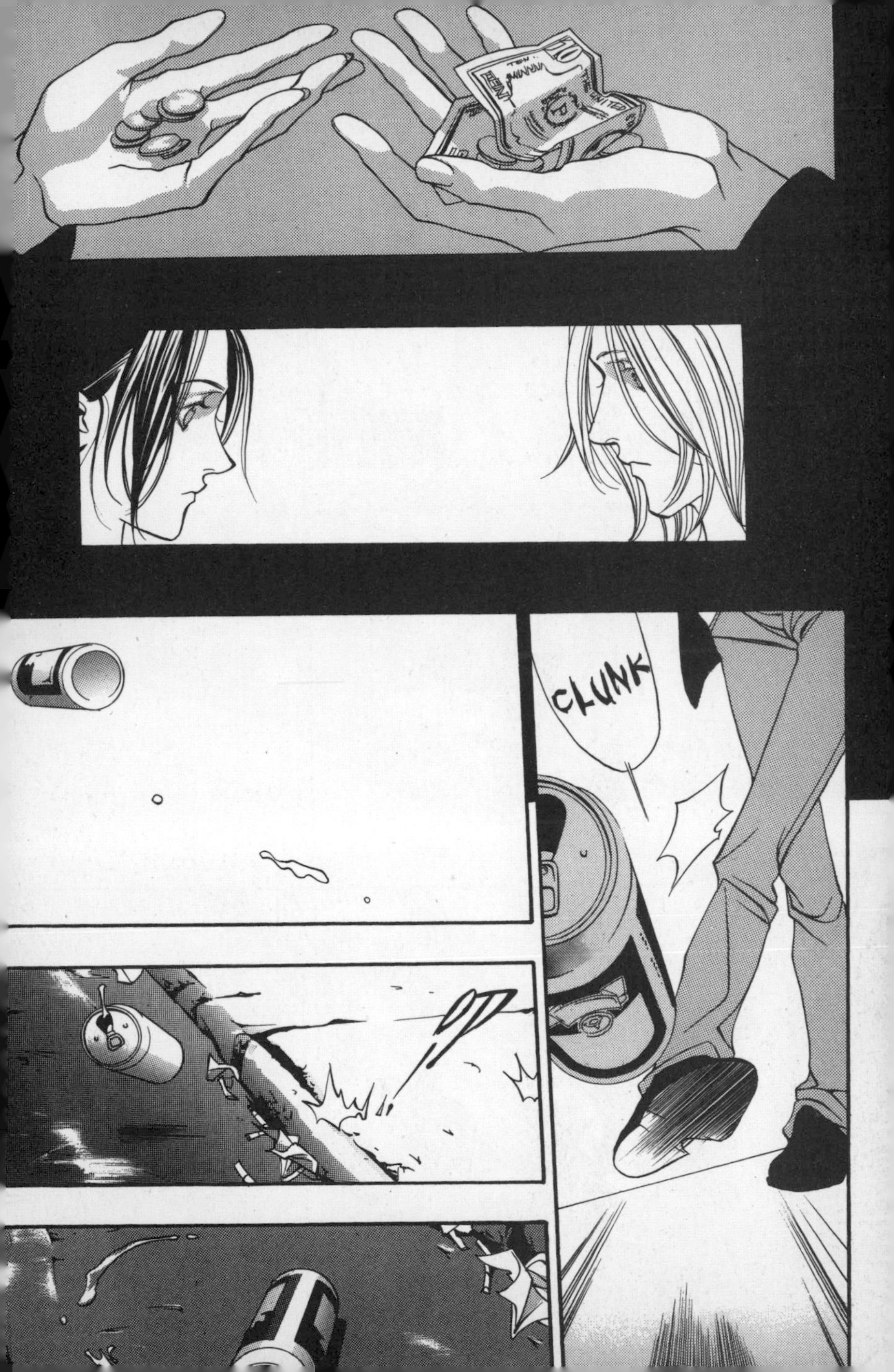
CLUNK

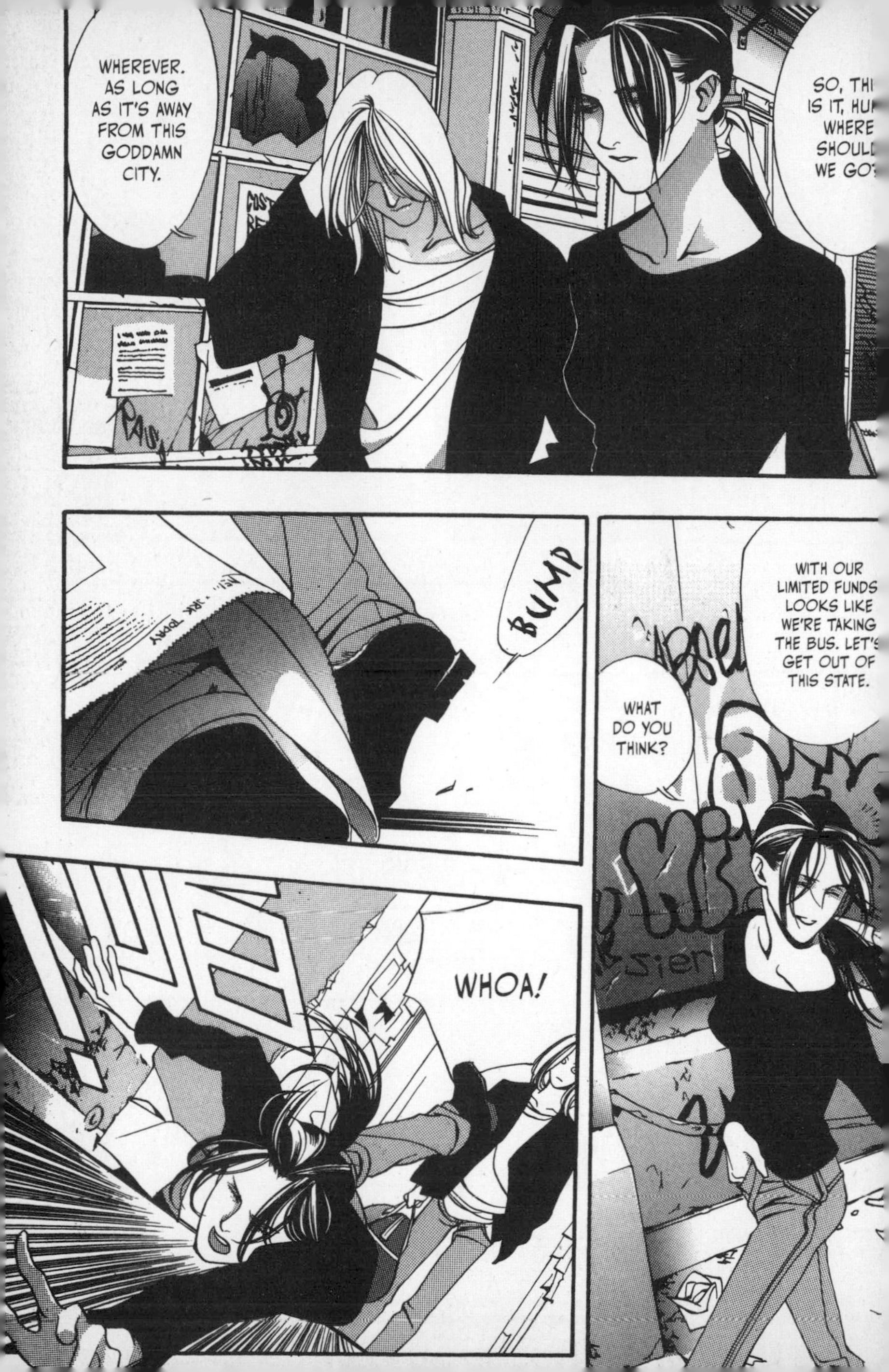
SO, THI IS IT, HU WHERE SHOULD WE GO
WHEREVER. AS LONG AS IT'S AWAY FROM THIS GODDAMN CITY.
WITH OUR LIMITED FUNDS LOOKS LIKE WE'RE TAKING THE BUS. LET'S GET OUT OF THIS STATE.
WHAT DO YOU THINK?
BUMP
WHOA!

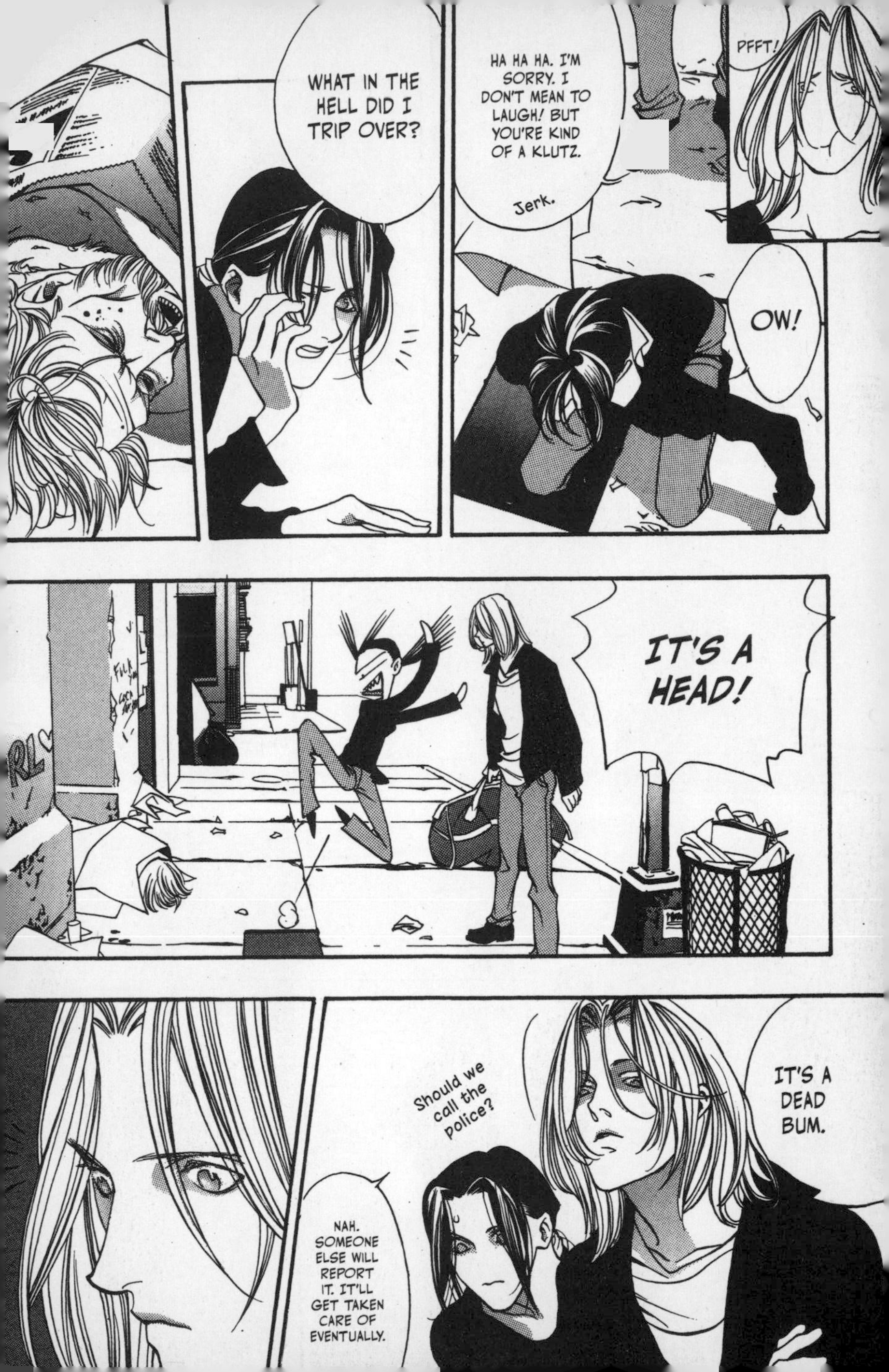

OW!
PFFT!
HA HA HA. I'M SORRY. I DON'T MEAN TO LAUGH! BUT YOU'RE KIND OF A KLUTZ.
Jerk.
WHAT IN THE HELL DID I TRIP OVER?
IT'S A HEAD!
IT'S A DEAD BUM.
Should we call the police?
NAH. SOMEONE ELSE WILL REPORT IT. IT'LL GET TAKEN CARE OF EVENTUALLY.

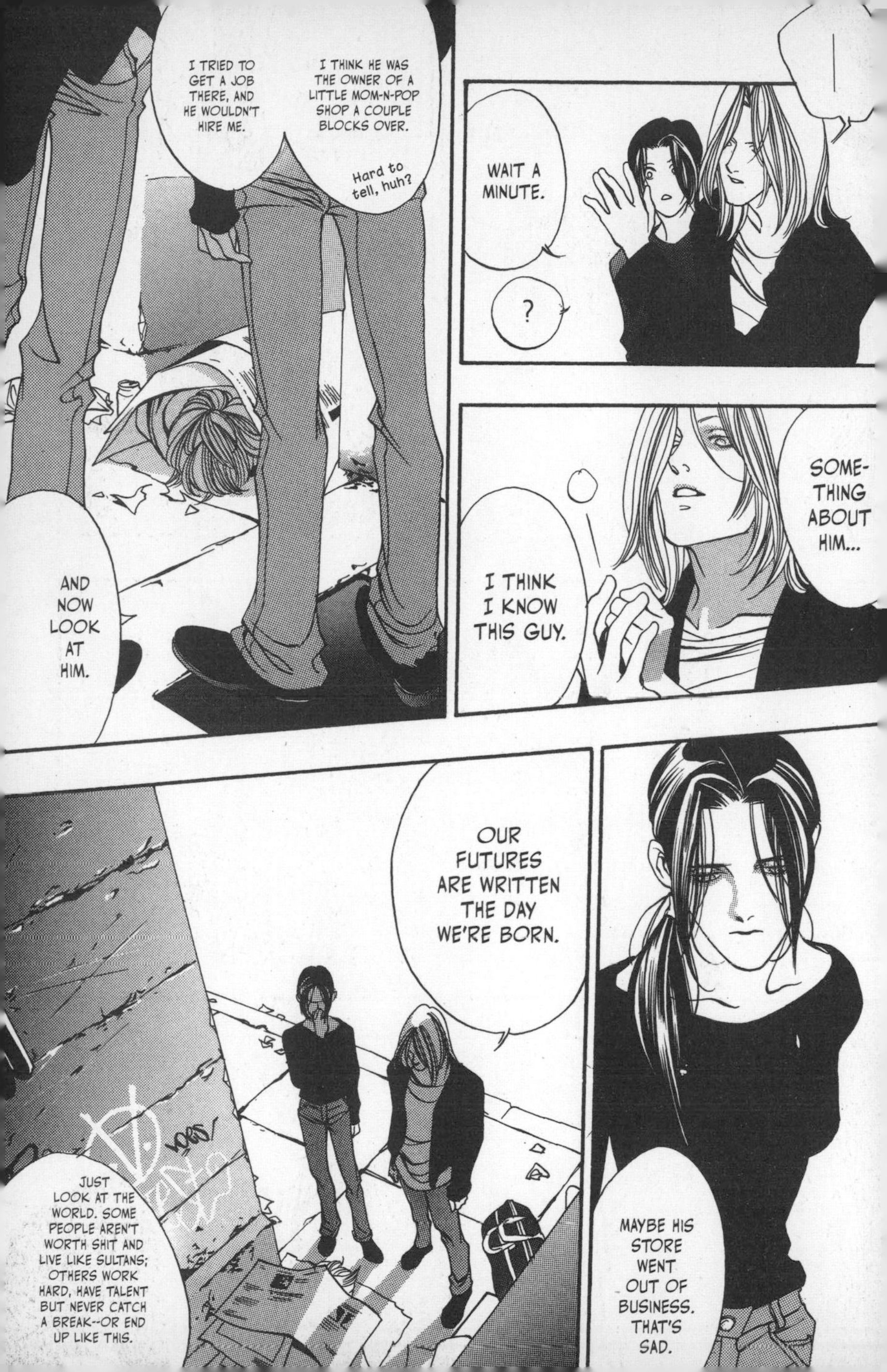
WAIT A MINUTE.
?
SOME-THING ABOUT HIM...
I THINK I KNOW THIS GUY.
I THINK HE WAS THE OWNER OF A LITTLE MOM-N-POP SHOP A COUPLE BLOCKS OVER.
I TRIED TO GET A JOB THERE, AND HE WOULDN'T HIRE ME.
Hard to tell, huh?
AND NOW LOOK AT HIM.
MAYBE HIS STORE WENT OUT OF BUSINESS. THAT'S SAD.
OUR FUTURES ARE WRITTEN THE DAY WE'RE BORN.
JUST LOOK AT THE WORLD. SOME PEOPLE AREN'T WORTH SHIT AND LIVE LIKE SULTANS; OTHERS WORK HARD, HAVE TALENT BUT NEVER CATCH A BREAK--OR END UP LIKE THIS.

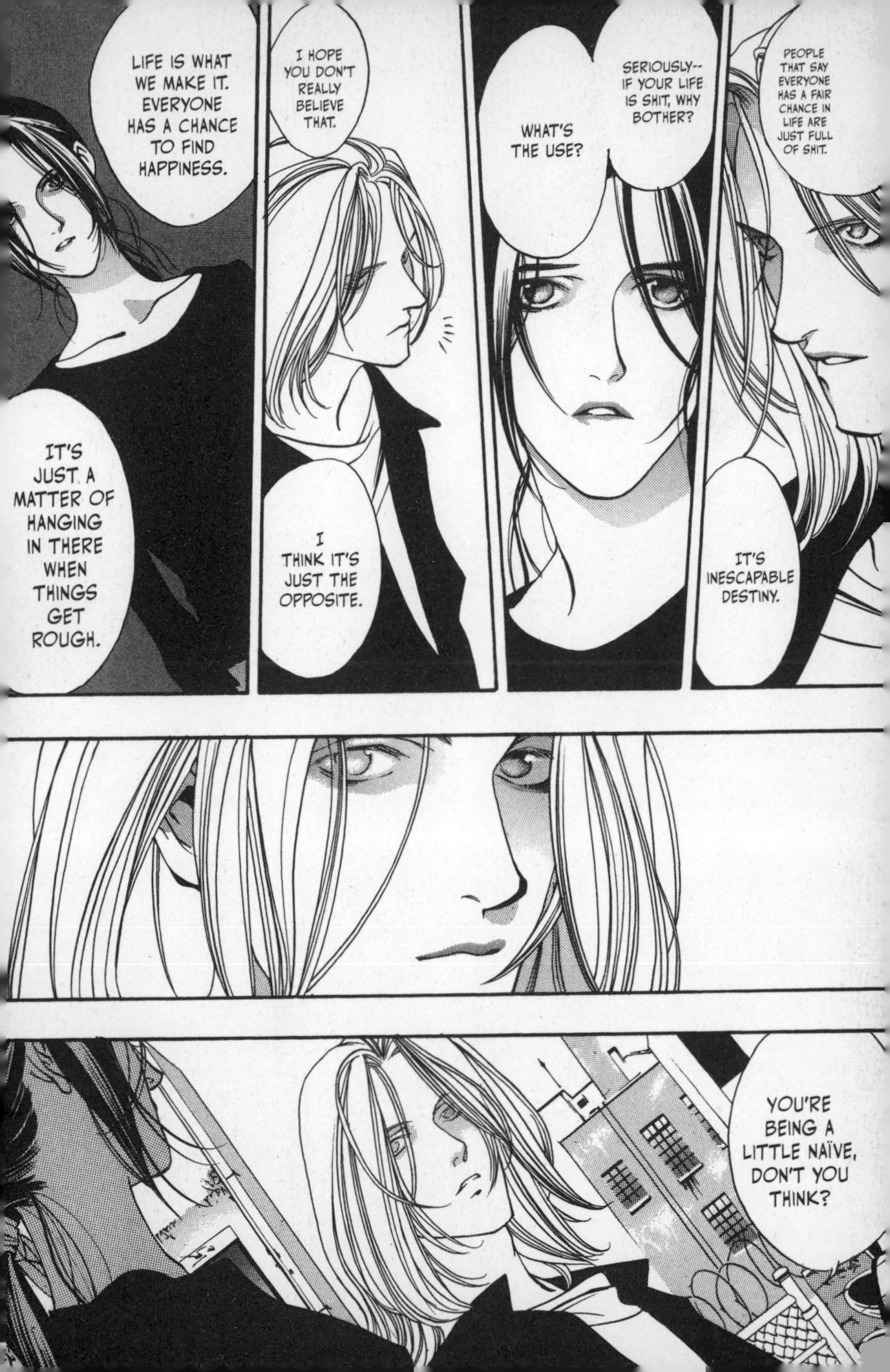
LIFE IS WHAT WE MAKE IT. EVERYONE HAS A CHANCE TO FIND HAPPINESS.
IT'S JUST A MATTER OF HANGING IN THERE WHEN THINGS GET ROUGH.
I HOPE YOU DON'T REALLY BELIEVE THAT.
I THINK IT'S JUST THE OPPOSITE.
SERIOUSLY-- IF YOUR LIFE IS SHIT, WHY BOTHER?
WHAT'S THE USE?
PEOPLE THAT SAY EVERYONE HAS A FAIR CHANCE IN LIFE ARE JUST FULL OF SHIT.
IT'S INESCAPABLE DESTINY.
YOU'RE BEING A LITTLE NAÏVE, DON'T YOU THINK?

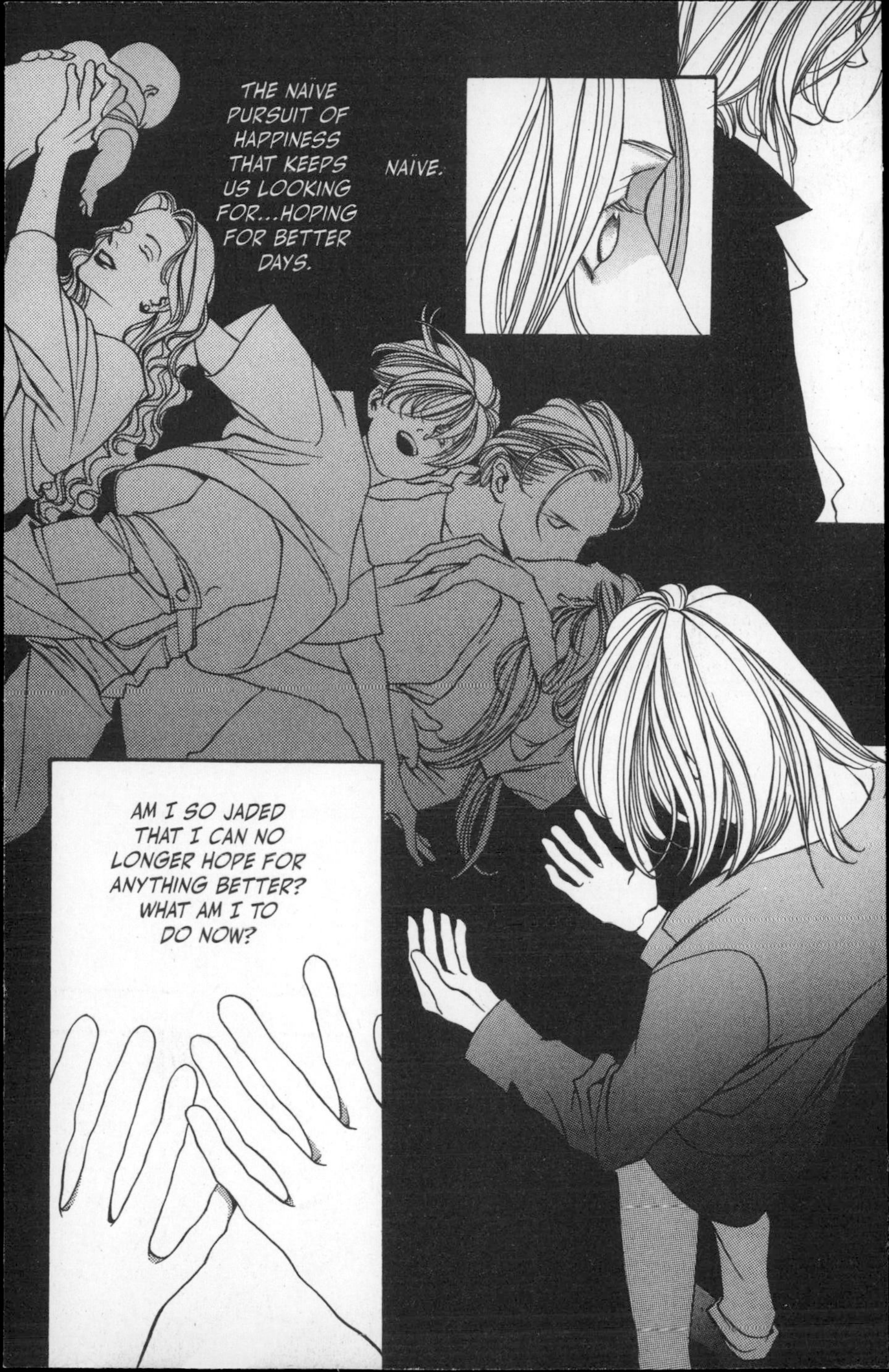
NAÏVE.
THE NAÏVE PURSUIT OF HAPPINESS THAT KEEPS US LOOKING FOR...HOPING FOR BETTER DAYS.
AM I SO JADED THAT I CAN NO LONGER HOPE FOR ANYTHING BETTER? WHAT AM I TO DO NOW?

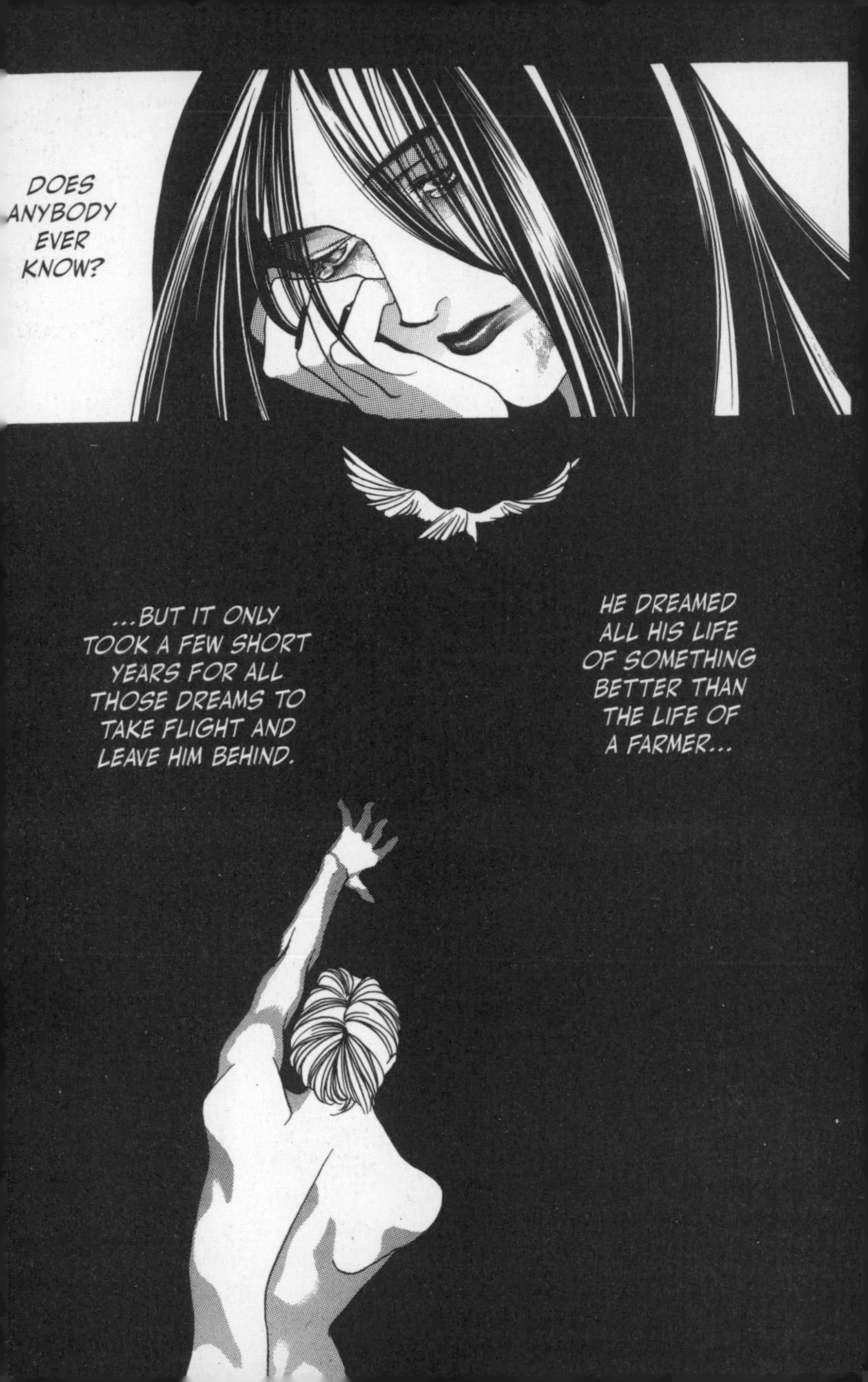
DOES ANYBODY EVER KNOW?
HE DREAMED ALL HIS LIFE OF SOMETHING BETTER THAN THE LIFE OF A FARMER...
...BUT IT ONLY TOOK A FEW SHORT YEARS FOR ALL THOSE DREAMS TO TAKE FLIGHT AND LEAVE HIM BEHIND.

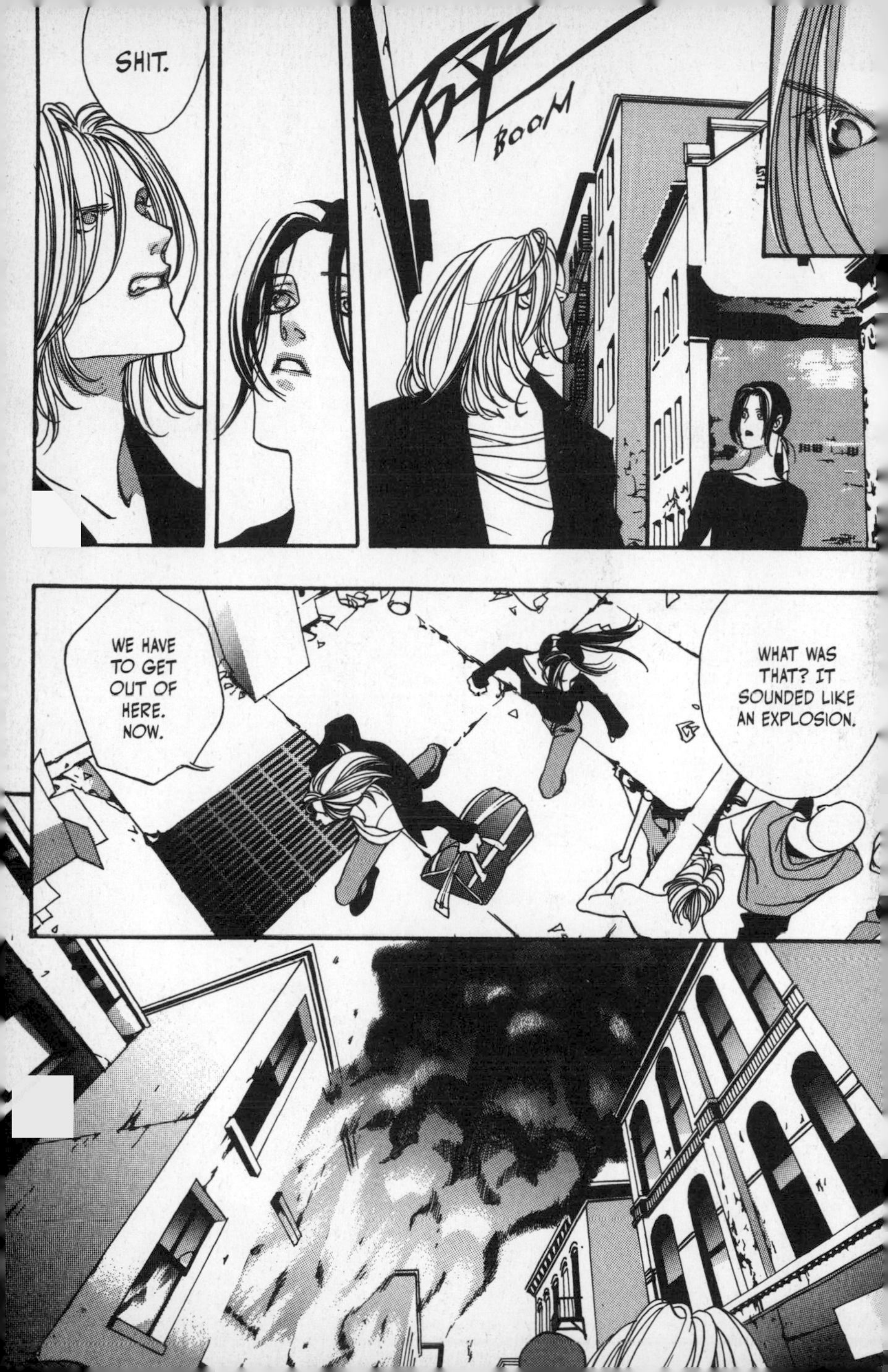
BOOM
SHIT.
WHAT WAS THAT? IT SOUNDED LIKE AN EXPLOSION.
WE HAVE TO GET OUT OF HERE. NOW.

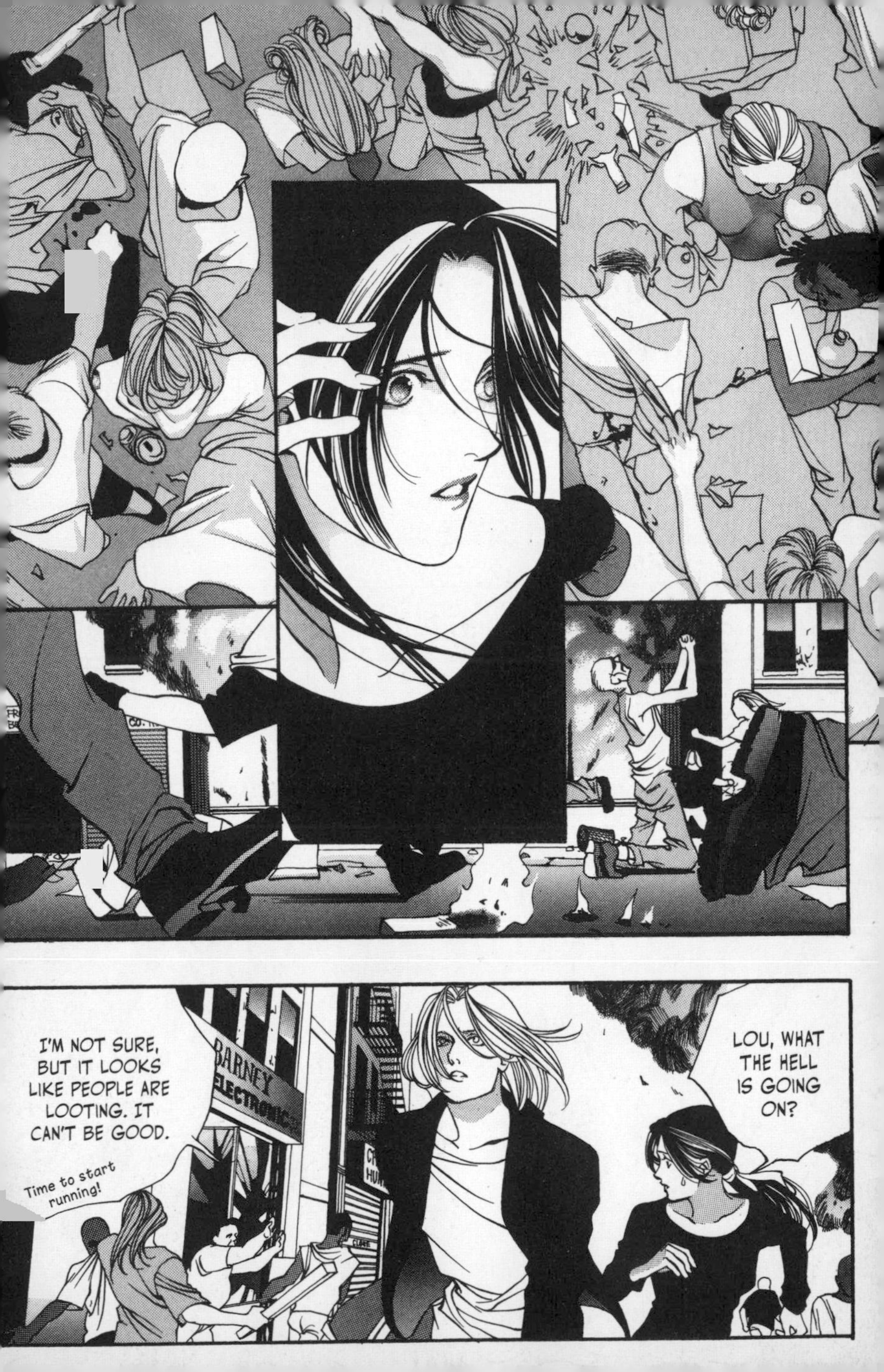
LOU, WHAT THE HELL IS GOING ON?
I'M NOT SURE, BUT IT LOOKS LIKE PEOPLE ARE LOOTING. IT CAN'T BE GOOD.
Time to start running!
BARNEY

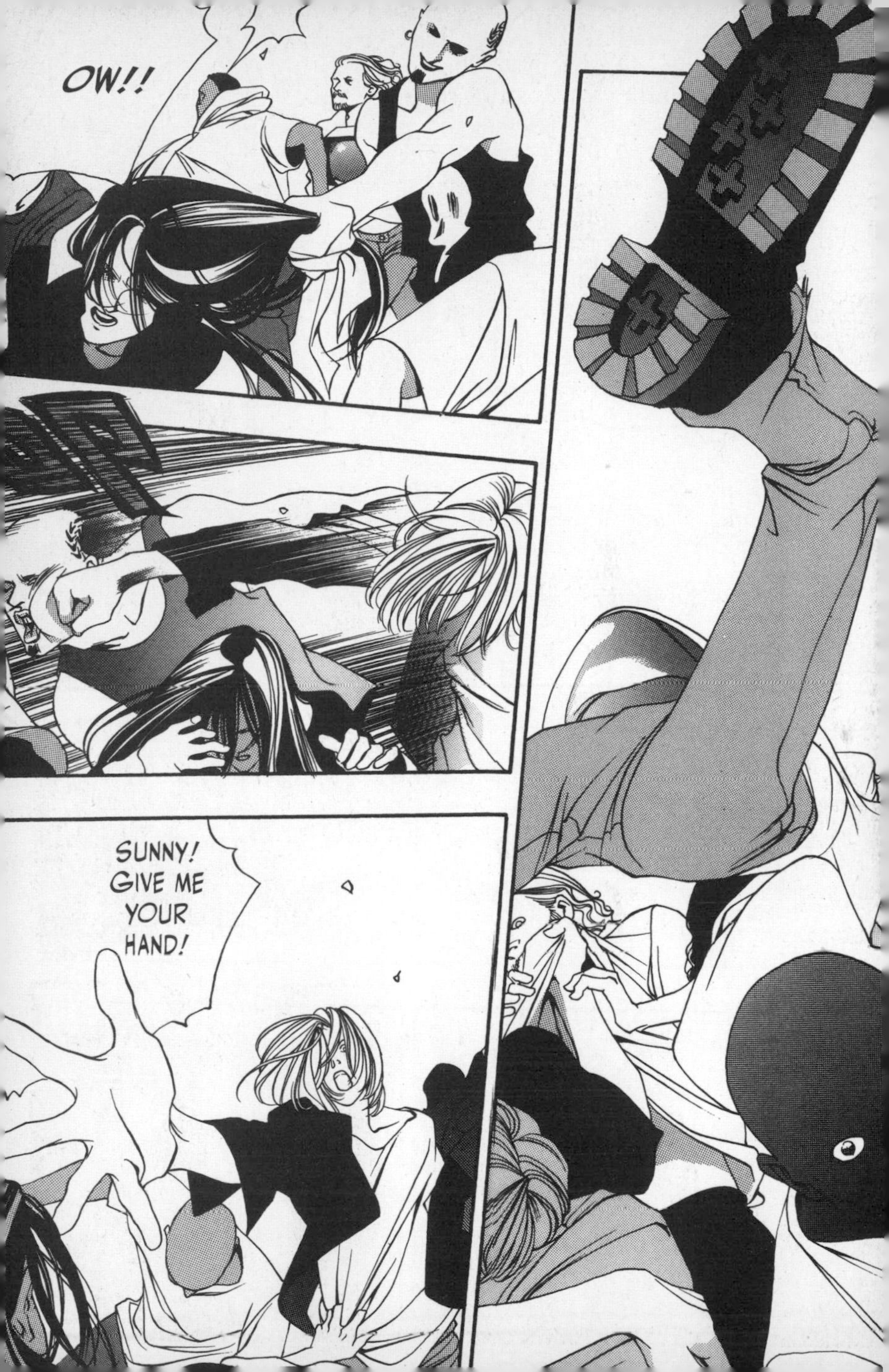
OW!!
SUNNY! GIVE ME YOUR HAND!

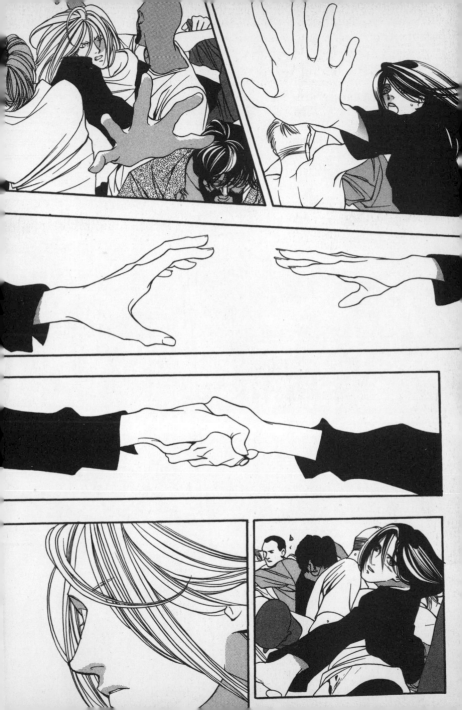

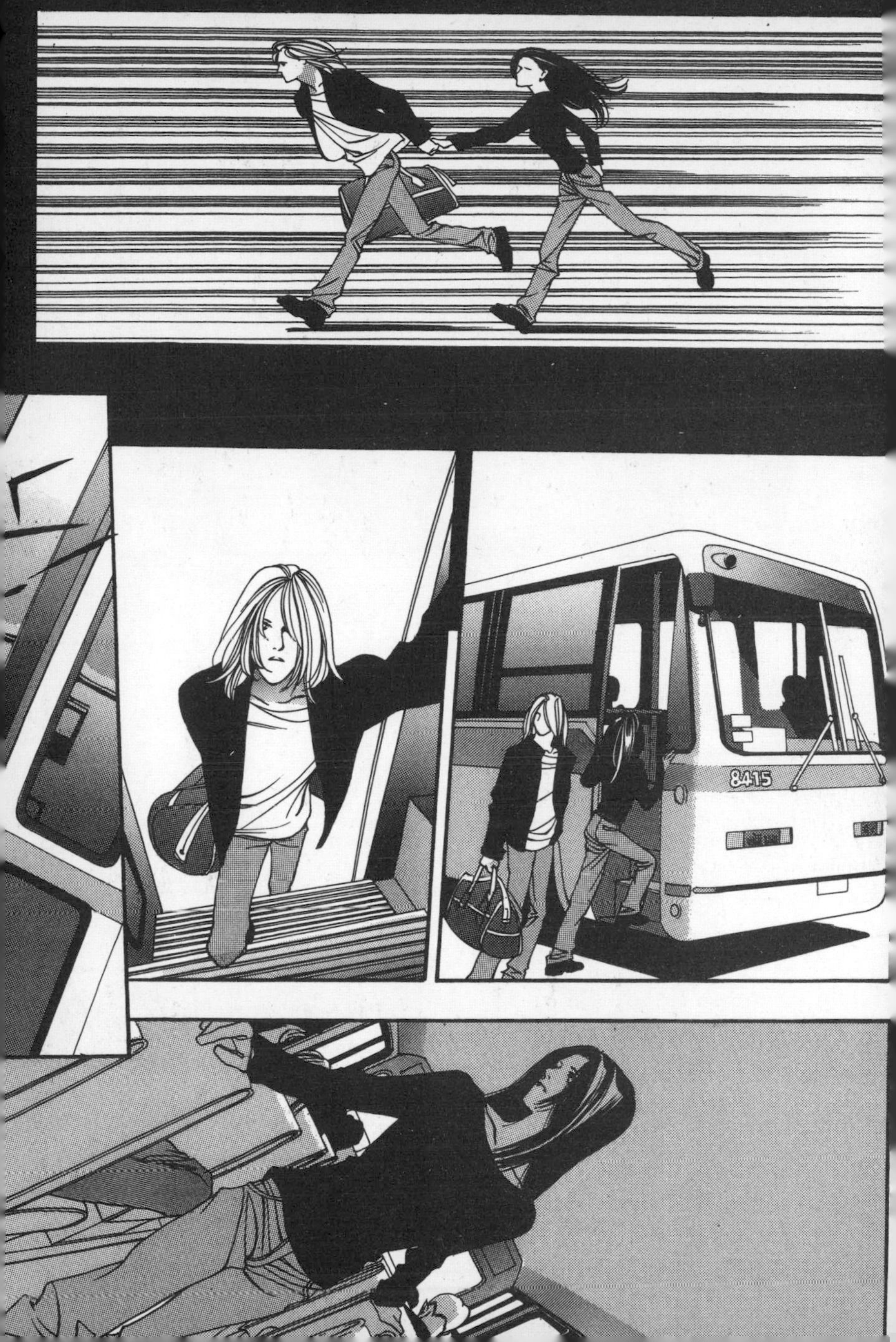
8415

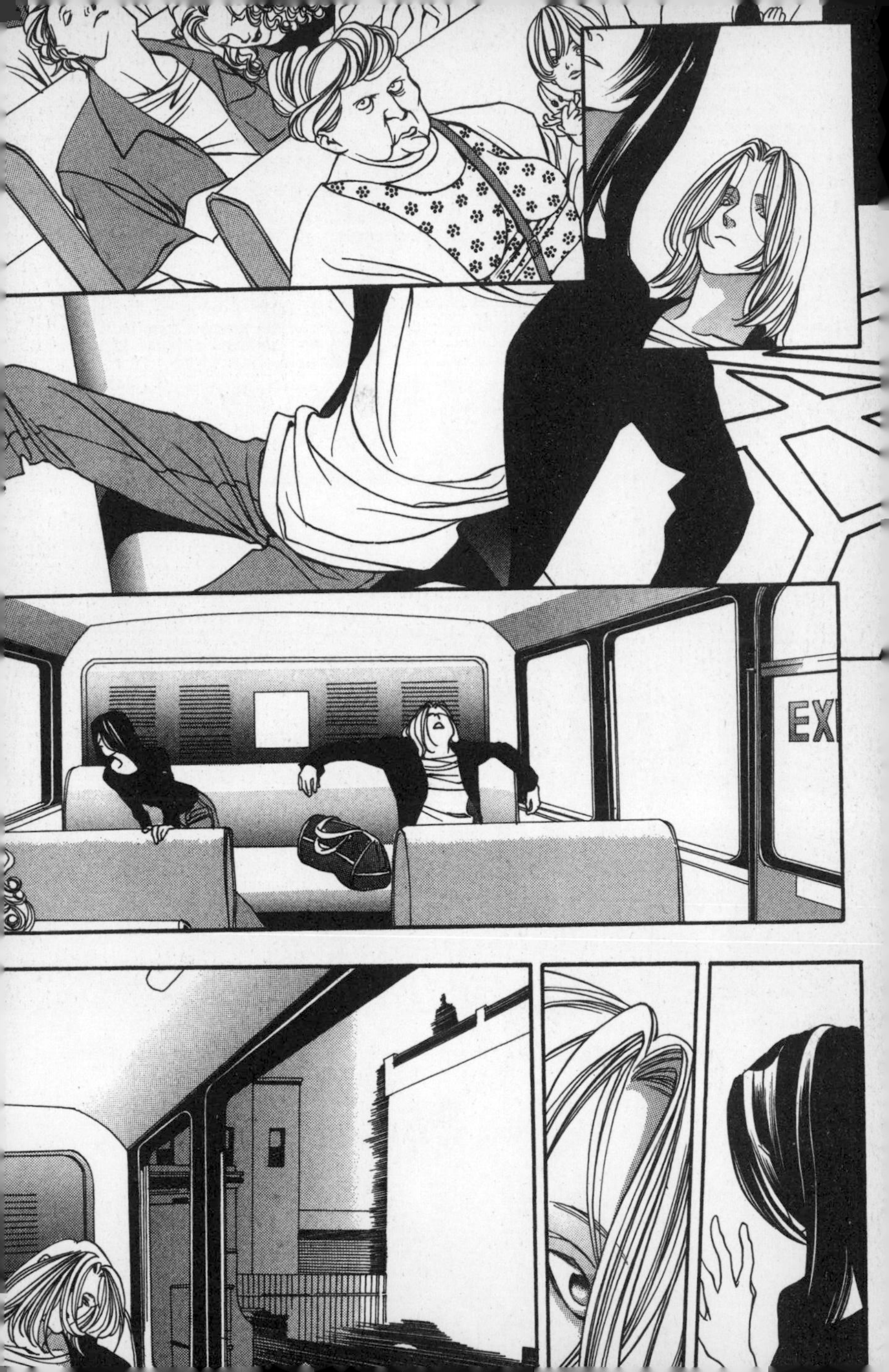
EX

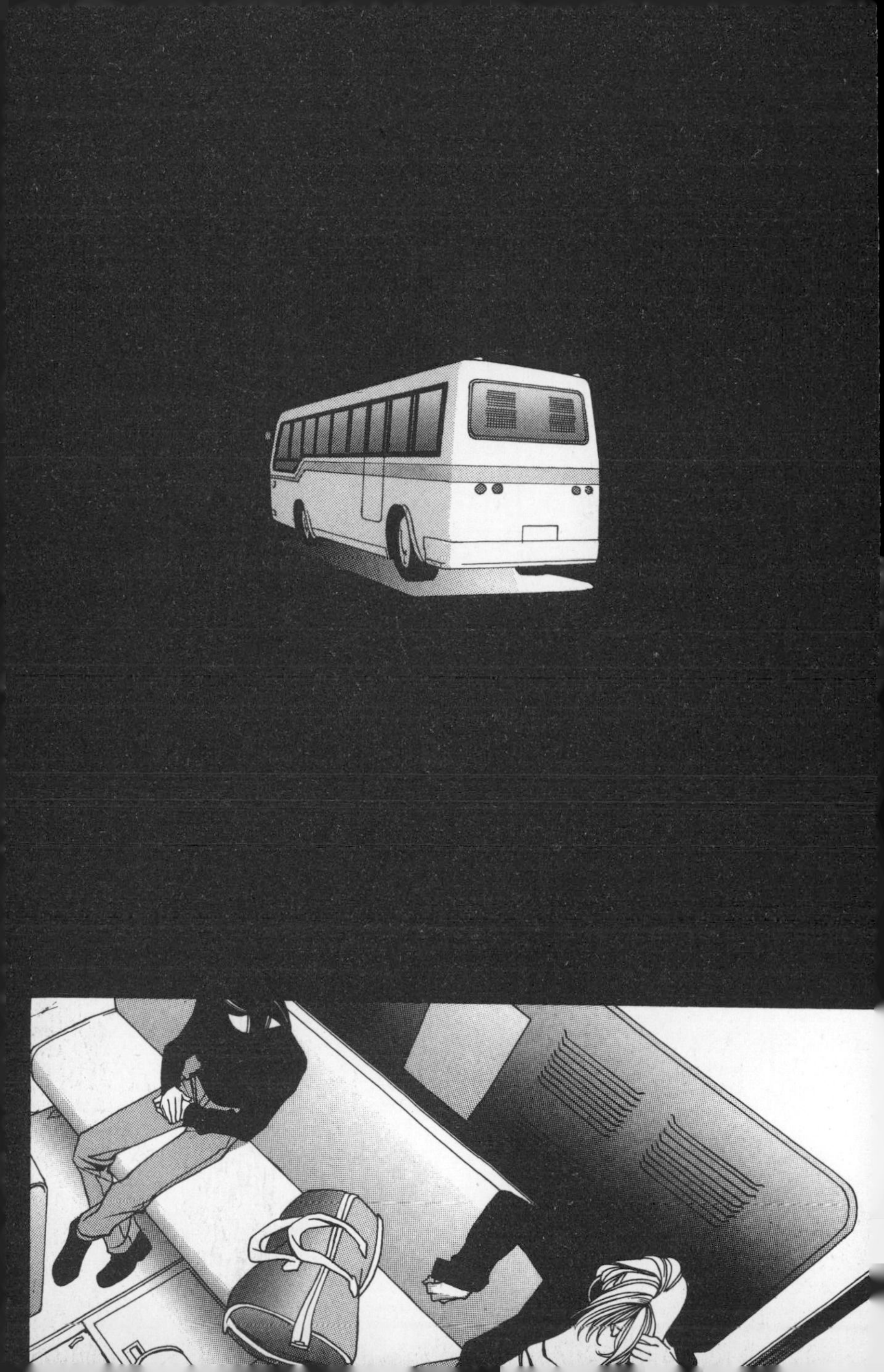

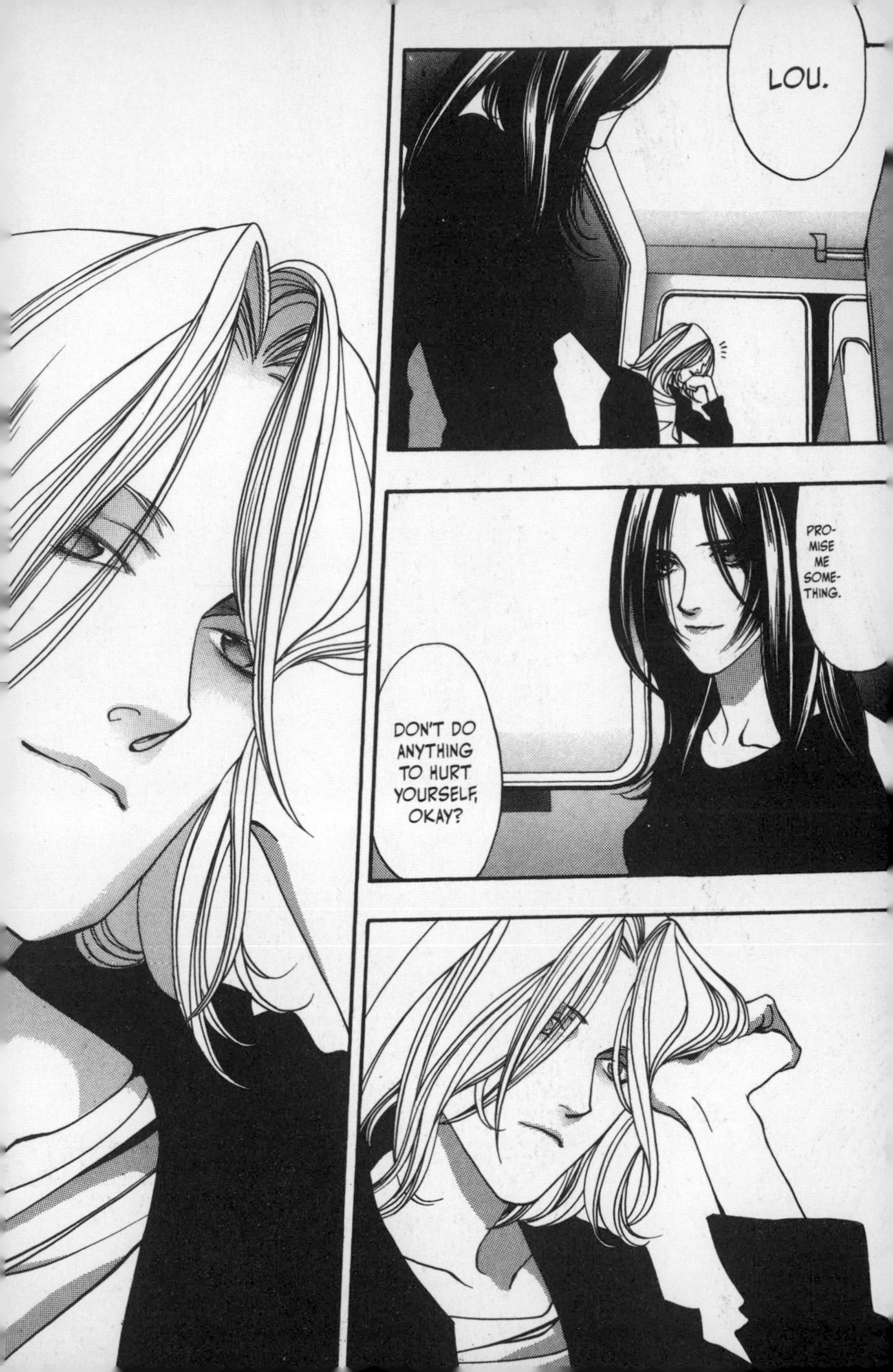
LOU.
PRO-MISE ME SOME-THING.
DON'T DO ANYTHING TO HURT YOURSELF, OKAY?

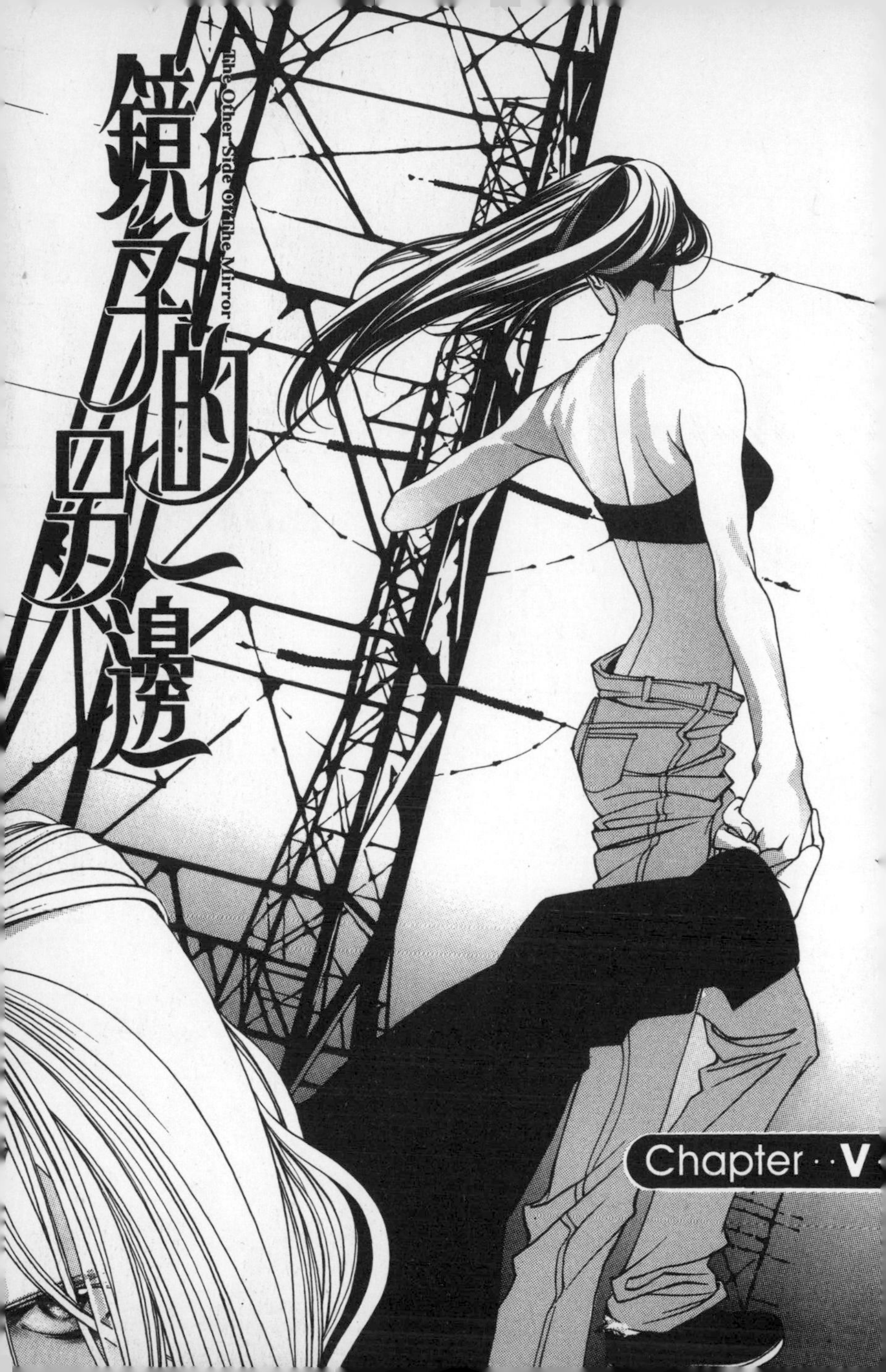
鏡子的另一邊
The Other Side Of The Mirror
Chapter · · V

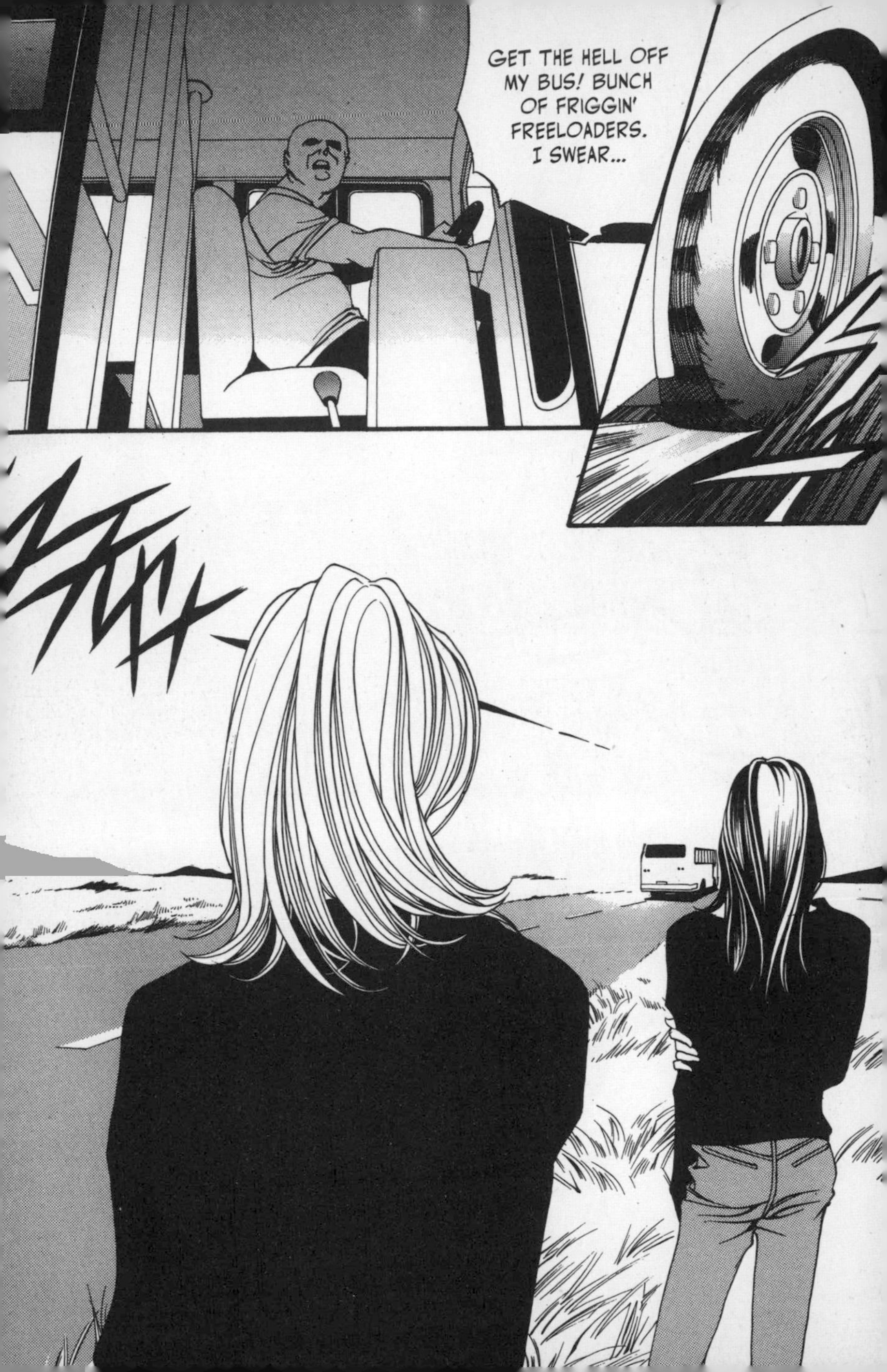
GET THE HELL OFF MY BUS! BUNCH OF FRIGGIN' FREELOADERS. I SWEAR...

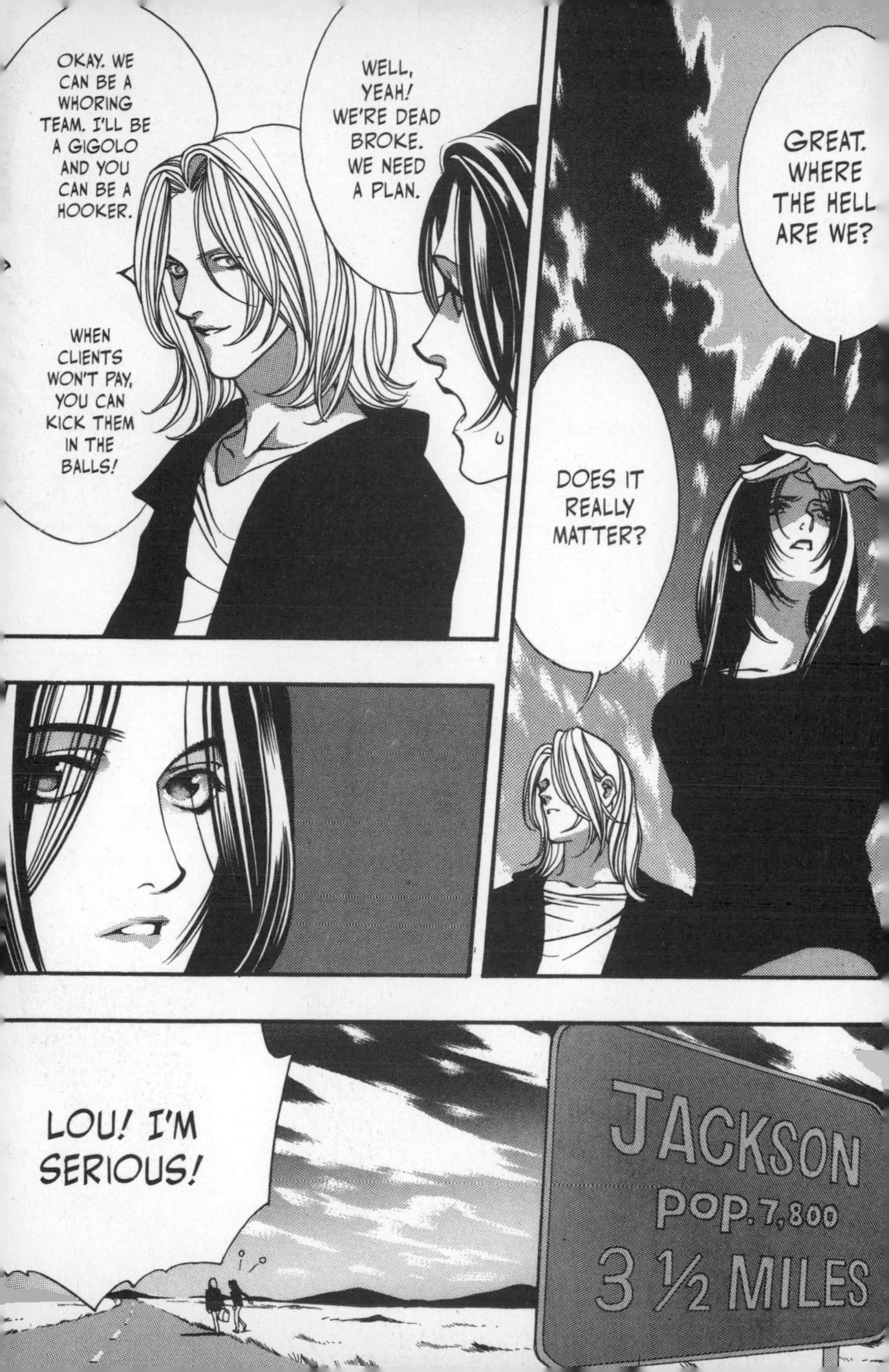
GREAT. WHERE THE HELL ARE WE?
DOES IT REALLY MATTER?
WELL, YEAH! WE'RE DEAD BROKE. WE NEED A PLAN.
OKAY. WE CAN BE A WHORING TEAM. I'LL BE A GIGOLO AND YOU CAN BE A HOOKER.
WHEN CLIENTS WON'T PAY, YOU CAN KICK THEM IN THE BALLS!
LOU! I'M SERIOUS!
JACKSON
POP. 7,800
3 ½ MILES

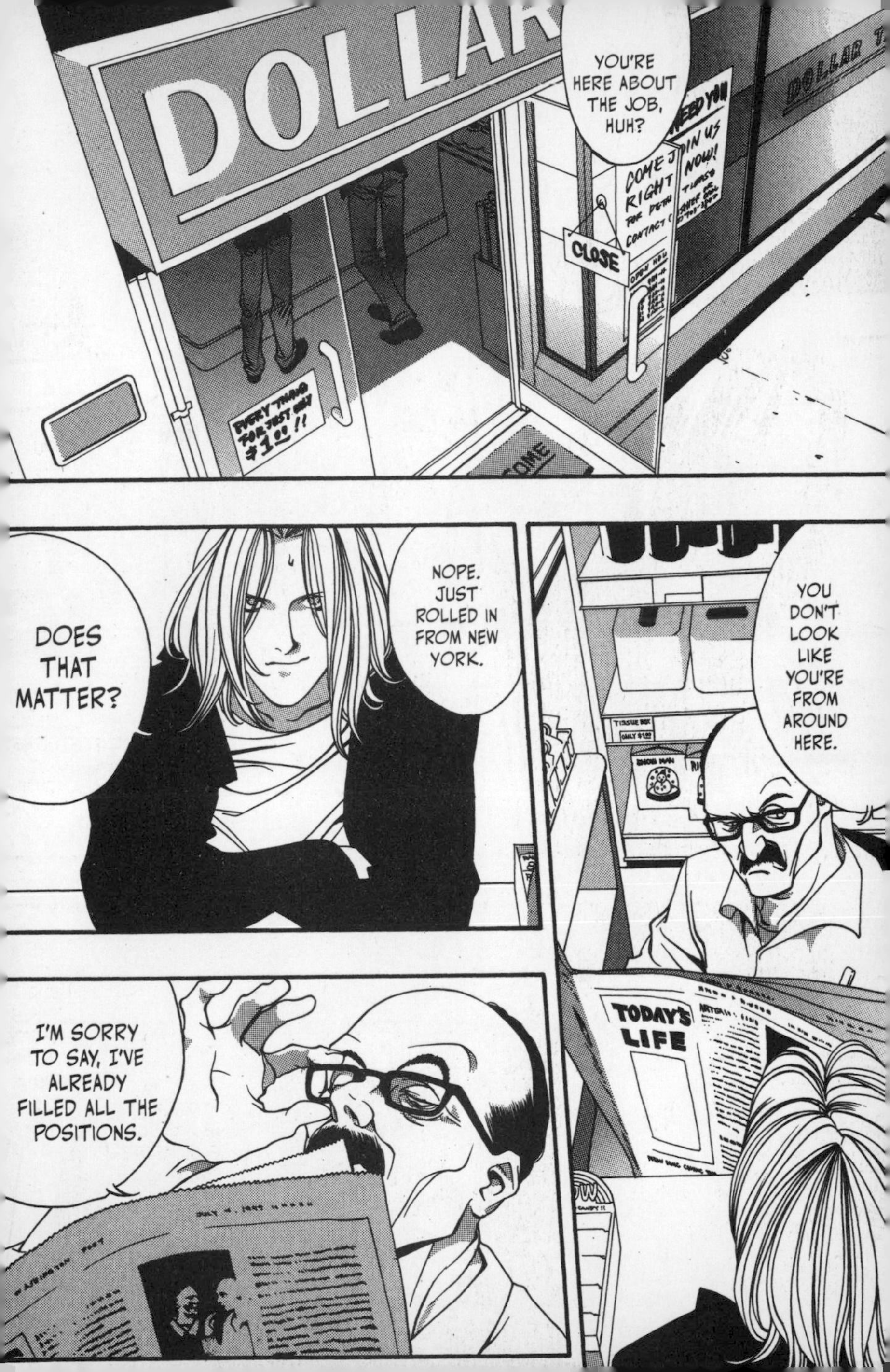
DOLLAR
YOU'RE HERE ABOUT THE JOB, HUH?
CLOSE
YOU DON'T LOOK LIKE YOU'RE FROM AROUND HERE.
NOPE. JUST ROLLED IN FROM NEW YORK.
DOES THAT MATTER?
TODAY'S LIFE
I'M SORRY TO SAY, I'VE ALREADY FILLED ALL THE POSITIONS.

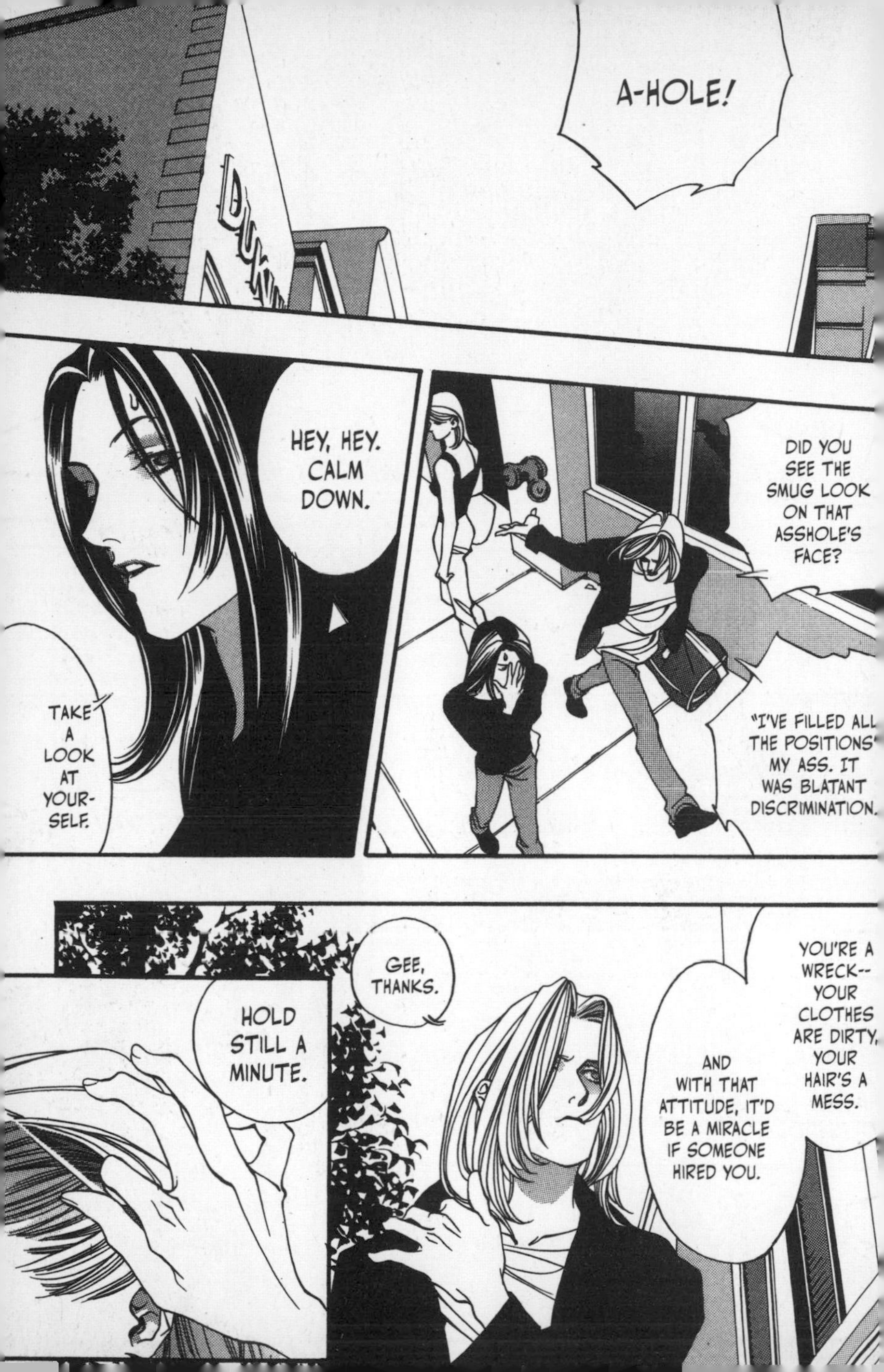
A-HOLE!
DID YOU SEE THE SMUG LOOK ON THAT ASSHOLE'S FACE?
"I'VE FILLED ALL THE POSITIONS" MY ASS. IT WAS BLATANT DISCRIMINATION.
HEY, HEY. CALM DOWN.
TAKE A LOOK AT YOURSELF.
YOU'RE A WRECK-- YOUR CLOTHES ARE DIRTY, YOUR HAIR'S A MESS.
AND WITH THAT ATTITUDE, IT'D BE A MIRACLE IF SOMEONE HIRED YOU.
GEE, THANKS.
HOLD STILL A MINUTE.

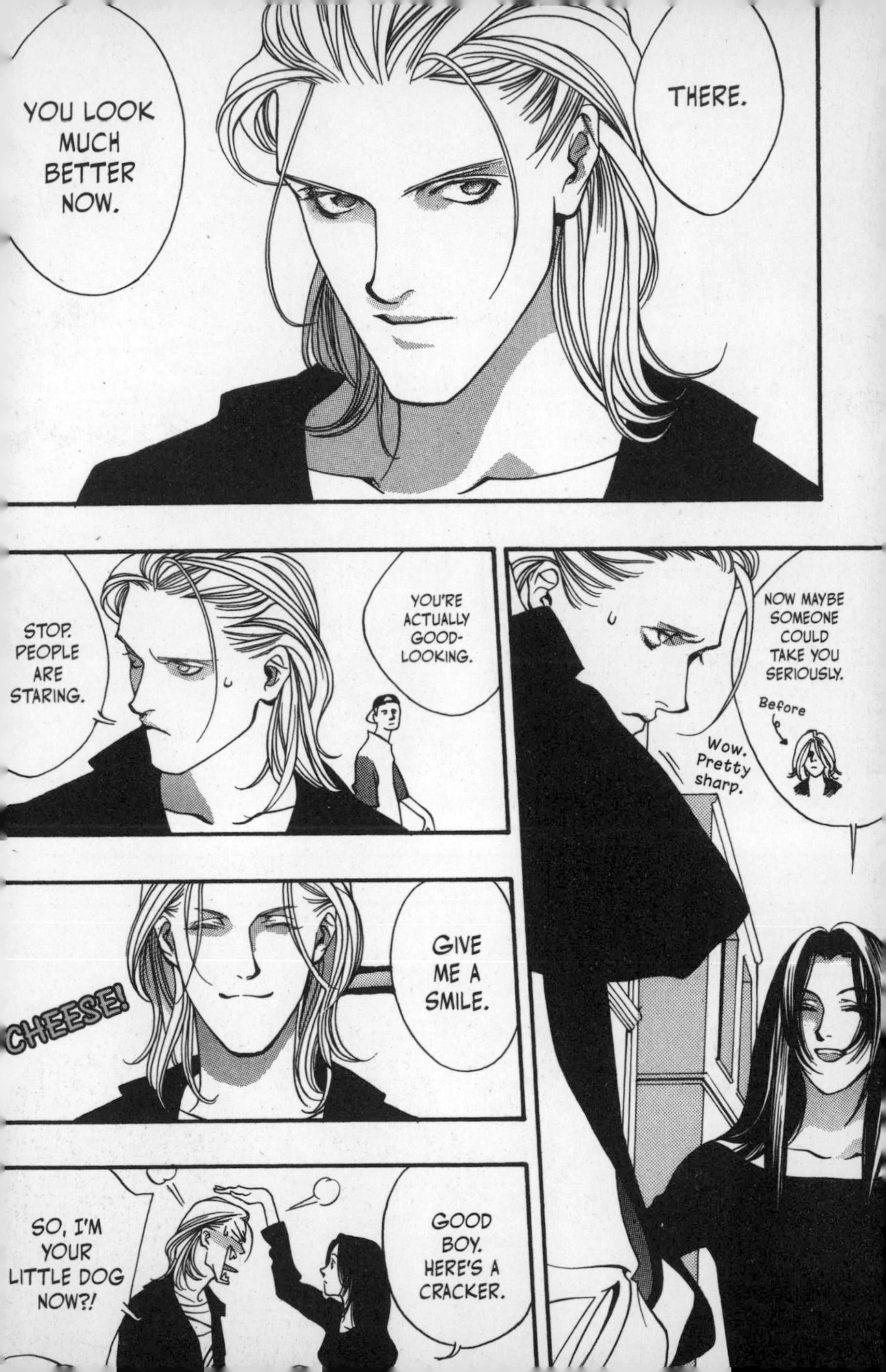
THERE.
YOU LOOK MUCH BETTER NOW.
NOW MAYBE SOMEONE COULD TAKE YOU SERIOUSLY.
Before
Wow. Pretty sharp.
YOU'RE ACTUALLY GOOD-LOOKING.
STOP. PEOPLE ARE STARING.
GIVE ME A SMILE.
CHEESE!
GOOD BOY. HERE'S A CRACKER.
SO, I'M YOUR LITTLE DOG NOW?!

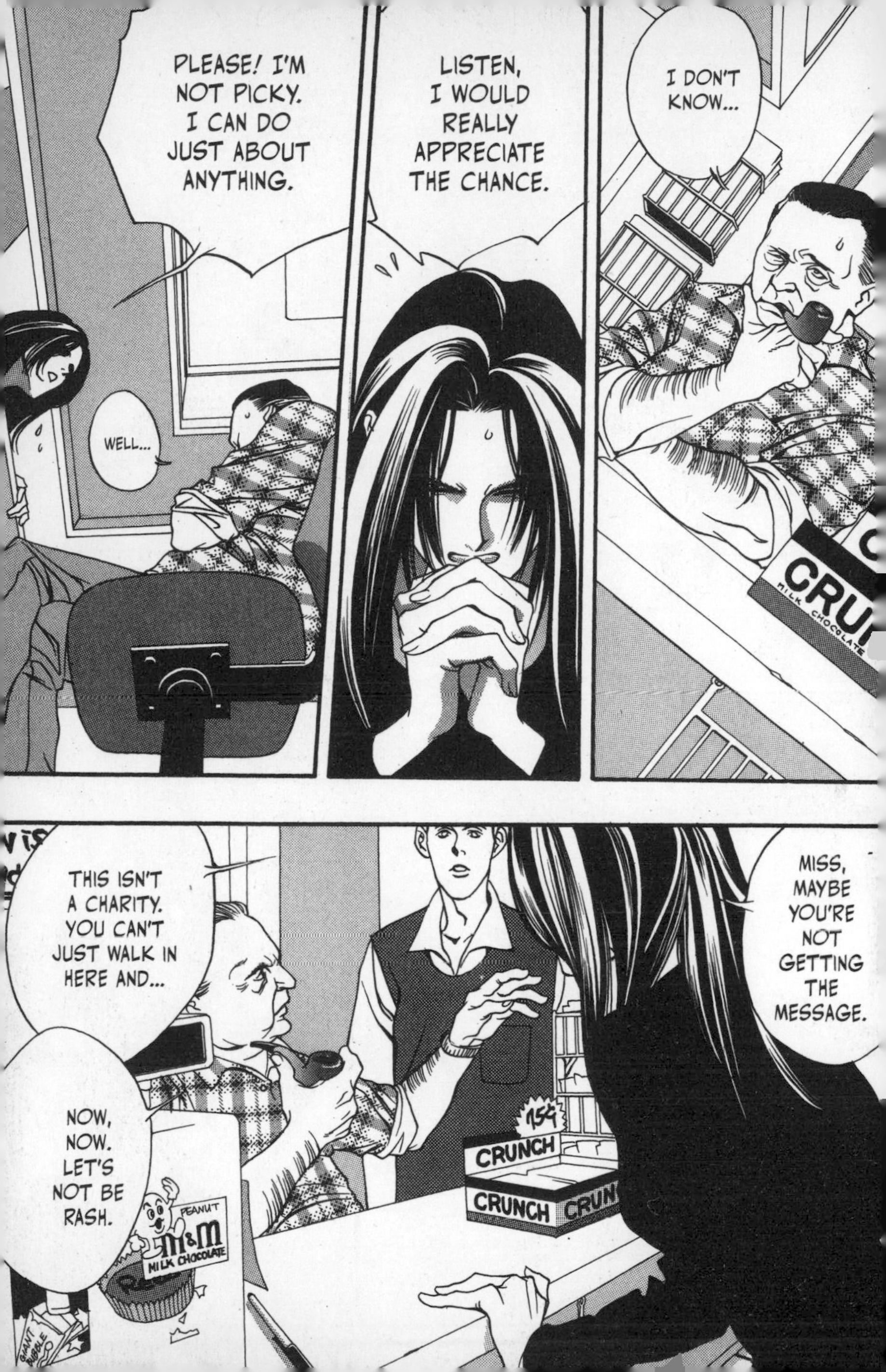
I DON'T KNOW...
CRUNCH
MILK CHOCOLATE
LISTEN, I WOULD REALLY APPRECIATE THE CHANCE.
PLEASE! I'M NOT PICKY. I CAN DO JUST ABOUT ANYTHING.
WELL...
MISS, MAYBE YOU'RE NOT GETTING THE MESSAGE.
THIS ISN'T A CHARITY. YOU CAN'T JUST WALK IN HERE AND...
15¢
CRUNCH
CRUNCH
NOW, NOW. LET'S NOT BE RASH.
PEANUT
M&M
MILK CHOCOLATE
GIANT BUBBLE

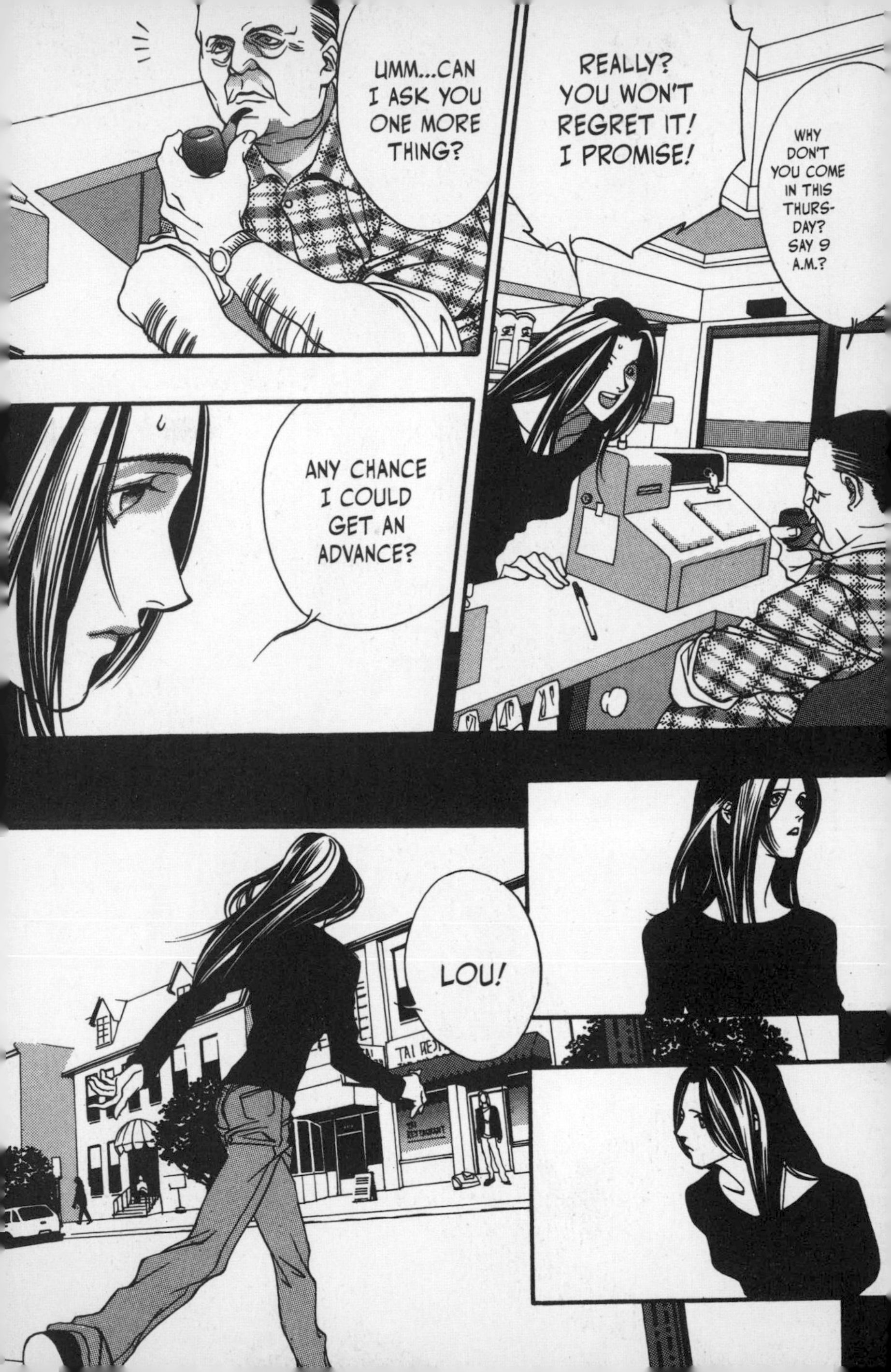
WHY DON'T YOU COME IN THIS THURS-DAY? SAY 9 A.M.?
REALLY? YOU WON'T REGRET IT! I PROMISE!
UMM...CAN I ASK YOU ONE MORE THING?
ANY CHANCE I COULD GET AN ADVANCE?
LOU!

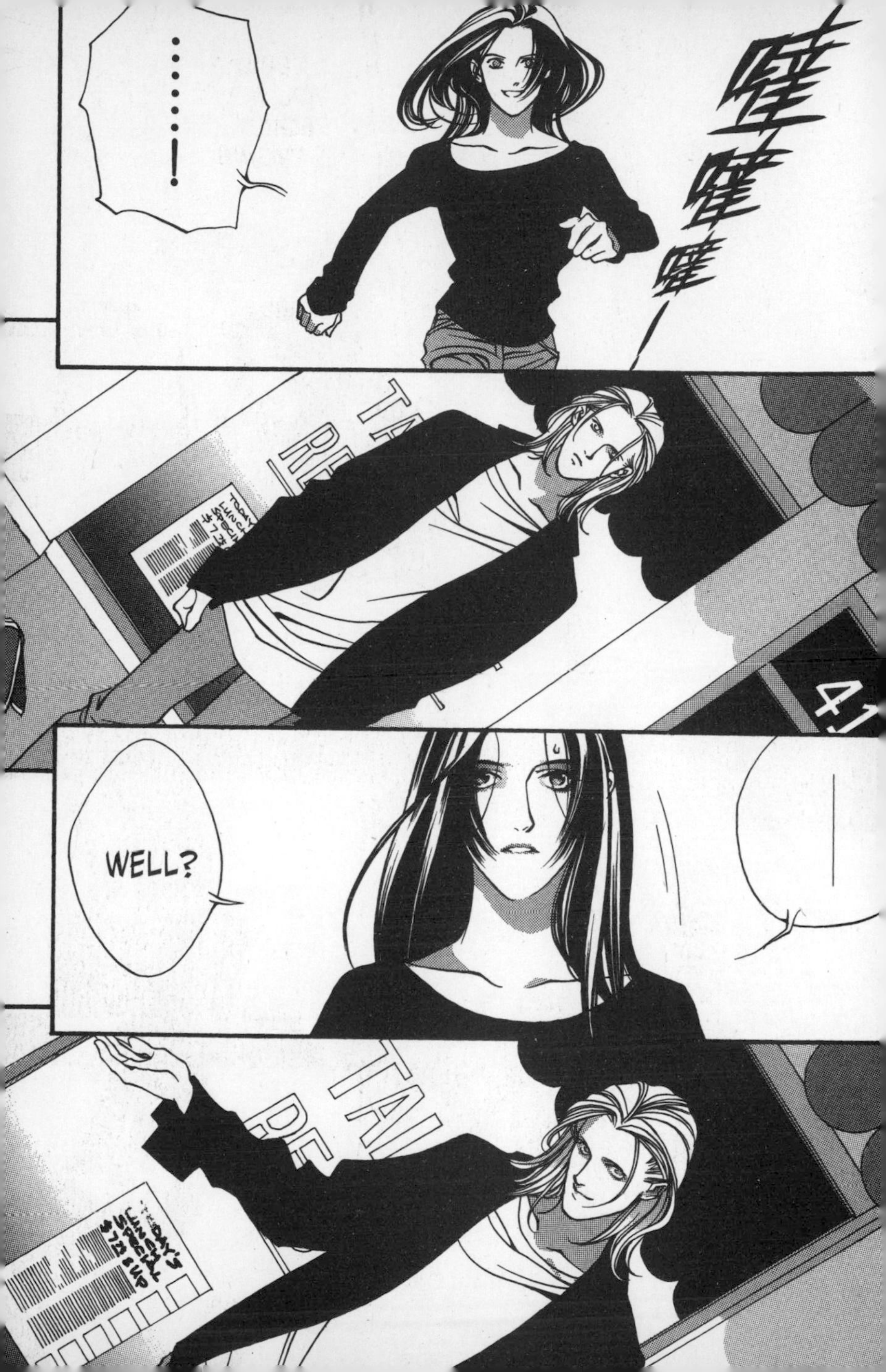
......!
WELL?

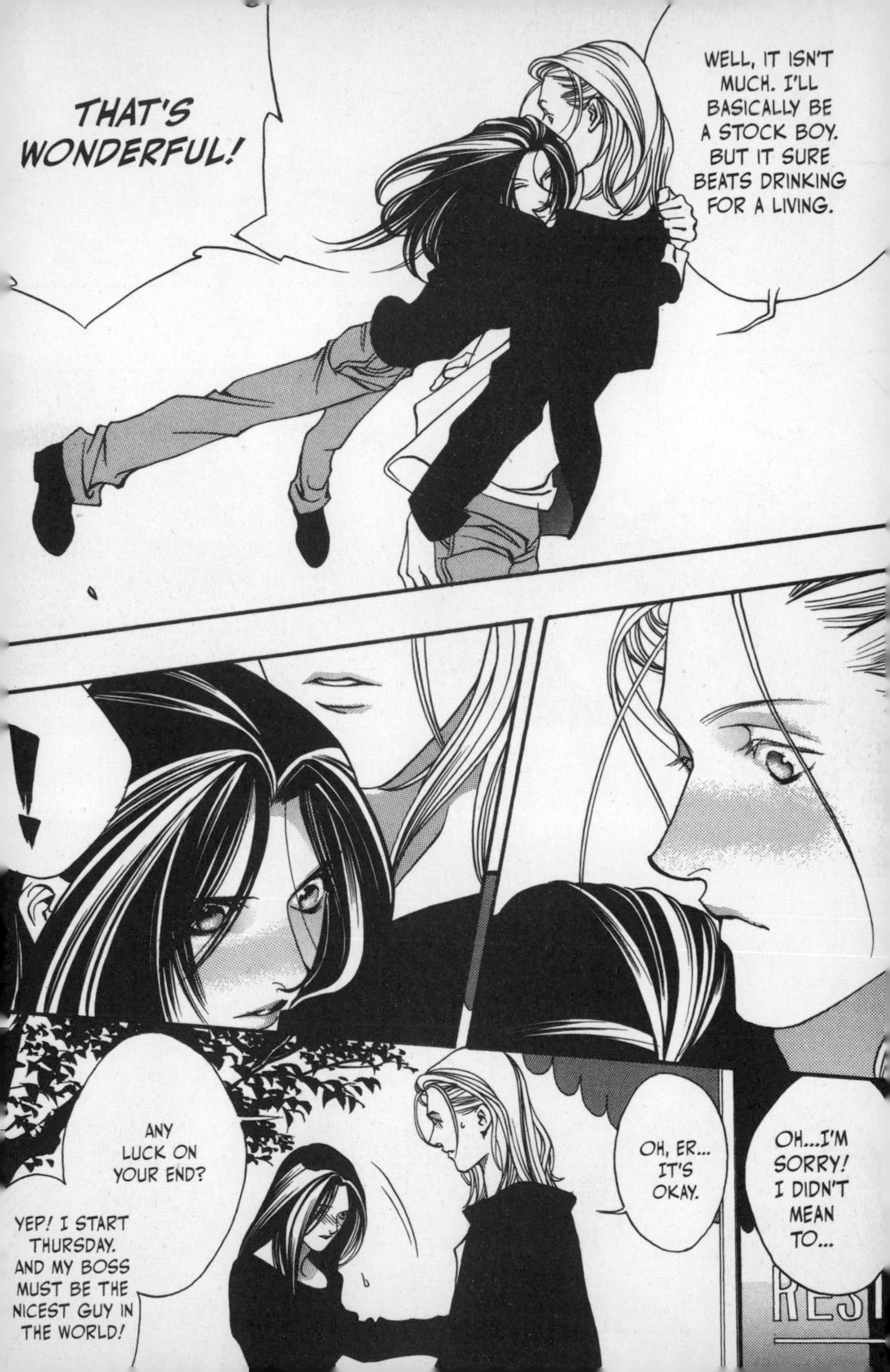
WELL, IT ISN'T MUCH. I'LL BASICALLY BE A STOCK BOY. BUT IT SURE BEATS DRINKING FOR A LIVING.
THAT'S WONDERFUL!
!
OH...I'M SORRY! I DIDN'T MEAN TO...
OH, ER... IT'S OKAY.
ANY LUCK ON YOUR END?
YEP! I START THURSDAY. AND MY BOSS MUST BE THE NICEST GUY IN THE WORLD!

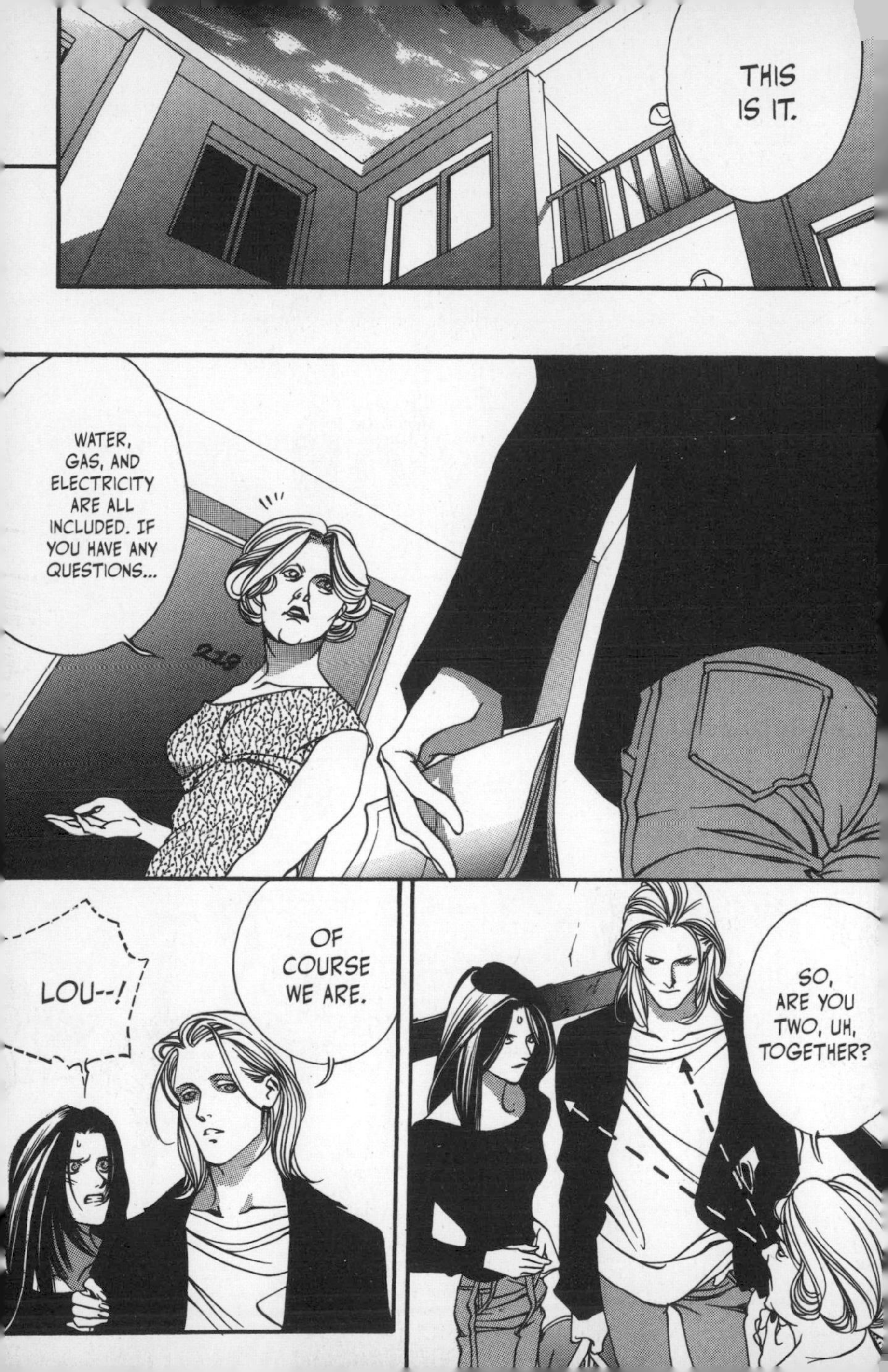
THIS IS IT.
WATER, GAS, AND ELECTRICITY ARE ALL INCLUDED. IF YOU HAVE ANY QUESTIONS...
SO, ARE YOU TWO, UH, TOGETHER?
OF COURSE WE ARE.
LOU--!

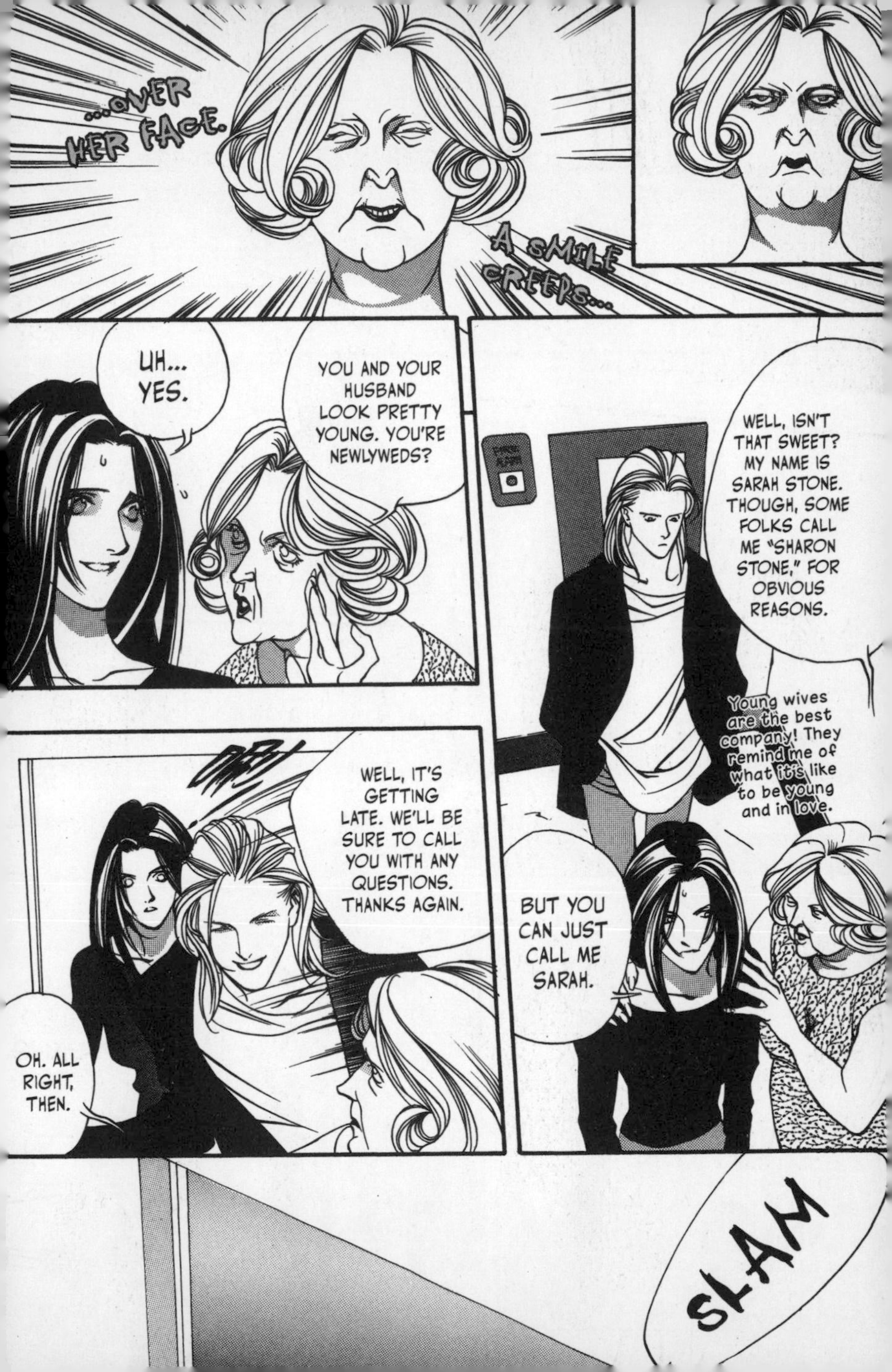
A SMILE CREEPS...
...OVER HER FACE.
YOU AND YOUR HUSBAND LOOK PRETTY YOUNG. YOU'RE NEWLYWEDS?
UH... YES.
WELL, ISN'T THAT SWEET? MY NAME IS SARAH STONE. THOUGH, SOME FOLKS CALL ME "SHARON STONE," FOR OBVIOUS REASONS.
Young wives are the best company! They remind me of what it's like to be young and in love.
BUT YOU CAN JUST CALL ME SARAH.
WELL, IT'S GETTING LATE. WE'LL BE SURE TO CALL YOU WITH ANY QUESTIONS. THANKS AGAIN.
OH. ALL RIGHT, THEN.
SLAM

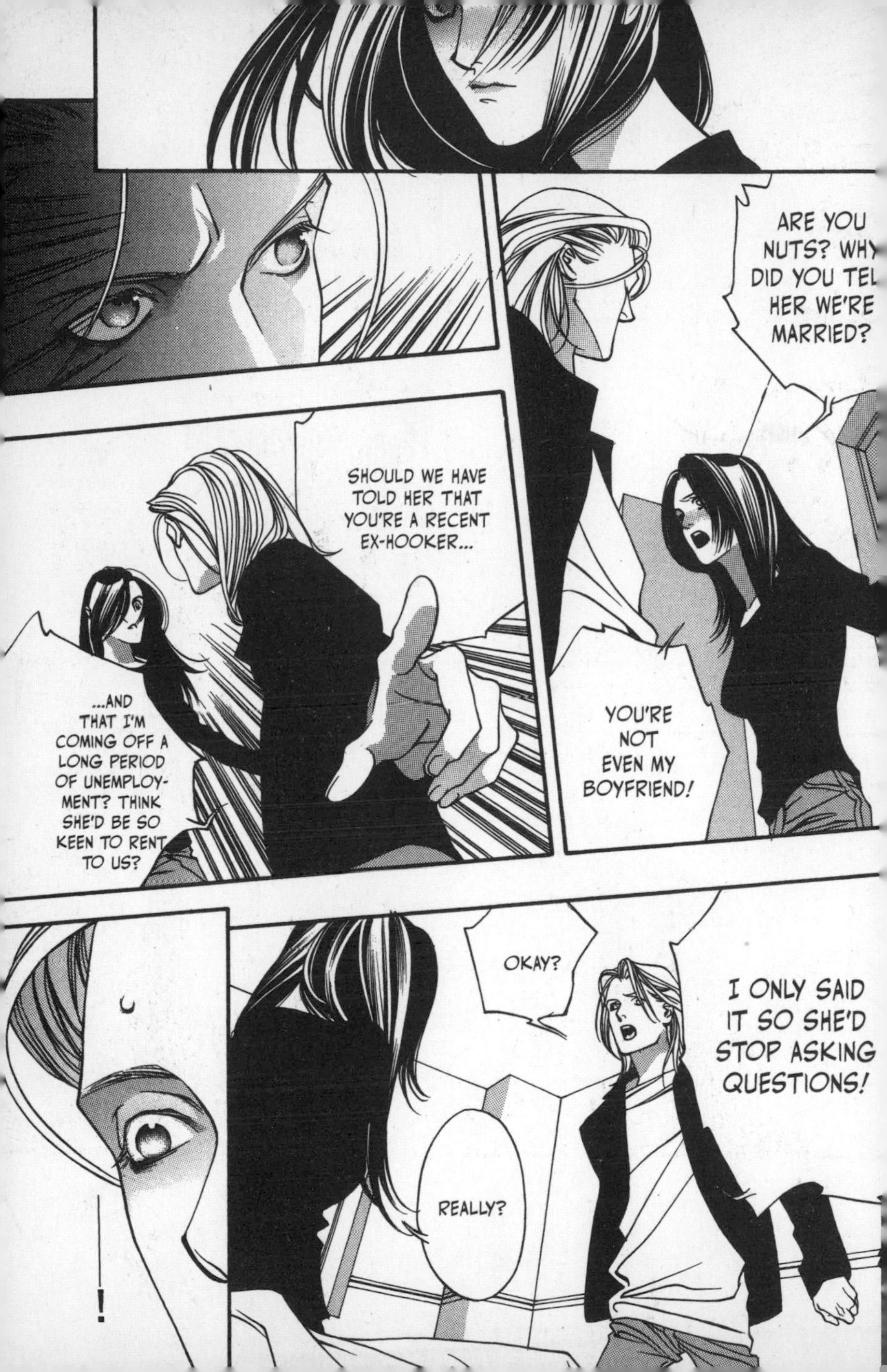
ARE YOU NUTS? WHY DID YOU TEL HER WE'RE MARRIED?
YOU'RE NOT EVEN MY BOYFRIEND!
SHOULD WE HAVE TOLD HER THAT YOU'RE A RECENT EX-HOOKER...
...AND THAT I'M COMING OFF A LONG PERIOD OF UNEMPLOY-MENT? THINK SHE'D BE SO KEEN TO RENT TO US?
I ONLY SAID IT SO SHE'D STOP ASKING QUESTIONS!
OKAY?
REALLY?
...!

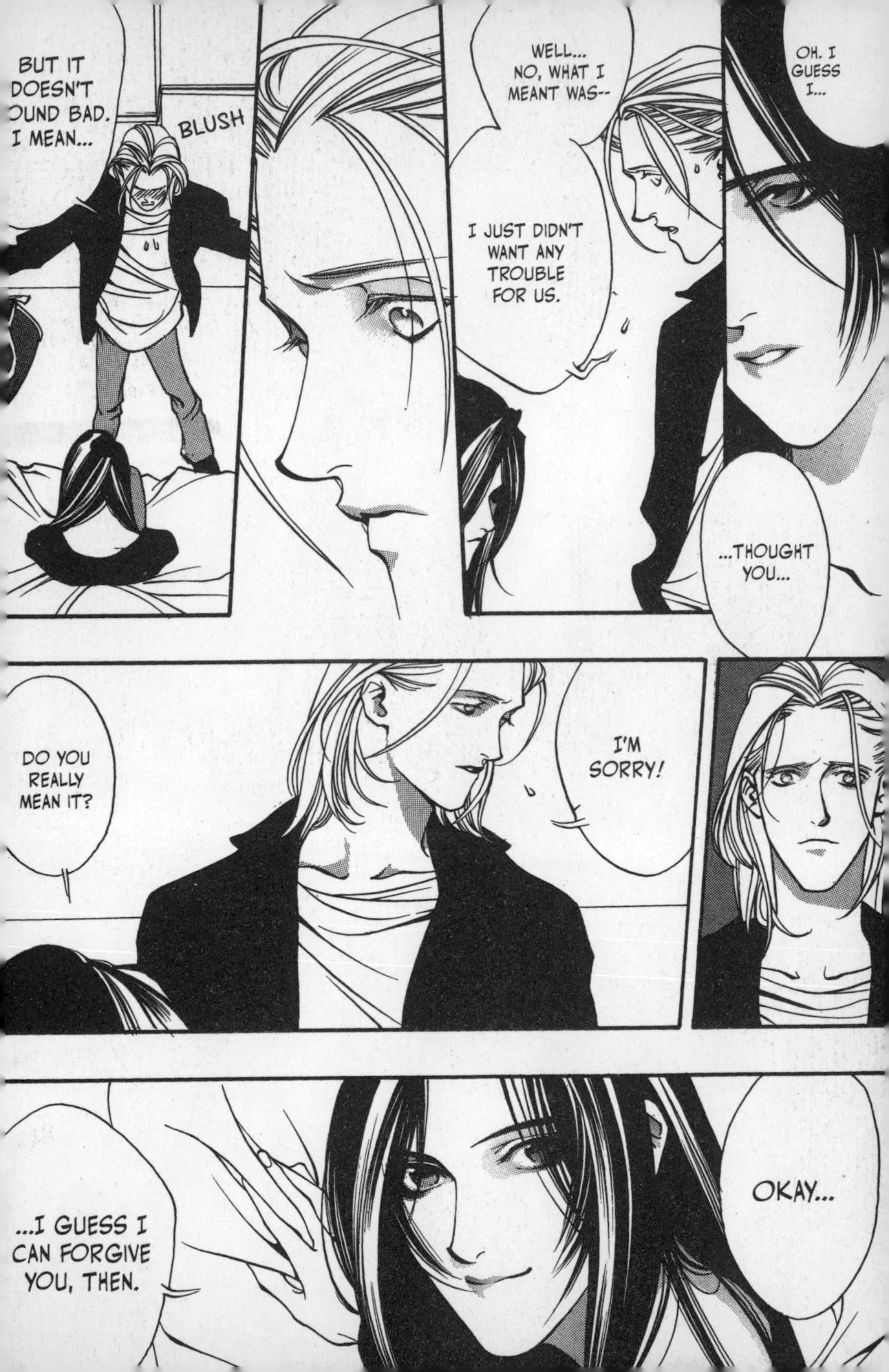

OH. I GUESS I...
...THOUGHT YOU...
WELL... NO, WHAT I MEANT WAS--
I JUST DIDN'T WANT ANY TROUBLE FOR US.
BUT IT DOESN'T OUND BAD. I MEAN...
BLUSH
I'M SORRY!
DO YOU REALLY MEAN IT?
OKAY...
...I GUESS I CAN FORGIVE YOU, THEN.

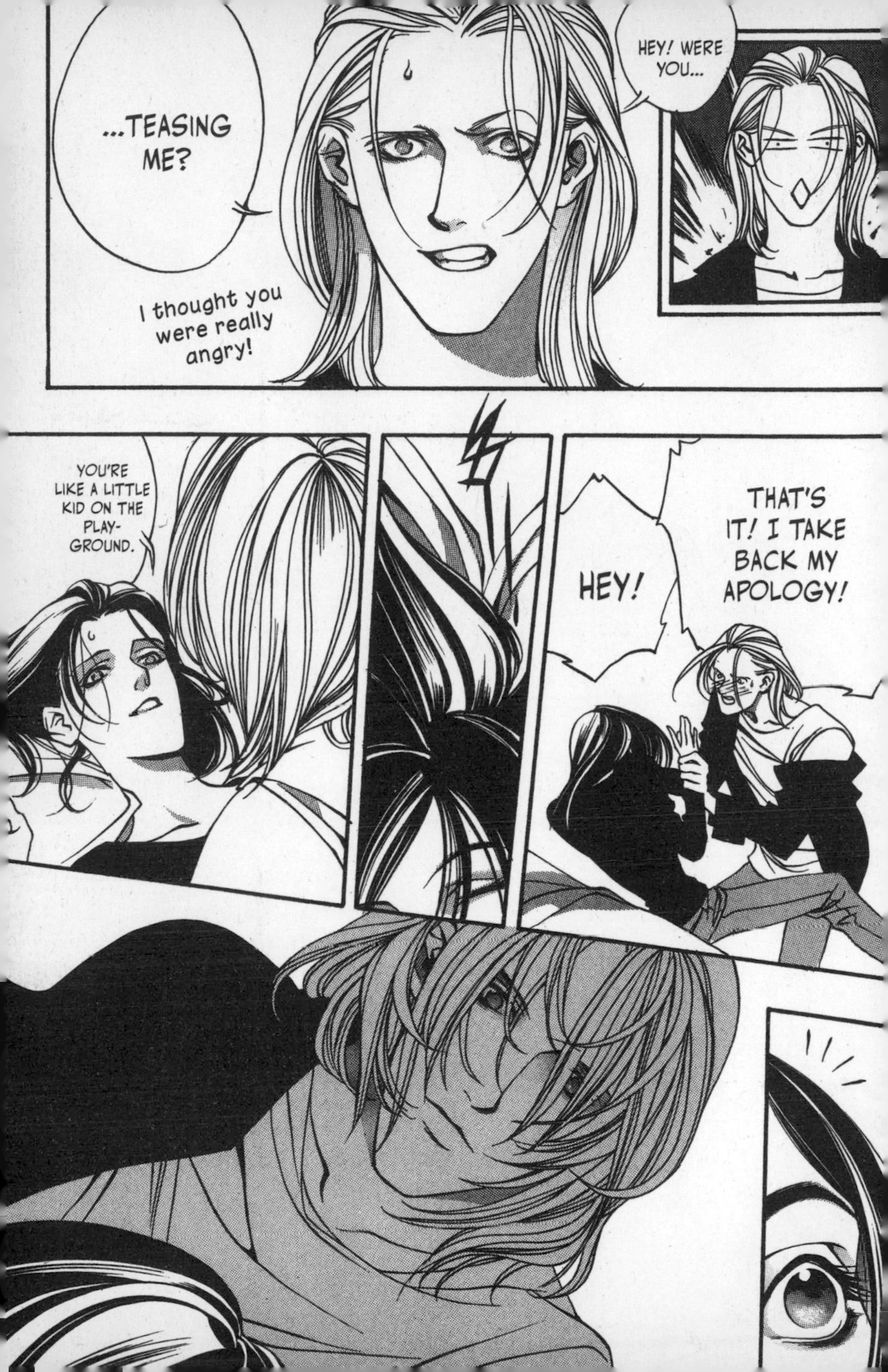
HEY! WERE YOU...
...TEASING ME?
I thought you were really angry!
THAT'S IT! I TAKE BACK MY APOLOGY!
HEY!
YOU'RE LIKE A LITTLE KID ON THE PLAY-GROUND.

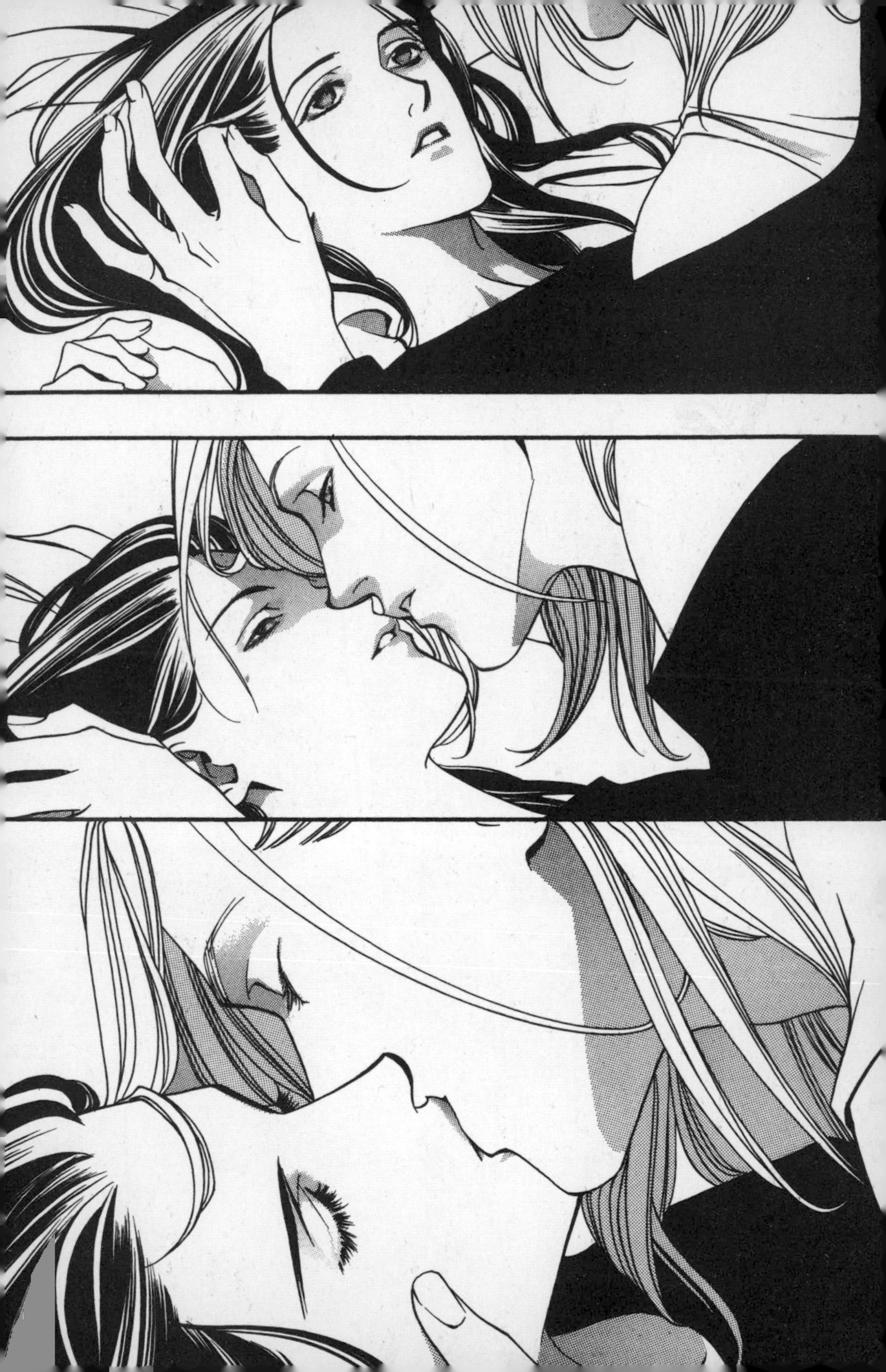

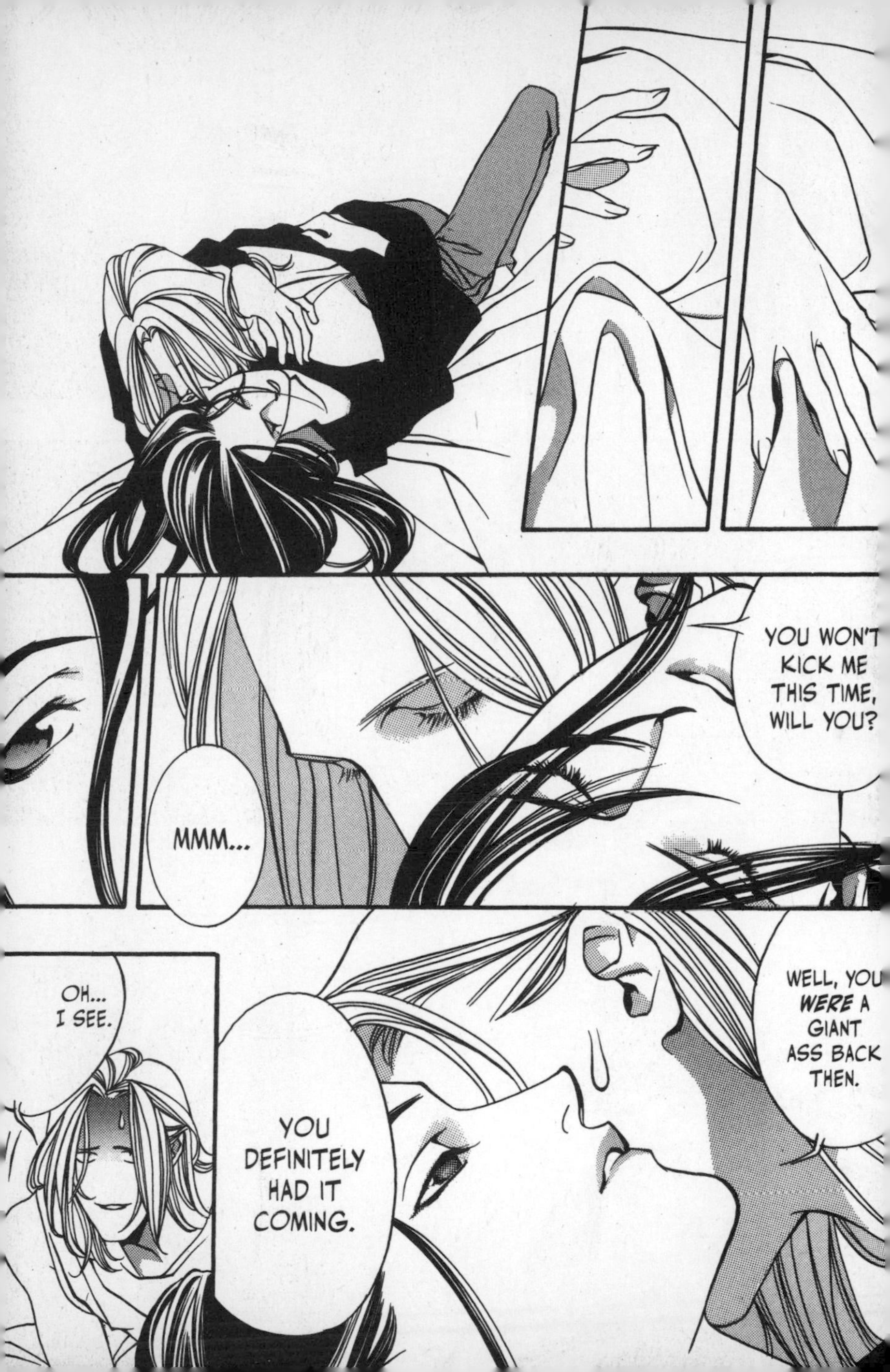
YOU WON'T KICK ME THIS TIME, WILL YOU?
MMM...
WELL, YOU *WERE* A GIANT ASS BACK THEN.
YOU DEFINITELY HAD IT COMING.
OH... I SEE.

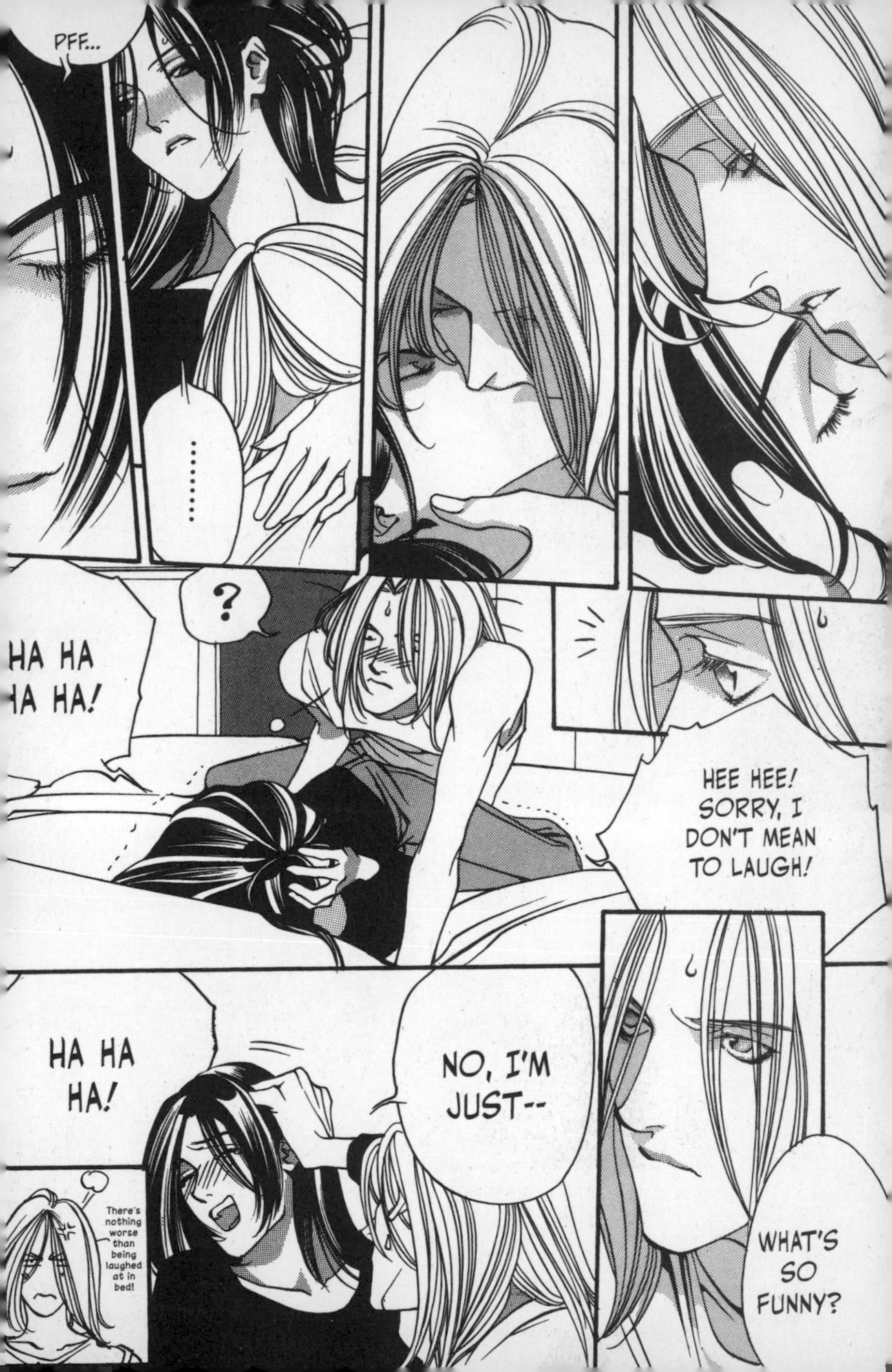
PFF...
......
HEE HEE! SORRY, I DON'T MEAN TO LAUGH!
?
HA HA HA HA!
WHAT'S SO FUNNY?
NO, I'M JUST--
HA HA HA!
There's nothing worse than being laughed at in bed!

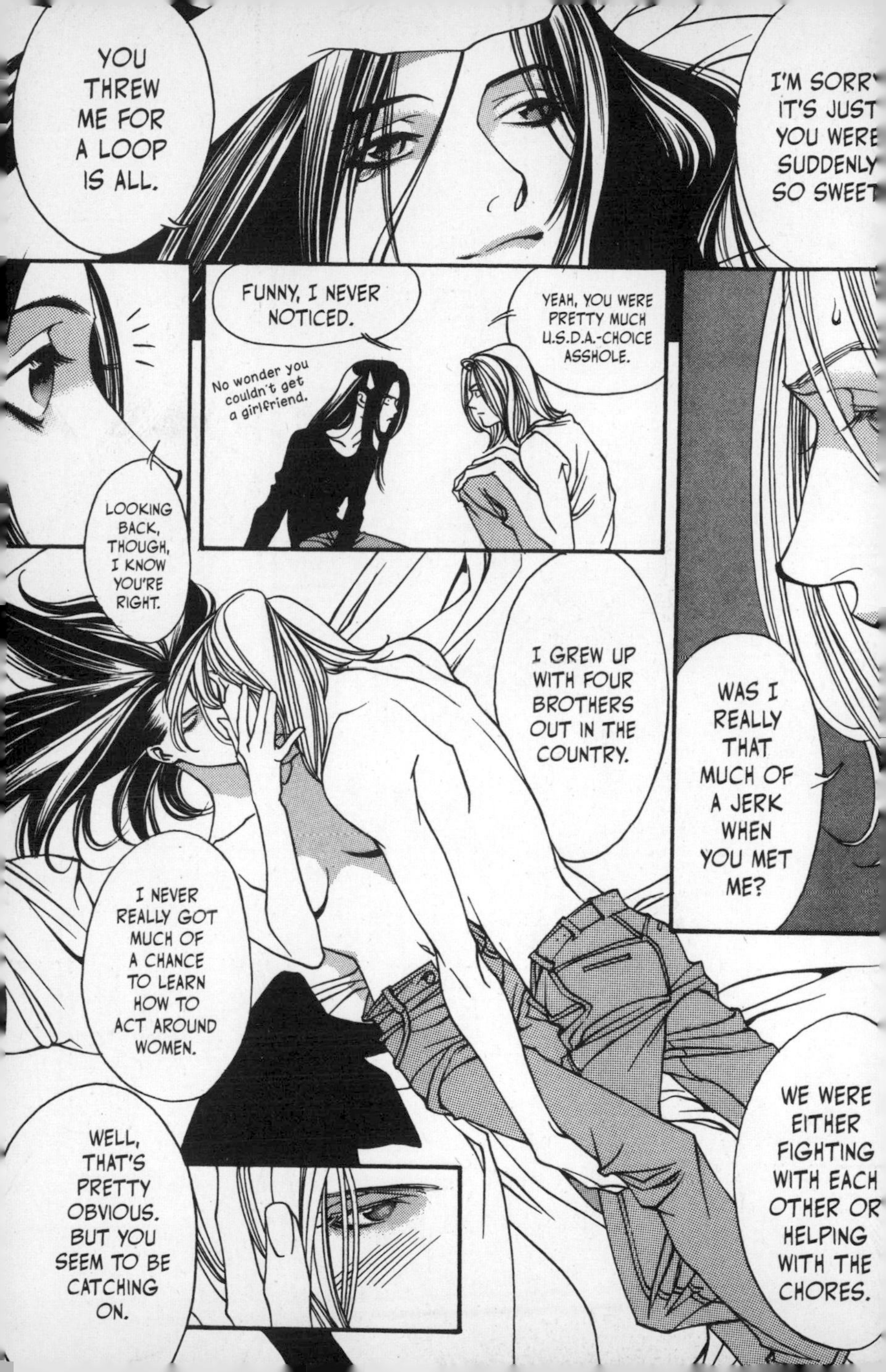
I'M SORR IT'S JUST YOU WERE SUDDENLY SO SWEE
YOU THREW ME FOR A LOOP IS ALL.
WAS I REALLY THAT MUCH OF A JERK WHEN YOU MET ME?
YEAH, YOU WERE PRETTY MUCH U.S.D.A.-CHOICE ASSHOLE.
FUNNY, I NEVER NOTICED.
No wonder you couldn't get a girlfriend.
LOOKING BACK, THOUGH, I KNOW YOU'RE RIGHT.
I GREW UP WITH FOUR BROTHERS OUT IN THE COUNTRY.
WE WERE EITHER FIGHTING WITH EACH OTHER OR HELPING WITH THE CHORES.
I NEVER REALLY GOT MUCH OF A CHANCE TO LEARN HOW TO ACT AROUND WOMEN.
WELL, THAT'S PRETTY OBVIOUS. BUT YOU SEEM TO BE CATCHING ON.

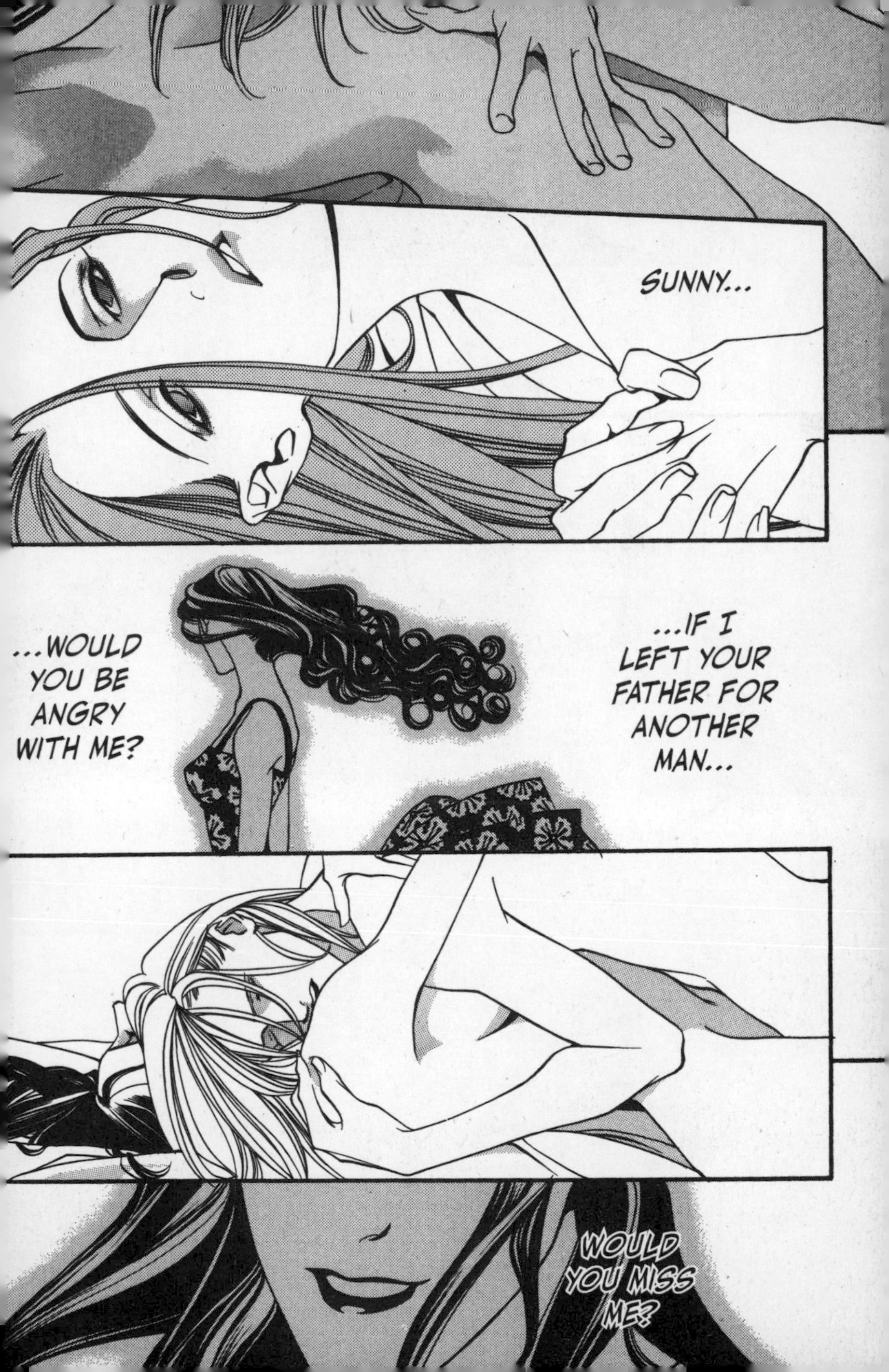
SUNNY...
...IF I LEFT YOUR FATHER FOR ANOTHER MAN...
...WOULD YOU BE ANGRY WITH ME?
WOULD YOU MISS ME?

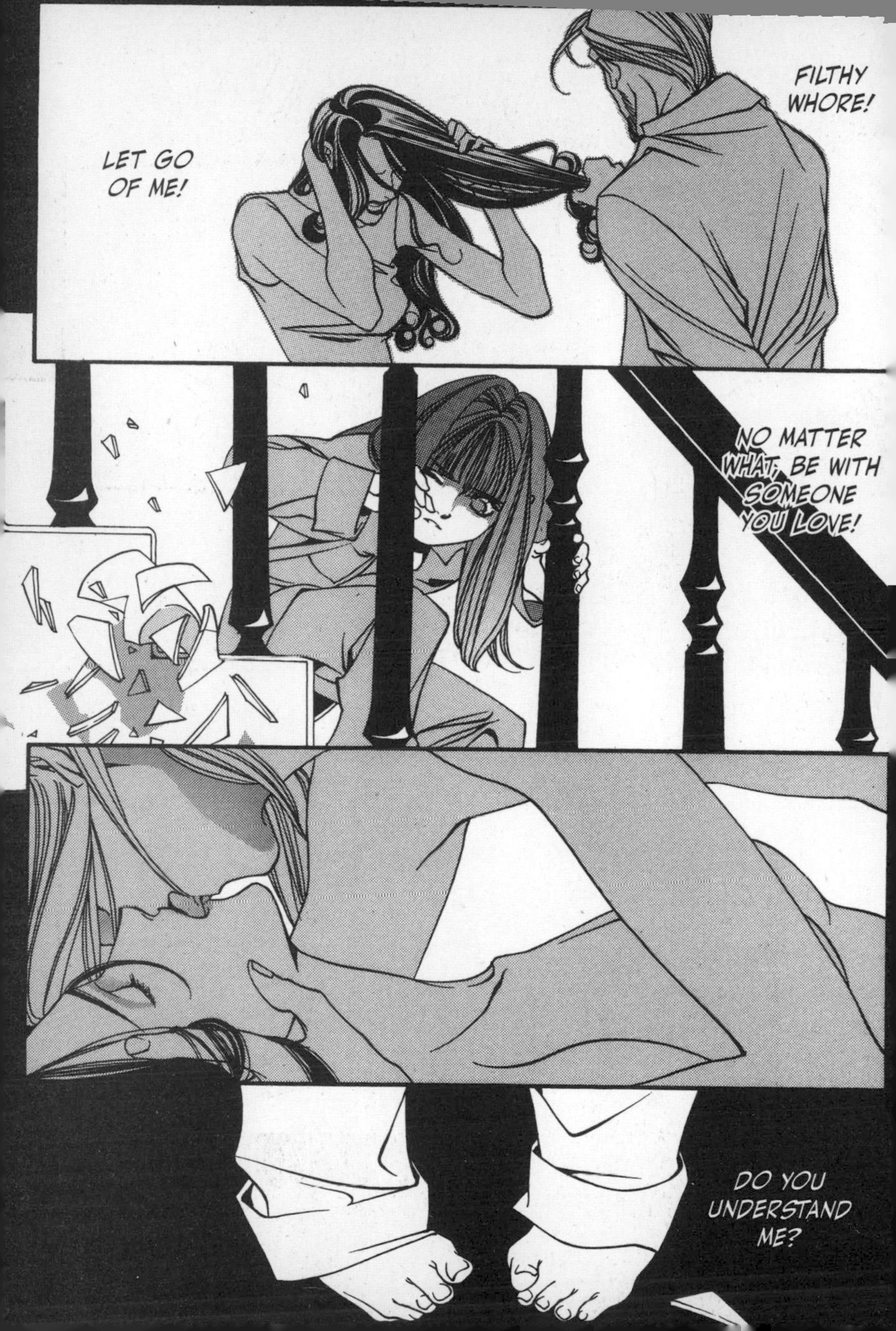
FILTHY WHORE!
LET GO OF ME!
NO MATTER WHAT, BE WITH SOMEONE YOU LOVE!
DO YOU UNDERSTAND ME?

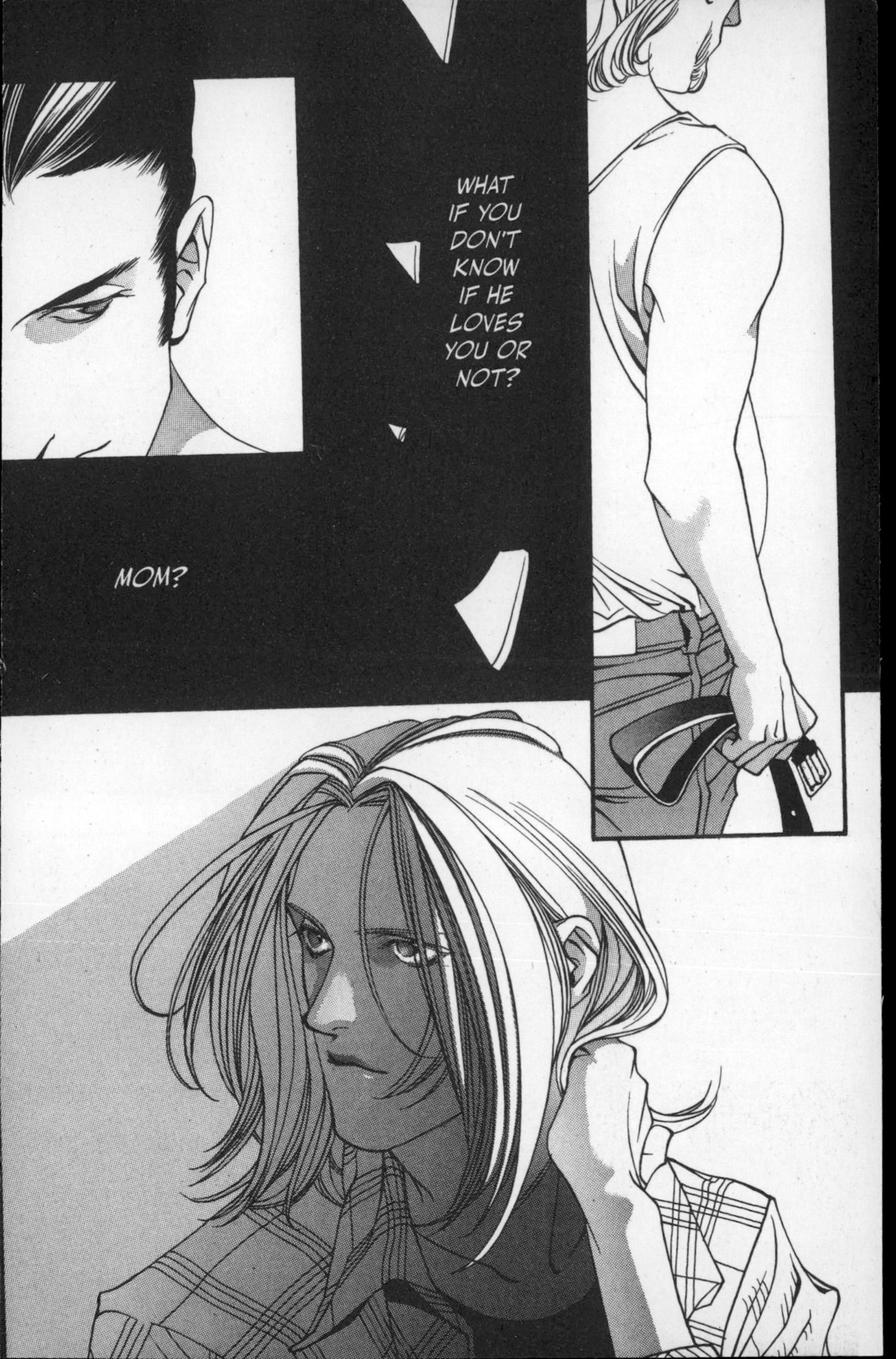
WHAT IF YOU DON'T KNOW IF HE LOVES YOU OR NOT?
MOM?

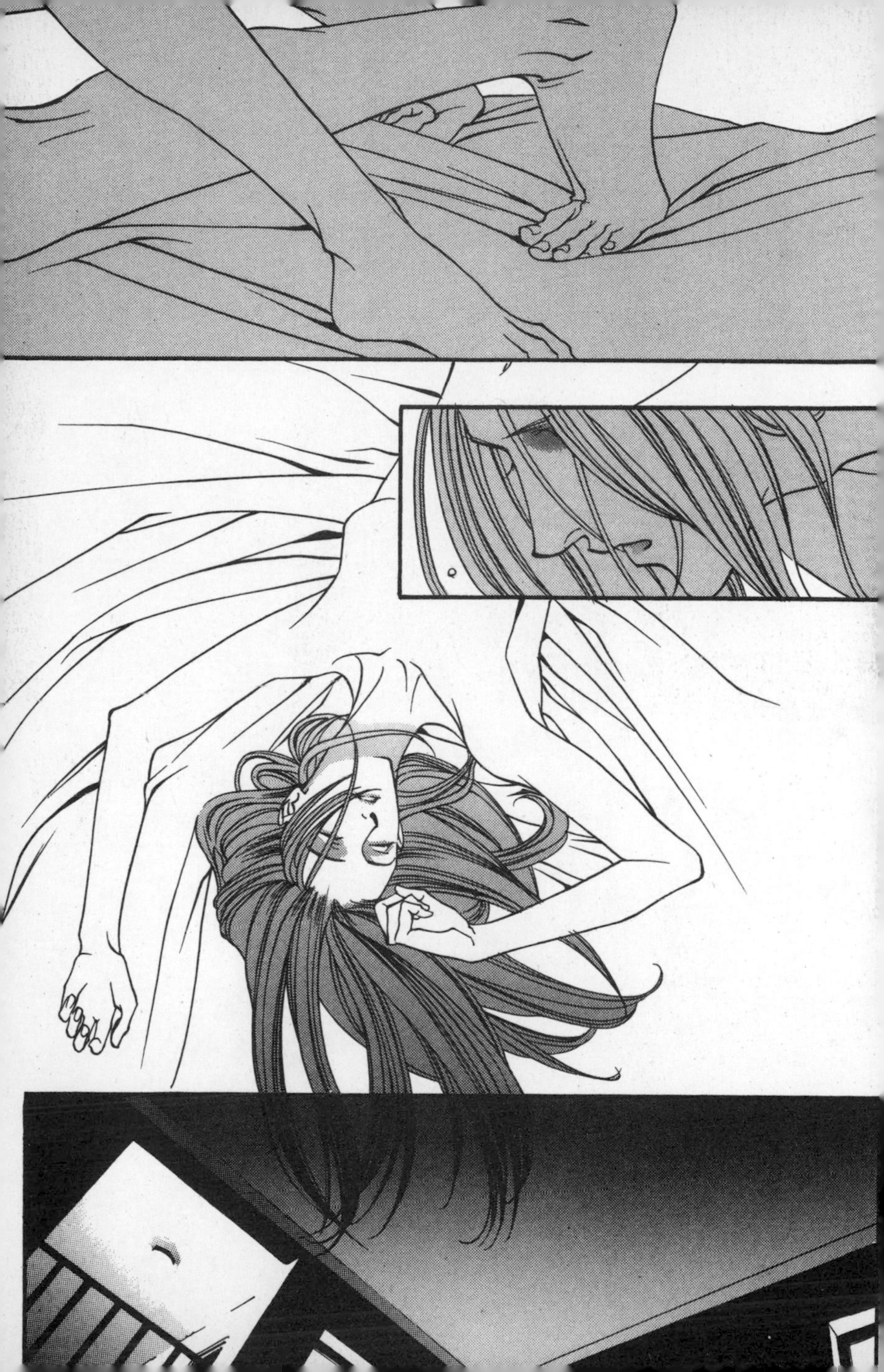

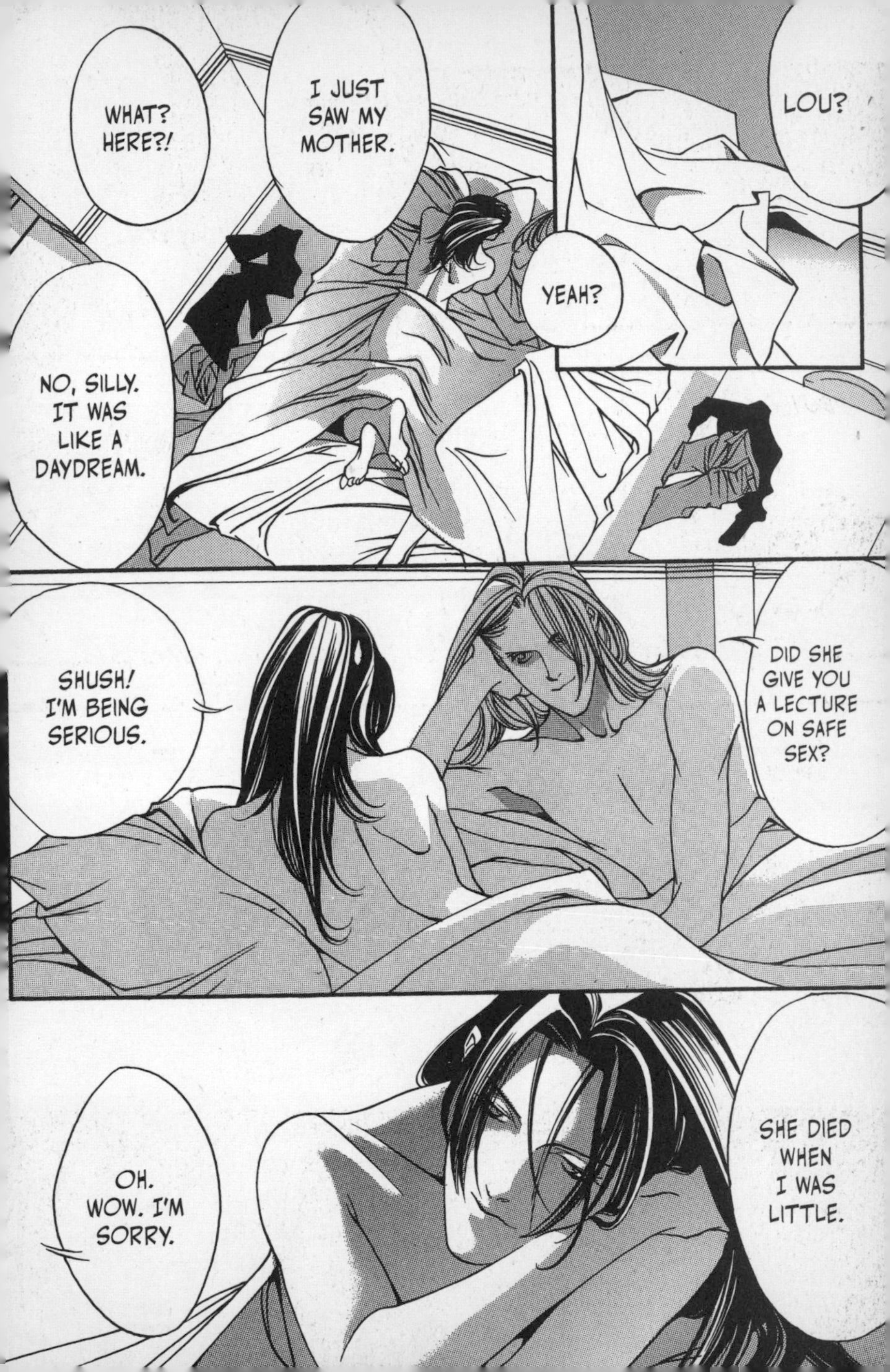
LOU?
YEAH?
I JUST SAW MY MOTHER.
WHAT? HERE?!
NO, SILLY. IT WAS LIKE A DAYDREAM.
DID SHE GIVE YOU A LECTURE ON SAFE SEX?
SHUSH! I'M BEING SERIOUS.
SHE DIED WHEN I WAS LITTLE.
OH. WOW. I'M SORRY.

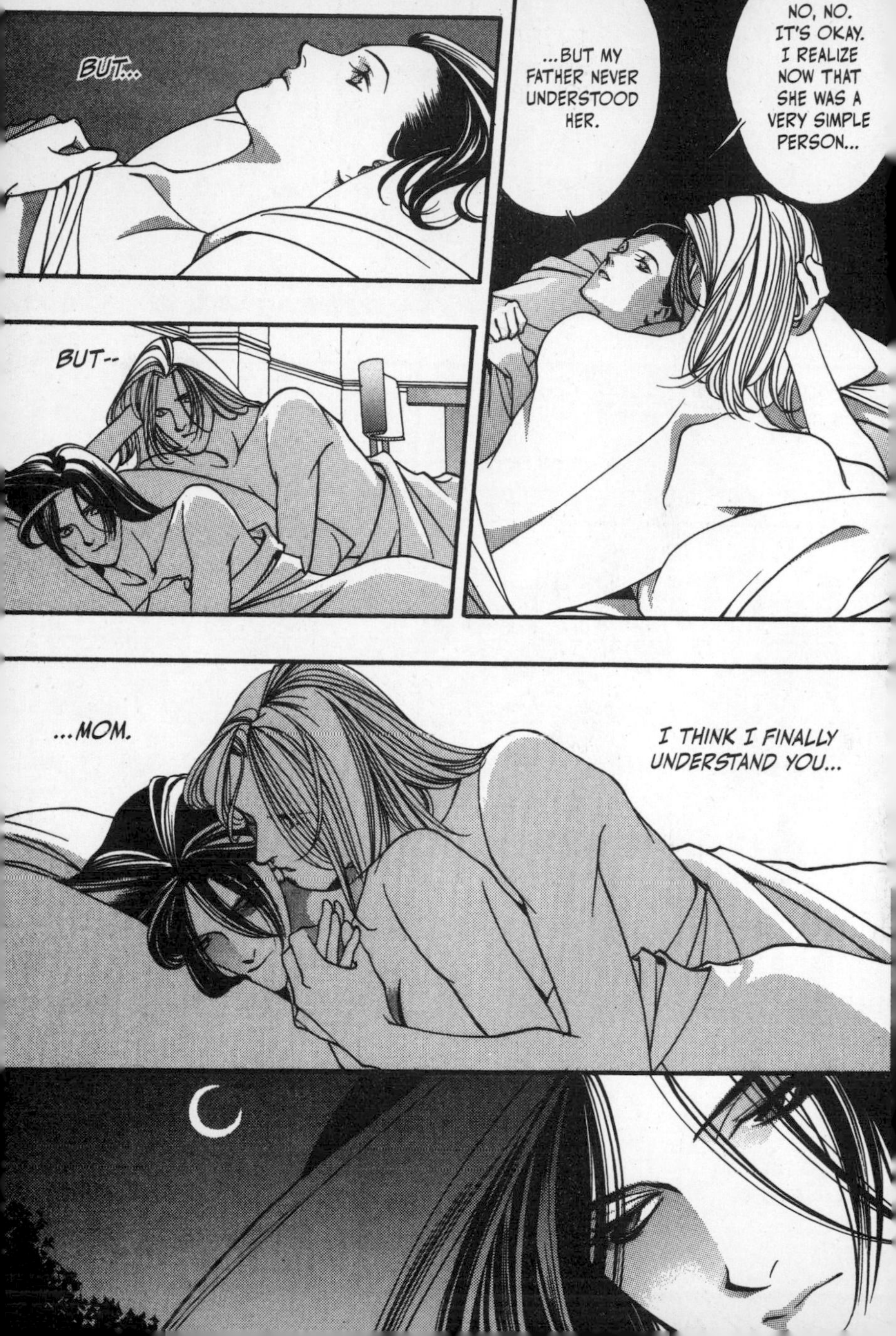
NO, NO. IT'S OKAY. I REALIZE NOW THAT SHE WAS A VERY SIMPLE PERSON...
...BUT MY FATHER NEVER UNDERSTOOD HER.
BUT...
BUT--
I THINK I FINALLY UNDERSTAND YOU...
...MOM.

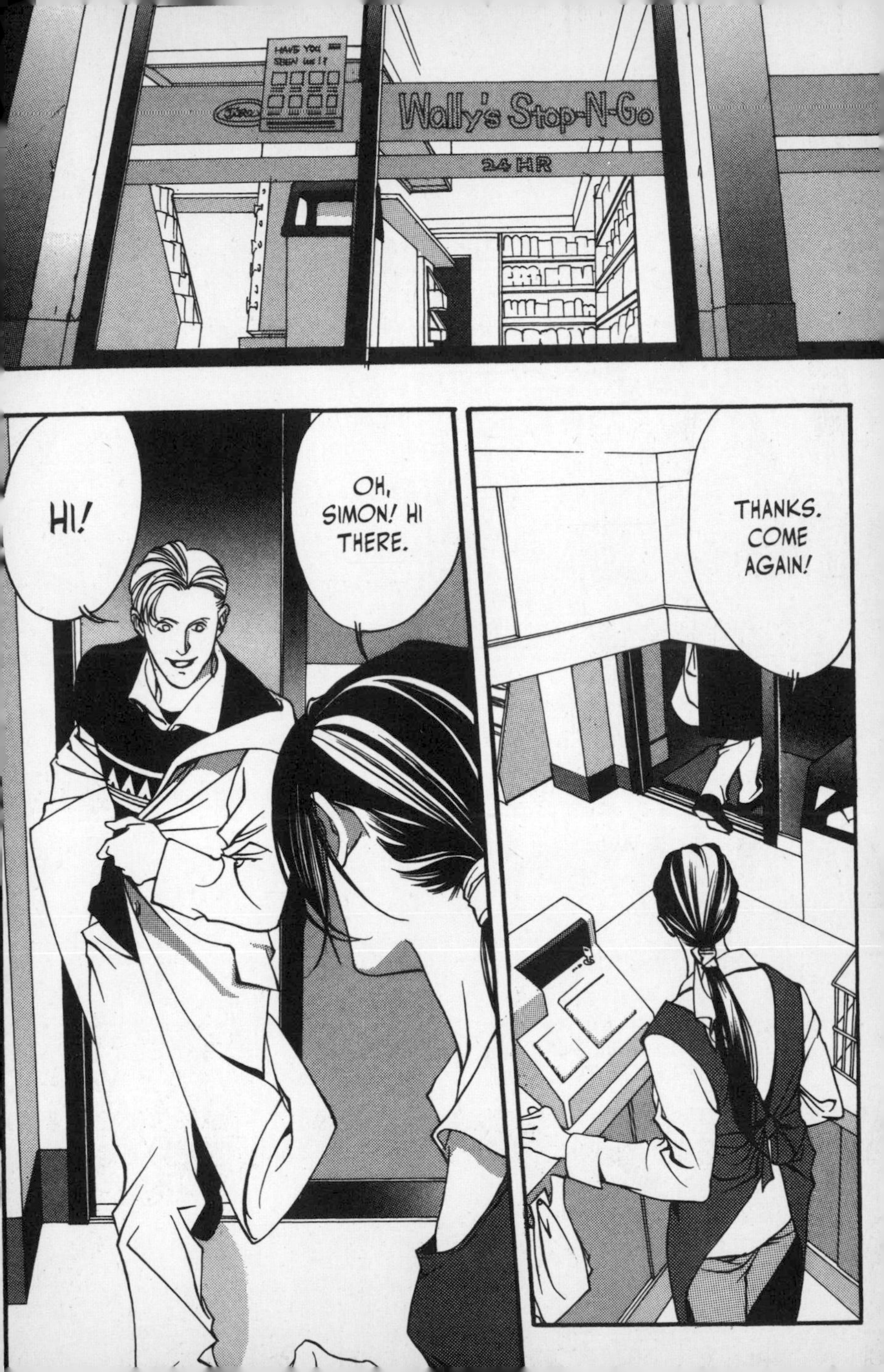
Wally's Stop-N-Go
24 HR
THANKS. COME AGAIN!
OH, SIMON! HI THERE.
HI!

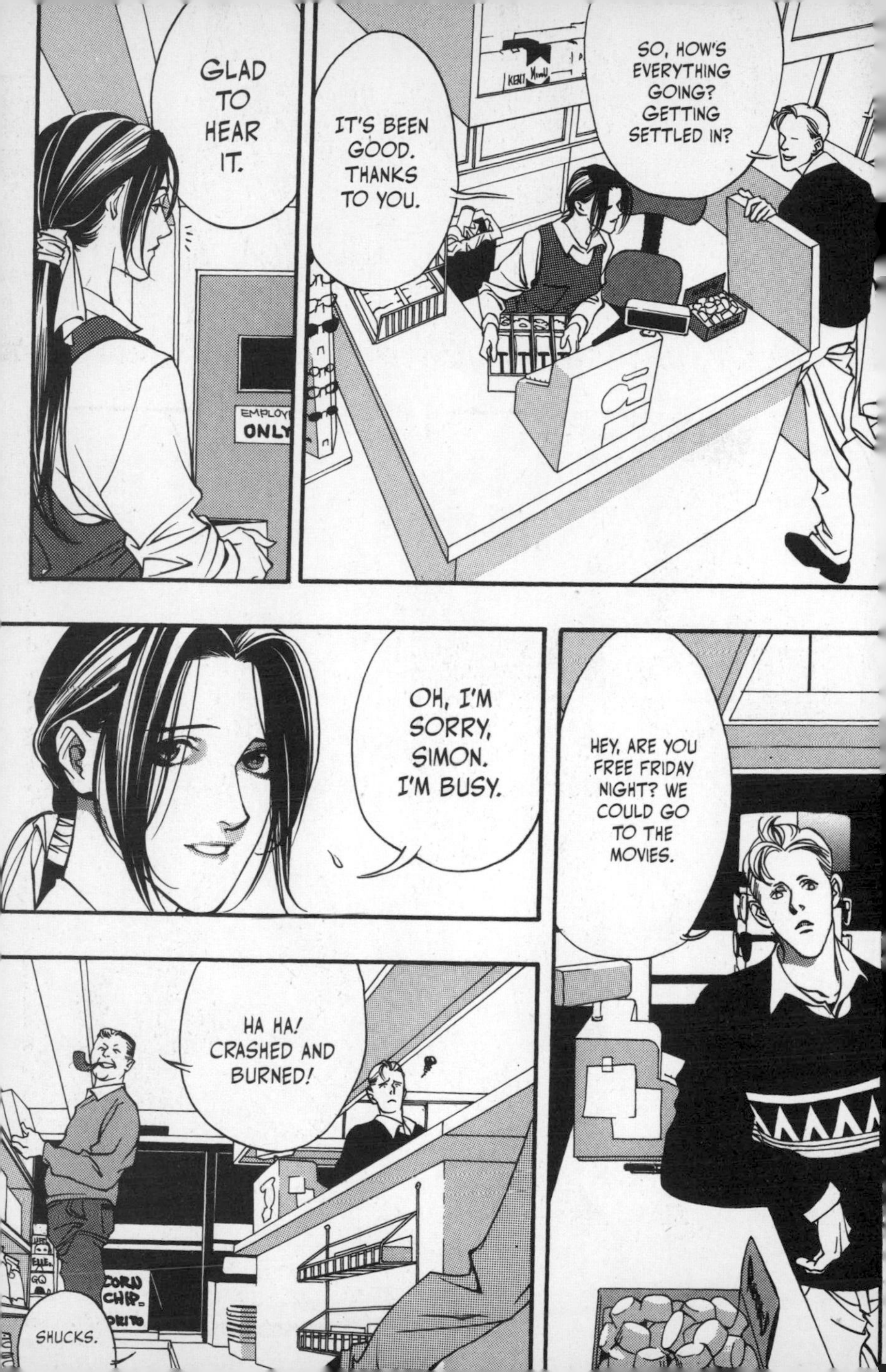
SO, HOW'S EVERYTHING GOING? GETTING SETTLED IN?
IT'S BEEN GOOD. THANKS TO YOU.
GLAD TO HEAR IT.
HEY, ARE YOU FREE FRIDAY NIGHT? WE COULD GO TO THE MOVIES.
OH, I'M SORRY, SIMON. I'M BUSY.
HA HA! CRASHED AND BURNED!
SHUCKS.

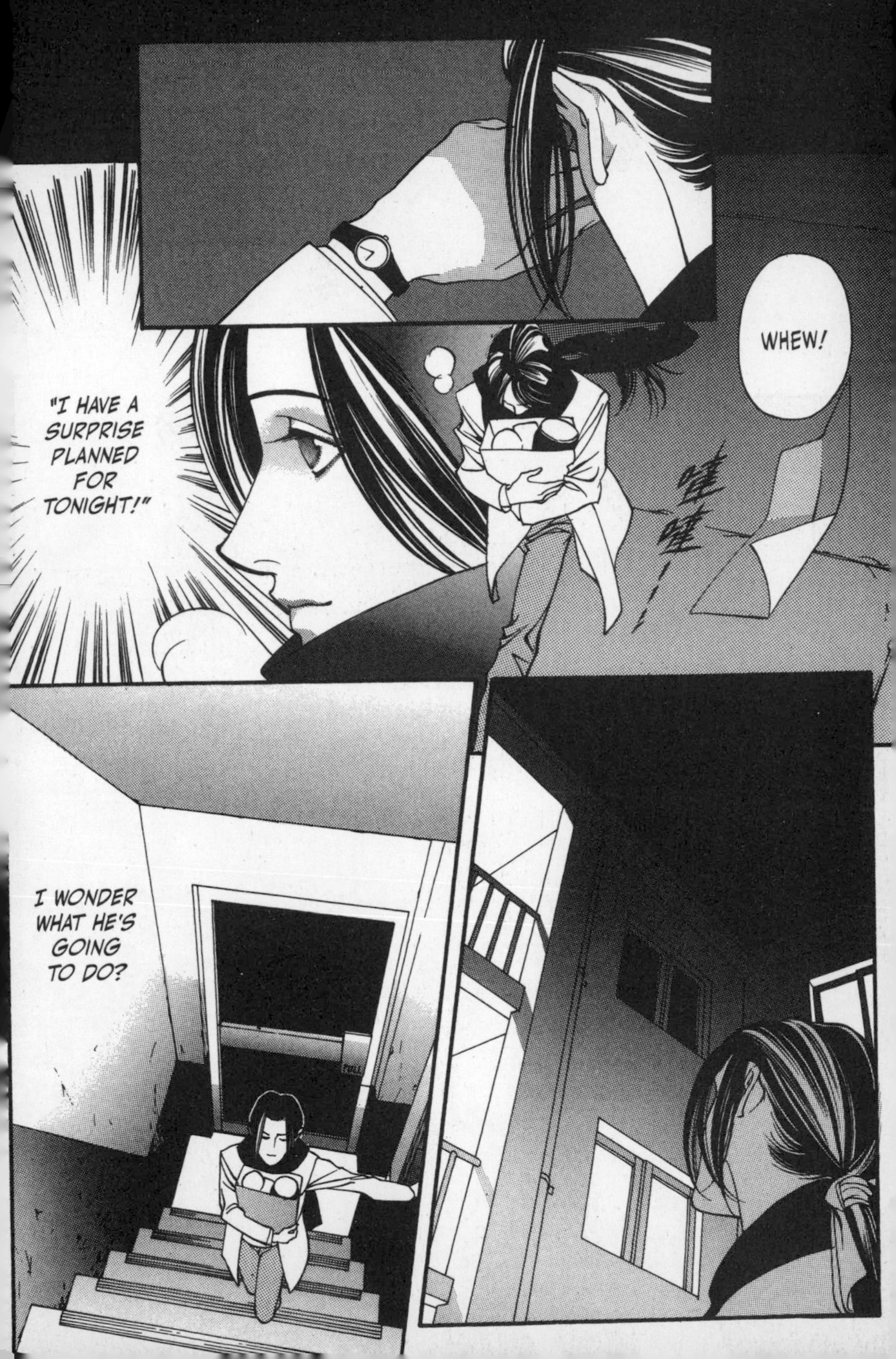
WHEW!
"I HAVE A SURPRISE PLANNED FOR TONIGHT!"
I WONDER WHAT HE'S GOING TO DO?

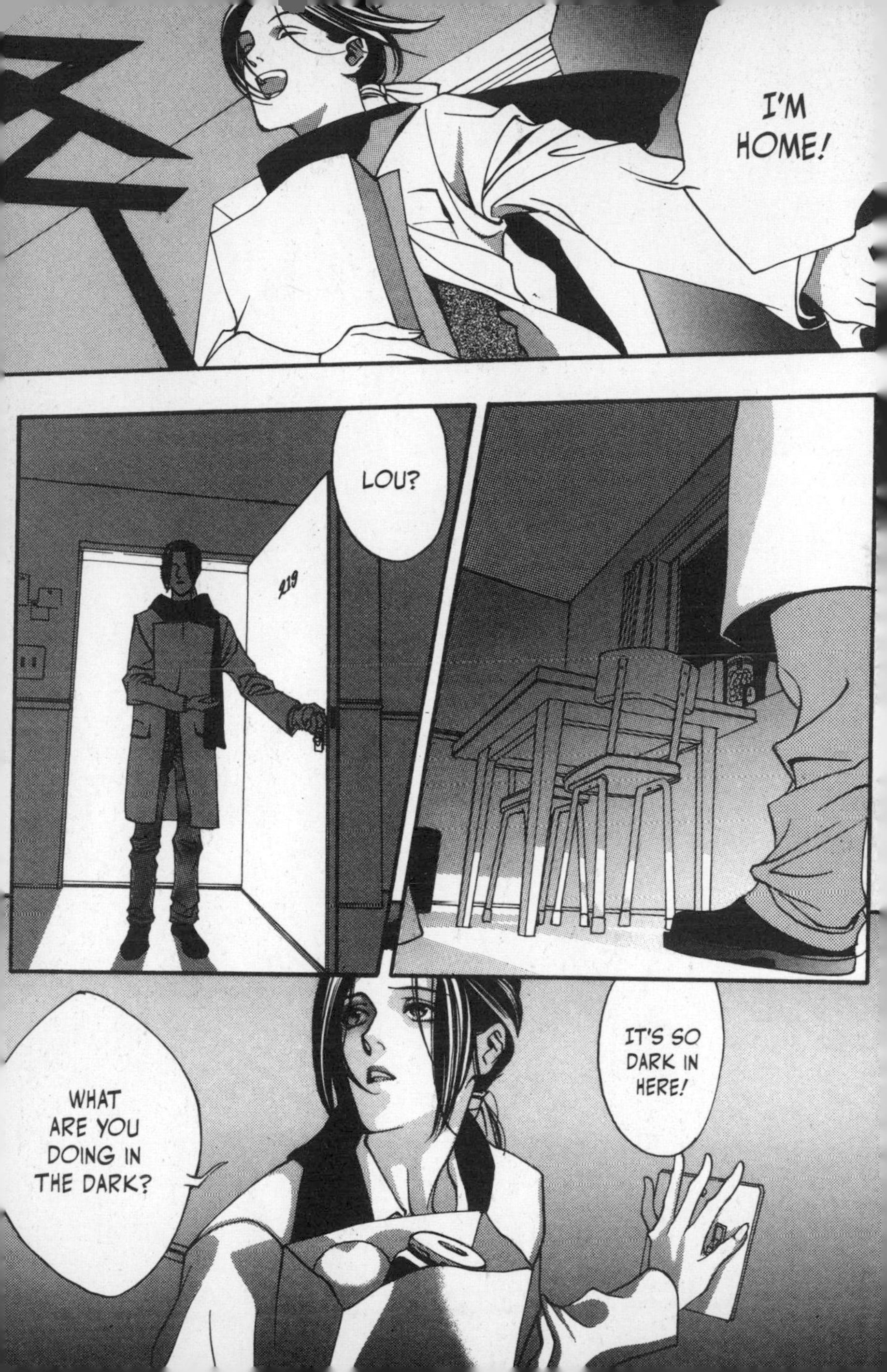
I'M HOME!
LOU?
219
IT'S SO DARK IN HERE!
WHAT ARE YOU DOING IN THE DARK?

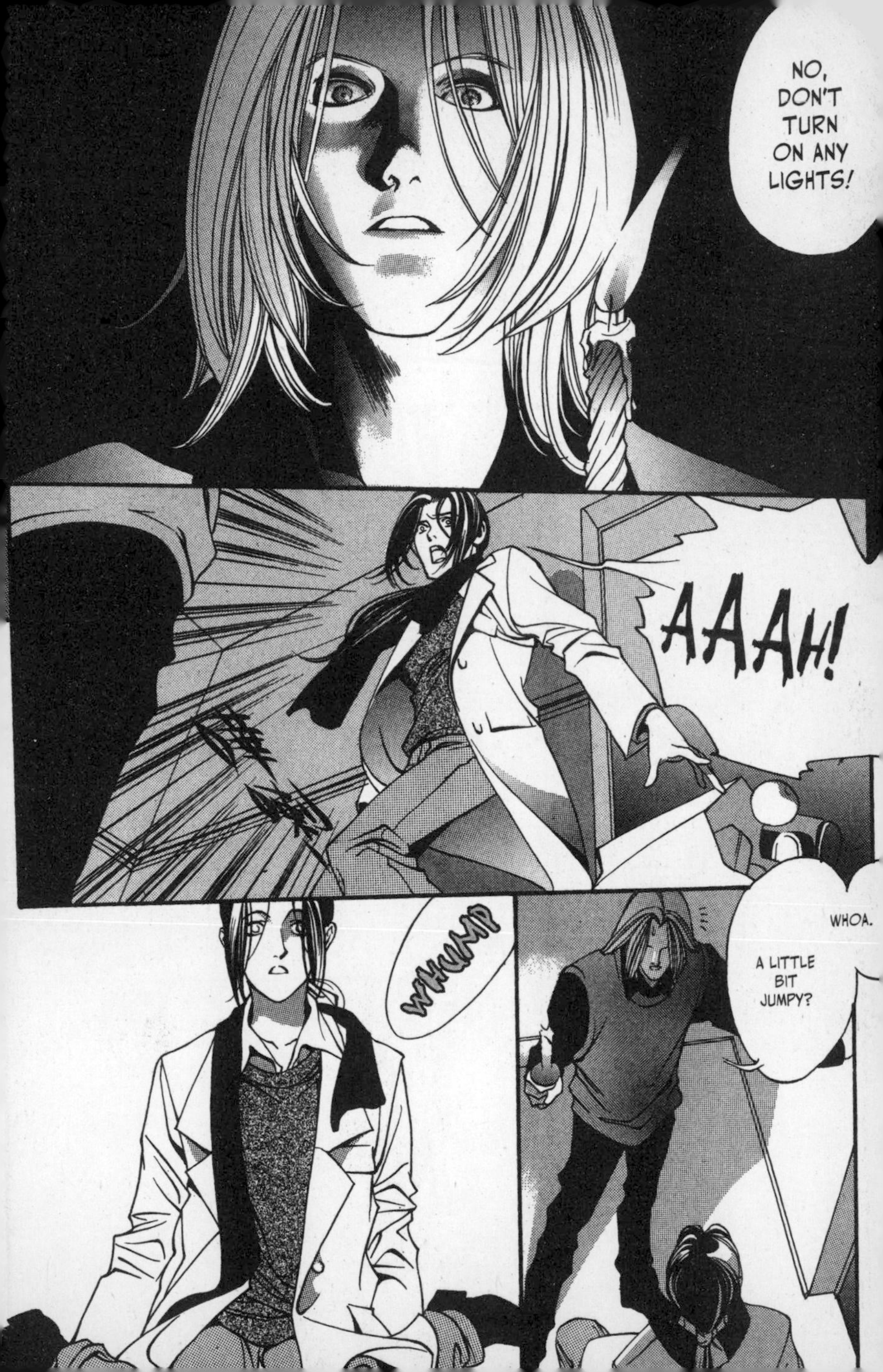
NO, DON'T TURN ON ANY LIGHTS!
AAAH!
WHOA.
A LITTLE BIT JUMPY?
WHUMP

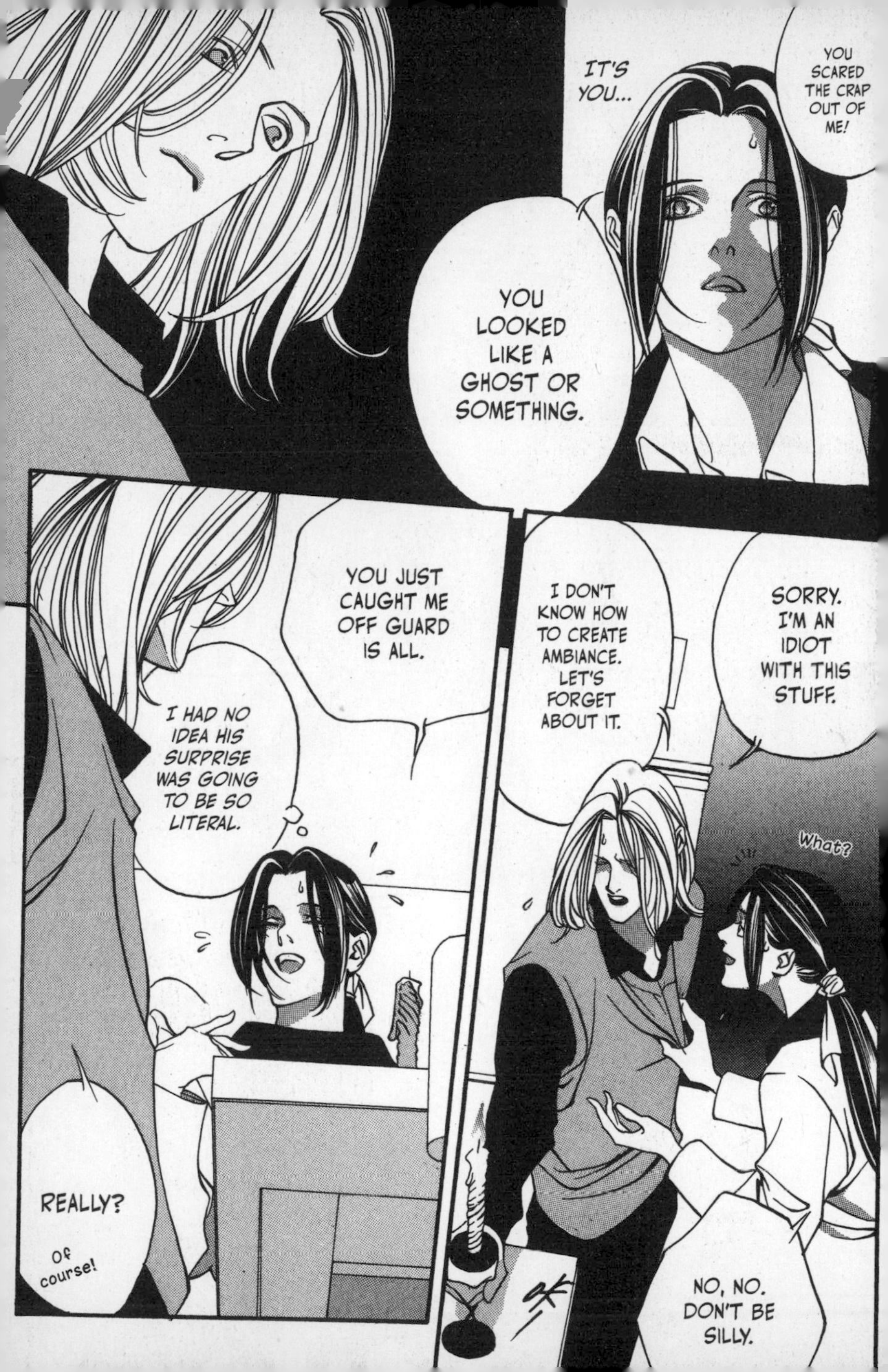
YOU SCARED THE CRAP OUT OF ME!
IT'S YOU...
YOU LOOKED LIKE A GHOST OR SOMETHING.
SORRY. I'M AN IDIOT WITH THIS STUFF.
I DON'T KNOW HOW TO CREATE AMBIANCE. LET'S FORGET ABOUT IT.
What?
NO, NO. DON'T BE SILLY.
YOU JUST CAUGHT ME OFF GUARD IS ALL.
I HAD NO IDEA HIS SURPRISE WAS GOING TO BE SO LITERAL.
REALLY?
Of course!

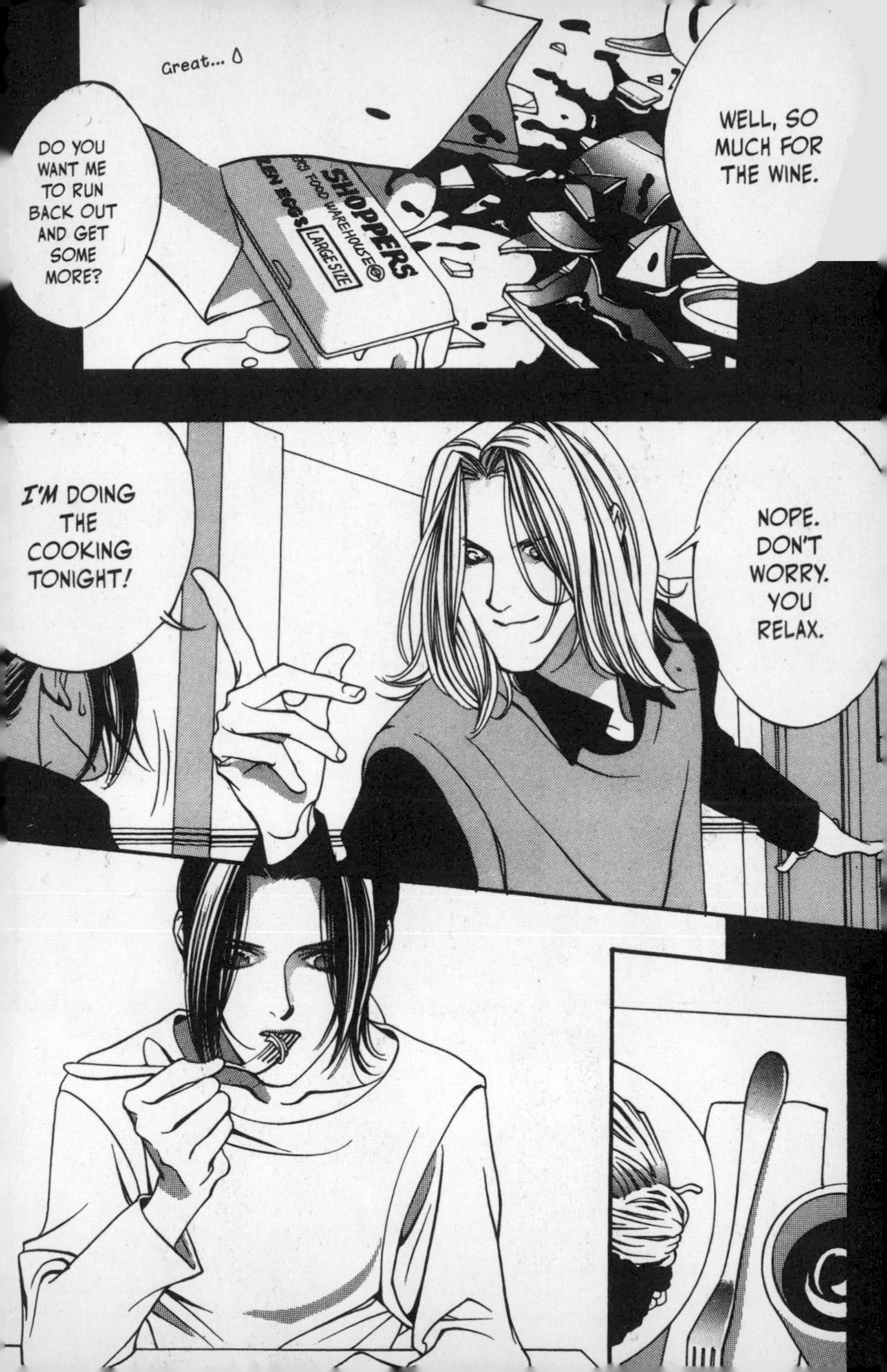
WELL, SO MUCH FOR THE WINE.
Great...
SHOPPERS
FOOD WAREHOUSE
LARGE SIZE
DO YOU WANT ME TO RUN BACK OUT AND GET SOME MORE?
NOPE. DON'T WORRY. YOU RELAX.
I'M DOING THE COOKING TONIGHT!

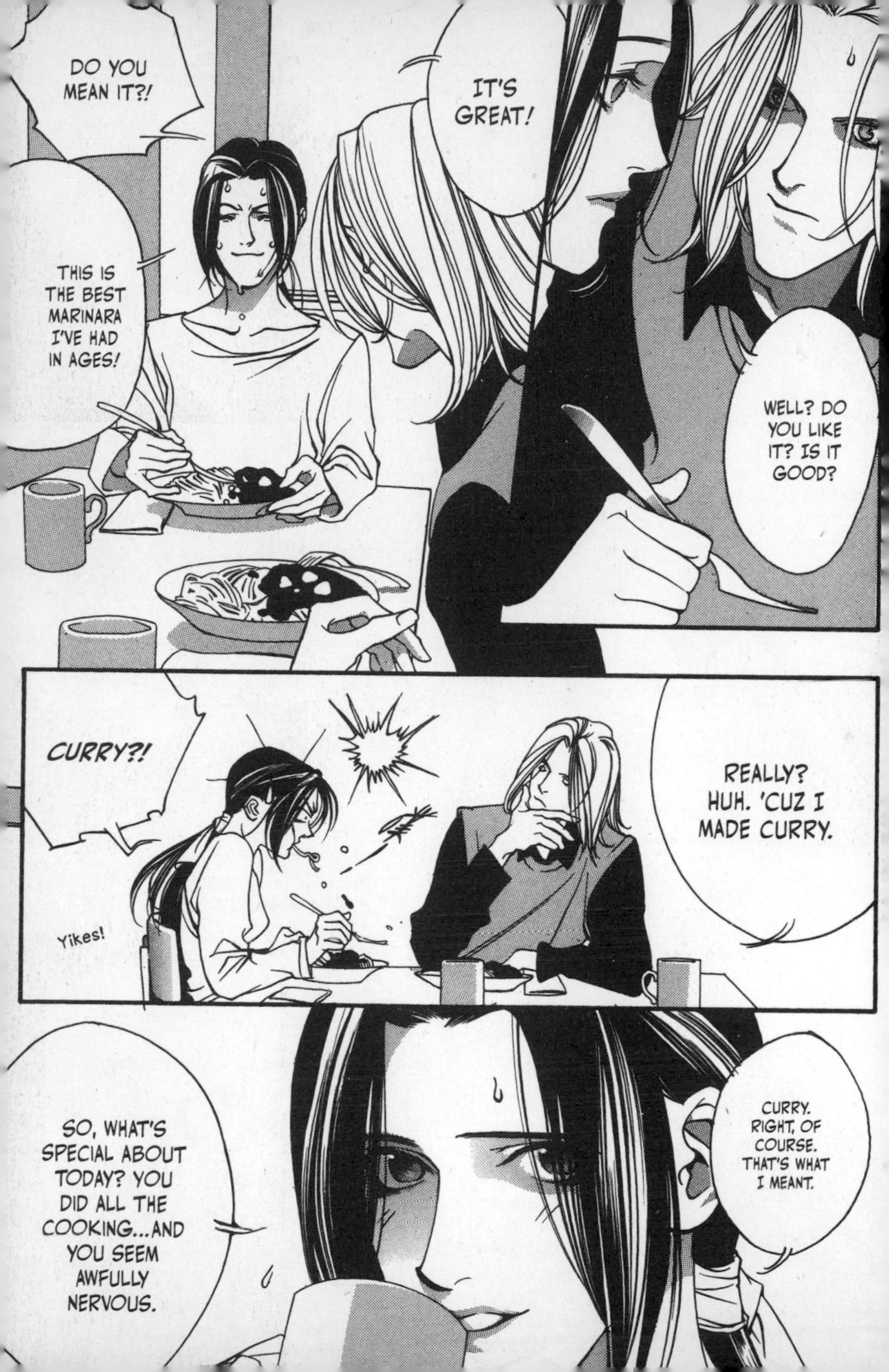
WELL? DO YOU LIKE IT? IS IT GOOD?
IT'S GREAT!
THIS IS THE BEST MARINARA I'VE HAD IN AGES!
DO YOU MEAN IT?!
REALLY? HUH. 'CUZ I MADE CURRY.
CURRY?!
Yikes!
CURRY. RIGHT, OF COURSE. THAT'S WHAT I MEANT.
SO, WHAT'S SPECIAL ABOUT TODAY? YOU DID ALL THE COOKING...AND YOU SEEM AWFULLY NERVOUS.

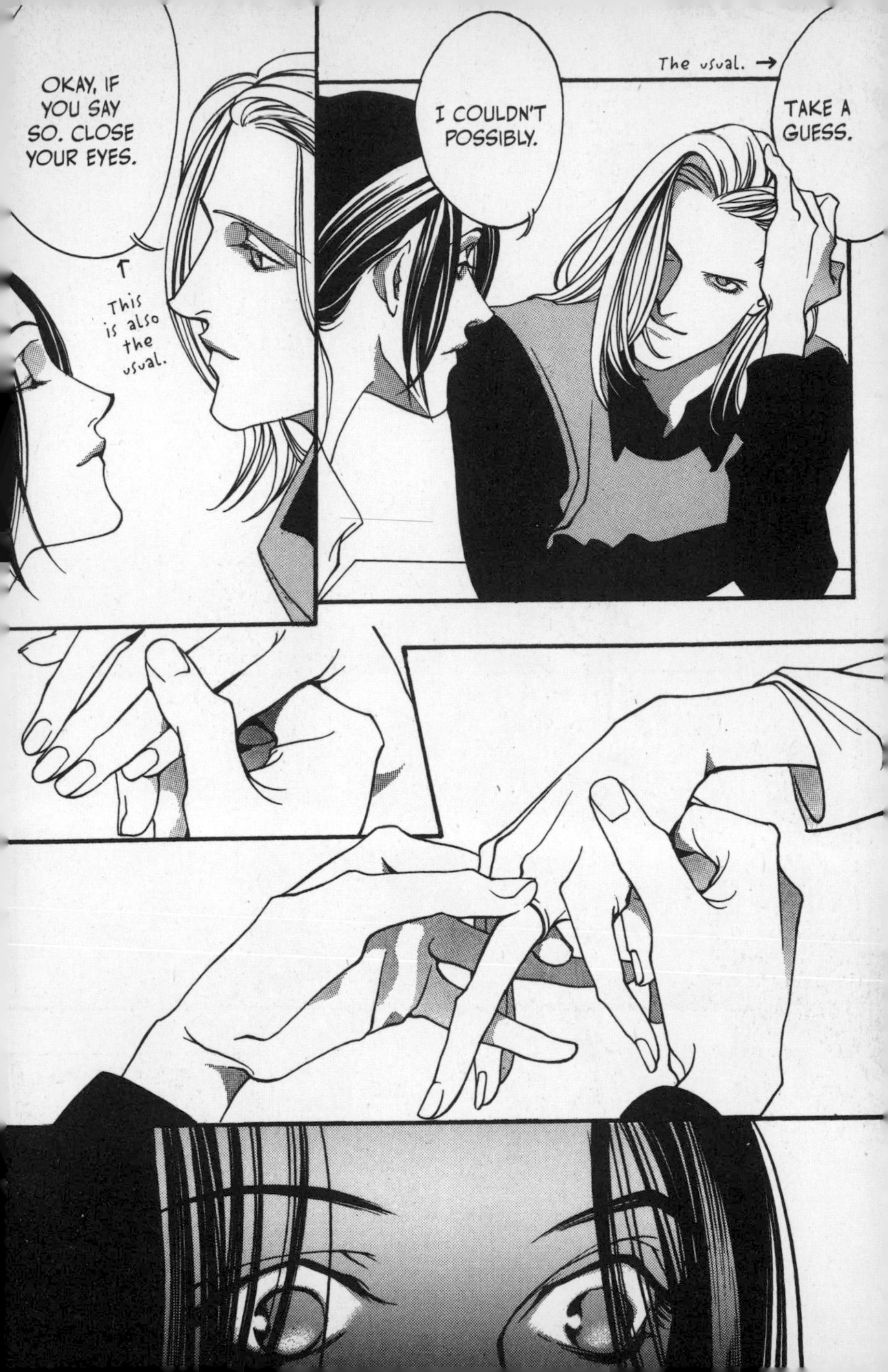

TAKE A GUESS.
The usual. →
I COULDN'T POSSIBLY.
OKAY, IF YOU SAY SO. CLOSE YOUR EYES.
↑ This is also the usual.

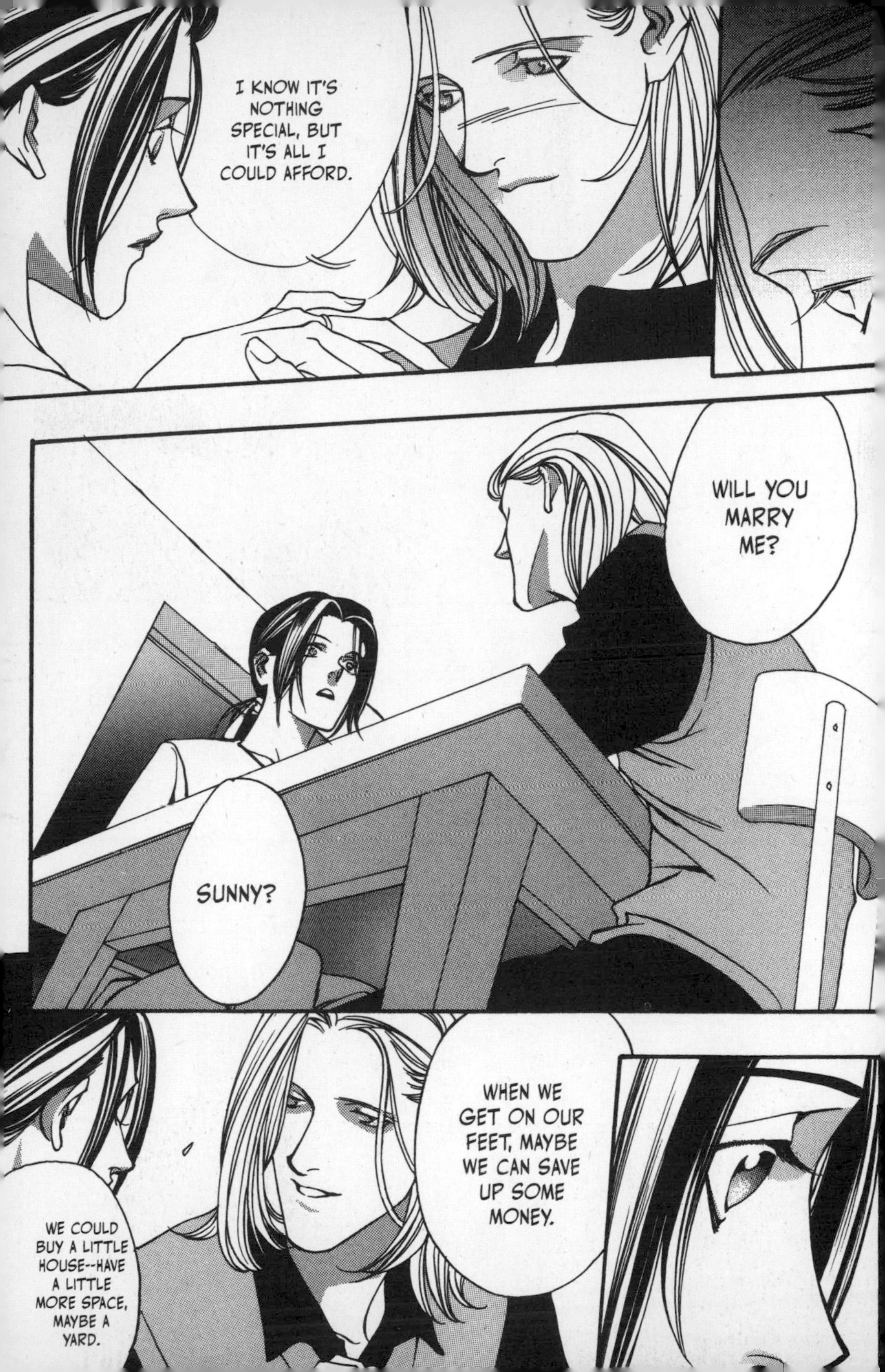
I KNOW IT'S NOTHING SPECIAL, BUT IT'S ALL I COULD AFFORD.
WILL YOU MARRY ME?
SUNNY?
WHEN WE GET ON OUR FEET, MAYBE WE CAN SAVE UP SOME MONEY.
WE COULD BUY A LITTLE HOUSE--HAVE A LITTLE MORE SPACE, MAYBE A YARD.

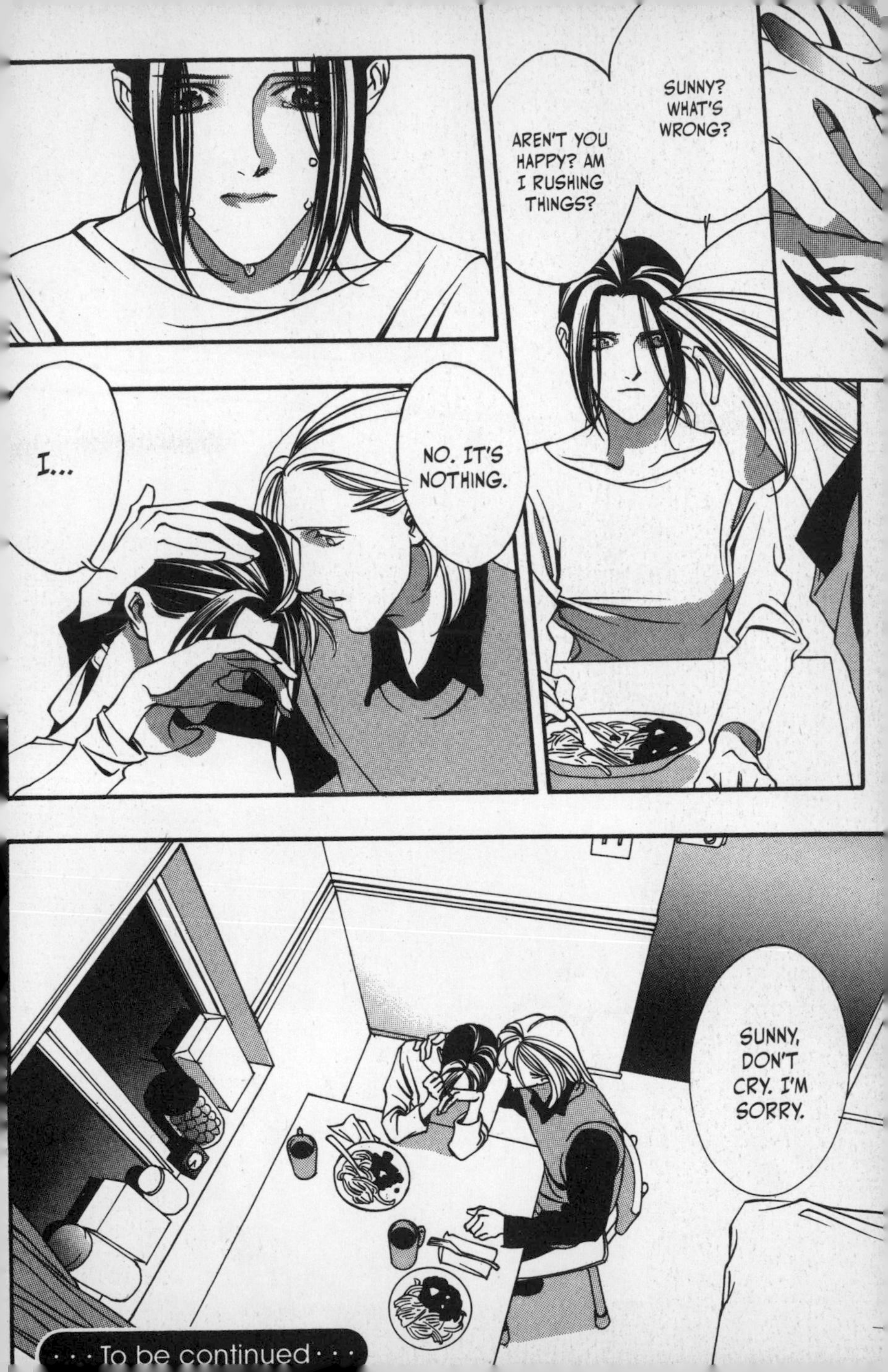
SUNNY? WHAT'S WRONG?
AREN'T YOU HAPPY? AM I RUSHING THINGS?
NO. IT'S NOTHING.
I...
SUNNY, DON'T CRY. I'M SORRY.
· · · To be continued · · ·

Ninety - nine Roses

99 Roses

HE WAS ALWAYS THERE, LINGERING FOR JUST A MOMENT, UNDER THE BALCONY.

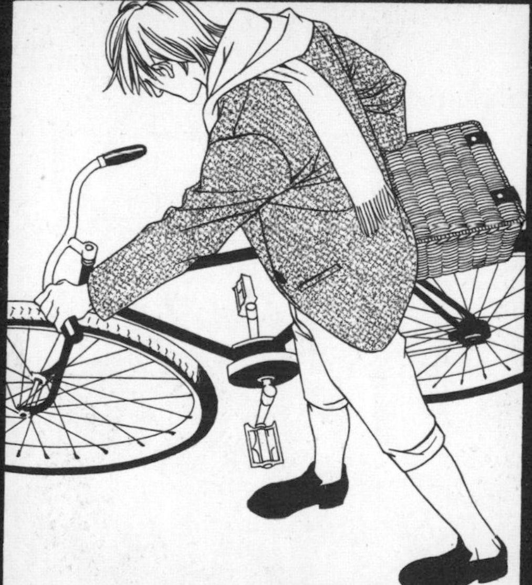

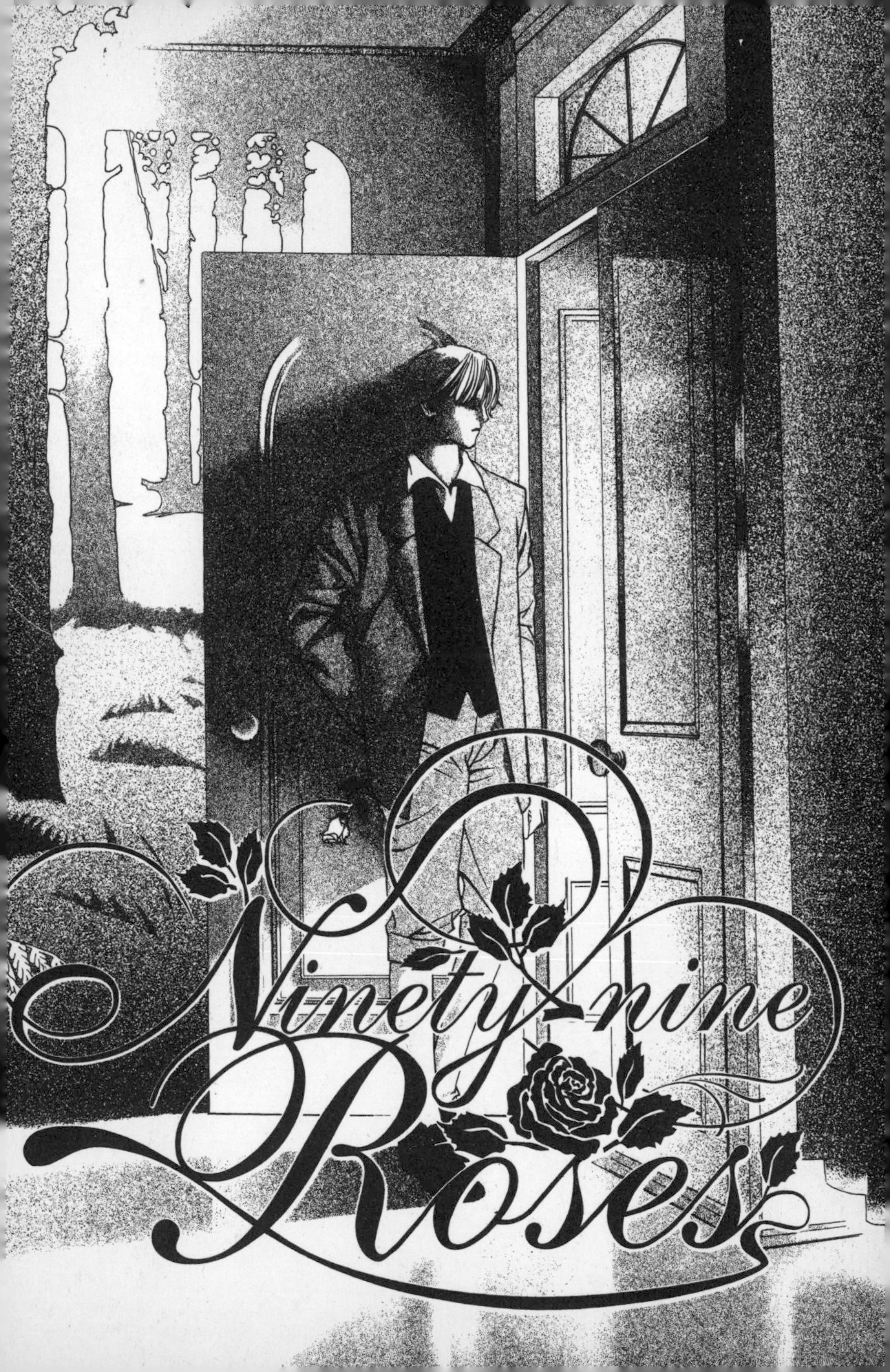
Ninety-nine Roses

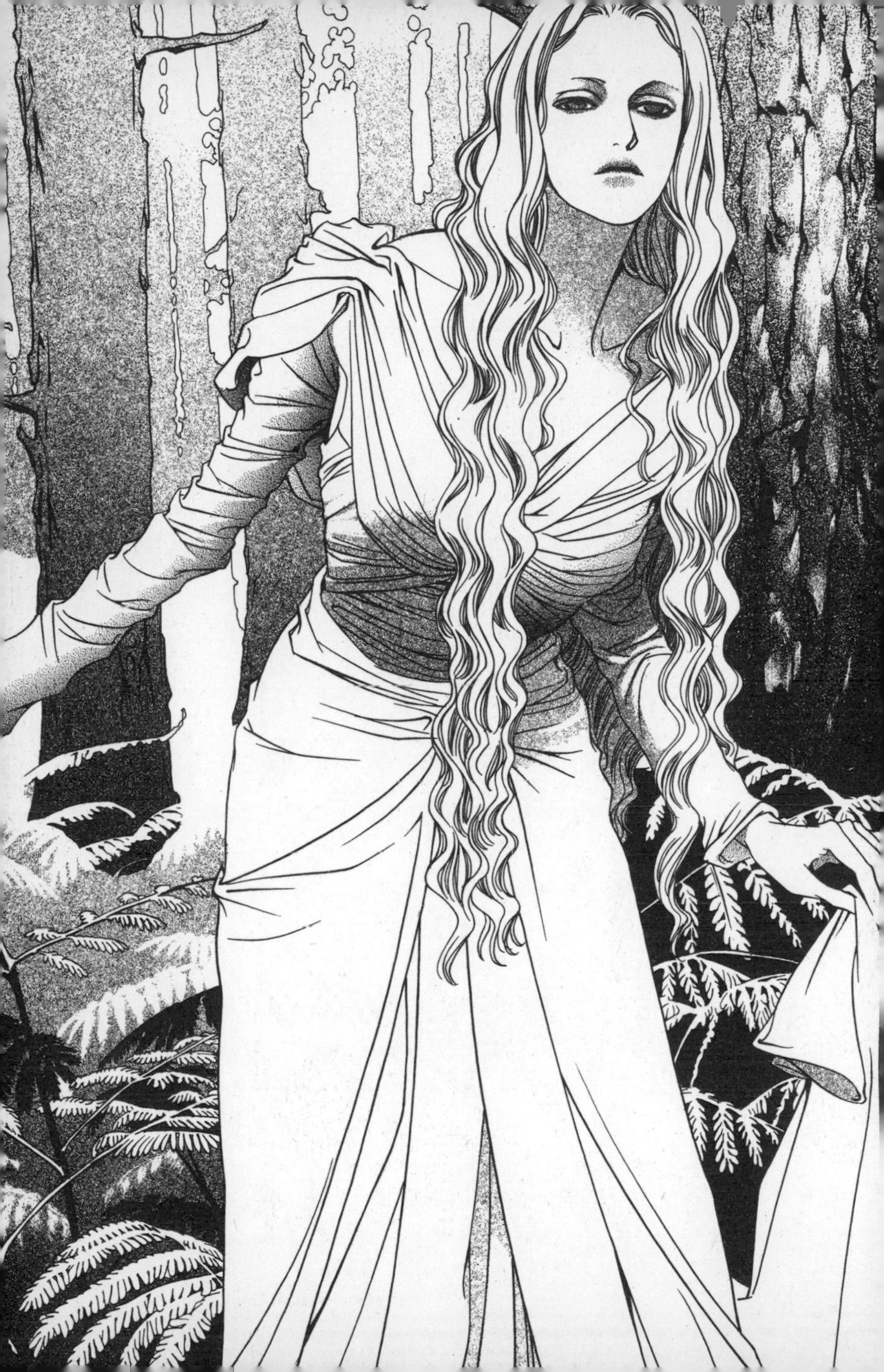

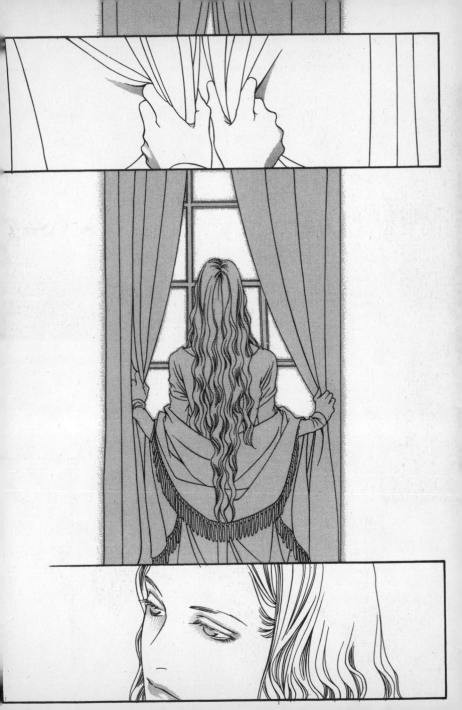

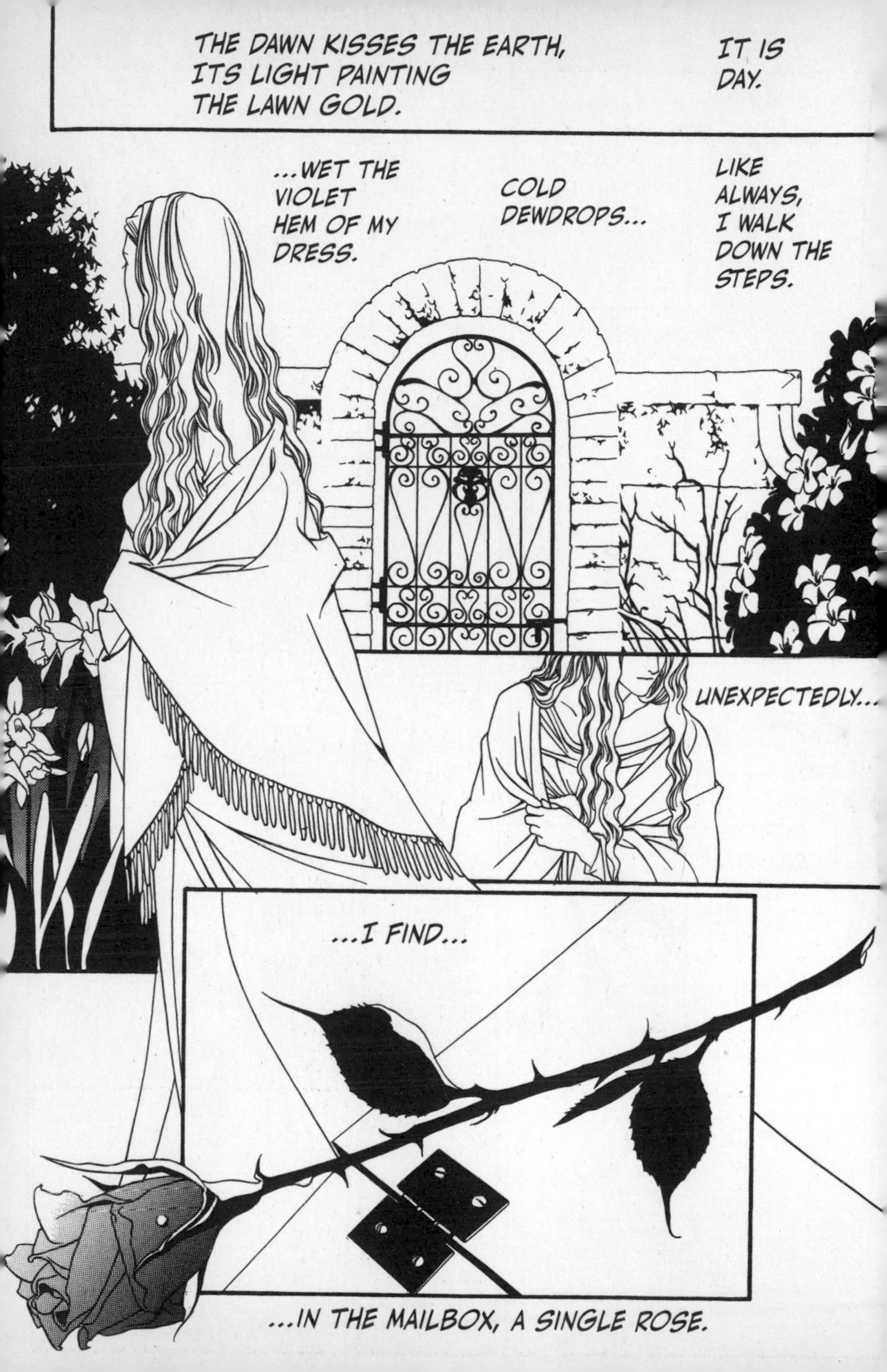
IT IS DAY.
THE DAWN KISSES THE EARTH, ITS LIGHT PAINTING THE LAWN GOLD.
LIKE ALWAYS, I WALK DOWN THE STEPS.
COLD DEWDROPS...
...WET THE VIOLET HEM OF MY DRESS.
UNEXPECTEDLY...
...I FIND...
...IN THE MAILBOX, A SINGLE ROSE.

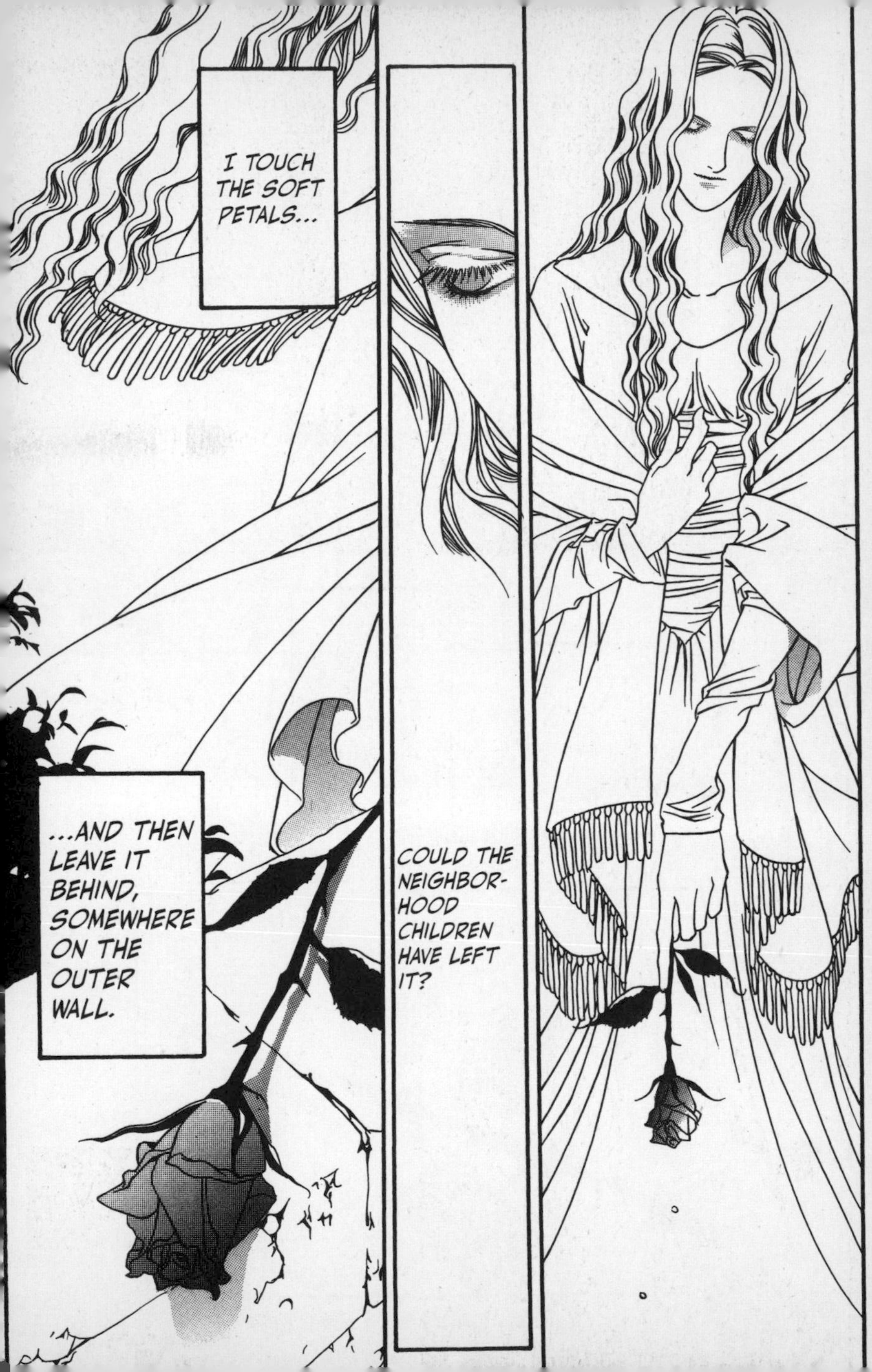
COULD THE NEIGHBORHOOD CHILDREN HAVE LEFT IT?
I TOUCH THE SOFT PETALS...
...AND THEN LEAVE IT BEHIND, SOMEWHERE ON THE OUTER WALL.

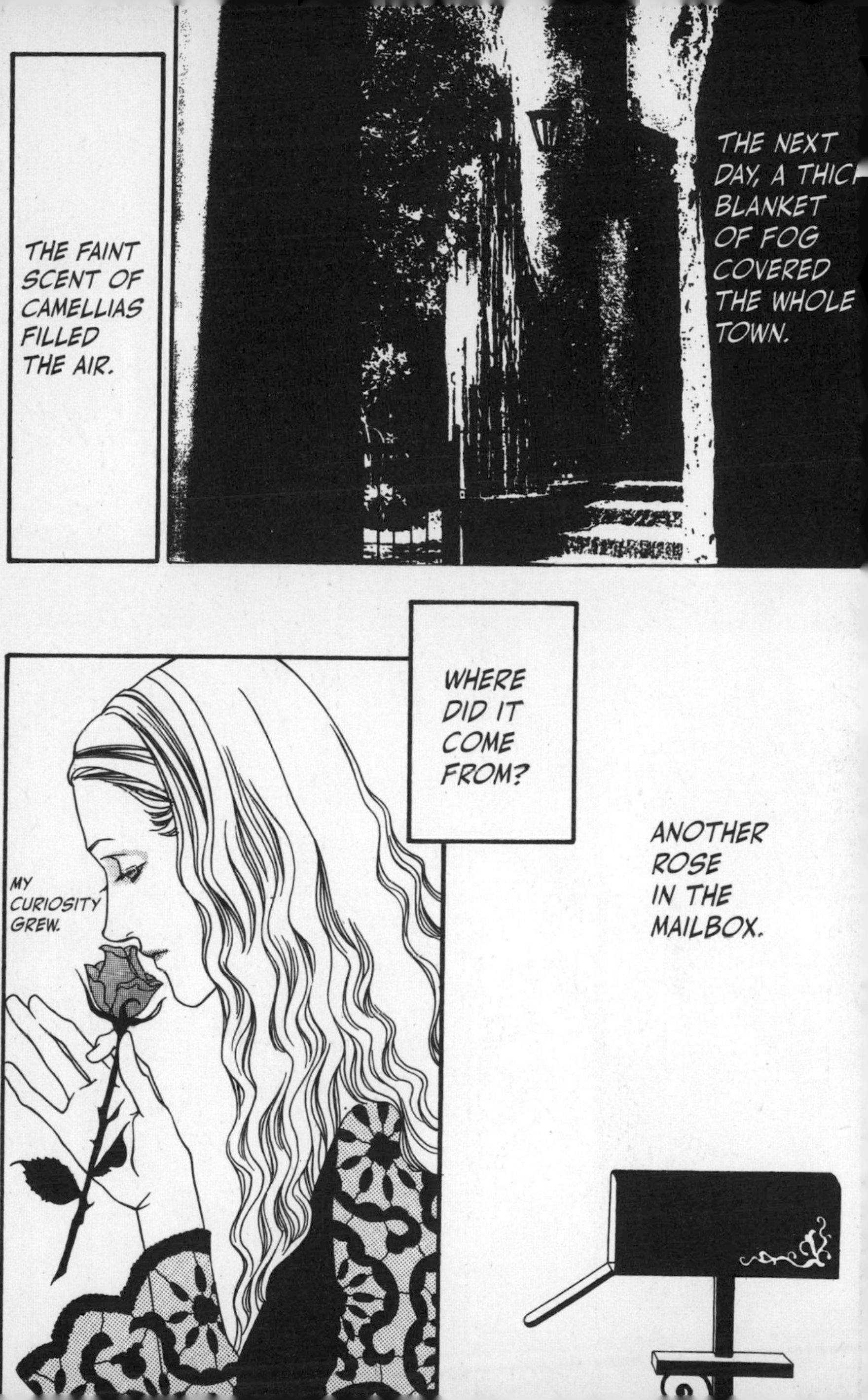
THE NEXT DAY, A THIC BLANKET OF FOG COVERED THE WHOLE TOWN.
THE FAINT SCENT OF CAMELLIAS FILLED THE AIR.
ANOTHER ROSE IN THE MAILBOX.
WHERE DID IT COME FROM?
MY CURIOSITY GREW.

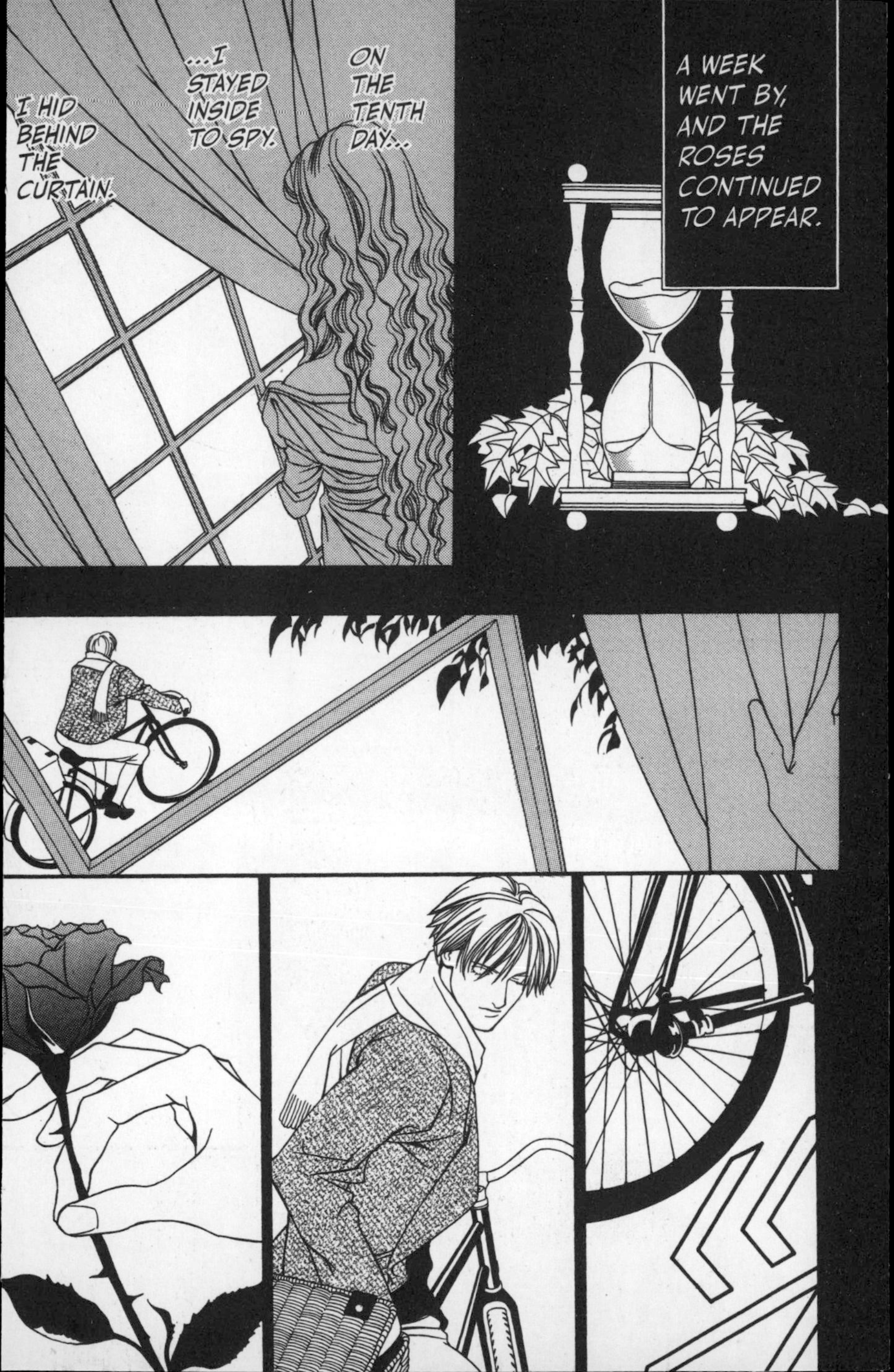
A WEEK WENT BY, AND THE ROSES CONTINUED TO APPEAR.
ON THE TENTH DAY...
...I STAYED INSIDE TO SPY.
I HID BEHIND THE CURTAIN.

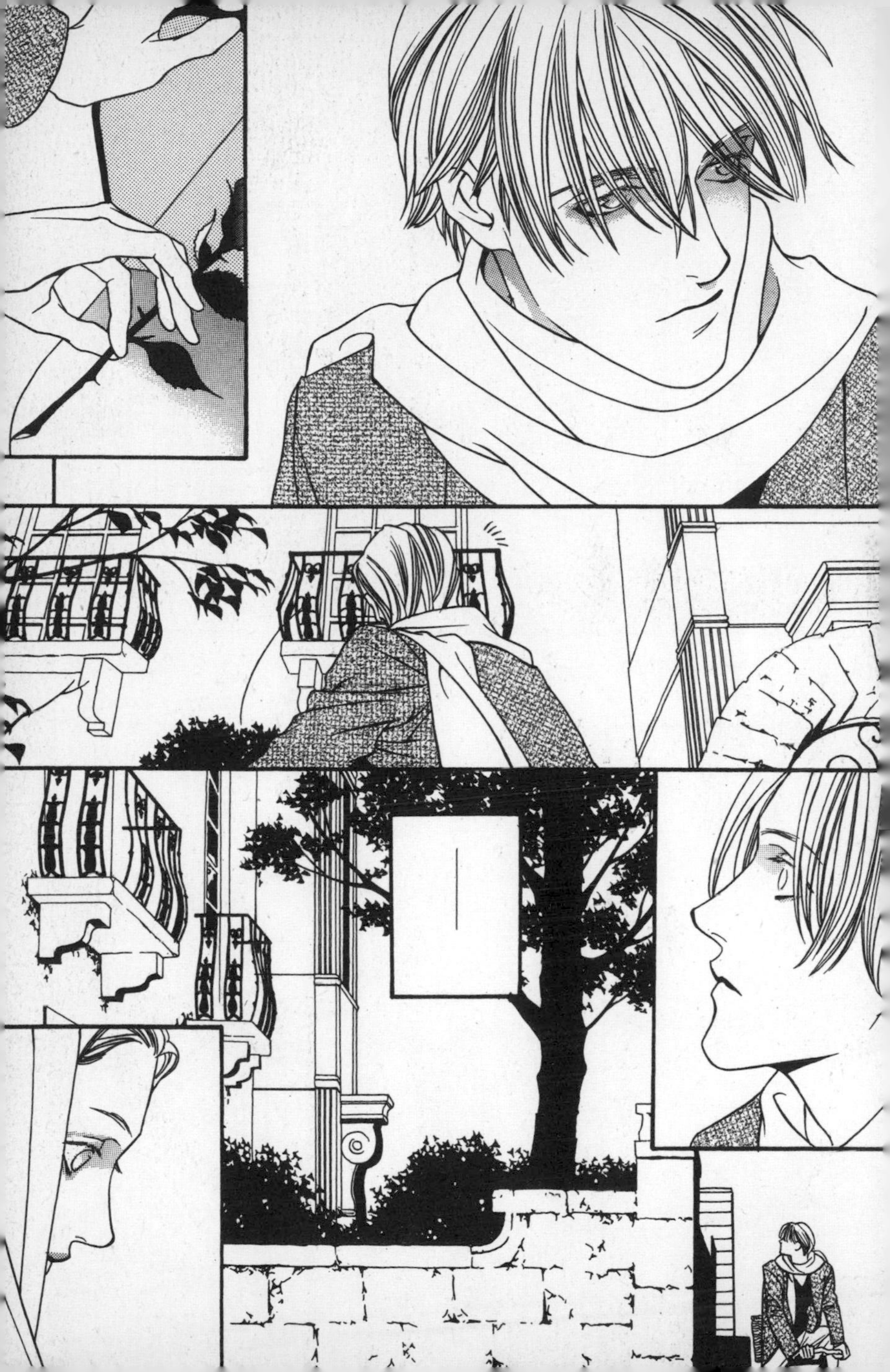

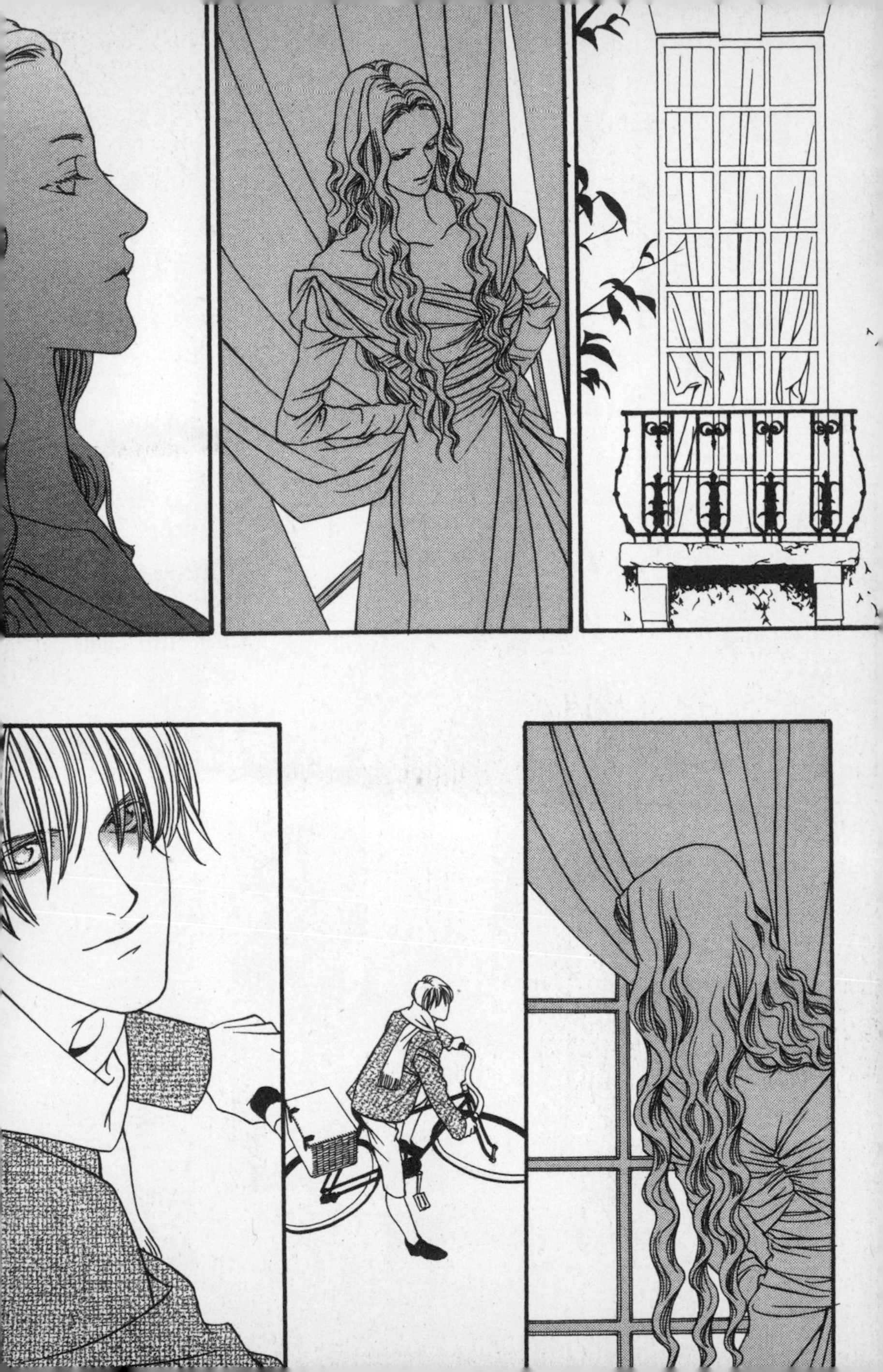

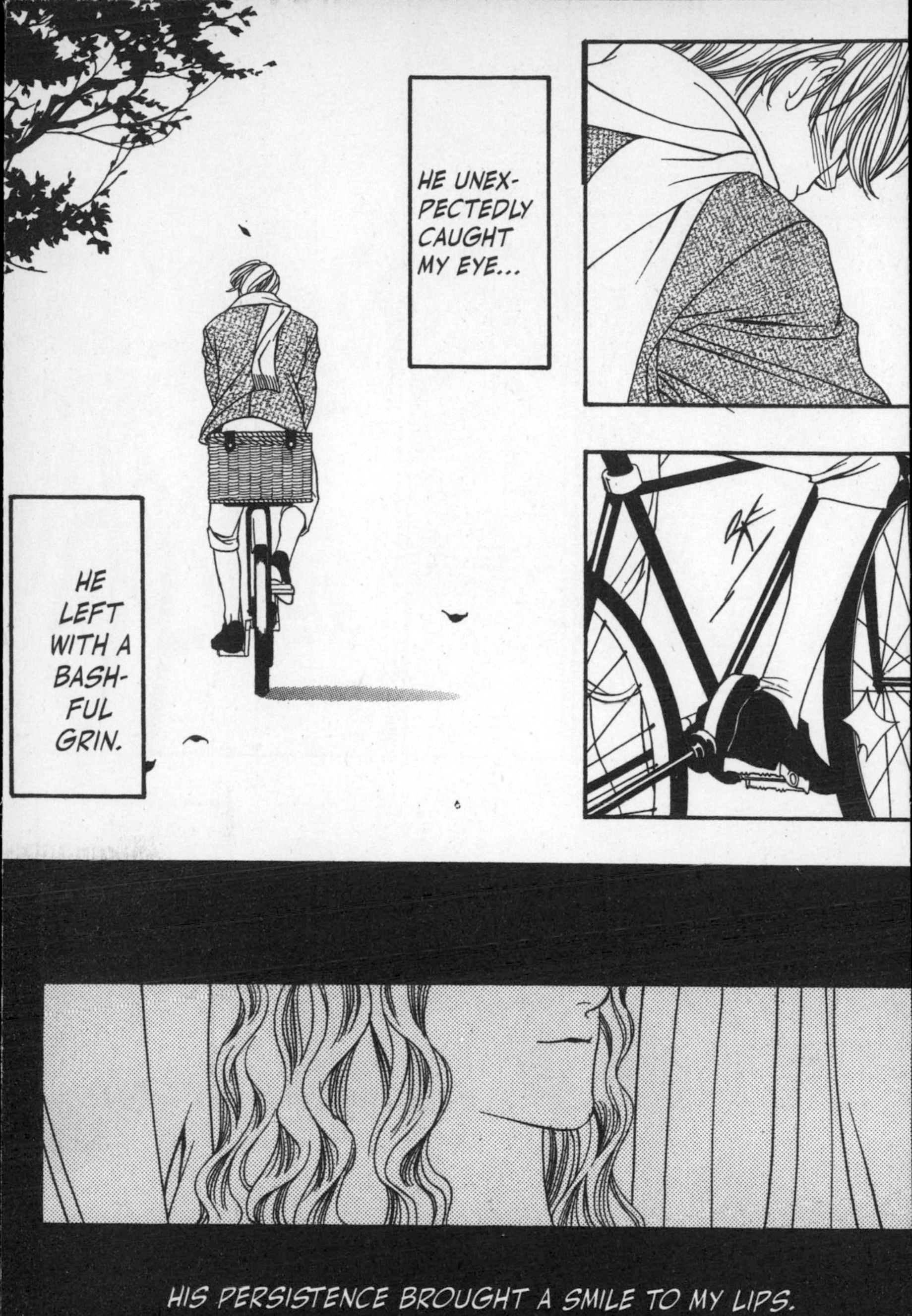
HE UNEXPECTEDLY CAUGHT MY EYE...
HE LEFT WITH A BASHFUL GRIN.
HIS PERSISTENCE BROUGHT A SMILE TO MY LIPS.

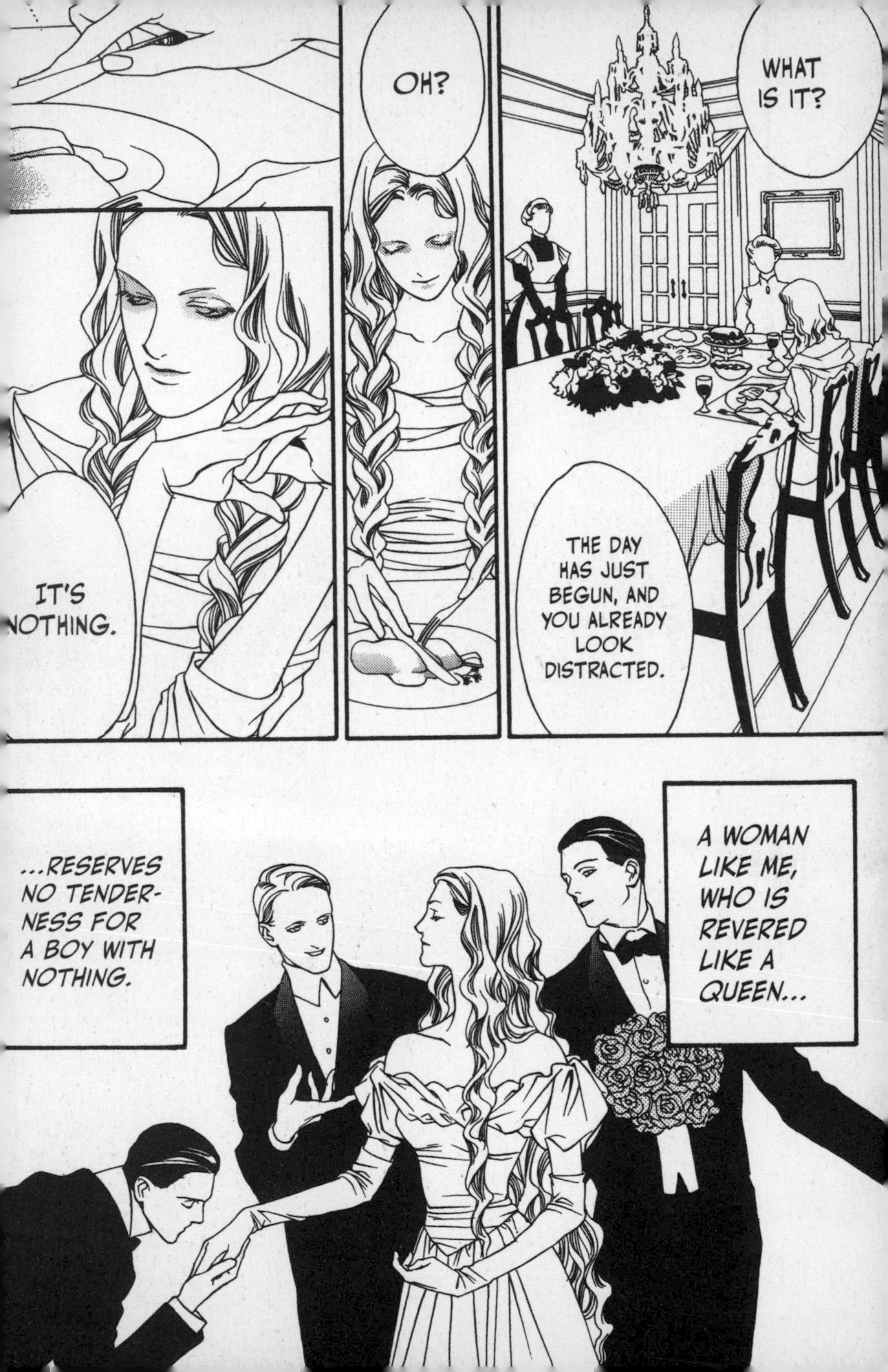
WHAT IS IT?
THE DAY HAS JUST BEGUN, AND YOU ALREADY LOOK DISTRACTED.
OH?
IT'S NOTHING.
A WOMAN LIKE ME, WHO IS REVERED LIKE A QUEEN...
...RESERVES NO TENDERNESS FOR A BOY WITH NOTHING.

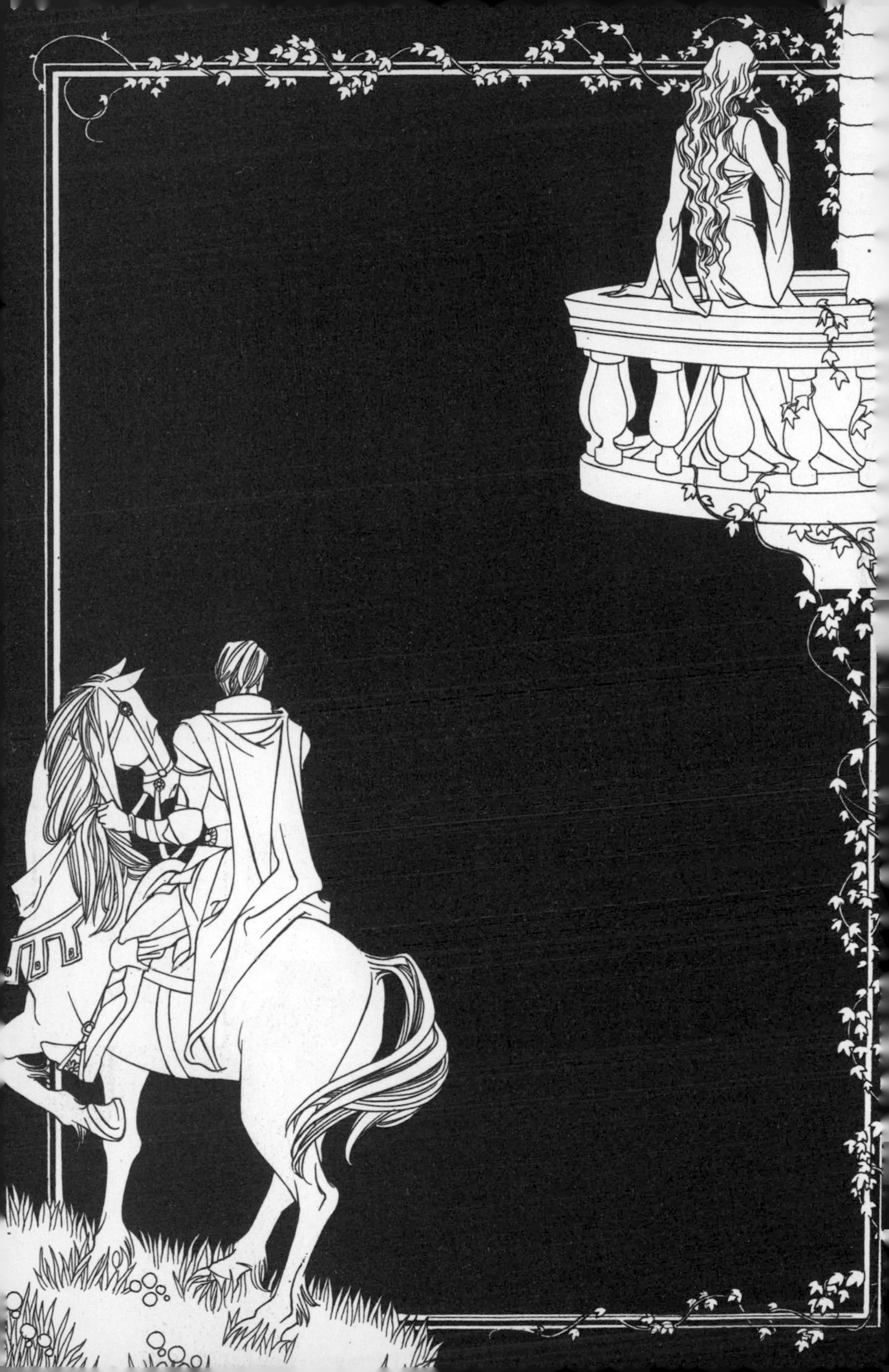

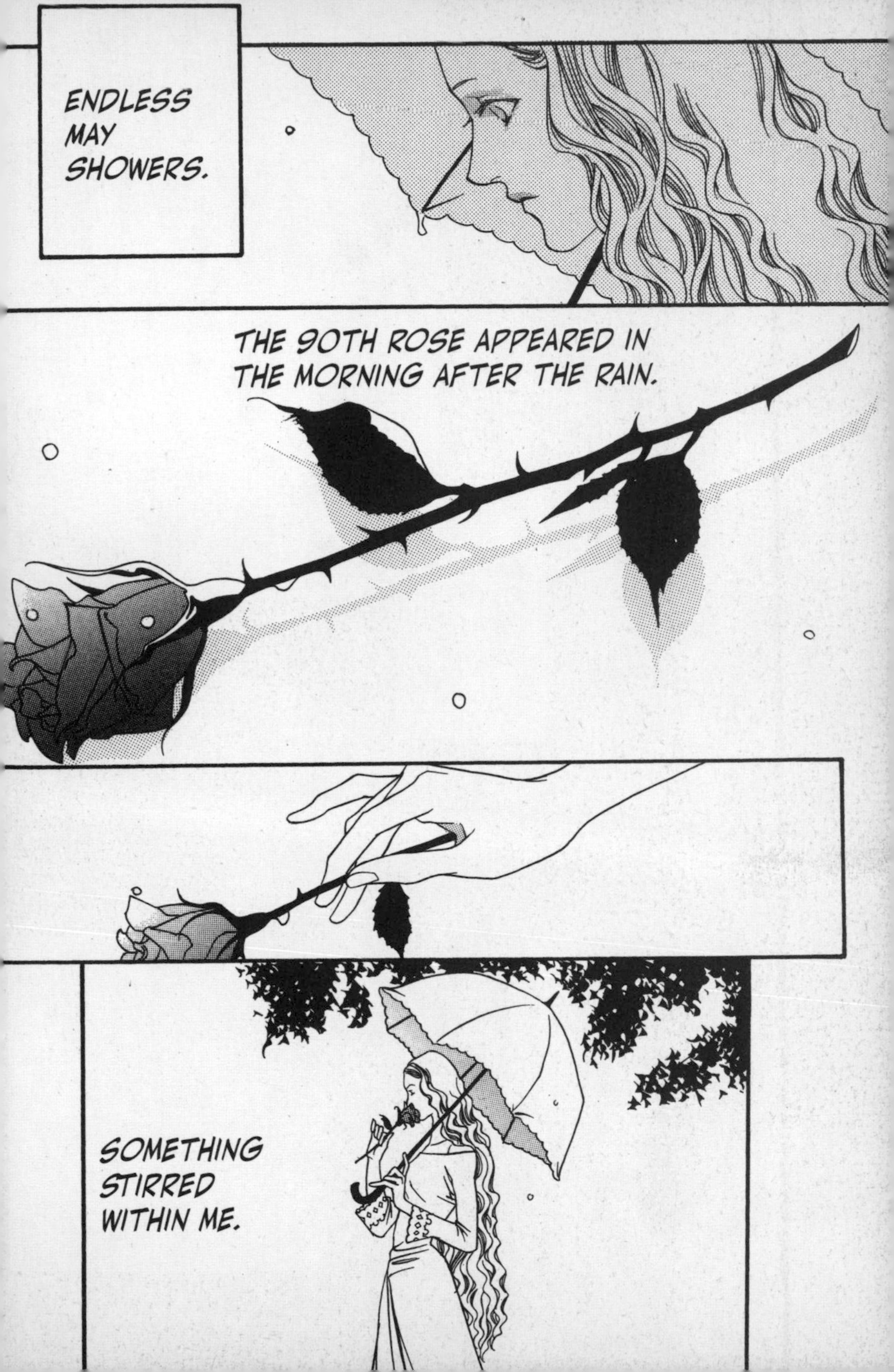
ENDLESS MAY SHOWERS.
THE 90TH ROSE APPEARED IN THE MORNING AFTER THE RAIN.
SOMETHING STIRRED WITHIN ME.

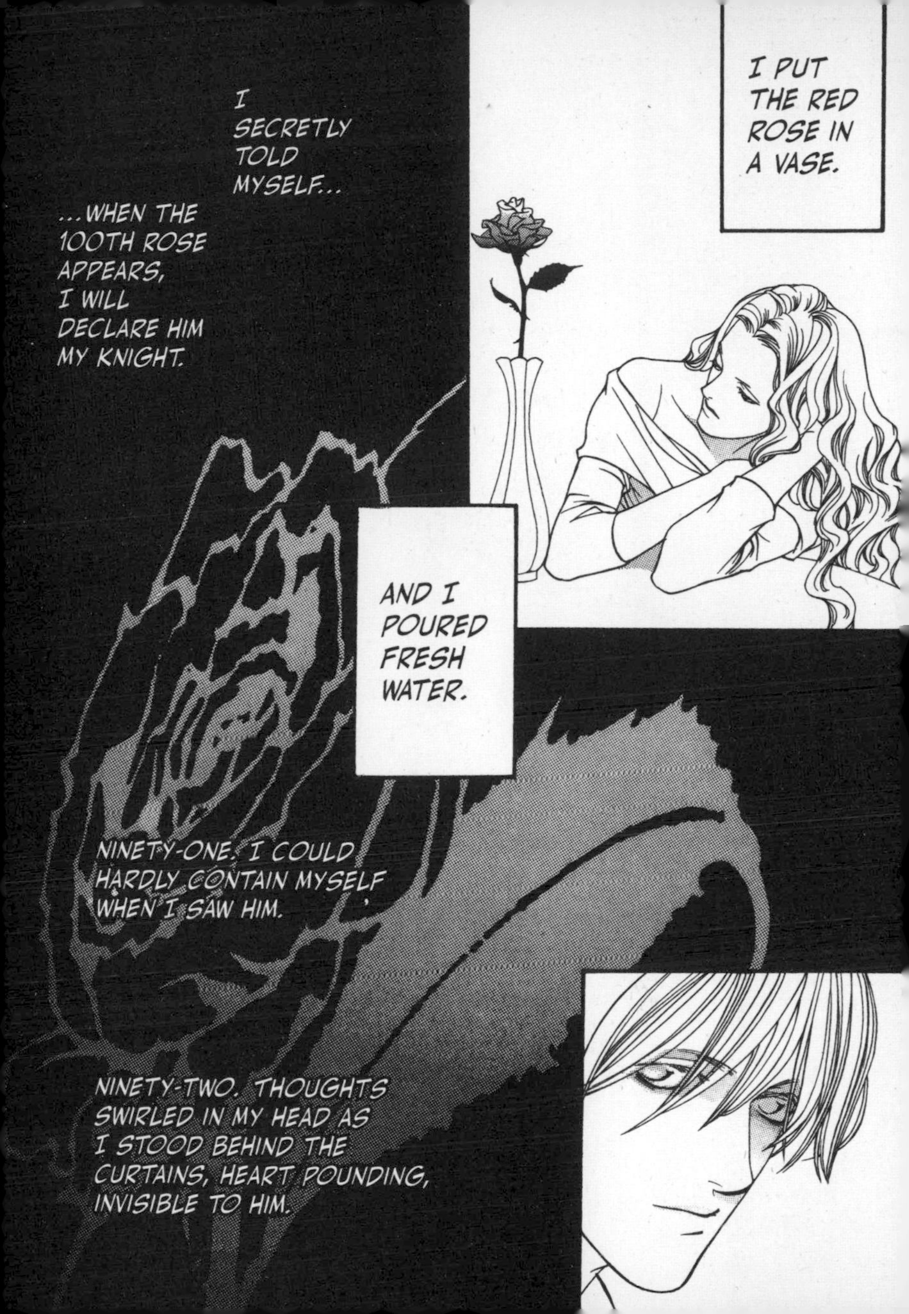
I PUT THE RED ROSE IN A VASE.
AND I POURED FRESH WATER.
I SECRETLY TOLD MYSELF...
...WHEN THE 100TH ROSE APPEARS, I WILL DECLARE HIM MY KNIGHT.
NINETY-ONE. I COULD HARDLY CONTAIN MYSELF WHEN I SAW HIM.
NINETY-TWO. THOUGHTS SWIRLED IN MY HEAD AS I STOOD BEHIND THE CURTAINS, HEART POUNDING, INVISIBLE TO HIM.

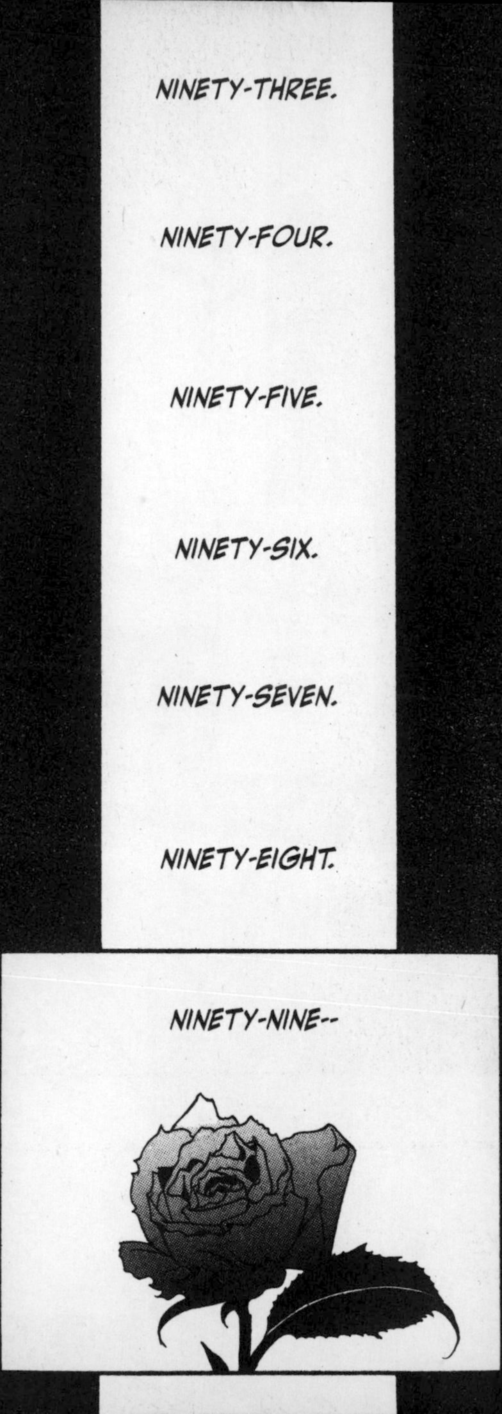
NINETY-THREE.
NINETY-FOUR.
NINETY-FIVE.
NINETY-SIX.
NINETY-SEVEN.
NINETY-EIGHT.
NINETY-NINE--

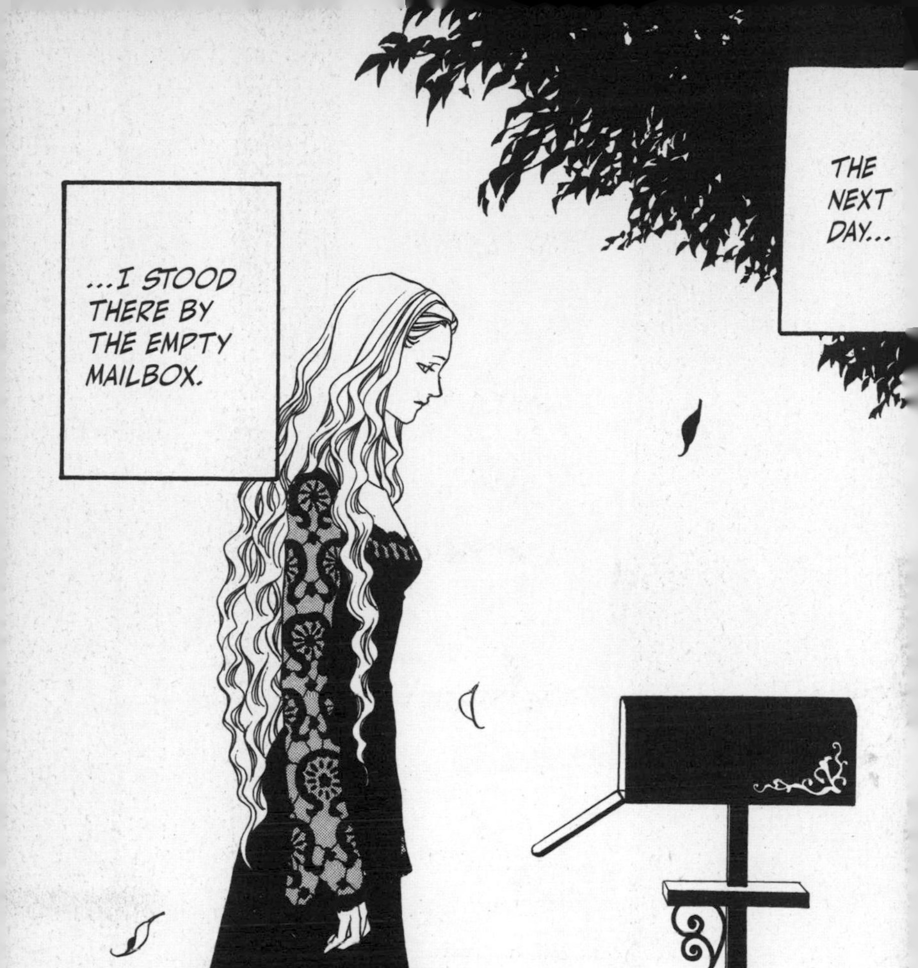
THE NEXT DAY...
...I STOOD THERE BY THE EMPTY MAILBOX.

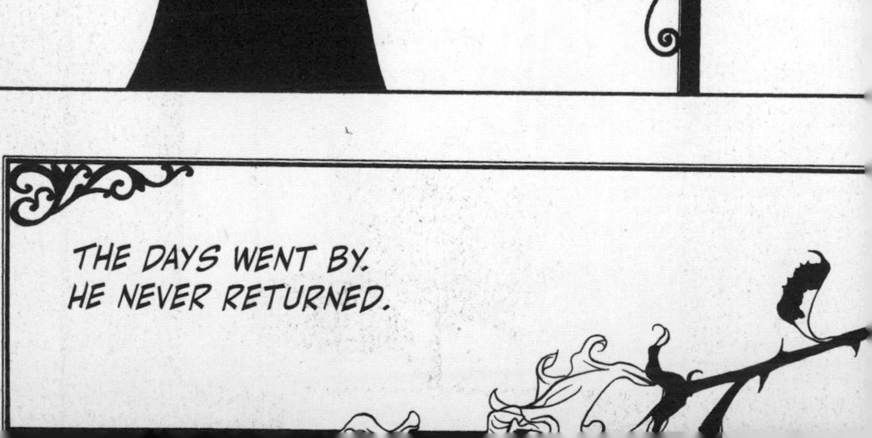
THE DAYS WENT BY. HE NEVER RETURNED.

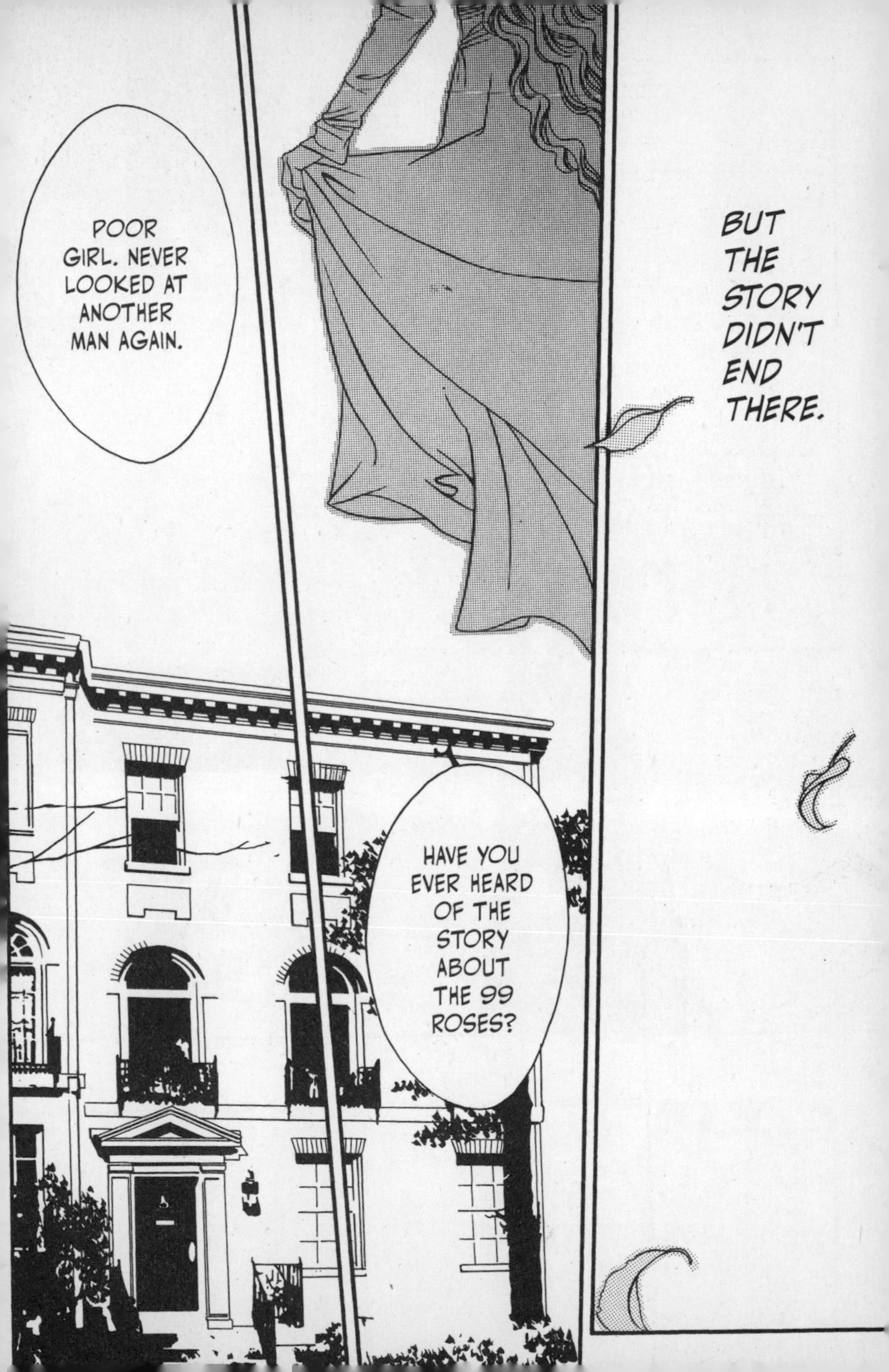
BUT THE STORY DIDN'T END THERE.
POOR GIRL. NEVER LOOKED AT ANOTHER MAN AGAIN.
HAVE YOU EVER HEARD OF THE STORY ABOUT THE 99 ROSES?

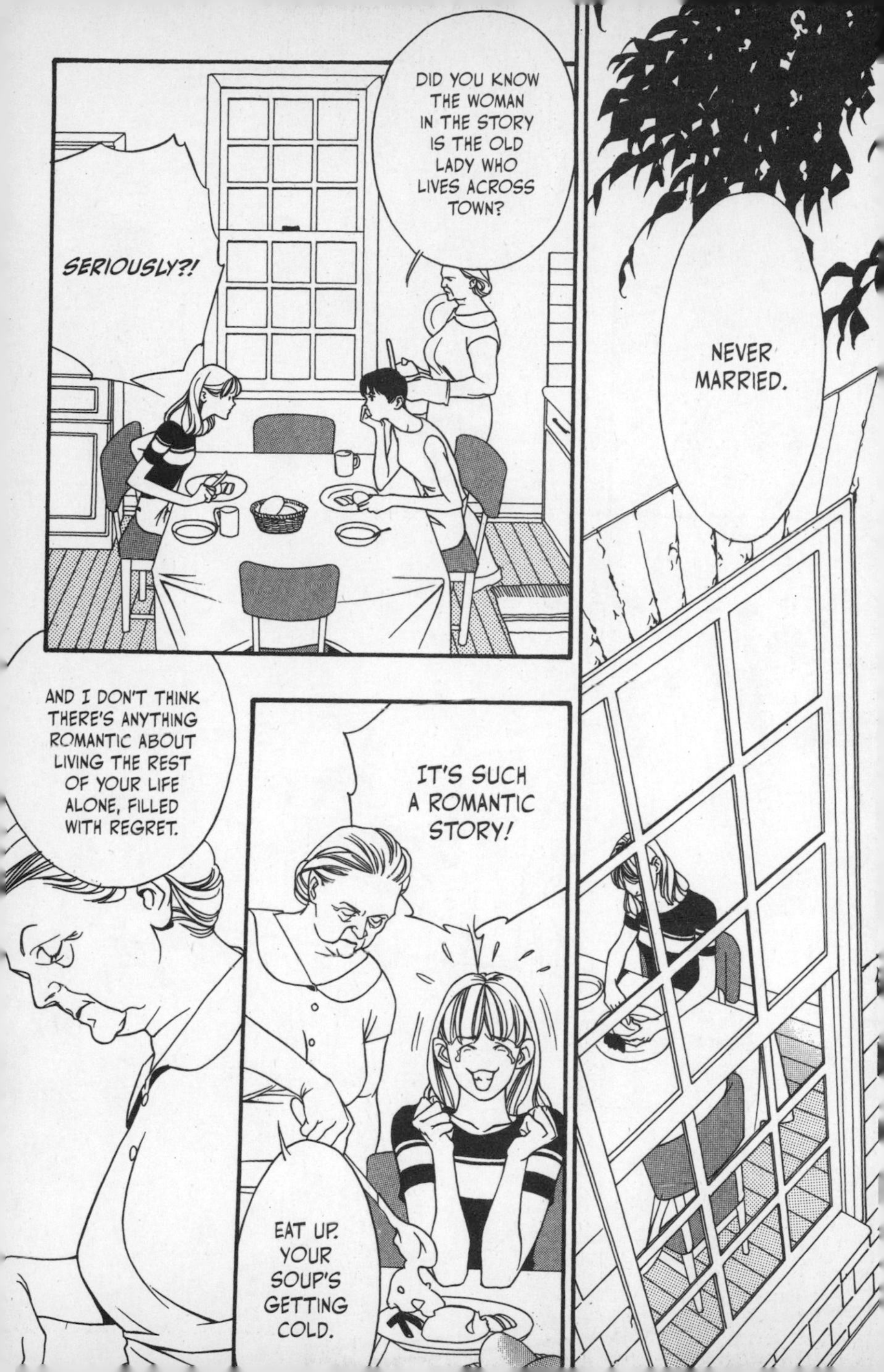
NEVER MARRIED.
DID YOU KNOW THE WOMAN IN THE STORY IS THE OLD LADY WHO LIVES ACROSS TOWN?
SERIOUSLY?!
IT'S SUCH A ROMANTIC STORY!
EAT UP. YOUR SOUP'S GETTING COLD.
AND I DON'T THINK THERE'S ANYTHING ROMANTIC ABOUT LIVING THE REST OF YOUR LIFE ALONE, FILLED WITH REGRET.

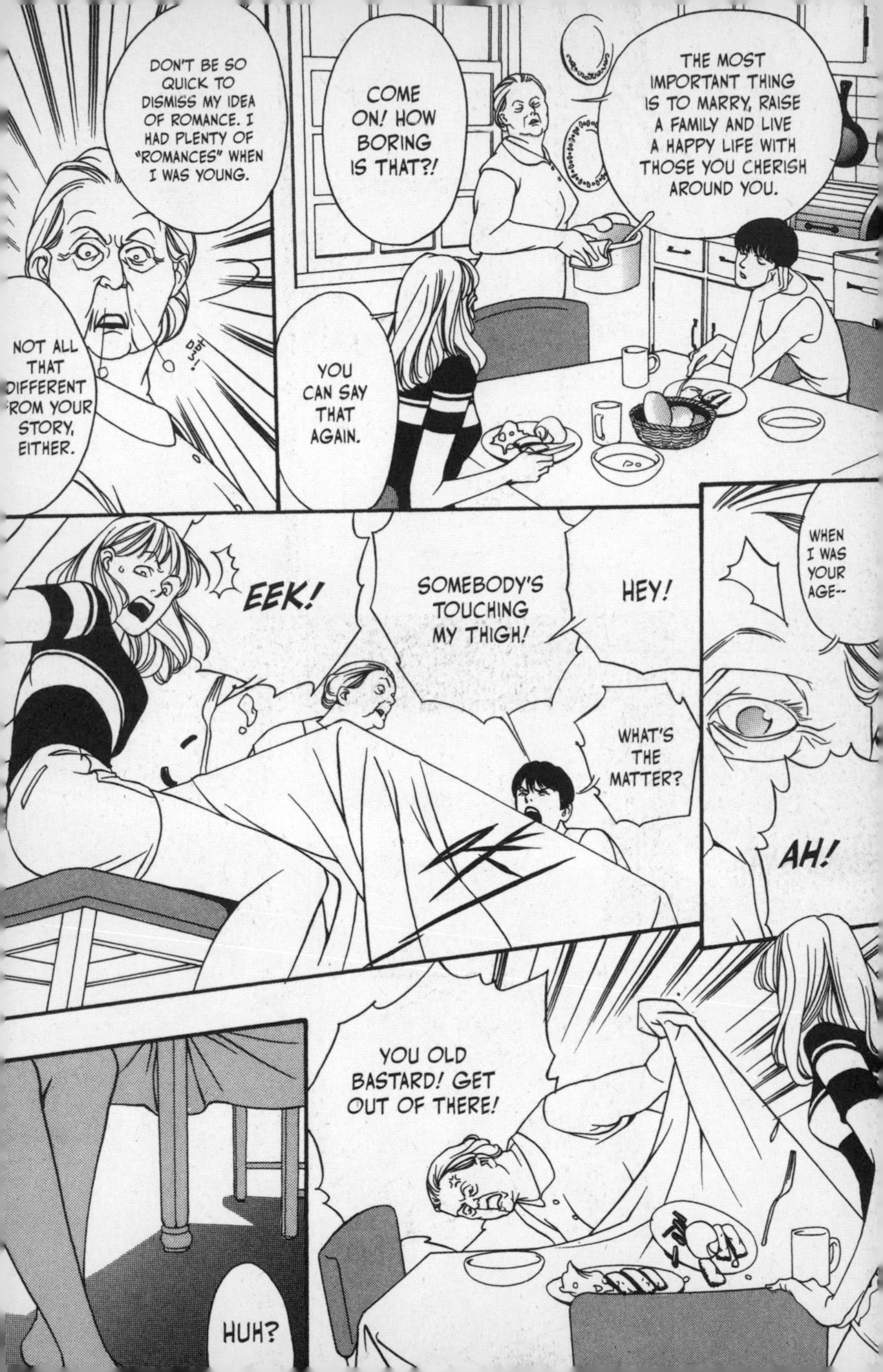
THE MOST IMPORTANT THING IS TO MARRY, RAISE A FAMILY AND LIVE A HAPPY LIFE WITH THOSE YOU CHERISH AROUND YOU.
COME ON! HOW BORING IS THAT?!
YOU CAN SAY THAT AGAIN.
DON'T BE SO QUICK TO DISMISS MY IDEA OF ROMANCE. I HAD PLENTY OF "ROMANCES" WHEN I WAS YOUNG.
NOT ALL THAT DIFFERENT FROM YOUR STORY, EITHER.
WHEN I WAS YOUR AGE--
AH!
HEY!
SOMEBODY'S TOUCHING MY THIGH!
EEK!
WHAT'S THE MATTER?
YOU OLD BASTARD! GET OUT OF THERE!
HUH?

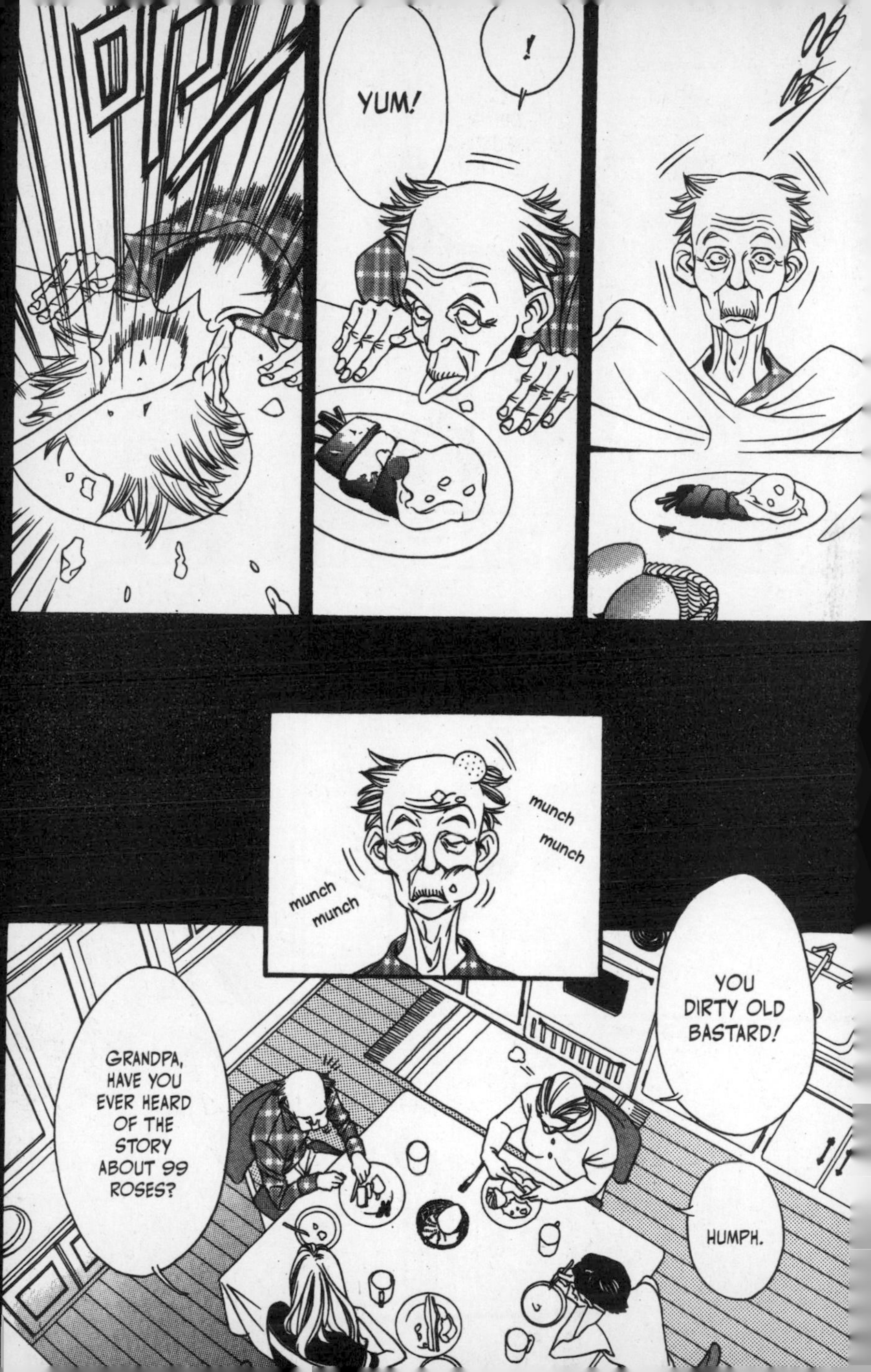
!
YUM!
munch munch
munch munch
YOU DIRTY OLD BASTARD!
HUMPH.
GRANDPA, HAVE YOU EVER HEARD OF THE STORY ABOUT 99 ROSES?

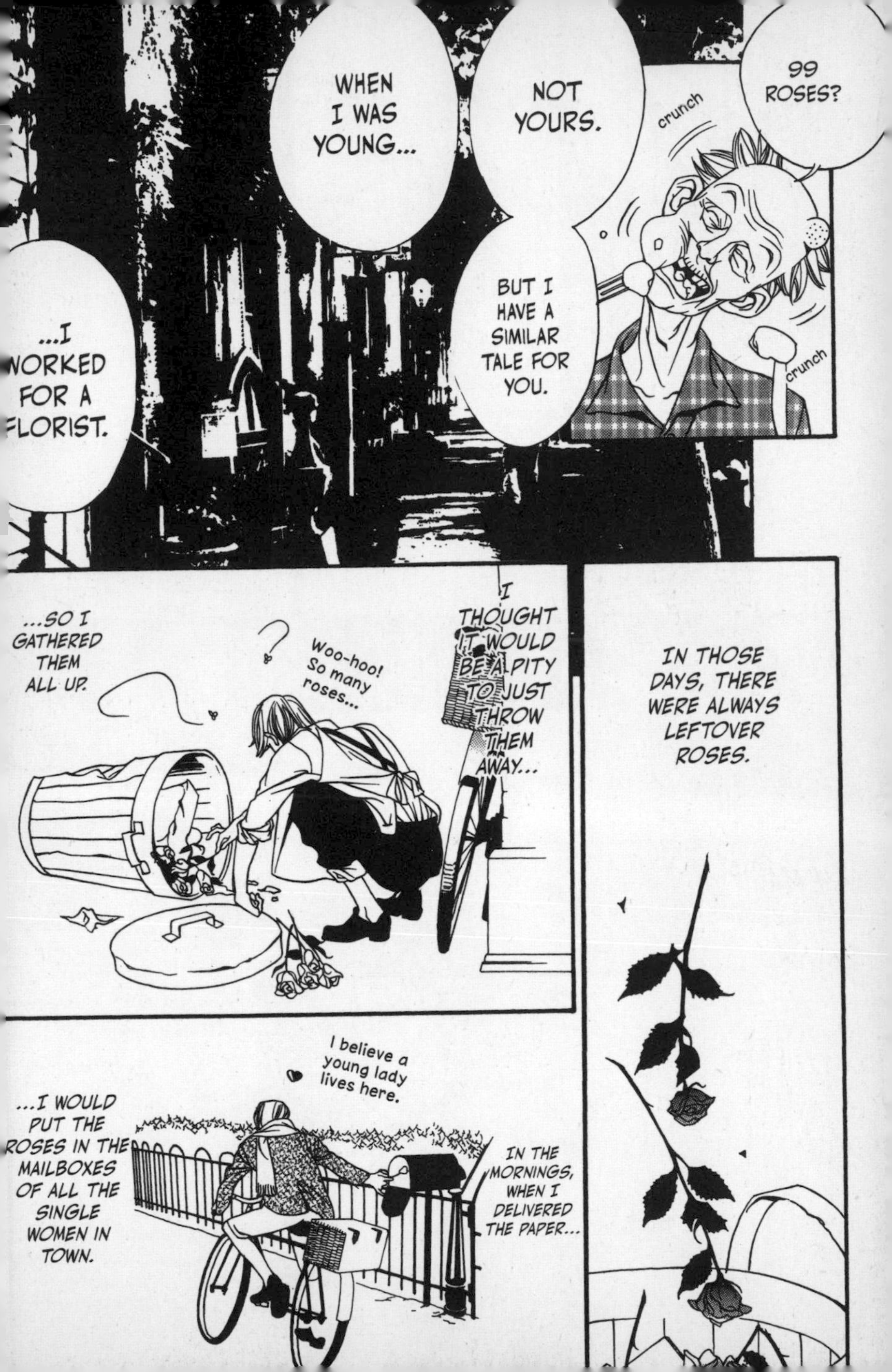
99 ROSES?
crunch
NOT YOURS.
BUT I HAVE A SIMILAR TALE FOR YOU.
crunch
WHEN I WAS YOUNG...
...I WORKED FOR A FLORIST.
IN THOSE DAYS, THERE WERE ALWAYS LEFTOVER ROSES.
I THOUGHT IT WOULD BE A PITY TO JUST THROW THEM AWAY...
Woo-hoo! So many roses...
...SO I GATHERED THEM ALL UP.
IN THE MORNINGS, WHEN I DELIVERED THE PAPER...
I believe a young lady lives here.
...I WOULD PUT THE ROSES IN THE MAILBOXES OF ALL THE SINGLE WOMEN IN TOWN.

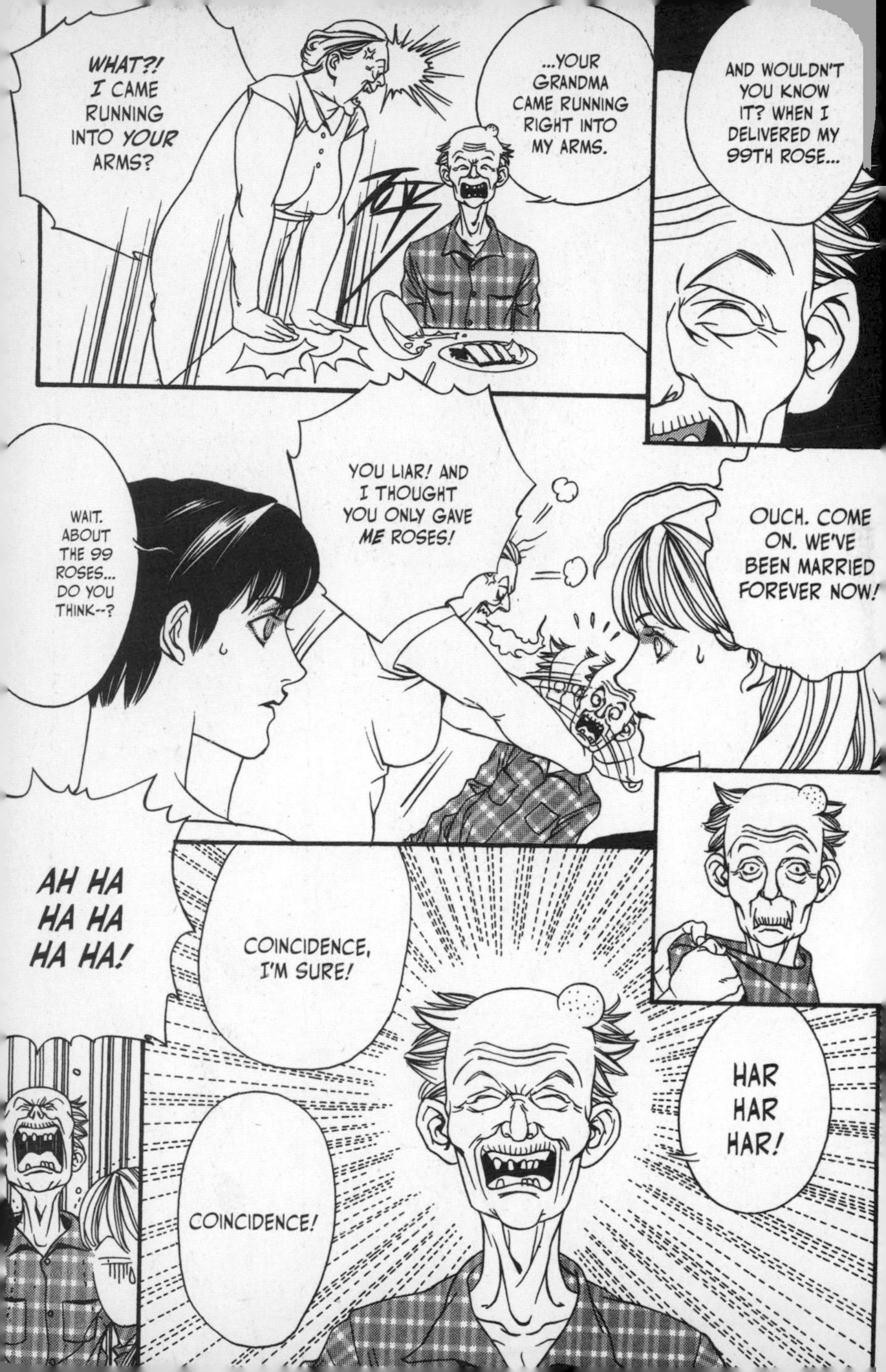
AND WOULDN'T YOU KNOW IT? WHEN I DELIVERED MY 99TH ROSE...
...YOUR GRANDMA CAME RUNNING RIGHT INTO MY ARMS.
WHAT?! I CAME RUNNING INTO *YOUR* ARMS?
OUCH. COME ON. WE'VE BEEN MARRIED FOREVER NOW!
YOU LIAR! AND I THOUGHT YOU ONLY GAVE *ME* ROSES!
WAIT. ABOUT THE 99 ROSES... DO YOU THINK--?
HAR HAR HAR!
COINCIDENCE, I'M SURE!
COINCIDENCE!
AH HA HA HA HA HA!

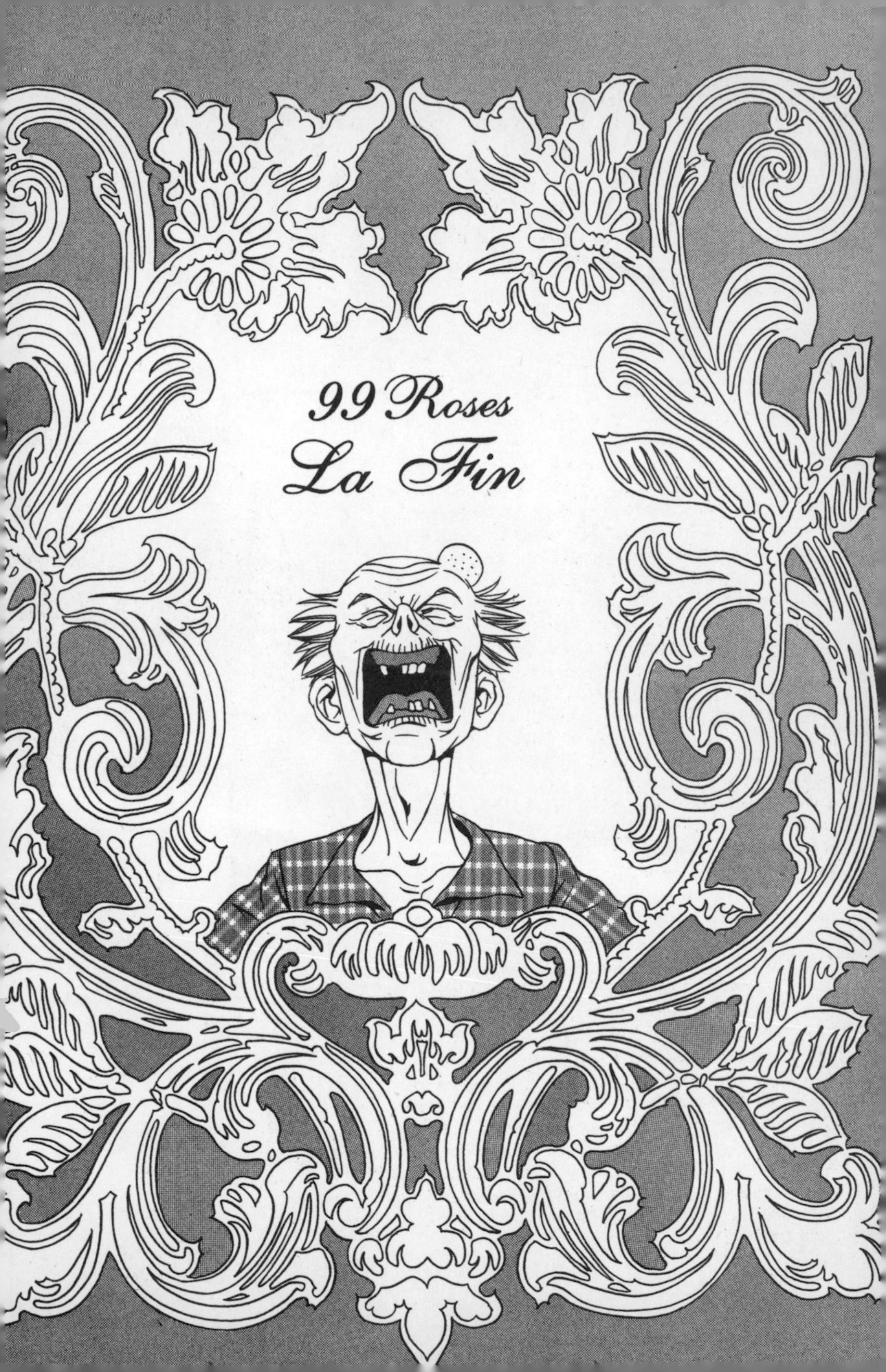
99 Roses
La Fin

Jo's Talk

Although I have experience drawing manga, the reality is that I find myself lacking in the ability to depict emotional nuances in my illustrations. It was a big challenge for me when I decided to do *The Other Side of the Mirror*, especially during the production stage. Because of my lack of experience in doing sequentials, I wasn't able to accurately express what I initially had in mind. For example, Sunny's story should have included this: She was born in South Carolina to a mother who was warm and inviting, who loved to sing and dance but who lacked the least bit of sophistication. Her mother's marriage to her father was the result of impulse. But that was not enough to sustain their marriage. Sunny's father never knew about his wife's affair. Only when she died did he find out that his wife's love was reserved only for her daughter and lover. He was nothing but a clown. As time went by, Sunny grew to resemble her mother physically. Insecure and bitter, Sunny's father believed that his daughter would also leave him, just like her mother. She became the object of his hatred, and in the end, she left him as a result. For better or for worse, Sunny inherited her mother's naïveté and optimism. She never gave up in the face of obstacles and worked hard to find happiness. By chance, she met Lou--miserable and disillusioned. (And, may I say, she was very lucky!) But in the end, it was Lou's story that was depicted in more detail. When I was drawing the first three chapters, I was still in the stages of finding the right voice for the characters and the right rhythm for the story. Because of this, both Lou and Sunny ended up like wanderers, with not much to tend to. These are the places in which I need to improve. As I read through *The Other Side of the Mirror* and wish that I had done a better job, I would very much like to thank my readers for their unwavering support. I will certainly work to polish and improve my work for you.

Thank you!

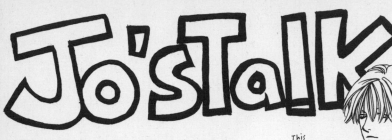

This person has nothing to do with this page.

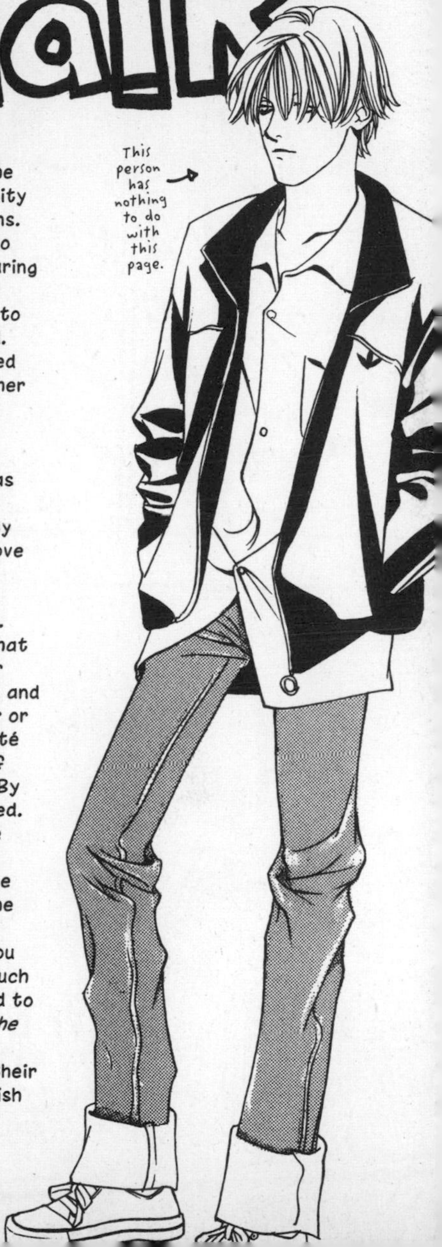

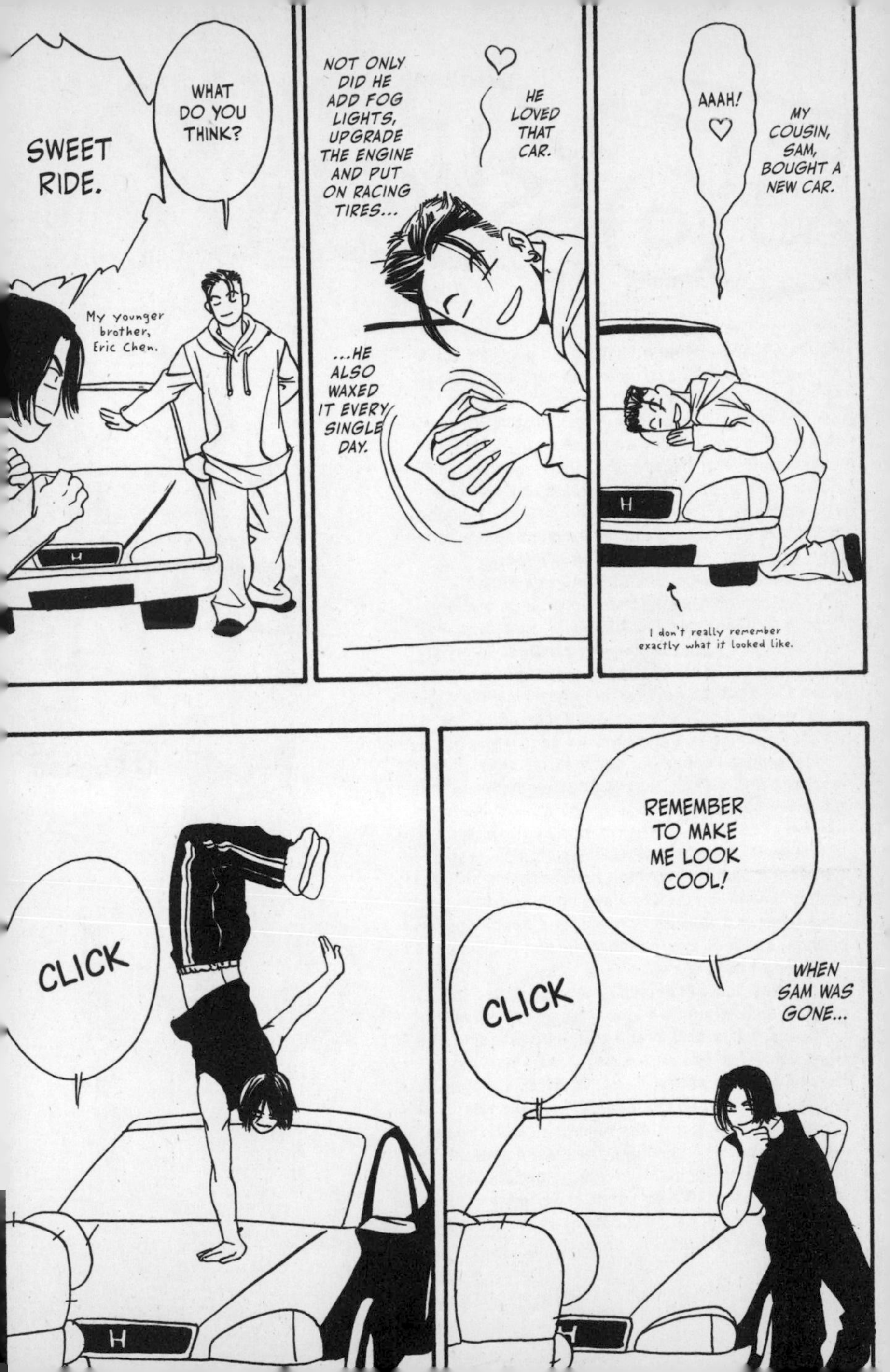
MY COUSIN, SAM, BOUGHT A NEW CAR.
AAAH! ♥
I don't really remember exactly what it looked like.
HE LOVED THAT CAR.
NOT ONLY DID HE ADD FOG LIGHTS, UPGRADE THE ENGINE AND PUT ON RACING TIRES...
...HE ALSO WAXED IT EVERY SINGLE DAY.
WHAT DO YOU THINK?
SWEET RIDE.
My younger brother, Eric Chen.
WHEN SAM WAS GONE...
REMEMBER TO MAKE ME LOOK COOL!
CLICK
CLICK

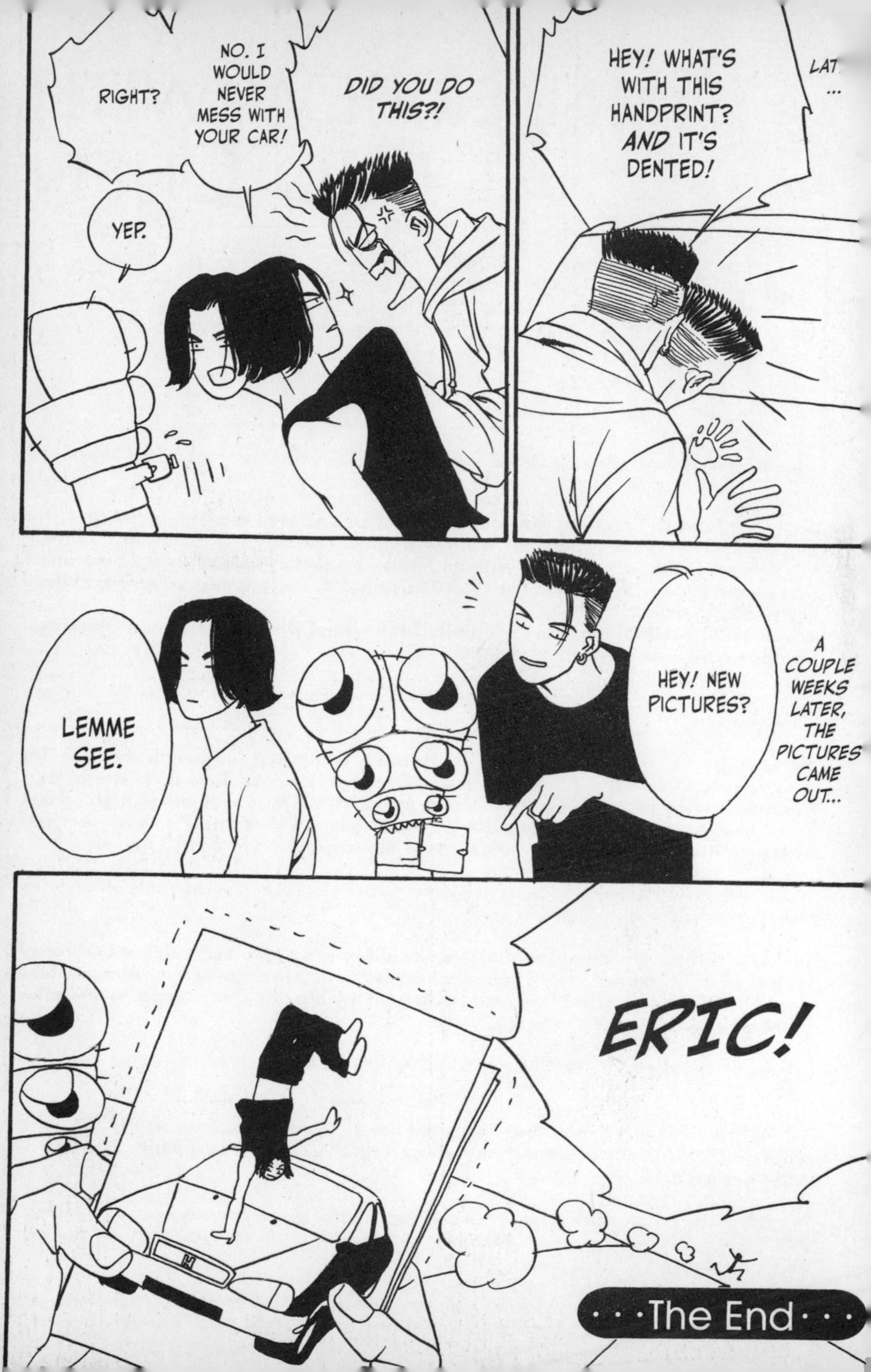
LAT ...
HEY! WHAT'S WITH THIS HANDPRINT? AND IT'S DENTED!
DID YOU DO THIS?!
NO. I WOULD NEVER MESS WITH YOUR CAR!
RIGHT?
YEP.
A COUPLE WEEKS LATER, THE PICTURES CAME OUT...
HEY! NEW PICTURES?
LEMME SEE.
ERIC!
· · · The End · · ·

INTERVIEW WITH JO CHEN

NAME:	JO CHEN
SPECIES:	LET ME CHECK.
CLASS:	LOADS OF IT.
WEAPON:	EXACTO KNIFE AND SHEETS AND SHEETS OF VERY STICKY SCREENTONE.
SKILLS:	CAN RENDER AN ANDROGYNOUS LOOKING MALE IN 60 SECONDS FLAT.

Perhaps you could first tell us a little about your background. Where did you live, how was school for you?

**Jo: I was born in Taipei on the island of Taiwan and was a pretty quiet and shy kid. I went everywhere my sister went and did everything she did. In fact, I didn't think that I could ever manage without her and it was simply a given in my mind that I would live with her and her future husband as her indentured servant when she finally married.
School was uneventful for me until junior high school when I started to make some friends because of my love of manga.**

The *Other Side of the Mirror* is your first published comic, correct? What stage in life were you while making it?

Jo: Well, it's not my first published work but it is my first full-length manga. The previous stuff I did for publishers amounted to short stories. I love short stories and I included a few of them in both volumes of the TOSOTM. I was still in high school when I began plotting the story but I'd never been in love and I'd never worked as a prostitute so some of the writing was me attempting to stretch myself.

The series deals with some heavy issues of lost dreams and destitution. Can you share with us some of the inspirations for the plot and/or characters?

Jo: Most of the characters and their personalities are pretty self evident and fairly typical of disillusioned young people. I myself was never quite that directionless since I always knew what I wanted to do with my life. So, there again, writing the script was terra incognito for me.

Any reason why the story is set in New York City? Does the location mean something special for you?

Jo: Not really. I just knew that I wanted the story to take place in the U.S. and what greater U.S. city is there than the Big Apple? L.A. just doesn't have that great and grim aspect to it.

Your artwork is clearly a mature and more lifelike take on what we normally associate with "manga" style. What sort of background education did you have in art, and who would you say are your biggest inspirations?

Jo: Comics and cartoons were sort of frowned upon by the faculty at Fu-Hsin Art and Trade school, where I received my formal art education. (cont'd on next page)

(cont'd from prev. page)

Manga was just something my friends and I did on the side, in addition to the traditional forms of art, graphics and design that were part of Fu-Hsin's curriculum. My style has changed much over the years. My first inspirations were Osamu Tezuka and Yoshikazu Yasuhiko both for their art and their storytelling prowess. Later, I became influenced by Yumi Tada. It is in this period that I worked on *TOSOTM* so you can see her influence in the way I drew my characters, even as I tried to create my own style. Today, I like a lot of artists but I would say James Jean and Zheng Wen are two artists that I respect quite a lot.

What do you find easiest when it comes to drawing? What's hardest?

Jo: The easiest? Hmmm...you mean aside from hot guys? The hardest is attempting something I've not done before and pulling it off in a convincing manner. I'd never done anything like the *Racer X* series when I took that job and I worked hard to create cool interiors about racing cars, military cabals, etc. Backgrounds aren't really difficult but they can be as ponderous to create as they are necessary to the story.

Since *Other Side*'s release, what other series or work has been keeping you busy? Any particular favorites?

Jo: Up until the middle of the summer, I was hard at work on both *Runaways* for Marvel and *Buffy the Vampire Slayer* for Dark Horse. There were other fun projects that I got to do so I keep as busy as I want to be. As for reading that keeps me busy, I am reading the Chinese translations of *Gundam The Origin* by Yoshikazu Yasuhiko, *Vagabond* by Takehiko Inoue, *Historie* by Hitoshi Iwaaki and *Mushishi* by Yuki Urushibara.

Aside from creating some amazing artwork, how do you like to spend your time?

Jo: Like most people, I enjoy seeing films, reading, eating good food and attempting to catch up on much needed sleep.

I've heard that you're sometimes recognized by your fans at conventions. Just how close are you to your fans, and have you had any funny encounters with them?

Jo: Yes, I've been approached by a few people at cons; especially San Diego Comic Con and Anime Expo. At Otakon, a few years back, this kid named Adam McClard, who is now a friend and a video game developer in China, started tailing me and my sister around the con. When the con closed down for the evening, we realized he'd spent all his money just getting to the con and had no place to sleep and was eyeing a park bench. So, we let him sleep on the floor of our hotel room, along with some of my sister's art students who came along with us. Unfortunately, he snored so we had to beat him with our shoes to quite him down. Not sure how much rest he got but afterward I slept great.

Any last minute advice for your fans who may be aspiring to become a writer and/or artist?

Jo: I'll say what I always say and that is to practice every waking moment you have. Drifting off to sleep, sketch. On the can, sketch. Break between classes, sketch. And keep a dream journal by your bed. I often awake from crazy, funny and horrific dreams and jot them down while they are still fresh. Reading them later might provide seeds for new stories.
Back to practicing; it's really the only way I know to hone one's craft to the point of excellence. That's what I did. I forsook dolls, boys, dancing and drinking in order to become better at what I did. It seemed to work for me.

Thanks again so much, Jo! We're all looking forward to the release of *The Other Side of the Mirror* volume 2!

BONUS GALLERY

In celebration of *The Other Side of the Mirror* being released in English for the first time, creator Jo Chen was kind enough to donate new never-before-seen sketches and roughs used in the early production stages of TOSM. She'll even shed light on the process of making manga, and all the thought that goes into it.

As an artist, I'm always interested in the processes other artists use to create manga. I assume you guys might be curious, as well. So here I am, digging through boxes and boxes of ancient (to me ^_^) works to display for your viewing pleasure. I finally managed to retrieve some notes, sketches and thumbnails I did a decade ago. It seems I've lost much of the rough work I'd done. What I did unearth isn't in a very good condition. It does, however, bring back a lot of memories. It also surprised me how different my style and mindset were back then. Hopefully, I've changed for the better. Nevertheless, I hope you guys enjoy these dusty nuggets (Hmmm…that doesn't sound too appetizing, does it?)

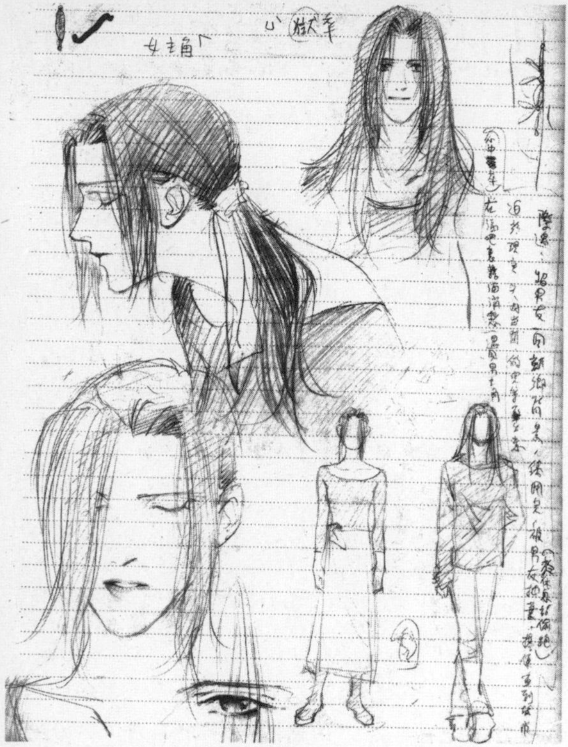

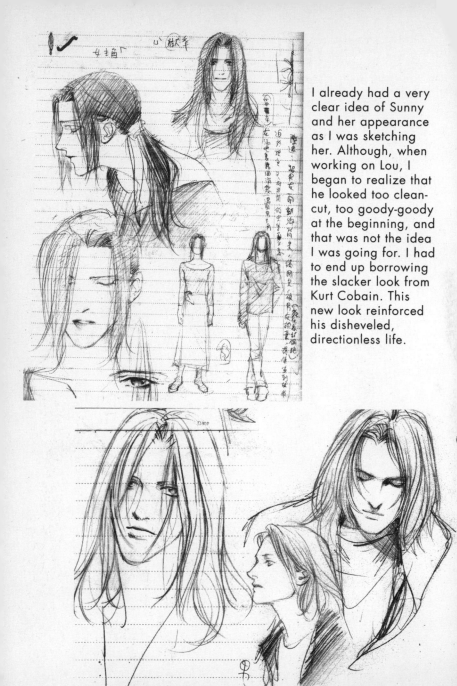

I already had a very clear idea of Sunny and her appearance as I was sketching her. Although, when working on Lou, I began to realize that he looked too clean-cut, too goody-goody at the beginning, and that was not the idea I was going for. I had to end up borrowing the slacker look from Kurt Cobain. This new look reinforced his disheveled, directionless life.

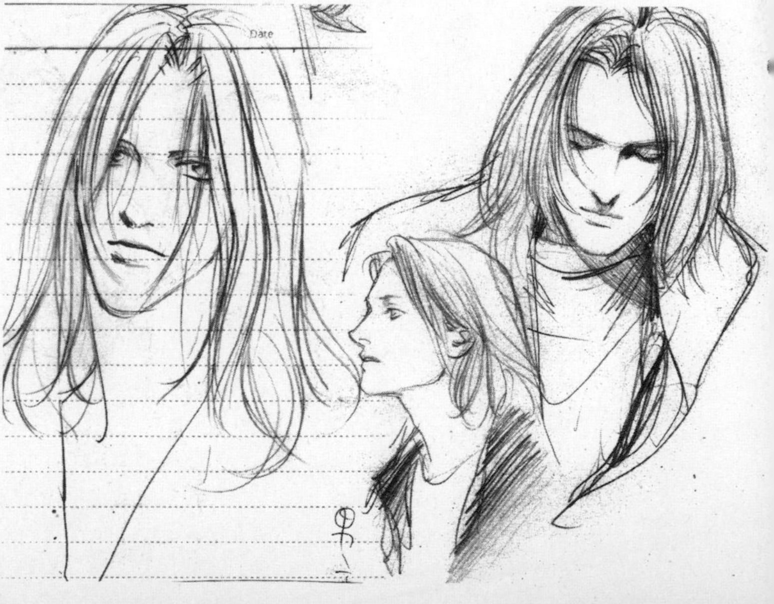

ar Girls Magazine was running a Valentine's Day special issue and asked me
› contribute a short story. However, I didn't want to write a saccharine piece like
verybody else. So I did the total opposite by creating a plot that contained a cliché
omantic opening to set false expectations then crush their gooey hopes at the end.
.egarding the style of the architecture and the main character's attire, they are
ıst part of the romantic set up. It was a happy cruel joke on my part. Heh heh.

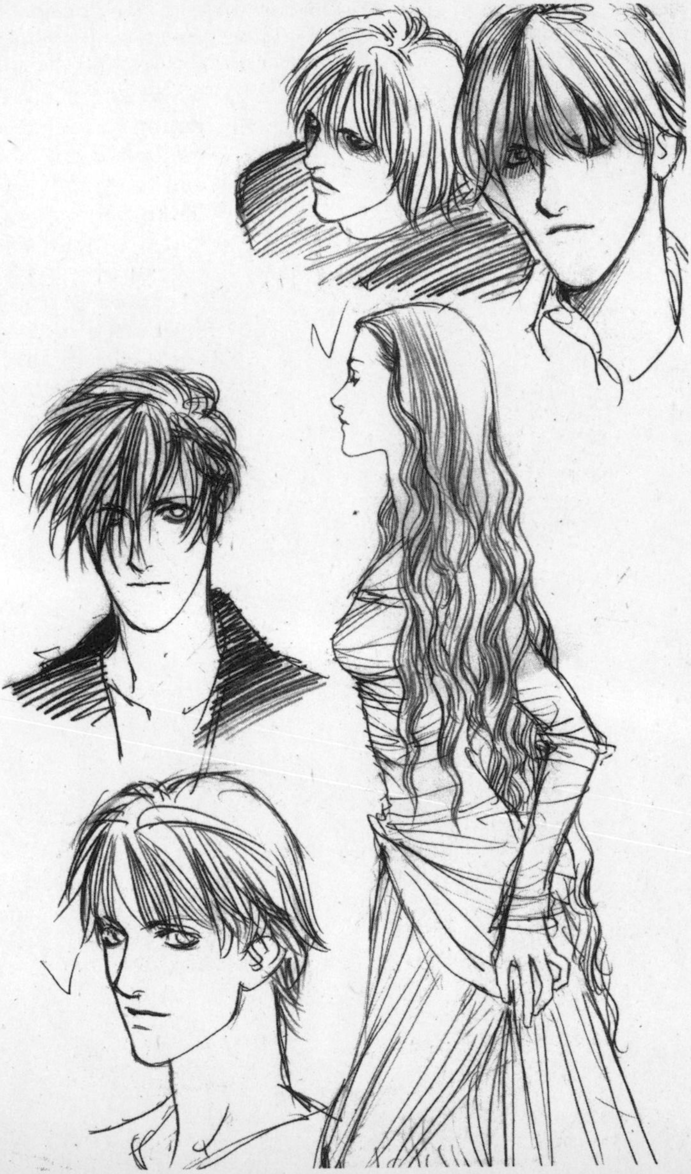

I actually turned in a goodly number of sketches. They picked two as potential candidates for the cover of *Star Girls Magazine*, which was to debut my book in serialized form. Of what you see here, sketch #5 and another (not displayed here purposefully) which was my least favorite of the lot. I then had to produce more detailed pencils of the two selections, and after submitting them, I couldn't believe it when they announced the one that I hated most was their choice for the magazine's cover. I was horrified, but what could I do? This seems to be a recurring theme... Editors picking my least favorite piece. By way of explanation, I was told that this illustration, of all that I had originally given them, suited the style of *Star Girls Magazine* better than any of the others. Whatever. Up to this day, that one magazine cover remains on my top 10 least favorite illustrations, ever.

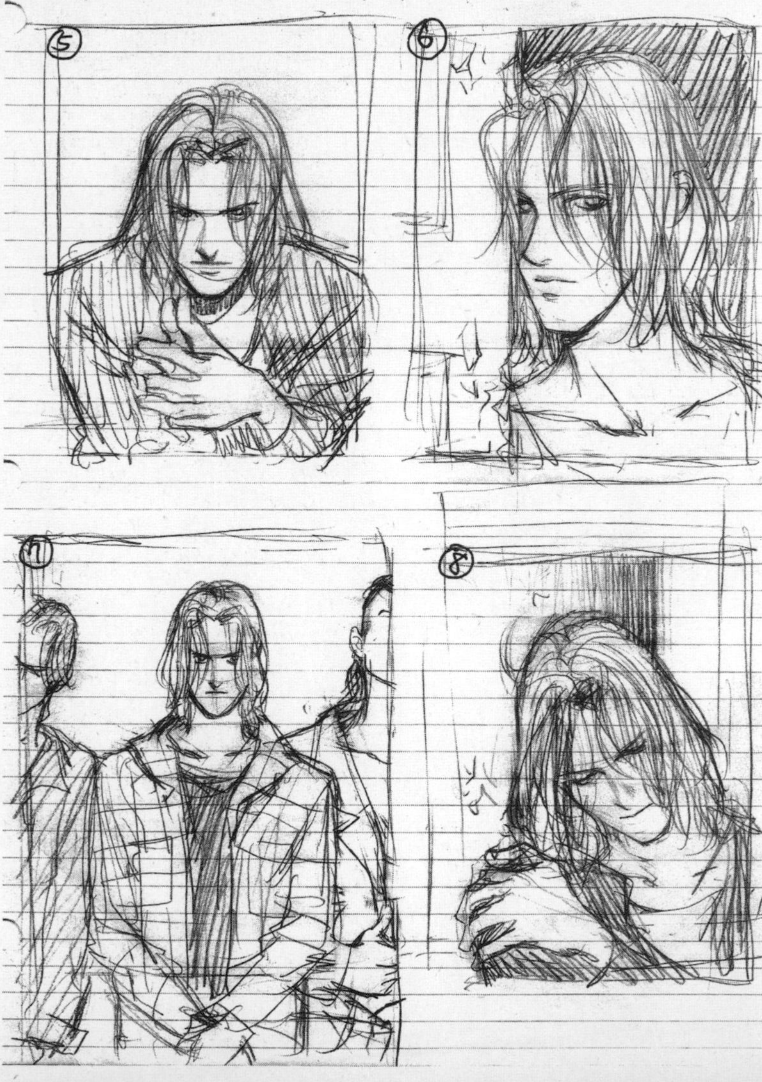
5
6
7
8

eft) To keep the ideas flowing and to minimize any distraction while
orking on the details of the story, I always laid the panels out first
s thumbnails and then rearranged and refined the panel composition
ater. Because I didn't leave enough room in the speech bubbles for
e existing dialogue, I had to add additional simplified text around
e margins of the pages, which I would review and edit later.

Below) This is just another sample of how I lay out panels. I've always
ttempted to give a cinematic feel to the way I create and layout a
age. It breaks up the monotony of having to view four to six perfectly
ordered cubes filled with artwork on each page of a comic book.

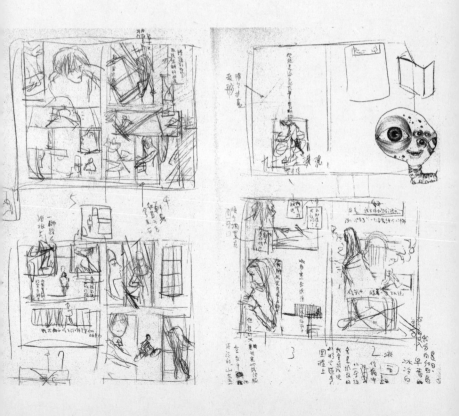

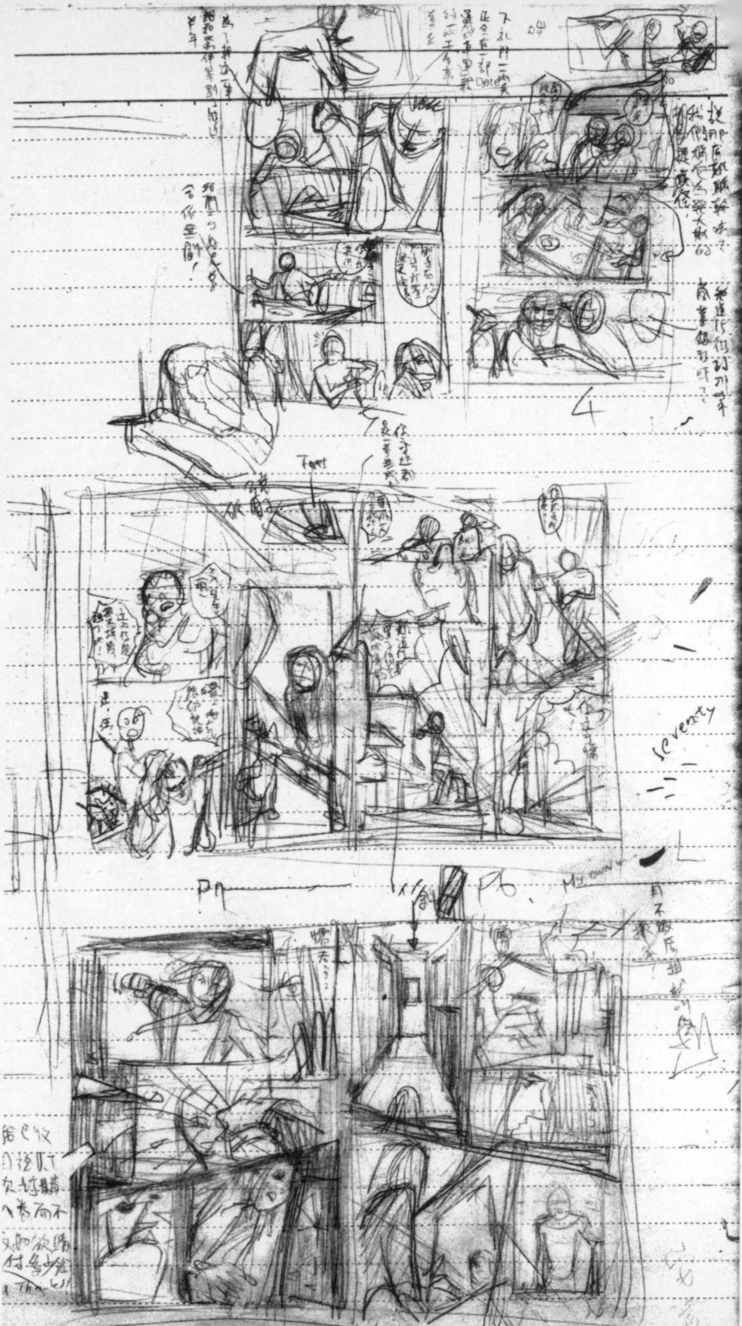
Date
4
seventy
MY OWN

What lies on the other side of the mirror...

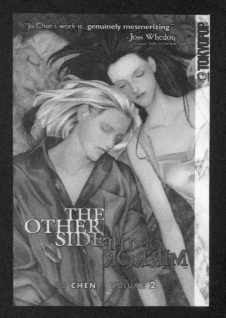

AFTER ESCAPING THE CONFINES OF NEW
YORK CITY, LOU AND SUNNY START A NEW
LIFE IN A SMALL TOWN. JUST AS THINGS ARE

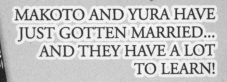

STOP!

This is the back of the book.
You wouldn't want to spoil a great ending!

This book is printed "manga-style," in the authentic Japanese right-to-left format. Since none of the artwork has been flipped or altered, readers get to experience the story just as the creator intended. You've been asking for it, so TOKYOPOP® delivered: authentic, hot-off-the-press, and far more fun!

DIRECTIONS

If this is your first time reading manga-style, here's a quick guide to help you understand how it works.

It's easy... just start in the top right panel and follow the numbers. Have fun, and look for more 100% authentic manga from TOKYOPOP®!